Exploring the Theory, Pedagogy and Practice
of Networked Learning

D1448150

Lone Dirckinck-Holmfeld · Vivien Hodgson
David McConnell
Editors

Exploring the Theory, Pedagogy and Practice of Networked Learning

 Springer

Editors
Lone Dirckinck-Holmfeld
Faculty of Humanities
Aalborg University
Aalborg, Denmark
lone@hum.aau.dk

Vivien Hodgson
Lancaster University Management School
Lancaster University
Lancaster, UK
v.hodgson@lancaster.ac.uk

David McConnell
Independent Consultant
in Higher Education
Stirling, Scotland, UK
dmcconnell@blumail.org

ISBN 978-1-4614-0495-8   e-ISBN 978-1-4614-0496-5
DOI 10.1007/978-1-4614-0496-5
Springer New York Dordrecht Heidelberg London

Library of Congress Control Number: 2011938140

Printed on acid-free paper

Springer is part of Springer Science+Business Media (www.springer.com)

Dedicated to the memory of Robin Mason and Bo Fibiger, two early and significant innovators in our field whose contribution is much missed

Foreword

In this centenary year of the birth of the Canadian media guru Marshall McLuhan, it is appropriate to see the publication of an important new book on network use in teaching and learning. Among McLuhan's most profound observations was that "we shape our tools and then the tools shape us." This observation, coupled with the profound increase in network use by people of all ages around the globe, helps us be cognizant of the most significant change in our "networked" society. We have created and are continually shaping our tools to applications in all domains – not excluding education. Now our tools are shaping us.

Education is made up of communications, information retrieval, and knowledge production – each of which is in the midst of massive and unprecedented change. As teachers and researchers of the applied science and practice of education, we need to have a very deep understanding of network and media effects. We need to understand and become skilled in exploiting the affordances of networks and networking tools to improve the content and the context, and most importantly the effectiveness and efficiency of the learning process.

In my own experiences (many echoed in the experiences related in this text) you will see the challenges faced and the successes achieved by innovators as they attempt to realize the new, while mitigating and confronting the disruptive effects of systems built and shaped by "old media." Networked learning challenges both rigid hierarchies and individualistic notions of learning; both centralized education administrations and individual teacher control of classrooms. It leads us to investigate more deeply the role of groups and sets as well as networks in individual and collective learning. And perhaps most challenging, it leads us to investigate our own notions of knowledge construction, information dissemination, privacy, and ownership.

One of the problems we all face in harnessing rapidly changing technologies is the sense that we are always behind and that we just can't keep up! This book doesn't solve that problem but the editors and the authors of each chapter serve the function of all explorers. They expand boundaries and borders. But as importantly they blaze trails for others to follow, create maps, and tell compelling stories when they return. Each chapter relates the experience and most provide empirical data to help us first understand these technologies and then judge which tools will likely make a difference in our teaching and individual learning contexts. They also provide insights into the best trails to use and maps that guide us on the path but as importantly show us the treasures that lie at the end of these paths.

Another of McLuhan's insightful quips was to turn an older aphorism on its head when he claimed that "I wouldn't have seen it if I hadn't believed it." Network effects are changing educational systems in very profound ways, and yet most of us are neither trained nor experienced in seeing, much less exploiting, these opportunities. Fortunately, you are not now, or will soon not be (after reading this text!), one of those lacking this vision – I am confident that you will believe in the educational power of these media after reading this text and thus not only be able to see but be able to use networks to improve your own teaching, researching, and learning. *Exploring the Theory, Pedagogy and Practice of Networked Learning* has helped me and I am sure will assist you in not only seeing but in believing in the many profound ways and opportunities we are facing in education today.

My only words of advice to the reader is to make use, explore, and test the networking approaches, tools, and pedagogies described in this book. It is useful to read about network applications, but there is no substitute for the experience of deep and profound learning that occurs as we develop and experience our own connected worlds. There is much to learn and an almost overwhelming need for better education – the tools and pedagogies described in this book are critically important in shaping ourselves and our world.

Athabasca, AB   Terry Anderson
                                                    Professor in Canada Research
                                                    Chair in Distance Education,
                                                    Athabasca University, Canada

Endorsements

Professor Peter Goodyear
Australian Laureate Fellow, University of Sydney, Australia.

The editors are to be congratulated in creating a valuable collection of writing by leading researchers in the fast-moving field of networked learning. The book offers some innovative ways of conceptualising learning and technology-mediated interaction; a number of empirical studies provide intriguing glimpses into emerging learning environments. Most important of all, the deep reflection on knowing and action, and on relations between the digital/material, social and mental, that is necessitated when trying to understand networked learning, leads the broader field of educational inquiry towards richer conceptualisations of theory and praxis. This is essential reading for anyone interested in the complex mix of ideas about how the social, technical, and personal combine in contemporary learning situations.

Professor Roger Säljö
Department of Education, Communication and Learning, University of Gothenburg, Sweden.

During 150 years of empirical research, scholars of learning have preferred to use the individual as their research object. The dominance of such approaches has diverted our attention from the more reasonable assumption that learning first and foremost emerges through collaboration and joint activity. In the present volume, the contributors give us the history of and the state-of-the-art networked learning. It is a rich account of lessons learned and potentials that have yet to be fully taken advantage of. In a globalized world it is natural that a large part of the research reported deals with the potentials of recent technologies. What makes the analyses especially interesting, however, is the foregrounding of learners and their concerns as they accommodate to, participate in and design their learning by engaging in contemporary forms of networking.

Gilly Salmon

Professor (Learning Futures) & Executive Director Australian.

Digital Futures Institute, University of Southern Queensland, Australia.

This book works carefully and scholarly through a sparkling web of networked learning and contributes to current and future debates around the ecology and sustainability of online collaboration. There's challenge to simplistic "solutions" and clarification of bridging and boundary crossing. For the student of educational change – in search of the transformation agenda – or even the New Academia – this book is a must for the desktop, dialogue, and debate.

Etienne Wenger

Independent thinker, researcher, consultant, author, and speaker;

Author of Communities of Practice, California, US.

We need new approaches to learning, and the networked learning conferences always bring together an interesting collection of researchers with a wide range of pursuits – including theory, pedagogy, design, culture, and technology. This book reflects this dialogue across perspectives, which is where promising innovation is most likely to flourish.

Acknowledgments

This book originates from the seventh international networked learning 2010 conference that took place in Aalborg, Denmark, May 3–4, 2010.

We would like to acknowledge the contributions and work of Chris Jones, Maarten de Laat, and Thomas Ryberg in running the conference. In addition we owe a huge debt to Alice Jesmont for both her assistance in preparing the book as well as her tireless work in supporting the organisation and administration of the networked learning conference series.

Contents

Author Biographies

Alevizou, Panagiota is a post-doctoral research fellow at the Open University's Institute of Educational Technology working on the Open Learning Networks project (Olnet). She has been engaging with numerous stakeholders and projects in the OER community to develop a working framework on the nature of openness and collaboration that characterizes the mediation of open resources, while addressing the opportunities and challenges relating to participatory interfaces, emerging pedagogies, adoption, and (re)use.

Prior to her current position she was an LSE fellow at the Department of Media and Communications. Her broader background is in media and communications with a particular emphasis on new media, knowledge systems, learning, and literacy. She has researched and published widely on collaborative communities, UGC and knowledge media.

Arnold, Patricia is a professor of socio-informatics at the University of Applied Sciences Munich, Germany. Her teaching, research, and development work focuses on facilitating learning communities with technologies, both in higher education and in the field of professional development. She received a PhD in educational sciences from Helmut-Schmidt University Hamburg, Germany, after having worked for several years in adult education and IT training. She studied educational science, mathematics, and sports in Hamburg, Germany and London, UK.

You will find her other publications and more details on http://www.patriciaarnold.wikispaces.com/

Boon, Stuart is a lecturer in the Centre for Academic Practice & Learning Enhancement at the University of Strathclyde. His main areas of research are in the fields of researcher development, information literacy, pedagogical uses/impacts of social software and simulations, phenomenography and variation theory, and identity and risk in the digital domain. As an active researcher, lecturer, educational developer, and sometimes student, Stuart is keenly aware of and greatly interested in transitional and transformative experiences in higher education and the creative potential that arises from them.

Brown, Cheryl is a Lecturer in the Centre for Educational Technology at the University of Cape Town. Over the past 7 years she has been researching issues of access to and use of ICTs for learning within higher education. She has also worked in the e-learning field in Australia where she managed the Multimedia Unit within Flexible Learning and Access Services at Griffith University. She has recently submitted her PhD in Information Systems, which focuses on students' perspectives about what technology really means to them as individuals and looks at how these meanings form the basis of their technological identities.

Buus, Lillian is part-time PhD Candidate at the research centre: E-learning Lab – Center for User Driven Innovation Learning and Design (http://www.ell.aau.dk). She has been participating in both national, international, and EU-projects with focus on ICT and learning in different contexts. In the PhD she is looking at the learning potentials within the use of web 2.0 in a problem-based learning approach, trying to develop a learning methodology for the use of web 2.0 in education. Her publications can be seen at: http://www.vbn.aau.dk/en/persons/lillianbuus %28ae29b162-ff83-4bac-8a31-4b2ed04fb1db%29.html

Bygholm, Ann is a professor in the Department of Communication and Psychology at Aalborg University and working in e-Learning Lab – center for user driven innovation, learning and design. Her research is in ICT implementation and evaluations processes. Focus is on knowledge organization and user involvement. The aim is to understand processes of transferring, translating, and transforming working practices by means of ICT and to identify what ICT mediation of work actually implies in concrete situations. Main domain of research is health and education.

Chu, Kar-Hai is a PhD candidate in the Communication and Information Sciences program at the University of Hawaii at Manoa. He is a member of the Laboratory for Interactive Learning Technologies, working under Dr. Dan Suthers. He received his B.S. at Johns Hopkins University and M.S. at Columbia University in computer science. His dissertation research is focused on technology-mediated interactions in online communities. Using social network analysis, Kar-Hai is examining how various patterns of these interactions can affect user relationships.

Conole, Gráinne is Professor of Learning Innovation and Director, Beyond Distance Research Alliance, University of Leicester. Prior to this, she was Chair of E-Learning, Institute of Educational Technology, The Open University, Professor of Educational Innovation in Post-Compulsory Education, University of Southampton, and Director of the Institute for Learning and Research Technology at the University of Bristol. Her research interests include the use, integration, and evaluation of Information and Communication Technologies and e-learning and the impact of technologies on organisational change. Two of her current areas of interest are focusing on the evaluation of students' experiences of and perceptions of technologies and how learning design can help in creating more engaging learning activities.

She has extensive research, development, and project management experience across the educational and technical domains; funding sources have included the

EU, HEFCE, ESRC, JISC, and commercial sponsors). She serves on and chairs a number of national and international advisory boards, steering groups, committees, and international conference programmes. She has published and presented over 200 conference proceedings, workshops, and articles, including over 50 journal publications on a range of topics, including the use and evaluation of learning technologies and is editor for the Association of Learning Technologies journal, ALT-J

Creanor, Linda is Development Director for Professional Practice in the Caledonian Academy, Glasgow Caledonian University, where she has responsibility for taking forward innovation in learning and teaching with a particular emphasis on technology-enhanced learning. Linda has successfully led several strategic initiatives and has been involved in a range of national and European projects as a researcher, designer, evaluator, and consultant. She is a Trustee of the Association for Learning Technology (ALT) in the UK, having previously served as Vice-Chair, Chair and President, and is a Fellow of the Higher Education Academy.

Czerniewicz, Laura is Associate Professor at the University of Cape Town, South Africa. Laura is the Director of Centre for Educational Technology (CET) and recently appointed Director of OpenUCT an institutional knowledge resources initiative. She has lead a research project for several years on students' digitally mediated practices and is exploring research dimensions of digital scholarship. She is interested in the relationships between policy and practice, as well as the conceptual underpinnings of this emerging domain of enquiry.

Danielsen, Oluf associated professor at Department of Communication, Business and Information Technologies, Roskilde University, Denmark. Educed as a physicist, but since 1978 at the Communication programme at Roskilde University. Research areas: the role of scientific knowledge in public discussions and decisions. For about 20 years member of the national research community of ICT and Learning. Since 2000 he has been member of the steering group and has functioned as researcher and supervisor at the Masters program ICT & Learning (MIL), a collaboration among four Universities in Denmark. From 2008 to 2014 member of the Dream research community working with projects on museums' and science parks' networked communication with its visitors and users.

Dirckinck-Holmfeld, Lone is professor in ICT and Learning at Aalborg University, Department of Communication, and from 2009 the Dean of the Faculty of Humanities. She holds a PhD from Roskilde University in computer-mediated communication and learning. Lone Dirckinck-Holmfeld has been a pioneer in developing the field of human centred informatics both as an academic field and as a practice. Main field of research is computer-supported collaborative learning (CSCL), networked learning and participatory design. She has co-authored a number of books within ICT and learning. Newest book: Dirckinck-Holmfeld, L., Jones, C., & Lindström, B. (Eds.) (2009). Analysing networked learning practices in higher education and continuing professional development. Rotterdam, the Netherlands: Sense Publishers.

Galley, Rebecca is project officer for the JISC funded Open University Learning Design Initiative project in the Institute of Educational Technology at the Open University in the UK. She is responsible for the monitoring and evaluation of the JISC-funded OULDI project, which includes facilitation and evaluation of the Cloudworks social networking site. She has led on the development of the evaluation framework for the site, and has identified a rich methodology for identifying and analysing user behaviour, including the theoretical framework on community indicators. She is also engaged in developing a set of strategies for promoting community engagement and working with users within and outside of the university to understand how these new social media spaces can be used to promote innovative approaches and lead to changes in practice. Her broader background is in work-based education and training.

Georgsen, Marianne is Associate Professor at Aalborg University (AAU), Department of Communication and Psychology. She is affiliated with the research centre: "E-learning lab – Center for User Driven Innovation, Learning and Design". Marianne did her PhD work within the field of CSCW and continues to do research on communication and collaboration in virtual environments. Another strong interest lies in methods, tools, and ways of working for teachers and other practitioners who wish to use ICT in teaching and learning. She has led and participated in both local and international research projects on this topic, as well as authored and co-authored several articles on the issue.

Hodgson, Vivien is Professor of Networked Management Learning in the department of Management Learning and Leadership at Lancaster University Management School, UK.

She has co-ordinated and participated in many networked learning and "e-learning" research projects and in the evaluation of development projects in both Europe and Latin America.

Between 1995 and 1998 she was seconded to the Socrates programme of the European Commission in Brussels where she was responsible for the Open and Distance Learning (Socrates) Action. She is the co-chair of the international bi-annual conference series "Networked Learning," which was held in May 2010 at Aalborg, Denmark.

She has written extensively on collaborative approaches to learning and the importance of dialogue and critical reflection in the design and process of networked learning. She is interested in how theoretical debates that exist, together with changes and advances in information and communications technology impact on the nature, design, and experience of learning. These interests include exploring ideas about the way experiences of relational dialogue contributes to the construction of a learner's online identity, what we learn about ourselves and how we view knowledge and our position in the world.

Further information about Professor Hodgson including her publications is available at; http://www.lums.lancs.ac.uk/dml/profiles/vivien-hodgson/

Chris, Jones is a Reader in the Institute of Educational Technology at the Open University. His research is focused on the relationship between technological arte-facts and social order and the ways in which policy affects practice in the field of networked learning. Chris has published journal articles and book chapters concerning the understanding of digital networks in relation to the network society. He has a particular research focus on the use of reifications and resources in teaching and learning and he has developed a distinctive research direction that incorporates an interest in investigating meso-level influences, including the role of infrastructural and institutional factors. Chris was the principal investigator for a UK Research Council funded project "The Net Generation encountering e-learning at university." Chris has published two edited collections and over 60 refereed journal articles, book chapters, and conference papers connected to his research.

Levinsen, Karin Tweddell is an associate professor in online education at university level at the Faculty of Arts at Aarhus University. She is a member of the internationally acknowledged Research Programme on Digital Media and ICT in a Learning Perspective. Currently her research is focused on both university pedagogy and ICT and ICT and learning in the primary school. Of special interest is the development of designs for teaching and learning that integrate ICT. Karin Tweddell Levinsen has many years of experience as a professional user-centred design developer of digital educational solutions, and she has been in the field since the two-screen solution and the laserdisc. Simultaneous with her professional carrier she has kept the contact with the research community and taught at several Danish Universities, including the Danish IT-University.

McConnell, David has held Professorial Chairs in Higher Education at the Universities of Sheffield, Open, Lancaster and Glasgow Caledonian. He is Visiting Professor at South China Normal University, China. He is a networked learning practitioner and researcher, and believes in the need for strong ties between research and practice. He has been a pioneer in developing the field of networked learning and has designed and directed several innovative networked learning higher education programmes, including the Masters in E-Learning at Sheffield University and the Doctoral PhD programme in E-Research and Technology Enhanced Learning at Lancaster University. He founded the International Networked Learning Conference in 1998 and now co chairs it with Vivien Hodgson at Lancaster University (see: http://www.networkedlearningconference.org.uk)

David McConnell's academic interests include adult and continuing education, the potential of the Internet for learning and teaching, open and distance learning, gender in education, professional development and qualitative research methods. He has worked on a wide variety of internationally funded research projects concerned with the development of higher education courses and initiatives across Europe, as well as UK funded projects concerned with e-community development, intercultural Sino-UK pedagogy, management development and networked collaborative learning.

He has written extensively on teaching, learning, and assessment in higher and continuing education and has published over 80 papers in refereed journals and co-authored several books in the above areas. His books on *Implementing Computer Supported Cooperative Learning* (Kogan Page, 2nd edition 2000), and *E-Learning Groups and Communities* (Maidenhead, SRHE/OU Press 2006) received enthusiastic acclaim.

Nielsen, Janni is professor at Center for Applied ICT at Copenhagen Business School. For the last two years she has worked with ICT and Innovation in a European-Latin American project. Her background is a Master in Psychology and a Ph.D. in Informatics, and her main publications are within Human Computer Interaction, where she has developed the MindTape method. During a sabbatical she worked in a design company in Barcelona and has studied design processes.

Nielsen, Jørgen Lerche associated professor at Department of Communication, Business and Information Technologies, Roskilde University, Denmark. For more than 10 years he has been part of the web-based cross-institutional Masters program ICT & Learning, a collaboration among four Universities in Denmark. His main focus is on learning processes in communities of practice, blended learning, challenges in problem oriented learning processes, networked learning, and change processes within higher education. 2001–2003 taken part in a EU Minerva supported project CLIENT – Collaborative learning in an International Environment, a collaboration between Roskilde University, Denmark, Salford University, UK, Maastricht, The Netherlands, and Tromsø, Norway.

Nyvang, Tom is an associate professor in the research center e-learning lab – center for userdriven innovation, learning and design at Aalborg University. His main interest is design for learning with focus on the relationship between organisational change and development of ICT based infrastructures for learning. In the past he has worked a lot with cases in universities and still does so. Recently he has developed a parallel interest in designs for e-government and citizen self-service applications. His research is based mainly in socio-cultural approaches to change, development and learning, theories of participatory design and organisational learning.

Raffaghelli, Juliana E. Higher degree in Psychology from the University of Buenos Aires, Master in Training Management from the University of Venice "Ca' Foscari", Scholarships Programme of the Italian Ministry of International Affairs, PhD in Cognitive and Educational Sciences.

Her research can be connected with intercultural pedagogy issues and intercultural teachers' training. Her PhD focus was internationalization of teachers' professionalism, with impact on teachers' professional identity.

In the last years she has been working in a number of international projects such as LLP-COMENIUS, Europaid, Latin America and Africa, INTERREG CARDS-PHARE Balkans, Programme of the Civil Society Dialogue Europe-Turkey, focusing on teachers' learning processes, international peers collaboration, and mobility. She has also explored international experiences in virtual space as an opportunity for reflection on personal and professional identity, and on an intercultural perspective for teaching. She is currently engaged in a post-doctoral research on multimodal analysis of learning processes in open Web 2.0 environment.

Richieri, **Cristina** has a Higher Degree in Foreign Languages, a Master in Didactic Research and Educational Counselling, and a PhD in Cognitive and Educational Sciences.

She teaches English and she is also a teacher trainer. She is a member of the A.N.F.I.S. editorial staff. She collaborates with CIRDFA (Inter-University Centre for Didactic Research and Advanced Training), she is a member of the RED Laboratory (Didactic and Educational Research) and the I.T. Laboratory for didactic and educational Research, both having their seat at CIRDFA (Porto Marghera, Venice).

She is the co-author of a number of English textbooks for primary and secondary school. She has published papers on foreign language teaching, self-directed learning, and reciprocity.

Ross, **Jen** is an associate lecturer at the University of Edinburgh, where she is part of the MSc in E-learning programme team and the Digital Cultures and Education research group, both based in the School of Education. She conducts research in the area of online learning, digital identity, reflective practices, and cultural and educational institutions online. More about her research and teaching can be found at http://www.jenrossity.net.

Ryberg, **Thomas** is Associate Professor in Aalborg University (AAU), Department of Communication and Psychology. He is part of the research centre: "E-learning lab – Center for User Driven Innovation, Learning and Design." He has participated in European and international research projects and networks. His primary research interests are within the field of Networked Learning and how new media and technologies transform our ways of thinking about and designing for learning. He has authored and co-authored several articles on networked learning and Learning and New media.

Sinclair, Christine observes higher education from several perspectives: as a student, a teacher, a researcher, and an educational developer. She is a lecturer in the Centre for Academic Practice and Learning Enhancement at the University of Strathclyde. This work encourages her to explore differences and intersections among academic "tribes" and the associated constantly changing environment for students. Her main interests are in academic writing, online learning, and student experience. She researches student experience by being a student herself, and recently graduated from the University of Edinburgh with an MSc in E-learning. Read her blog about her experiences at: http://www.e-learningconfessions.blogspot.com/

Smith, **John David** helps communities, their leaders, and their sponsors with research and coaching about technology, learning and politics. He has years of experience in the design and production of community events, self-assessments, and the selection, configuration, and use of technologies. He is the community steward for CPsquare, an international community of practice on communities of practice. He worked at the University of Colorado as a planner, institutional researcher, administrator, and technologist. He received a Bachelor's degree from St. John's College and a master's degree in planning and architecture from the University of New Mexico. He was born and raised in Humacao, Puerto Rico.

You can find out more about John, his work and clients at http://www.learning alliances.net

Susan, M. Smith manages the knowledge exchange initiatives in the Institute for Entrepreneurship and Enterprise Development within Lancaster University Management School. She is the Director of the LEAD programme which focuses on developing the management and leadership of SME owner managers. The programme has successfully been rolled out in England and Wales and she supports the deliverers of LEAD through a provider network, which seeks to engage in reflexive practice. Her research focuses on how SME owner managers learn through peer-to-peer learning and how Higher Education Institutions can support regional development through knowledge exchange.

Suthers, Daniel D. is Professor in the Department of Information and Computer Sciences at the University of Hawaii at Manoa, where he directs the Laboratory for Interactive Learning Technologies. His research is generally concerned with cognitive, social, and computational perspectives on designing and evaluating software for learning, collaboration, and community. His current focus is on multilevel analysis of socio-technical systems to understand how local interaction leads to emergent phenomena, and the role of technology media in this emergence. His research on social affordances of digital media has examined how software interfaces both influence and are appropriated by small groups.

Thompson, Terrie Lynn is a post-doctoral fellow at Athabasca University, Canada's Open University. She is also appointed as the Researcher-in-Residence for Digital Opportunity Trust, an international NGO focused on ICT for social and economic development.

Her research focuses on exploring how web technologies are changing ways of working and learning as well as conceptions of work and learning spaces. She has studied how web-based technologies can facilitate human development; the politics and ethics of ICTs; informal work-related learning online of the self-employed; and the pedagogical impact of technology integration into the formal school system at all levels, including higher education.

Trayner, Beverly is an independent learning consultant helping organizations convene communities of practice and networks. She is particularly interested in social systems that span national boundaries, disciplines, or professions and has been a pioneer in the use of social media for learning.

Her current published work focuses on new forms of leadership associated with convening social learning spaces and a recent paper providing a framework for promoting and assessing value creation in communities and networks, co-authored with Etienne Wenger and Maarten de Laat.

You can find out more about Beverly, her work, and clients at http://www. bevtrayner.com

Walker, Steve is a lecturer in the Dept. of Communication and Systems, Faculty of Mathematics, Computing and Technology, where he is a member of the Society and Information Research Group. Steve's research interests are in the broad fields of social informatics, and most particularly in learning technologies, the design and use of ICT in civil society. He has worked with trade unions on their use of ICT since the 1980s, and specifically on a series of e-learning in trade union education projects since the mid-1990s. He is a Member of the British Computer Society and is a Fellow of the Higher Education Academy. He blogs very occasionally at http://www.stevewalker.wordpress.com/

Part I
Introduction

Chapter 1
Networked Learning: A Brief History and New Trends

David McConnell, Vivien Hodgson, and Lone Dirckinck-Holmfeld

Introduction

The chapters in this book emerge from selected conference papers given at the Networked Learning conference 2010 in Aalborg. In this chapter, we first offer a short review of the history of networked learning. We examine how it has developed in both the UK and Denmark as well as in other parts of Europe and the USA. The chapter first outlines the philosophical and pedagogical roots of networked learning and, in addition, describes some of the history of the development of the Networked Learning Conference itself.

It considers how developments in the World Wide Web and Web 2.0 in particular have given fresh impetus and support to the basic principles and ideas behind networked learning as a pedagogical approach. That is, an approach that takes a critical and inquiring perspective and focuses on the potential of information and communication technology (ICT) to support connections and collaboration.

The chapter concludes with a summary of the structure and content of the rest of the book.

D. McConnell (✉)
Independent Consultant in Higher Education, Stirling, Scotland, UK
e-mail: dmcconnell@blumail.org

V. Hodgson
Lancaster University Management School,
Lancaster University, Lancaster, UK

L. Dirckinck-Holmfeld
Faculty of Humanities, Aalborg University, Aalborg, Denmark

L. Dirckinck-Holmfeld et al. (eds.), *Exploring the Theory, Pedagogy and Practice of Networked Learning*, DOI 10.1007/978-1-4614-0496-5_1,
© Springer Science+Business Media, LLC 2012

A Short History of the Theory and Practice of Networked Learning

The development of networked learning has largely been influenced by understanding of developments in technology to support learning alongside thinking stemming from the traditions of open learning and other radical pedagogies and humanistic educational ideas from the likes of Dewey, Freire, Giroux and Rogers.

In the UK, the tradition of open learning was an influence on early thinking associated with the development of networked learning. After Coffey (1977), open learning can be considered from the perspective of removing administrative and/or educational constraints to learning. "Administrative" constraints include the location, timing and cost of study. "Educational" constraints include the setting of learning objectives, methods of study, assessment methods, etc. Harris (1987) in an analysis of the development of the UK Open University (OU) demonstrated, however, that much of the early open and distance learning (ODL) initiatives and courses, such as The UK Open University established in 1971, were more about administrative openness than educational openness. As Morrison (1989) explained, distance education in its then stage of development was not addressing or overcoming cultural, economic or educational barriers to learning.

In work being developed at places like Lancaster University and the then North East London Polytechnic, there were however programmes that sought to reflect greater degrees of educational openness. Boot and Hodgson (1987), in a study of the pedagogical principles and assumptions that separated these more educationally open programmes from administratively open programmes, claimed that there were essentially two orientations to open learning: one that took a dissemination orientation to open learning (and in practice offered "administrative" openness) and those that took a development orientation (i.e. offered more educational openness).

In their analysis, they identified "other people as an inherent part of the learning venture, providing challenge and collaboration in the construction of personal meaning" and, in addition, assessment as being "part of the learning process, based on collaborative assessment against mutually agreed criteria". Their analysis identified what were to become important principles for networked learning; together with the idea that the tutor role within a development orientation was one of facilitator, "resource person and co-learner. Meanings he/she attribute to events no more valid than anyone else's".

Technology-Mediated Learning Experiments and Initiatives

At the same time, while the UK Open University was predominately offering administrative openness in its approach, there was some interesting experimental work taking place there. This included pre-Internet experiments with innovatory ICTs with a view to evaluating their potential to support student learning. An early development was the Cyclops shared screen telewriting conferencing system that was trialled as a means of supplanting face-to-face tutorials, which were the norm. Cyclops allowed groups of students in study centres to link with other groups throughout the country via a teleconferencing network. Students could talk to each other and share ideas on a TV screen through the use of a light pen. Teaching material could be prepared in advance on cassettes and distributed to all groups via the TV screen during the tutorial. The meetings were synchronous and were facilitated by the tutor (McConnell 1982). These early pioneering trials indicated the real, practical possibilities of ICT to support learning. They demonstrated that students and tutors could adapt to new technologies and methods and showed the potential of such technologies in the teaching and learning process. The research drew on theory from the social psychology of telecommunications (Short et al. 1976) and pointed to ways forward in our understanding of the effects of these technologies on social presence, tutorial processes and learning outcomes (Howe and McConnell 1984; McConnell 1983, 1984, 1986; McConnell and Sharples 1983), issues that were to re-emerge in the networked learning era.

Trials of early versions of computer conferencing as a practical means of supporting distant learners, and as a vehicle for facilitating cooperative student–tutor design and collaborative assessment of in-service teacher education, were also being conducted at the OU. These early trials of the emerging technologies were underpinned by the humanistic values and radical pedagogy of Carl Rogers and Malcolm Knowles (values that were later to underpin the pedagogy of networked learning) with a view to overcoming some of the factors that limit meaningful learning:

> when we put together in one scheme such elements as a prescribed curriculum, similar assignments for all students, lecturing as almost the only mode of instruction, standard tests by which all students are externally evaluated, and instructor-chosen grades as a measure of learning, then we can almost guarantee that meaningful learning will be at an absolute minimum (Rogers 1983).

The aim of the trials was to establish if it was possible to engage in a radical pedagogy in the context of distance learning mediated by technology and to support learning, where students were able to make personal decisions about their learning (Knowles 1975, 1985) in a cooperative and collaborative learning context. These trials foreshadowed some of the thinking about learning using technology that developed into what we now call networked learning. The outcomes indicated that students were quick to see the potential benefits of learning via new technologies as a means of supporting them at a distance, offering them opportunities to interact, participate in discussions, share ideas and support each other (Emms and McConnell 1988; McConnell 1988a, b), characteristics that later became important aspects of networked learning processes.

Despite these early exploratory ideas and research projects showing that the use of new ICTs in learning could be as effective as traditional face-to-face methods in terms of achieving tutorial tasks and outcomes (McConnell 1986), some tutors and students felt that the new methods could not fully match the rich experience of face-to-face meetings that they were used to. This foreshadowed similar concern voiced at the introduction of computer conferencing and Internet-based learning systems that began to emerge in the late 1980s and early 1990s. For many present-day networked learning students and tutors, the perception that learning technologies lack social presence and do not match the experience of face-to-face meetings still persists, and despite much evidence to the contrary (as the contents of this book testify) it remains one of the major barriers to the widespread uptake of networked learning in higher education.

Information Technology-Supported Open Learning

Following on from these early studies and trials, there was a UK Training Agency-supported Information Technology-Based Open Learning ("ITOL") project. This was an innovative project that set out to optimise and research the growing potential and possibilities of rapid developments in ICT to offer greater degrees of educational openness (Hodgson et al. 1989). The ITOL project became a precursor for a whole series of projects and initiatives that was to encapsulate the pedagogical approach and model of learning now known as networked learning. It led in 1989 to an early trial case study based on an existing part-time MA in Management Learning at Lancaster University (Hodgson and McConnell 1992).

Figure 1.1 shows the model of the electronic environment that was subsequently developed and adopted for the MA based on the trial. As Hodgson et al. (1989) explained, ITOL was a working model where all the parts, actors and objects relate to each other and:

> ... allows any individual to communicate with a tutor, or tutors, or facilitator(s) (most likely University based people, but not exclusively) with other learners and with a series of collections of both University and non-University based resources (p. 139).

It is important to note that it was not the technology itself that made the MA more educationally open but the way it was able to contribute to implementing the learning design and processes that underpinned the programme. The key features of the design of the MA were and remain: (1) a learning community approach, (2) an open structure and curriculum, (3) learning sets, (4) free choice of topics for all course work and (5) peer involvement in feedback and assessment of assignments.

A significant follow-up project to ITOL was the European-funded Framework 3 DELTA project, JITOL, followed by a Joint Information Systems Committee (JISC) of the UK higher education funding council project. The JISC project's working title was "*Networked Learning in Higher Education*". It began in January 1999, and was based on the original ITOL model. It offered what has turned out to be a surprisingly enduring first definition of networked learning, i.e.:

> We define 'networked learning' as learning in which information and communications technology (ICT) is used to promote connections: between one learner and other learners, between learners and tutors; between a learning community and its learning resources.

This definition has persisted remarkably well and was reiterated in the book that came out of that project (Steeples and Jones 2001) and confirmed by Goodyear et al. (2004). But as Goodyear (2001) commented, "while the richest examples of

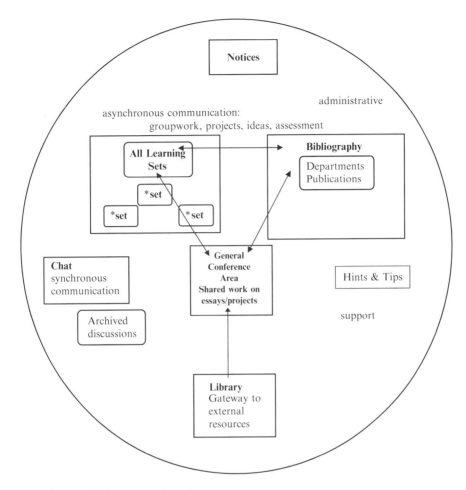

Fig. 1.1 CM MAML – electronic environment

networked learning involve interaction with on-line materials *and* with other people. But use of on-line materials is not a *sufficient* characteristic to define networked learning".

The principle not emphasised in this early definition of networked learning, but which was always present and has become to be seen as an important and integral aspect of networked learning, is the one of collaboration. Collaboration and cooperation were identified in the early research and trials as important features of a development orientation to open learning. They were significant aspects in the early literature of "networked learning" and were explicitly identified in the writing of, for example, Hodgson and McConnell (1992) writing about the ITOL model and Goodyear and Steeples (1992) writing about the JITOL model. Hodgson and

McConnell (1992) explain that the aspirations of the ITOL project were, as described in Hodgson et al. (1989), to strive to pursue an approach to open learning, where:

> We have sought to take a 'developmental' orientation to our work and see open learning as allowing learners to define their own learning and personal development needs through processes of negotiation, collaboration and cooperation (p. 137).

To all intents and purposes, the ITOL model they depict and describe in that paper was an early variation of a VLE but underpinned by an identifiable and distinct pedagogy which assumed "*negotiation, collaboration and cooperation*".

That cooperative and collaborative learning was always seen as an important feature in the work of both ITOL and JITOL is clearly stated by Hodgson and McConnell (1995) when describing the work of "cooperative learning and development network" (CLDN). The CLDN was another initiative that was conducted as part of the JITOL project, where the "very purpose of the trial was to set up a cooperative learning and support group" or network.

A Pedagogic Framework for Networked Learning

Drawing on the above work and the evaluation of online learning courses, and associated theory of education and computer-supported collaborative learning (CSCL), McConnell attempted to provide a pedagogic foundation for the application of the emerging ideas on networked learning (1994, 2006). Posing the question "what constitutes a "useful design" for networked learning, and what issues need to be addressed in designing such courses", he suggested six broad areas of pedagogy that need to be addressed when designing networked learning courses.

Openness in the educational process. The Learning Community: Being open in the teaching and learning process was seen to be a key factor in the design of networked learning. Openness leads to meaningful learning and can be facilitated by the development of a learning community, where one works for oneself and for others and where development occurs. Learning is seen to occur in a social context, and as a consequence learners begin to address learning from a qualitatively different, meta-level. When asked about their willingness to work collaboratively in groups, 96% of students said it depended on the degree of openness in the group (McConnell 2006, p. 72).

Self-determined learning. Self-determined learners take primary responsibility for identifying their own learning needs, and help others in determining theirs. In these processes, learners become aware of how they learn, and develop deep approaches to learning. When asked, a large proportion of students (91%) say that studying in this way has made them more aware of the strengths and weaknesses of their own learning processes (McConnell 2006, p. 80).

A real purpose in the cooperative process. Much higher education learning is abstract and often unrelated to real situations, and many students struggle to see the purpose of it. If learners have a real purpose in learning, they engage with the learning process in a qualitatively different way. Problem-based learning (PBL) and action learning/research are two ways in which learners can define the focus of their learning in meaningful and relevant contexts. This promotes positive interdependence:

> Positive interdependence is the knowledge that you are linked closely with others in the learning task and that success .... depends on each person working together to complete the tasks ... (McConnell 1994, p. 94).

Outcome interdependence – the desired goals of learning – provides learners with a means of relating to the group and its tasks. Means interdependence is the action required by each group member.

A supportive learning environment. A supportive learning environment is one where learners encourage and facilitate each other's efforts. Being supportive does not, however, mean a lack of intellectual challenge. Learners need to be able to work without fear: where there is a cloud of uncertainty, they act with caution.

Collaborative assessment of learning. Collaborative self–peer–tutor assessment processes are central to networked learning; they are a corollary of cooperative learning and support the cooperative process. Reflection on the process of collaborative assessment helps those involved learn from the process and helps them be better prepared and skilled for the next assessments (McConnell 2006). With experience, collaborative assessment is often the most positively thought of aspect of networked learning.

Assessment and evaluation of the ongoing learning process. Assessing and evaluating the networked learning course is also a cooperative tutor–learner process. Learners must feel that there is a real opportunity to change the design of the course; this can be achieved by the tutor and learners working together in regular group processing. The norms and roles associated with networked learning groups help eliminate some of the competitive nature of traditional educational environments. Learners need to work at mutual acceptance, and develop skill in working cooperatively.

Using this framework, the first virtual Masters in Networked Collaborative Learning was launched in 1996 at Sheffield University (McConnell 1998). The course ran completely virtually and was offered globally. It developed and changed over the years as a consequence of the cooperative tutor–learner evaluation process (McConnell 2000, 2006) and was the basis for the design of a TEL doctoral PhD programme first offered at Lancaster University in 2007.

The Networked Learning Conference

As the practice of networked learning developed and research emerged, the need for a good academic outlet for this new field became apparent. The Networked Learning conference was founded in 1998 by David McConnell with the specific purpose of offering an international conference that focused primarily on the educational aspects of learning that is supported by new information technologies, rather than a focus on the technology itself, as was the case with many other conferences at that time. McConnell made specific mention to the importance of collaboration to a learning approach based on networked learning. In the special issue of JCAL that published a selection of papers from that conference, he explained in his editorial:

What is Networked Learning

Many terms are emerging to describe the use of electronic communication and the Internet in education and training. My preference is for 'networked learning' since it places emphasis on networking people and resources; and on collaboration as the major form of social relationships within a learning context. The emphasis is empathically on learning and not on technology (McConnell 1999).

By the third networked learning Conference in 2002, this was a firmly embedded aspect of the Networked Learning Conference calls for papers. The 2002 call stating:

We invite you to the above conference which is an opportunity to participate in a forum for the critical examination and analysis of research in networked learning i.e. learning and teaching carried out largely via the Internet/Web which emphasises collaborative and cooperative learning, learning through dialogue and group work together with interaction with online materials, and collaborative knowledge production.

At that conference, a Manifesto called "*Towards E-quality in Networked e-learning in Higher Education*" was presented from the work of the participants of an ESRC seminar series on Understanding the Implications of Networked Learning for Higher Education.

In the 2002 Manifesto, the working definition of networked learning offered was:

Networked e-learning refers to those learning situations and contexts which, through the use of ICT, allow learners to be connected with other people (for example, learners, teachers/ tutors, mentors, librarians, technical assistants) and with shared information rich resources. Networked e-learning also views learners as contributing to the development of these learning resources and information of various kinds and types (E-Quality Network 2002).

While again the idea of collaborative learning does not appear in the definition in the Manifesto itself, the Manifesto states very explicitly that technology used to support e-learning affords two significant capabilities:

1. Its ability to support distributed collaborative interaction and dialogue
2. Its ability to support access to information-rich resources

These were two capabilities which the signatories of the manifesto felt had been considered unequally. One of the aims of the manifesto was to rebalance the debate on e-learning to give greater attention to the processes which support interaction and dialogue – or in other words "*collaborative* and cooperative learning, learning through dialogue and group work together with interaction with online materials, and collaborative knowledge production" (c.f. NLC 2002 call for papers).

To this date, the Networked Learning Conference series refers to networked learning as an approach that emphasises dialogical and collaborative learning, the NLC 2010 call for papers saying much the same as the 2002 call, i.e.:

The conference is an opportunity to participate in a forum for the critical examination and analysis of research in networked learning i.e. learning and teaching carried out largely via the Internet/Web which emphasises dialogical learning, collaborative and cooperative learning, group work, interaction with on-line materials, and knowledge production.

McConnell (2006) explains that collaboration can help to clarify ideas and concepts through discussion, develop critical thinking and provide opportunities for learners to share information and ideas. He further suggests that it "also helps to develop communication skills, provide a context where the learners can take control of their own learning in a social context and offer or provide validation of individuals' ideas and ways of thinking through conversation (verbalising); multiple perspectives (cognitive restructuring) and argument (conceptual conflict resolution)" (McConnell 2006).

Cousin and Deepwell (2005), like other writers in the field, make a direct connection to the overlap between the collaborative pedagogic values of networked learning and Lave and Wenger's theory of situated learning within communities of practice. The connection to the idea of learning as described by Lave and Wenger (1991) as emerging from collaborative and situated practice was recognised early in the development of networked learning (cf. Goodyear and Steeples 1992; Hodgson and Fox 1995). Taking this further within the context of networked learning, Ferreday et al. (2006) claim that online collaboration that adopts a critical relational dialogue perspective can provide learners with opportunities to articulate their social and cultural experiences and to develop critical thinking.

At the NLC 2010 conference on which this book is based, Beaty, Cousin and Hodgson "revisited" the E-Quality in Networked e-Learning in Higher Education Manifesto stating:

> In the paper we argue that the time is right to simply use the term networked learning and drop the 'e' in networked e-learning. This is because we think it is more important to foreground connectivity as a specific and important pedagogical feature of networked learning. We claim that an updated definition of networked learning should not only refer to being a pedagogy based on connectivity and the co-production of knowledge but also one that aspires to support e-quality of opportunity and include reference to the importance of relational dialogue and critical reflexivity in all of this (2010).

They also alluded to networked learning as being a "pedagogy of inquiry" and one suited for the twenty-first century.

Networked Learning in a Danish Setting

This far, we have focused essentially on the development of networked learning in the UK and how this influenced and led to the Networked Learning Conference series and current networked learning definition.

At the same time, however, similar pedagogical ideas and practices were being developed elsewhere. In a Danish setting, the primary educational exploration of ICT at university level was also linked to developments within open–distance learning.

In the late seventies and beginning of the eighties, Jutland Open University, in a joint initiative between Århus University and Aalborg University, was established. The objective was to offer university programmes as open–distance learning. This initiative was especially taken up by the faculties within the Humanities. Denmark has not had a long tradition of distance education as the other Scandinavian countries, and this gave a kind of freedom to the learning approaches adopted. Where many international distance learning programmes at that time were based on a delivery mode, Jutland Open University was based on a critical educational tradition building on critical investigations and dialogues. At the same time, developments within ICTs provided the opportunities for new infrastructures for learning. Jutland Open University became, in the Danish setting, the spearhead to explore these opportunities; and especially computer conferencing was seen as an interesting tool to explore due to the focus on many-to-many communication, which provided an infrastructure for dialogues and for collaboration as a prerequisite for an educational approach of critical enquiry and dialogue.

There were strong contacts to Hiltz and Turoff, two networked learning pioneers from New Jersey Institute of Technology, who developed the idea of the networked nation (1978) and the virtual classroom (Hiltz 1990) based on the design and use of computer conferencing. But due to practical circumstances, it became PortaCOM, a computer conferencing system originally developed by the Swedish Government's Defence Research Institute (Palme 2000), which was used in the first development projects in Denmark (Dirckinck-Holmfeld 1990). Jutland Open University and the PICNIC group at Aalborg University became some of the pioneers in a Scandinavian setting. PICNIC was the acronym for "Project in Computer Networks in Distance Education Curricula" – a project supported by the Danish Research Council running in the late 1980s (Lorentsen 2004).

A particular focus in the Danish setting, originally developed by the PICNIC team and further developed within the Human Centred Informatics group (later e-Learning Lab) at Aalborg University, and also in the national research network on Multimedia and Learning with partners from most of the Danish universities (later the MIL-group), was the focus on how problem and project-based learning could become the pedagogical foundation for the integration of ICT in a pedagogy of open–distance learning (Danielsen et al. 1999; Dirckinck-Holmfeld 1990; Dirckinck-Holmfeld and Fibiger 2002).

The pedagogical framework, which we labelled (POPP) as an abbreviation of problem-oriented project pedagogy, has its roots in critical pedagogy and socio-constructivist and socio-cultural approaches to the understanding of ICT and learning. It incorporates a series of integrated didactical principles as basis for the design of a learning environment: problem formulation, inquiry of exemplary problems, participant control, interdisciplinary approaches, joint projects and action learning (Dirckinck-Holmfeld 2002; Kolmos et al. 2004). In this approach, (1) students have to go through different systematic stages: preliminary inquiry, problem formulation, theoretical and methodological considerations, experimentation and reflection; (2) the learning content is related to the real world and to the learners' experience – which promotes the students' motivation and comprehension; (3) the projects are carried out in collaboration with companies and public institutions and (4) learning takes place by doing, and through dialogue, communication and collaboration in joint groups (Coto 2010).

Along the way, there were of course other inspirations for the development of POPP. One of the greatest inspirations was the work of Lave and Wenger (1991) and Wenger (1998). In the early nineties, scholars from Aalborg University had an opportunity to engage with the Institute for Research on Learning in Palo Alto, where the principles of learning in communities of practice were being shaped. It became obvious that the principles of learning within communities of practice (Wenger 1998) together with the principles from the critical educational tradition around problem and project-based learning provided a theoretically productive framework to understand principles of collaboration, meaning making and identity within an open–distance learning landscape (Dirckinck-Holmfeld 1995).

Since the early experimentation in the beginning of the eighties using computer conferencing to support problem and project-based learning, the pedagogical approach was further developed theoretically and practically through the early nineties. A great number of educational master programmes have been established and are now being offered on a regular basis. This has provided a solid background for the development of sustainable pedagogical practices integrating the principles of problem and project-based learning and communities of practice.

One of these master's programmes is the MIL-programme, Master in ICT and Learning. It was established in 2000 and has been running for more than 10 years. It is itself a network based on mutual and equal collaboration between five university institutions, and as such a forerunner for the organisational principles of the networked society and new institutional set-ups as described by, among others, Castells (2000).

The Master of ICT and Learning can in a Danish context be seen as a prototypical example of a networked learning environment. Even if it has not from the beginning defined itself within the networked learning framework, it has become evident that it shares some of the same values and principles. ICT has never been a goal in itself. On the other hand, ICT is viewed as a many-fold and complex learning infrastructure, which mediates the learning taking place and which enables the students, students and supervisors and coordinators to work together on shared enterprises to build up shared repertoires and engagements through promoting connections between one learner and other learners, between learners and tutors and between the learning community and its learning resources (Goodyear et al. 2004). In the POPP approach to networked learning, it is however not so much "connections" which are viewed as the core motor for development as more engaged interdependencies between the group members that is seen as the driving force for meaningful learning (Fjuk and Dirckinck-Holmfeld 1997).

Given this opportunity to look back into the history of networked learning in a Danish context, it seems as if the pioneers of networked learning in Denmark have been following many of the same paths as the pioneers of networked learning in the UK. In periods, they have also been engaged in shared activities. The New Jersey Institute of Technology was a kind of shared anchor point at that time and so were activities and seminars organised around Open University in the UK (Mason and Kaye 1990).

Later researchers from Denmark engaged in EQUEL, a European project, and at the Networked Learning Conference in 2004 the EQUEL participants presented five symposia that each explored a dimension of "E-quality in e-learning". Each symposium shared ideas and perspectives and theoretical principles on various practices and experiences of networked learning. Some of the same actors got an opportunity to engage in the European Research Team on "Productive Learning within Networked Learning" within Kaleidoscope, a Network of Excellence on Technology Enhanced Learning, supported by the EU Framework programme 6. This work, reported in Dirckinck-Holmfeld et al. (2009), researched networked learning practices within higher education and continuing professional development to provide a meso-level perspective.

Finally, through the collaboration organising the 7th International Conference on Networked Learning, which took place in Aalborg in 2010 and this book, we have become much more aware of the parallel histories, which have been going on in the various academic communities in the search for productive ways to engage with ICT to serve meaningful learning. In this work, the International Networked Learning Conference along with other conferences in the field, among others the international conference on Computer Supported Collaborative Learning, has played an important role in bringing scholars within education and technology and practitioners together.

Impact of World Wide Web Developments on Networked Learning

Developments of the World Wide Web in the mid 1990s stimulated the emergence of new practices within networked learning and more broadly within e-learning (electronic mediation of learning). The WWW provided new services, graphical interfaces and more user-friendly and accessible environments, and most important the Web has become used by many people for many and various different purposes. The first generation of WWW was dominated by a content delivery metaphor and to make information accessible. Within education courses, delivery systems, such as Black Board, Fronter and Web CT, became widespread. These systems were, due to their design and their focus on content delivery, not so supportive of networked learning approaches. Networked learning communities have been more oriented towards community-oriented systems, as FirstClass, Quickplace or Moodle (Pilkington and Guldberg 2009; Tolsby et al. 2002). With the development of social software sites, first My Space, later Face Book, Second Life, etc., there was a real breakthrough in the use of the Internet. It was estimated (for 2010) that more than a quarter of Earth's population use the services of the Internet (http://www.internetworldstats.com/stats.htm).

Web 2.0 technologies have given unprecedented access to both information and the world and ways of being and interacting. The diffusion of Web 2.0 has given a dramatic rise in the integration of ICT for social and leisure activities. As well as within all kinds of professional activities, Web 2.0 principles are being used. The basic design principles of Web 2.0 are set within a social and participative perspective of interaction that does not depend on expert's meaning and understanding so much as that of members and participants, who negotiate the meaning of the design and the content (Ryberg and Dirckinck-Holmfeld 2010). As such, the Web 2.0 technologies are more in line with the basic pedagogical principles of networked learning focussing on engaged connections and collaborations.

From the history of networked learning, it becomes evident that the focus on engaged connections and collaborations is not caused by the emergence of Web 2.0; however, Web 2.0 technologies may be used in ways, which are more in line with the basic pedagogical principles of networked learning. Thus, Web 2.0 may provide the support for a shift in learning infrastructure, and bring networked learning out of the research lab and into practice providing many different learning designs.

Summary of the Development of Networked Learning

We can begin to delineate more clearly what networked learning is from this review and history of its development. The various scholars and practices associated with networked learning have an identifiable educational philosophy that has emerged out of those educational theories and approaches that can be linked to radical emancipatory and humanistic educational ideas and approaches. It can on the one hand be seen to emulate and reflect principles associated with areas of educational thinking, such as critical pedagogy (cf Freire 1970; Giroux 1992; Negt 1975) and democratic and experiential learning (cf. Dewey 1916; Kolb et al. 1974). While on the other hand it is seen as an approach and pedagogy within the general field of technology-mediated learning especially exploring the socio-cultural designs of learning as mediated by ICT and enacted by networked learning participants.

Structure of the Book

In the previous section, we considered the evolution of networked learning and highlighted some important theoretical, conceptual and practice issues that have occurred over the past 30 years and which have in many ways shaped the way in which networked learning has developed and is practiced today. This section now considers the main recent developments in the theory, practice and pedagogy of networked learning which form the basis of the chapters of this book. There are five sections, followed by a concluding chapter by ourselves. The sections are: developing understandings of networked learning; new landscapes and spaces for networked learning; dynamics of changing tools and infrastructures; understanding the social material in networked learning, and identity, cultural capital and networked learning. The final chapter attempts to consider what has gone before in the book and some important questions addressing the nature of networked learning.

Section 1: Developing Understandings of Networked Learning

In his chapter on *"Networked Learning, the Net Generation and Digital Natives"*, Chris Jones looks at the ways in which young people at the end of the twentieth century have undergone a step change in the use and perception of new technologies in their everyday lives. It is often assumed that the net generation have a fundamentally different orientation to the use of new technologies, and are able and appreciative users. It is also often assumed that because of this, they are or will be positive about the potential use of new technologies in the learning and teaching process and that this has implications for networked learning. In comparing the situation in the year 2000, when broadband was still a novelty and mobile devices relatively sparsely used by young people, with that 10 years later when there is ubiquitous use of the Internet, Web 2.0 and social networking systems, Chris Jones concludes that little has changed in young people's perception of the potential use of these technologies in the learning process. There is no generational divide. Young people use technology in modest ways, focussing on simple tasks of accessing course materials and resources provided by universities. Students are not seeking radical changes in pedagogy that require innovative uses of technology. Jones concludes that self-report and interview studies of the past, often suggesting simple dichotomies and crude determinism, now need to be complemented by in-depth studies looking at the actual use of technology in the learning process. By doing this, we will be able to gain greater insight into the potential for student learning of new technologies.

The chapter by Thomas Ryberg, Lillian Buus and Marianne Georgsen on *"Identifying Differences in Understandings of Networked Learning Theory and Interactional Interdependencies"* asks some fundamental questions about the nature and purpose of networked learning in relation to emerging ideas on "connectivism", which has strong links with Web 2.0 and social networking. They indicate that ideas, such as collaboration, sharing, creation and production, which are commonly associated with Web 2.0 can also be seen in the practice of networked learning. Connections and networking appear to be shared notions in networked learning and "connectivism". The authors explore the theoretical challenges to networked learning by new ideas emerging from "connectivism", and they explore the subtle but important differences in the meaning of shared terms that may point to important differences in pedagogy and the values that underpin learning and teaching in networked learning and in "connectivist" contexts.

Section 2: New Landscapes and Spaces for Networked Learning

The chapter titled *"Mediators of Socio-Technical Capital in a Networked Learning Environment"* by Dan Suthers and Kar-Hai Chu considers the restrictions of existing virtual learning environments (such as WebCT) in supporting what they call overlapping communities: that is, communities of learners that exist between different courses of study. They suggest that the potential for developing wide-ranging social capital is lost by the use of VLEs. They draw on the concepts of "bridging" (Granovetter) and "boundary spanning" (Levina and Vaat) in order to show how the design of a new software environment (called disCourse) can be used to facilitate inter-group communication. They call this "bridging socio-technical capital". Here, users can develop networks of weak ties *outside of their specific course circle* that provide access to a greater number of potential collaborators and resources that often are not available in strong tie circles. They call these "transcendent communities" and suggest that they provide useful networked learning opportunities for higher education students that are additional to those normally embedded communities designed into courses.

Panagiota Alevizou, Rebecca Galley and Gráinne Conole write about "*Collectivity, performance and self-representation: Analysing Cloudworks as a public space for networked learning and reflection*" and describe how the Web-based Cloudworks is a specialised networking site that uses the interfaces of social media within an educational context to permit participants to share resources and exchange ideas in a public space. The authors suggest that Cloudworks is an example of "productive network learning" and it is a place for collective intelligence and expressive interactions. The use of Cloudworks blurs formal and informal cultural learning and networked learning. Cloudworks exists somewhere between micro-blogging practices and the use of Twitter communications. It supports the link between the personal and the community, and provides a location for individuals to meet, discuss personal and collective issues and share resources. The networked learning practices evident in Cloudworks are informal in nature and often have a short lifespan. The chapter shows that issues of performance and identity, the transcendence of boundaries, processes of negotiation of the private and the public and resource sharing are all evident in Cloudworks.

The complex issue of networked learning processes between communities from different language and cultural backgrounds is examined by Juliana Raffaghelli and Cristina Richieri in their chapter titled "*A classroom with a view Networked Learning strategies to promote intercultural education*". The authors suggest networked learning as a place to bring about intercultural education and as a place to meet equal-but-diverse people: a place of interculturalism rather then one of multiculturalism, where relationships are of mutual respect that may lead to cultural exchange. They suggest that instructional design principles and the management of diversity in networked learning are not enough and do not in themselves lead to greater intercultural learning. The authors conclude by inquiring into the possibility of influencing teachers' practices towards creating greater intercultural teaching in networked learning environments, and suggest some interesting future research that may realise this concern.

Section 3: The Dynamics of Changing Tools and Infrastructures

Working from the position of a "technology steward", that is someone who takes a leading role in considering which tools to introduce into a community, Patricia Arnold, John David Smith and Beverly Trayner in their chapter titled "*The challenge of introducing 'one more tool' – a community of practice perspective on networked learning*" examine the intricate relationships between communities and technologies. Their research shows that the social fabric of learning is made up of communities and networks, and both enhance social learning processes. The introduction of "one more tool" – the focus of their work – with the aim of supporting and extending a community's learning – can blur boundaries and create new ones. They show that the interplay among domain, practice and community is affected when "one new tool" is introduced in the community, bringing about changes in identity with the community and methods of engagement.

The chapter on "*Identifying the appropriate network for learning*" by Tom Nyvang and Ann Bygholm considers the conditions under which an institution decides on which ICTs are adopted for supporting networked learning. The authors focus on the shift from the use of one particular learning platform to another in order to show the intricacies of decision making in the process of change. By focussing on three main users of technology – students and teachers, management and support personnel – the authors show that there are various motives, goals and conditions that surround the use of learning technologies by each group. The case study approach adopted by the authors shows that the requirement for change is complex and at times contradictory. They argue that dissatisfaction with the existing system may not be addressed by changing to a new system. The reasons for change of the existing system are around user dissatisfaction in the use of the system, whereas the reasons put forward for adopting a new system focus on the operation, support and management of the system. This apparent contradiction is explained by the authors in terms of poor institutional guidance in the use of the existing system and an absence of explicit policy in the educational purpose of the system. They suggest that issues such as these will not be addressed solely by moving to a new system.

Section 4: Understanding the Social Material in Networked Learning

Terrie Lynn Thompson's chapter "*Who's taming who? Tensions between people and technologies in cyberspace communities*" adopts a socio-material approach to the exploration of various online networks in which self-employed people interact with Web technologies. With more people looking to the Web as a place for seeking human–human learning opportunities in online communities, concern is rising over the ways in which they negotiate the *materiality* of the net: that is the human–non-human pathways through the various discussion boards, chat forums and access to social networking systems and so on. The author shows that there is a series of passages through which users move, and in doing this they experience stabilising and disrupting community relations. It seems that users' attempts to "tame" the technology are counteracted by the technology attempting to "tame" users. These relationships can be described as entanglements of hybrid or socio-technical constructions, which raise a series of interesting questions which the author addresses.

The focus of the chapter by Linda Creanor and Steve Walker titled "*Learning Technology in context: a case for the sociotechnical interaction framework as an analytical lens for networked learning research*" is socio-technical approaches in networked learning, and how they can provide useful concepts that are underutilised in the networked learning literature. Widespread technological determinism often describes relationships between people, technology and learning, contributing to gaps in our understandings of the use of learning technologies and learning. The authors argue for the use of socio-technical interaction network (STIN) (Kling) as a little used but useful method for understanding the complexities of contemporary learning. They argue that there is good reason to approach the examination of networked learning through the lens of social agency, ownership and control. Although there is a call for an emphasis on epistemic fluency (Goodyear et al.) in networked learning, existing theories (e.g. networked theory; actor network theory; communities of practice and so on) seem to have little widespread utility in mainstream HE practice. The chapter argues for a better balance between understandings of social agency and individual autonomy in the networked learning field. The authors feel that socio-technical frameworks can complement the use of socio-cultural theories, and help us make sense of the new interactions and analyse their consequences.

Section 5: Identity, Cultural Capital and Networked Learning

The advent of the use in higher education of blogging, reflective e-portfolios and other forms of online communication requiring high levels of reflection and disclosure raises serious questions about the kinds of new literacies required by students who are asked to use these tools as part of the formal learning and teaching process. This leads to the need to assist students in developing new forms of digital literacies which they can draw on in their course work. This concern for developing in students new forms of digital literacies is the subject of the chapter titled "*Just what is being reflected in online reflection? New literacies for new media practices*" by Jen Ross. The background to the chapter is a study examining how students and teachers negotiate issues of identity, authenticity, ownership, privacy and performativity in high-stakes online reflection in higher education. Jen Ross shows how the wider cultural societal context of blogging, where there is often a high degree of risk taking and personal disclosure, affects expectations in the use of these tools in higher education contexts. Conflicting expectations and norms are often associated with blogging, relating to authenticity, risk, pretence, commodification, othering and narcissism. Student and teacher assumptions and practices are affected, which suggests that we need to give greater consideration to the nature of online reflective writing and to the associated tensions that as a consequence arise.

The study by Laura Czerniewicz and Cheryl Brown titled "*Objectified cultural capital and the tale of two students*" examines the ways in which students use cell phones as a central and important means of accessing higher education resources. The authors explain that in South Africa, there is considerably greater ownership of cell phones by students than there is of personal computers. They take this as their impetus to examine the digitally mediated worlds of South African students, and to explore how the identities of students are forged through the use of cell phones as they access and contribute to the resources of higher education.

The chapter provides two students as illustrative cases of mobile-centric and computer-centric digital practices. Bourdieu's concept of cultural capital (in its objectified and embodied forms) is used as a lens to examine the students' differences and similarities, their convergences over time and their disparate histories. The different types of objectified cultural capital available to each student are described, as are the processes of appropriation of embodied cultural capital. The relationship between these different types of capital and their influence on the students' attitudes to and choices about using ICTs for learning is especially relevant. Of particular note is the role that the cell phone as objectified capital plays. The case studies surface complexities, which need unravelling, and point to the research questions to be explored when grappling with participation in higher education in a digital age.

The focus of the chapter by Sue Smith titled "*How do SME leaders learn within networked learning? The situated curriculum and social identity*" is a networked learning programme set up for the owner-managers of small businesses (SMEs). It draws on the ideas of communities of practice and situated curriculum in particular to discuss how the owner-managers through participation in the "LEAD" programme acquire/construct an identity as LEAD delegates. The chapter argues that through the process of participation and constructing an identity as a LEAD delegate the programme participants learn and acquire an identity of leaders of their SMEs. What is significant in this process is that the participative pedagogy and networked learning approach of the programme are used to encourage critical reflection through dialogue. It is claimed that the pedagogical approach and spaces for learning that the programme provides, enabled by the programme facilitators, encourage the delegates to become leaders that are critically reflective and are open to challenging their own taken-for-granted assumptions and practice. Sue Smith concludes that given the importance of the enablers' roles in this process, critical reflexivity is essential for this networked learning role.

How do higher education practitioners develop new designs for learning in online settings in the face of widespread changes in higher education that require learners to acquire new digital skills, and for teachers to produce high-quality learning experiences and learning outcomes in the context of increased demands for productivity? The chapter by Karin Tweddell Levinsen and Janni Nielsen titled "*Innovating Design for Learning in the Networked Society*" attempts to address these and other important, but difficult-to-answer, questions. The authors note that their study is situated in the widespread social, political and economic changes in society brought about by a move from the industrial to the networked society and that these changes have a profound effect on education and on the identities of teachers and students. They ask the question: How can the educational system meet the challenge of the changing conditions? Is there a conflict between the call for higher education to be more productive while also continuing to produce high-quality learning, which takes time? Within the context of a system where teachers have to produce more with fewer resources, the authors explore the development of what they call a "Design for Learning Model" intended to provide forms of networked learning that support learners in the new demands they face in taking on heavier workloads in the context of greater pressure on their time.

In Jorgen Lerche Nielsen's and Oluf Danielsen's chapter titled "*Problem-oriented project studies – the role of the teacher as supervising the study group in its learning processes*", the authors consider an emerging change in the role of the teacher in supporting PBL students (or students involved in problem-oriented project studies, as they prefer to call their form of PBL) from that of the teacher who acts as expert and decides on the curriculum to be followed by students, provides lectures, sets tasks and unilaterally assesses learning outcomes to that of a supervisor and facilitator, supporting students in examining problems that they themselves have adopted and wish to focus on. This new teacher role produces a shift in relations between the student and the teacher, the latter now focussing on processes and methodological issues and ensuring a strong reflective element of the overall process, rather than ensuring that students follow "correct" and accepted procedures for examining problems. In the chapter, the authors explore the challenges for teachers and students in this new relationship, drawing on the literature to inform practice and to suggest ways of understanding what these new relationships may mean for the learning and teaching process.

The many transformative experiences encountered by academics in adjusting to, and participating in, networked learning environments is discussed in the chapter by Stuart Boon and Christine Sinclair, titled "*Life Behind The Screen: Taking the Academic Online*". The transition by academics from contexts of familiar practice to the new one of being an online practitioner results in some disconnectedness. Academics continue to have a stake in existing practices as they become immersed in their new, virtual environments. This has implications for identity as they find themselves operating in both kinds of environment simultaneously. Identity, language, time and engagement are viewed as both barriers and enablers in the movement from behind the screen to full participation in networked learning environments. In exploring sites of transformation and highlighting the process of transition involved in taking the academic online, the authors identify potential challenges and opportunities experienced in stepping out from behind the screen and projecting themselves into networked learning environments.

Concluding Chapter: The Theory, Pedagogy and Practice of Networked Learning

In the final chapter, we reflect on what has gone before in the central chapters of the book and consider four important questions concerning the theory, pedagogy and practice of networked learning. These questions are:

1. Is networked learning a theory, practice or pedagogy?
2. What are the pedagogical values that underpin networked learning?

3. What is the relevance and challenges of networked learning to mainstream higher education?
4. What new possibilities and challenges is Web 2.0 bringing to networked learning?

References

Beaty, E., Cousin, G., & Hodgson, V. (2010). Revisiting the e-quality in networked learning manifesto. In Dirckinck-Holmfeld, L., Hodgson, V., Jones, C., McConnell, D., & Ryberg, T. (Eds.), *Proceedings of the 7th International Conference on Networked Learning 2010.* Aalborg, Denmark: Aalborg University. ISBN978-1-86220-225-2.

Boot, R., & Hodgson, V. (1987). Open learning: Meaning and experience. In V. Hodgson, S. Mann, & R. Snell (Eds.), *Beyond distance teaching: Towards open learning* (pp. 5–15). Buckingham: Open University Press.

Castells, M. (2000). *The rise of the network society* (2nd ed.). Oxford: Blackwell.

Coffey, J. (1977). Open learning opportunities for mature students. In C. Davies (Ed.), *Open learning systems for mature students, CET Working Paper 14.* London: Council for Educational Technology.

Coto, M. C. (2010). *Designing for change in university teaching practices. A community of practice approach to facilitate university teacher professional development in ICT and project-oriented problem pedagogy.* PhD thesis, Department of Communication and Psychology, Aalborg University, Aalborg.

Cousin, G., & Deepwell, F. (2005). Designs for network learning: A communities of practice perspective. *Studies in Higher Education, 30*(1), 57–66.

Danielsen, O., Dirckinck-holmfeld, L., Sørensen, B. H., Nielsen, J., & Fibiger, B. (1999). *Læring og multimedier [Learning and multimedia].* Aalborg: Aalborg University Press.

Dewey, J. (1916). *Democracy and education: An introduction to the philosophy of education (1966 edn).* New York: Free Press.

Dirckinck-Holmfeld, L. (1990). *Kommunikation på trods og på tværs* [Project pedagogy and computer-mediated communication in distance education] Dissertation, Aalborg University, Aalborg.

Dirckinck-Holmfeld, L. (1995). Tilbage til praksis [Back to practice]. *Humaniora, 9*(2), 25–27.

Dirckinck-Holmfeld, L. (2002). Designing virtual learning environments based on problem oriented project pedagogy. In L. Dirckinck-Holmfeld & B. Fibiger (Eds.), *Learning in virtual environments* (pp. 31–54). Frederiksberg C: Samfundslitteraturess.

Dirckinck-Holmfeld, L., & Fibiger, B. (Eds.). (2002). *Learning in virtual environments.* Frederiksberg C: Samfundslitteratur.

Dirckinck-Holmfeld, L., Jones, C., & Lindström, B. (Eds.). (2009). *Analysing networked learning practices in higher education and continuing professional development.* Rotterdam: Sense Publishers.

Emms, J., & McConnell, D. (1988). An evaluation of tutorial support provided by electronic mail and computer conferencing. *Aspects of Educational Technology, 21,* 263–270.

E-Quality Network (2002). *Towards e-quality in networked e-learning in higher education 'manifesto.* Presented at the Networked Learning 2002 Conference, Sheffield. Retrieved August 7, 2011 from http://csalt.lancs.ac.uk/esrc/manifesto.htm

Ferreday, D. J., Hodgson, V. E., & Jones, C. (2006). Dialogue, language and identity: Critical issues for networked management learning. *Studies in Continuing Education, 28*(3), 223–239.

Fjuk, A., & Dirckinck-Holmfeld, L. (1997). Articulation of actions in distributed collaborative learning. *Scandinavian Journal of Information Systems, 9*(2), 3–24.

Freire, P. (1970). *Pedagogy of the oppressed.* New York: Continuum.

Giroux, H. (1992). *Border crossings: Cultural workers and the politics of education*. New York: Routledge.

Goodyear, P. (2001). *Effective networked learning in higher education notes and guidelines*. Retrieved August 7, 2011 from http://csalt.lancs.ac.uk/jisc/

Goodyear, P., Banks, S., Hodgson, V., & McConnell, D. (2004). Research on networked learning: An overview. In P. Goodyear, S. Banks, V. Hodgson, & D. McConnell (Eds.), *Advances in research on networked learning*. Dordrecht: Kluwer.

Goodyear, P., & Steeples, C. (1992). IT-based open learning tasks and tools. *Journal of Computer Assisted Learning, 8*(3), 163–176.

Harris, D. (1987). *Openness and closure in distance education*. Lewes: Falmer Press.

Hiltz, S. R. (1990). Evaluating the virtual classroom. In L. Harasim (Ed.), *Online education: Perspectives on a new environment*. New York: Praeger.

Hiltz, S. R., & Turoff, M. (1978). *The network nation: Human communication via computer* (1st ed.). Reading, MA: Addison-Wesley.

Hodgson, V., & Fox, S. (1995). Understanding networked learning communities. In P. Held & W. F. Kugemann (Eds.), *Telematics for education and training*. Proceedings of Delta 94 Conference, Dusseldorf, Germany.

Hodgson, V., Lewis, R., & McConnell, D. (1989). *IT-based open learning: A study report*. ESRC InTER Programme Occasional Paper 12/89, Lancaster University, Lancaster, England.

Hodgson, V. E., & McConnell, D. (1992). IT-based open learning: A case-study in management learning. *Journal of Computer Assisted Learning, 8*(3), 136–158.

Hodgson, V. E., & McConnell, D. (1995). Co-operative learning and development networks. *Journal of Computer Assisted Learning, 11*(4), 210–224.

Howe, A., & McConnell, D. (1984). The use of the Cyclops telewriting system for teaching electronics. *International Journal of Electrical Engineering Education, 21*, 234–249.

Knowles, M. (1975). *Self-directed learning*. New York: Associated Press.

Knowles, M. (1985). *Andragogy in action*. San Francisco: Jossey Bass.

Kolb, D. A., Rubin, I. M., & McIntyre, J. M. (1974). *Organizational psychology: A book of readings* (2nd ed.). Englewood Cliffs, NJ: Prentice-Hall.

Kolmos, A., Fink, F. K., & Krogh, L. (Eds.). (2004). *The Aalborg PBL model: Progress, diversity and challenges*. Aalborg: Aalborg University Press.

Lave, J., & Wenger, E. (1991). *Situated learning: Legitimate peripheral participation*. Cambridge: Cambridge University Press.

Lorentsen, A. (2004). Quality in master programmes in continuing education through problem based project work. In A. Kolmos, F. K. Fink, & L. Krogh (Eds.), *The Aalborg PBL mode l: Progress, diversity and challenges* (pp. 263–283). Aalborg: Aalborg University Press.

Mason, R., & Kaye, A. (1990). Towards a new paradigm for distance education. In L. Harasim (Ed.), *Online education: Perspectives on a new environment*. New York: Praeger.

McConnell, D. (1982). Cyclops telewriting tutorials. *Teaching at a Distance, 22*(Autumn), 20–25.

McConnell, D. (1983). Sharing the screen: Cyclops teleconference tutorials. *Media in Education and Development, June*, 59–63.

McConnell, D. (1984). Cyclops shared-screen teleconferencing. In A. W. Bates (Ed.), *The role of technology in distance education* (pp. 139–153). London: Croom Helm.

McConnell, D. (1986). The impact of Cyclops shared-screen teleconferencing in distance tutoring. *British Journal of Educational Technology, 17*(1), 37–70.

McConnell, D. (1988a). Computer conferencing in teacher inservice education: A case study. In D. Harris (Ed.), *World yearbook of education, 1988: Education for the new technologies* (pp. 199–218). London: Kogan Page.

McConnell, D. (1988b). Co-operative student/tutor design of an educational technology and development course for adults. *Aspects of Educational Technology, 21*, 64–71.

McConnell, D. (1994). *Implementing computer supported cooperative learning*. London: Kogan Page.

McConnell, D. (1998). Developing networked learning professionals: A critical perspective. In Banks, S., Graebner, C., & McConnell, D. (Eds.), *Networked lifelong learning: Innovative approaches to education and training through the Internet* (pp. v.1-v.x11). Proceedings of the International Conference, University of Sheffield, DACE, Sheffield, England. ISBN 1 899 323 05 1 (pp. 430). Retrieved August 7, 2011 from http://www.networkedlearningconference.org.uk/past/nlc1998/

McConnell, D. (1999). Networked learning [Guest editorial]. *Journal of Computer Assisted Learning, 15*(3), 177–178.

McConnell, D. (2000). *Implementing computer supported cooperative learning* (2nd ed.). London: Kogan Page.

McConnell, D. (2006). *E-learning groups and communities*. Maidenhead: SRHE/OU Press.

McConnell, D., & Sharples, M. (1983). Distance teaching by Cyclops: An educational evaluation of the open university's telewriting system. *British Journal of Educational Technology, 14*(2), 109–126.

Morrison, T. R. (1989). Beyond legitimacy: Facing the future in distance education. *International Journal of Lifelong Education, 8*(1), 3–24.

Negt, O. (1975). *Sociologisk fantasi og eksemplarisk indlæring* (B. Nielsen et.al., Trans.). Frederiksberg: Roskilde University Press. (Original work published 1971)

Palme, O. (2000). *History of the KOM Computer Conferencing System*. Retrieved January 19, 2011 from http://people.dsv.su.se/~jpalme/s1/history-of-KOM.html

Pilkington, R., & Guldberg, K. (2009). Conditions for productive networked learning among professionals and carers: The WebAutism case study. In L. Dirckinck-Holmfeld, C. Jones, & B. Lindström (Eds.), *Analysing networked learning practices in higher education and continuing professional development*. Rotterdam: Sense Publishers.

Rogers, C. (1983). *Freedom to learn for the eighties*. Columbus, OH: C. E. Merrill.

Ryberg, T., & Dirckinck-Holmfeld, L. (2010). Analysing digital literacy in action: A case study of a problem-oriented learning process. In R. Sharpe, H. Beetham, & S. de Freitas (Eds.), *Rethinking learning for a digital age* (pp. 170–183). New York: Routledge.

Short, T. J., Williams, E., & Christie, B. (1976). *The social psychology of telecommunications*. London: Wiley.

Steeples, C., & Jones, C. (Eds.). (2001). *Networked learning in higher education*. Berlin: Springer Verlag.

Tolsby, H., Nyvang, T., & Dirckinck-Holmfeld, L. (2002). A survey of technologies supporting virtual project based learning. In S. Banks (Ed.), *The third international conference on networked learning* (pp. 572–581). Sheffield: University of Sheffield.

Wenger, E. (1998). *Communities of practice: Learning, meaning, and identity*. New York: Cambridge University Press.

Part II
Developing Understandings
of Networked Learning

Chapter 2
Networked Learning, Stepping Beyond the Net Generation and Digital Natives

Chris Jones

Introduction

This chapter critically examines an idea that has become common during the past 10 years that young people have undergone a generational change in which their exposure to digital and networked technologies, the bits and bytes of the twenty-first century, has caused a step change in the character of a whole generation. The empirical and theoretical basis for this argument is reviewed and critical theoretical perspectives are assessed. The discussion begins by reexamining the outcomes of a research project that studied the experience of networked learning in English universities that took place at the very end of the twentieth century. Evidence from that research is compared and contrasted with evidence gathered from students who were the very first students that could be described as part of the new generation, gathered approximately 10 years later.

The argument for a generational break is put clearly by Marc Prensky the originator of the term digital native when he states that young people have:

> ... not just changed incrementally from those of the past ... A really big discontinuity has taken place. One might even call it a "singularity" – an event which changes things so fundamentally that there is absolutely no going back (Prensky 2001, p. 1).

The claim for such a dramatic change rests on powerful anecdotal and popular evidence. Many educators and parents connect with an idea which identifies young people as more naturally adept with new technologies than they find themselves or others of the same age. The claim made by the author is that the material context constituted by widespread computing and digital networks has led to young people developing an instinctive aptitude and high skill levels in relation to the new technologies.

C. Jones (✉)
The Institute of Educational Technology, Open University, Milton Keynes, UK
e-mail: c.r.jones@open.ac.uk

L. Dirckinck-Holmfeld et al. (eds.), *Exploring the Theory, Pedagogy and Practice of Networked Learning*, DOI 10.1007/978-1-4614-0496-5_2,
© Springer Science+Business Media, LLC 2012

Those older people who grew up in an analogue world, prior to the new digital technologies, are portrayed as always being behind, as being immigrants to this new world, and never likely to reach the levels of skill and fluency developed effortlessly by those who have grown up with new digital technologies.

The issue is important to networked learning because these claims include specific claims about approaches to learning in the new generation. The young learner is characterized as exhibiting known qualities that can be assumed to apply to an entire generation. The language used about the new generation of learners is directive and contains few qualifications. For example, Tapscott says this in his most recent book:

> In education they [the Net Generation] are forcing a change in the model of pedagogy, from a teacher-focused approach based on instruction to a student-focused model based on collaboration (Tapscott 2009, p. 11).

The language is firm and commanding and the claim is that like it or not a new generation is forcing change and the character of that change is student-focused and based on collaboration. The claim that the new generation is likely to have a profound effect on education suggests that educational reform arises out of pressure from a new generation of digitally native students.

The general idea that the Internet would change learning practices was sketched out in the late 1980s and early 1990s. Harasim et al. (1995) wrote in terms of network learning and suggested that:

> Network learners of the future will have access to formal and informal education of their choice, wherever they are located, whenever they are able to participate ... The network learner will be an active participant ... learning with and from experts and peers wherever they are located (p. 273).

The development that has occurred in the past 10 years is that the mechanism for change has moved from choice to become identified with a transformation in the character of a new generation of young people that have grown up with new technologies. Marc Prensky has recently written *Teaching Digital Natives* (Prensky 2010), a book in which he argues that because of the technological environment in the twenty-first century:

> It is inevitable ... that change would finally come to our young peoples' education as well, and it has. But there is a huge paradox for educators: the place where the biggest educational changes have come is not our schools; it is everywhere else but our schools (p. 1).

Prensky is not alone in suggesting that institutional change has been slow and is likely to arise as an outcome of an inevitable process consequent on generational change. Don Tapscott (2009), for example, devoted an entire chapter in his recent book to the Net Generation as learners. It is clear from his writing that Tapscott views education as one of the central locations for the broad institutional changes he associates with the new generation, something he has developed further elsewhere (Tapscott and Williams 2010). Palfrey and Gasser (2008) also devote a chapter to learners in their book *Born Digital* and they also go on to promote the argument that: "The educational establishment is utterly confused about what to do about the impact of technology on learning" (p. 238). All these authors encourage the idea that education has to change because there has been a generational change caused by a process of technological change. In this view, technological change is seen as arising independently and then having an impact on other dependant domains in society. Even when technological change is not seen as independent, it is often described as an inevitable outcome of social development. Writing in 2003, Selwyn noted that the problem with such discourses is that they fail to reflect the diversity and complexity to be found in real lives. This weakness can have an impact and become embedded in policy and "the framing of children, adults and technology within these determinist discourses tends to hide the key shaping actors, the values and power relations behind the increasing use of ICT in society" (Selwyn 2003 p. 368).

This chapter takes a critical stance in relation to the arguments put forward for there being a new Net Generation of digital native students and explores the consequences of these ideas from the standpoint of networked learning. Networked learning is defined in this chapter as:

> learning in which information and communication technology ... is used to promote connections: between one learner and other learners, between learners and tutors; between a learning community and its learning resources (Goodyear et al. 2004, p. 1).

A key term in this definition is the word connections. It is the interactions that connectivity allows, including human interactions with materials and resources, but most particularly the human–human interactions enabled through digital and networked technologies that are the key to networked learning. The definition of networked learning takes a relational stance in which learning takes place both in relation to others and in relation to learning resources.

This definition was applied in a research project that took place at the end of the twentieth century which aimed to explore students' experiences of networked learning in higher education (Goodyear et al. 2001). At that time, there was relatively little research that examined undergraduate use of networked technologies in what would now be described as a blended setting, that is, sustaining courses in which networked technologies were supported by face-to-face contact (Goodyear et al. 2005; Jones and Bloxham 2001; Jones and Asensio 2001). This chapter looks back at the outcomes of that research in the context of recent research examining the terms Net Generation and digital native in both England and broader global contexts. The aim of this retrospective review is to suggest that ways in which the changes that have taken place in networked technologies and students' attitudes toward them can be more adequately theorized in relation to the idea of networked learning.

Networked Learning in Higher Education

The research that took place between 1999 and 2000, in the networked learning in higher education project, used a mixed method approach, including whole course surveys and interviews with staff and students from a range of courses in English HE. The findings from the research established that there were no strong links between students' judgments about their experience of networked learning and either their conceptions of learning or their approach to study. A practical implication of this research was that it was reasonable to expect *all* students to have positive experiences on well-designed and well-managed networked learning courses, and positive experiences were not likely to be restricted to those students with more sophisticated conceptions of learning or deep approaches to study (Goodyear et al. 2003). Prominent among our research goals was to see firstly whether there were significant differences between students' expectations about networked learning and their reports of their experience of networked learning at the end of a course, and secondly whether expectations and experiences differed between different groups of students. Students' views were generally positive at the start and at the end of each course, though their attitudes became more moderate over time. The structure of students' reported feelings remained relatively stable over time and there was no evidence to suggest that male or younger students had more positive feelings about networked learning. The thoroughness with which new technologies were integrated into a networked learning course appeared to be a significant factor in explaining differences in students' feelings and as might be expected, a well-integrated course was associated with more positive experiences (Goodyear et al. 2005). At the dawn of the new millennium, there was no evidence in the study of courses in England using networked learning of a generational divide, rather the course context, and particularly the degree to which networked learning was embedded in the course, appeared to be a key factor.

Empirical Research on Digital Natives and the Net Generation

A persistent call has been for the introduction of good empirical evidence into the debate about the existence of a Net Generation and digital natives. Recently, there has been a significant effort to ground the Net Generation and digital native debate in evidence and there are a range of nationally and regionally focused research studies. These include studies in the USA (Hargittai 2010; Salaway et al. 2008; Smith and Borreson Caruso 2010; Smith et al. 2009) and Canada (Bullen et al. 2009; Salajan et al. 2010), Australia (Judd and Kennedy 2010, 2011; Kennedy et al. 2006, 2007, 2008, 2010; Oliver and Goerke 2007; Waycott et al. 2009), the UK (Jones and Cross 2009; Jones and Healing 2010a; Jones and Hosein 2010; Jones et al. 2010; Margaryan et al. 2011; Selwyn 2008), other European countries (Schulmeister 2010; Ryberg et al. 2010; Pedró 2009), South Africa (Brown and Czerniewicz 2010; Czerniewicz et al. 2009; Thinyane 2010), Chile (Sánchez et al. 2010), and Hong Kong (McNaught et al. 2009). This empirical evidence from around the world, in contrasting economic conditions, shows that today's young students repeatedly prove to be a mixture of groups with various interests, motives, and behaviors, and never a single generational cohort with common characteristics.

Rather than showing a Net Generation of digital native students, who were naturally proficient with technology due to their exposure to the technology-rich environment, the empirical evidence showed that students' experiences with technologies varied. Not all students were equally competent with technologies and their patterns of use varied considerably when moved beyond basic and entrenched technologies (Hosein et al. 2010b; Jones et al. 2010; Kennedy et al. 2008). There were variations among students within the Net Generation age band (Bullen et al. 2009; Hosein et al. 2010b; Jones et al. 2010) and students' selection of tools were related to other characteristics, including age, gender, socioeconomic background, academic discipline, and year of study (Brown and Czerniewicz 2008; Hargittai 2010; Jones et al. 2010; McNaught et al. 2009; Selwyn 2008).

Although there has been a considerable growth in university students' access to a range of computing technologies and online technological tools, their use of technologies has often been for social and entertainment purposes rather than learning (Oliver and Goerke 2007) and there were differences in students' use of technology for social and leisure purposes and for academic use (Corrin et al. 2010; Hosein et al. 2010a; Kennedy et al. 2008). Furthermore, empirical studies showed that students' high levels of use and skill did not necessarily translate into preferences for increased use of technology in the classroom (Schulmeister 2010) and a large number of students still hold conventional attitudes toward teaching (Margaryan et al. 2011). In my own work, the research focused on first-year university students and there was no evidence that students arrived at university with high expectations for ICT use that the university could not fulfil (Hosein et al. 2010a; Jones and Hosein 2010; Jones et al. 2010). The findings also showed that students used ICT more than they were required to but they tend to use the same technologies that are required to use for their courses. This suggests that the range of technologies that students are familiar with, and which they expect to be available, are not radically different to those currently supplied by English universities and that students are still using ICT in somewhat predictable ways, e.g., to communicate with their tutors and to access course materials. The longitudinal analysis of our data suggested that in a similar way to the data gathered almost 10 years earlier, students become slightly less firm in their opinions about the usefulness of ICT for learning during their studies and their opinion becomes slightly less positive with regard to some university provision, such as online library resources and specialist software.

There is now a need to return to the theories that contend for attention in explaining both the changes the evidence shows are taking place and how these changes relate both to students' age and a variety of other demographic and contextual influences.

Theory, Criticisms, and Alternative Approaches

Several authors (Bayne and Ross 2007; Buckingham and Willett 2006; Herring 2008) have pointed to the importance of commercial and market interests in perpetuating the idea of a new generation and we noted earlier the strong anecdotal appeal of generational arguments for parents and educators. However, such arguments lead to some highly negative consequences. Bayne and Ross, for example, note that digital native arguments lead to a paradoxical one-way determinism in which institutions and teachers are forced to change but each person is said to be fixed in their own generational position. This provides a contradictory account in which older people are expected to change, though they are generationally fixed, and become more like the new generation. In education, this can lead to a deficit model of professional development in which academic staffs who are outside the new generation can only ever be "immigrants," never able to fully bridge the gap with "natives" arising from their generational position (Bayne and Ross; Bennett et al. 2008).

Bennett et al. (2008) have noted that the discourse surrounding technology and generational change resembles an academic "moral panic," in that it restricts critical and rational debate and because the new generation is identified as a positive but threatening presence in relation to the existing academic order. The Net Generation and digital native discourse is one that provides a series of binary distinctions, new generation or old generations; technically capable and inclined or technically challenged; and finally between students and their teachers. These authors do not dismiss the potential for change related to developments in digital and networked technology, rather they argue for the collection of evidence and the adoption of a cautious attitude when advocating technologies as a vehicle for educational reform.

The Generational Argument

The idea of a Net Generation composed of digital natives has a strong generational component. Howe and Strauss wrote *Millennials Rising* (2000) several years after the book *Generations: The History of America's Future and The Fourth Turning: An American Prophecy* (1991). The idea of a Millennial generation is related to a cyclic view of history that suggests that the history of the USA has followed a regular and predictable pattern since the 16th century. From this perspective, the Millennials are simply the most recent outcome of a long historical process. Millennials, although described by their digital and networked technological context, are part of a process rooted in human history, biology, and culture. In this scheme, they are the most recent form of the "Civic" generational type, who are said to be heroic, collegial, and rationalistic. Interestingly, they are also said to have core values that include community, technology, and affluence. The idea of the Net Generation was associated with the historical idea of a Millennial generation through the work of Oblinger and Oblinger (2005).

The authors who use the term Net Generation do not generally advance this cyclical argument about generations, but the generational argument has had a clear influence on thinking about young people in education. Oblinger and Oblinger (2005, Ch. 2) explicitly build on the ideas of Howe and Strauss in the book Educating the Net Generation. While Oblinger and Oblinger are careful to state their claims cautiously, they associate a new generation, drawn directly from Howe and Strauss, with the Net Generation defined in terms of its exposure to technology (Jones 2011).

Palfrey and Gasser in their book Born Digital (2008) and subtitled "understanding the first generation of digital natives" suggest that the term generation is an overstatement and prefer to call the new cohort a "population" (p. 14). Their intention in this is clearly to reclaim the term digital native, but I fear their cause is lost. By identifying a population by their access to technology, it ceases to have full generational coverage because technology access is not a universal condition within the age group. They also note that access to technology is partly dependant upon a learned digital literacy. However, if being part of the population of digital natives requires learning, then the group cannot be "Born Digital" and it is not clear what benefits there are in retaining the idea of being a digital "native." Even in the authors' own terms, digital native is at best misleading and the idea of generational change needs to be abandoned.

As we have noted, Kennedy et al. (2008) found that the use of technologies among first-year Australian students showed significant diversity when looking beyond the basic and entrenched technologies. They found that the patterns of access to, use of, and preference for a range of other technologies varied considerably among students of a similar age. Similarly, in my own work (Jones et al. 2010), I have reported that English first-year students show significant age-related variations and that these are not generational in character. The Net Generation age group is itself divided internally and both of these empirical studies suggest that while age is a factor there is no single Net Generation or digital native group and that first-year university students of a similar age show a diversity that is inconsistent with a generational hypothesis.

Agency and Affordance

The arguments used to support the contention that there has been a significant generational change rely on a form of structural, specifically technological, determinism. The argument suggests that because young people have been exposed to a range of digital and networked technologies there has been a consequent change in their attitudes and natural skill levels with these technologies and they are radically different from preceding generations. In this account, technology behaves as an independent and external structural factor acting on social forms but not being conditioned by them. Alternative accounts understand young people as active agents in the process of engagement with technology. The notion of agency has been widely discussed as a contrasting framework to structure in the social sciences. Structure describes the factors enabling and constraining what human agents do. Agency, in contrast, is concerned with the shaping of processes by the intentions and projects of humans. Czerniewicz et al. (2009) have investigated student agency in relation to university students' use of new technology by applying the critical realist approach of Archer (2002, 2003).

Archer's opinion is that agency can be viewed as a "distinct strata of reality" (Archer 2003, p. 2), in which agency is emergent and cannot be reduced to structure nor vice versa. In Archer's writing, there is an association of the agent with the person and the self and social identity for Archer is a "subset" of personal identity. It is the individual who holds the power to be active and reflexive:

> In a nutshell, the individual, as presented here in his or her concrete singularity, has powers of ongoing reflexive monitoring of both self and society (Archer 2002, p. 19).

The strength of this approach is the rejection of social as well as technological determinism and its focus on the active mediation between structure and agency. Archer also argues that agency is fundamentally a human characteristic. Czerniewicz et al. (2009) agree with this approach and argue that: "The particular value of Archer's work is her interest in the relation between agency and structure from the perspective of the agent, or the person" (Czerniewicz et al. 2009, p. 83).

The research I have conducted (Jones and Healing 2010a) illustrates the way in which the structural conditions that students face at university are, at least in part, the outcomes of collective agency. The research showed how staff members designed and redesigned courses in relation to available technologies and how the availability of the technologies themselves was an outcome of decisions and actions taken elsewhere in the university. For this reason, I have suggested expanding the notion of the agent to include persons acting not on their own behalf, but enacting roles in collective organizations, such as courses, departments, schools, and universities. Furthermore, individual students are working in settings that have increasing amounts of active technologies that replicate the aspects of human agency. Increasingly, the digital networks through which education is mediated are able to become interactive and I reported that distraction is already recounted by students who suggest it is caused by the intervention of automated processes, such as notifications from social networking sites. While it may be correct to argue that there is not a complete symmetry between human and machine agency, there is an increasing likelihood that students will interact with humans and machines in similar ways.

Networked Individualism and Networked Sociality

Manuel Castells is possibly the most widely known author to place networks at the centre of contemporary society (2000). Building on work by Wellman (see Wellman et al. 2003), Castells has used the term "networked individualism" to describe the form of sociality in such societies. Networked individualism relates to the way social relations are realized in interaction between online and off-line social networks and to a move from physical communities to personalized or privatized virtual networks. This social trend raises fundamental questions about the relationships between the emerging networked society and the organization of learning environments in both formal education and training. Networked individualism might suggest that we need to take a more critical approach to the theories of education and learning that are based on community and collaboration. The term also suggests that we can do this without ruling out the central place of communication and dialogue in education and learning (Jones and Dirckinck-Holmfeld 2009). The term networked individualism suggests a move away from place-to-place interaction toward interactions that are person to person in character. The pattern of social life enabled by networked digital technologies is one that allows for a sociability based on the person rather than classic notions of community and collaboration. The new networks rely as much on weak ties as they do on the strong ties of traditional groups and communities (Jones et al. 2008).

The emphasis on the person and choice in networked individualism contrasts with the deterministic arguments that support the Net Generation and digital natives. Bennett and Maton (2010) suggest that networked individualism places the focus on the individuals who navigate through their own personal networks. This focus on choice is welcome, but it may be insufficient as the choices people make are in conditions that they themselves are not able to control (Jones 2011). Jones and Healing (2010a) argue that choices are made at various levels of social scale, including in universities, departments, and whole institutions. Their argument suggests that choice cannot be restricted to the individual and that decisions about what kind of infrastructures to provide for students have an impact on the range of choices which students have.

If educational designers and university policy makers respond to networked individualism by individualizing networked learning, they are not only responding to a social pressure, they are adding to it by constituting a privatized context within which students make educational and technological choices. The more radical arguments for PLEs suggest an extremely individualized and learner-centric view of learning. This radical view ignores the political and institutional requirements built into educational systems for social cohesion (Dirckinck-Holmfeld and Jones 2009), and seen from a social cognitive or a social pedagogical perspective such a radical version of PLEs may be counterproductive. Networked learning offers an alternative vision of a learning environment that allows for individualization but emphasizes connections rather than the privatization involved in PLEs. While networked learning does not necessarily privilege the strong ties involved in collaboration or community, it still involves a connectedness of some kind, whether reliant on strong or weak ties.

The University and the Net Generation

The Net Generation and digital natives debates are not restricted to describing young people or predicting their approaches to learning. The authors of some of these ideas have a more radical agenda, one that predicates deep institutional change on the speculative arguments about the character of this new generation (Margaryan et al. 2011). Tapscott and Williams provide the following account of the necessity for radical change:

> Change is required in two vast and interwoven domains that permeate the deep structures and operating model of the university: (1) the value created for the main customers of the university (the students); and (2) the model of production for how that value is created. First we need to toss out the old industrial model of pedagogy (how learning is accomplished) and replace it with a new model called collaborative learning. Second we need an entirely new modus operandi for how the subject matter, course materials, texts, written and spoken word, and other media (the content of higher education) are created (2010, p. 10).

These fundamental changes in the university are predicated on a new cohort of students bringing about a generational clash. The determinism forms a complete circle in which young people are determined by their technological environment to form a new generational cohort and then the Net Generation go on to force deep changes to the fundamental nature of the university. Tapscott and Williams propose an entirely new approach to the place and role of the university in society. The answer that Tapscott and Williams suggest is the adoption of a free market approach in which private initiative and the market replace existing models of the university. The government's role would be reduced to building the digital infrastructure, such as broadband networks, that would allow such private commercial providers to succeed. In the context of severe budget reductions, following the banking crisis, these calls for a reduced role for the state and increased private provision fall on fertile ground and they find a strong echo in the UK Government-commissioned Browne Report (2010).

Like Bates (2010), I argue that the future of university provision is a choice and not the result of a technologically determined process. Technological change can assist many kinds of changes in university teaching and learning and in relation to the broader role of the university. Technological change does not require universities to change in one particular way rather than another and it certainly does not lend itself to simple solutions based on generational stereotypes. Resistance to educational reform can arise from issues of funding and the significant divergences in vision that different social groups have for universities. Change is not hindered by the state-organized nonmarket form of organization in the university sector, and a neoliberal approach to markets and privatization offers no simple solution. The key issue that this chapter addresses is the determinism inherent in Net Generation and digital natives arguments that obscures the role of political choice.

Concluding Remarks

The networked learning in higher education project was completed almost 10 years ago. It was reporting on a population of students that would have been born in the early 1980s at the beginning of the age group that has become known as the Net Generation and digital natives. It was a period in which broadband network connections were still a novelty and ADSL, using copper wire subscriber lines, was launched commercially only in 2000. The provision of wired broadband in student study bedrooms was still a novelty and almost certainly unavailable, outside of some workplaces, for distance learners (Jones and Healing 2010b). Mobile phones were relatively new and while Vodafone took the first mobile call in 1985 the GSM 2G phone system, enabling SMS text messaging, was introduced only in the 1990s. Mobile Internet is a very recent service, introduced with 3G networks after the new millennium had begun. One of the conclusions we drew in 2000 was that there was no evidence of a generational divide. We also noted that students' views of networked learning were generally positive but that these views moderated over time following exposure to their networked learning course. A key factor we identified was the integration of networked learning within the course and positive experiences were associated with the most integrated courses. Ten years later and despite the increased availability of computing devices, fast broadband access, the development of mobile technologies, and all the rhetoric about new generations, we find very similar results in research from across the world. In my own research, in the UK, I have found no evidence of the much hyped generational divide. I have found that students are generally satisfied with university provision and that they are quite unlike the picture found in Net Generation and digital native literature. The students were not radicals adopting the most recent innovations, skilled in the latest technologies, and forcing change on reluctant faculty and resistant universities. Their requirements were modest and remained focused on the kinds of communication tools and services that enable access to the study resources that the universities are already providing.

There is now a mounting empirical base on which we must begin to develop theories to adequately account for the changes that we can clearly see from research across the world. The availability of cheap computing, broadband, and mobile networks and a range of Web-based services is clearly changing the way both students study and the way the universities they attend conduct their work. These changes involve choice and they cannot be read from a predetermined script that relies on a crude form of determinism. I agree with Bennett and Maton (2010) that one of the things we require now is a more theoretically informed body of research that moves away from simple dichotomies. We need to understand the changes that are taking place while avoiding the hyperbole that has characterized much of the debate in the past 10 years. We need to reengage with research agendas and step outside the narrow confines of the recent debate. In the research 10 years ago, we drew on the relational tradition of research that suggested that there might be a relationship between teachers' approaches to teaching and learners' approaches to learning (Jones et al. 2000). Margaryan et al. (2011) noted that: "Our findings show that, regardless of age and subject discipline, students' attitudes to learning appear to be influenced by the teaching approaches used by lecturers." (p. 10). This is a line of research that could usefully be further developed, for example by investigating the way faculty's use of new technologies can influence the take up and use of new technologies by students for educational purposes.

In researching the relationship between students and technology, much of the research effort has gone into self-report, largely through the use of surveys but also in interview data. There is a need to move beyond this kind of data using new methods to access data that reveals the actual use of new technologies. Recently, Judd and Kennedy (2010) reported a 5-year study of medical students that described actual rather than reported use. Their innovative approach provided quantitative data, but there are also the beginnings of qualitative approaches that go beyond simple interviews by engaging the students themselves in capturing data. Ryberg (2007) conducted an interesting, ethnographically inspired study of "power users" of technology. The study investigated whether young "power users" might be learning, working, and solving problems differently as a result of their more intensive use of technology. Jones and Healing (2010b) have reported their experience of using a cultural probe and the self-collection by students of video and textual records prompted by SMS text messages. Corrin et al. (2010) have used a similar experience sampling approach in their work.

Overall, the importance of the debate about the new generation of students is that determinist arguments about the new generation of students can close down debate about the role and purposes of higher education. Networked learning relies on these debates for its existence and it would be impoverished if the radical market-driven solutions that are associated with Net Generation and digital native arguments succeed.

References

Archer M. (2002). Realism and the problem of agency. *Journal of Critical Realism, 5*, 11–20.

Archer M. (2003). *Structure, Agency and the Internal Conversation*. Cambridge: Cambridge University Press.

Bates, T. (2010). *A critique of Tapscott and William's views on university reform*. Retrieved January 24, 2011, from http://www.tonybates.ca/2010/02/14/a-critique-of-tapscott-and-williams-views-on-university-reform

Bayne, S., & Ross, J. (2007). *The 'digital native' and 'digital immigrant': A dangerous opposition*. Paper presented at the Annual Conference of the Society for Research into Higher Education, Brighton 11–13th December 2007. Retrieved January 24, 2011, from http://www.malts.ed.ac.uk/staff/sian/natives_final.pdf

Bennett, S., & Maton, K. (2010). Beyond the 'digital natives' debate: Towards a more nuanced understanding of students' technology experiences. *Journal of Computer Assisted Learning, 26*(5), 321–331.

Bennett, S., Maton, K., & Kervin, L. (2008). The 'digital natives' debate: A critical review of the evidence. *British Journal of Educational Technology, 39*(5), 775–786.

Brown, C., & Czerniewicz, L. (2008). *Trends in student use of ICTs in higher education in South Africa*. Paper presented at the 10th Annual Conference of WWW Applications. Retrieved January 24, 2011, from http://www.cet.uct.ac.za/files/file/ResearchOutput/2008_wwwApps_UseTrends.pdf

Brown, C., & Czerniewicz, L. (2010). Debunking the 'digital native': Beyond digital apartheid, towards digital democracy. *Journal of Computer Assisted Learning, 26*(5), 357–369.

Browne, J. (2010). *Securing a sustainable future for higher education: An independent review of higher education funding and student finance*. Retrieved January 24, 2011, from http://hereview.independent.gov.uk/hereview/report/

Buckingham, D., & Willett, R. (Eds.). (2006). *Digital generations: Children, young people and new media*. Mahwah, NJ: Erlbaum.

Bullen, M., Morgan, T., Belfer, K., & Qayyum, A. (2009). The Net generation in higher education: Rhetoric and reality. *International Journal of Excellence in eLearning, 2*, 1–13.

Castells, M. (2000). *The rise of the network society* (2nd ed.). Oxford: Blackwell.

Corrin, L., Lokyer, L., & Bennett, S. (2010). Technological diversity: An investigation of students' technology use in everyday life and academic study. *Learning Media and Technology, 35*(4), 387–401.

Czerniewicz, L., Williams, K., & Brown, C. (2009). Students make a plan: Understanding student agency in constraining conditions. *ALT-J, The Association for Learning Technology Journal, 17*(2), 75–88.

Dirckinck-Holmfeld, L., & Jones, C. (2009). Issues and concepts in networked learning: Analysis and the future of networked learning. In L. Dirckinck-Holmfeld, C. Jones, & B. Lindström

(Eds.), *Analysing networked learning practices in higher education and continuing professional development*. Rotterdam: Sense Publishers.

Goodyear, P., Asensio, M., Jones, C., Hodgson, V., & Steeples, C. (2003). Relationships between conceptions of learning, approaches to study and students' judgements about the value of their experiences of networked learning. *Association for Learning Technology Journal, 11*(1), 17–27.

Goodyear, P., Banks, S., Hodgson, V., & McConnell, D. (2004). Research on networked learning: An overview. In P. Goodyear, S. Banks, V. Hodgson, & D. McConnell (Eds.), *Advances in research on networked learning*. Dordrecht: Kluwer.

Goodyear, P., Jones, C., Asensio, M., Hodgson, V., & Steeples, C. (2001). *Students' experiences of networked learning in higher education, final project report (2 vols)*. Bristol: Joint Information Systems Committee (JISC).

Goodyear, P., Jones, C., Asensio, M., Hodgson, V., & Steeples, C. (2005). Networked learning in higher education: Students' expectations and experiences. *Higher Education, 50*(3), 473–508.

Harasim, L., Hiltz, S. R., Teles, L., & Turoff, M. (1995). *Learning networks: A field guide to teaching and learning*. Cambridge, MA: MIT.

Hargittai, E. (2010). Digital na(t)ives? Variation in internet skills and uses among members of the "Net Generation". *Sociological Inquiry, 80*(1), 92–113.

Herring, S. (2008). Questioning the generational divide: Technological exoticism and adult construction of online youth identity. In D. Buckingham (Ed.), *Youth, identity and digital media* (pp. 71–92). Cambridge, MA: MIT.

Hosein, A., Ramanau, R., & Jones, C. (2010a). Learning and living technologies: A longitudinal study of first-year students' frequency and competence in the use of ICT. *Learning Media and Technology, 35*(4), 403–418.

Hosein, A., Ramanau, R., & Jones, C. (2010b). *Are all net generation students the same? The frequency of technology use at university*. IADIS International Conference e-Learning 2010, Freiburg, Germany.

Howe, N., & Strauss, W. (1991). *Generations: The history of America's future and the fourth turning: An American prophecy*. Oxford: Oxford University Press.

Howe, N., & Strauss, W. (2000). *Millennials rising: The Next greatest generation*. New York: Vintage Books.

Jones, C. (2011). Students, the net generation and digital natives: Accounting for educational change. In M. Thomas (Ed.), *Deconstructing digital natives*. New York: Routledge.

Jones, C., & Asensio, M. (2001). Experiences of assessment: Using phenomenography for evaluation. *Journal of Computer Assisted Learning, 17*(3), 314–321.

Jones, C., Asensio, M., & Goodyear, P. (2000). Networked learning in higher education: Practitioners' perspectives. *Association for Learning Technology Journal, 8*(2), 18–28.

Jones, C., & Bloxham, S. (2001). Networked legal learning: An evaluation of the student experience. *International Review of Law, Computers and Technology, 3*(15), 317–329.

Jones, C., & Cross, S. (2009). Is there a Net generation coming to university? In H. Damis, & L. Creanor (Eds), *"In dreams begins responsibility"- choice evidence and change: The 16th Association for Learning Technology Conference, Manchester 2009* (pp. 10–20). Retrieved August 3, 2011, from http://oro.open.ac.uk/18468/

Jones, C., & Dirckinck-Holmfeld, L. (2009). Analysing networked learning practices: An introduction. In L. Dirckinck-Holmfeld, C. Jones, & B. Lindström (Eds.), *Analysing networked learning practices in higher education and continuing professional development*. Rotterdam: Sense Publishers.

Jones, C., Ferreday, D., & Hodgson, V. (2008). Networked learning a relational approach – weak and strong ties. *Journal of Computer Assisted Learning, 24*(2), 90–102.

Jones, C., & Healing, G. (2010a). Net generation students: Agency and choice and the new technologies. *Journal of Computer Assisted Learning, 26*(5), 344–356.

Jones, C., & Healing, G. (2010b). Networks and locations for student learning. *Learning Media and Technology, 35*(4), 369–385.

Jones, C., & Hosein, A. (2010). Profiling university students' use of technology: Where is the net generation divide? *International Journal of Technology Knowledge and Society, 6*(3), 43–58.

Jones, C., Ramanau, R., Cross, S. J., & Healing, G. (2010). Net generation or digital natives: Is there a distinct new generation entering university? *Computers in Education, 54*(3), 722–732.

Judd, T., & Kennedy, G. (2010). A five-year study of on-campus Internet use by undergraduate biomedical students. *Computers in Education, 55*(1), 564–571.

Judd, T., & Kennedy, G. (2011). Measurement and evidence of computer-based task switching and multitasking by 'Net Generation' students. *Computers in Education, 56*(3), 625–631. doi:10.1016/j.compedu.2010.10.004.

Kennedy, G., Dalgarno, B., Gray, K., Judd, T., Waycott, J., Bennett, S., et al. (2007). The net generation are not big users of web 2.0 technologies: Preliminary findings. In *ICT: Providing choices for learners and learning*. Proceedings of ASCILITE Singapore 2007. Retrieved January 24, 2011, from http://www.ascilite.org.au/conferences/singapore07/procs/kennedy.pdf

Kennedy, G., Judd, T., Dalgarno, B., & Waycott, J. (2010). Beyond natives and immigrants: Exploring types of net generation students. *Journal of Computer Assisted Learning, 26*(5), 332–343.

Kennedy, G., Krause, K.-L., Judd, T., Churchward, A., & Gray, K. (2006). *First year students' experiences with technology: Are they really digital natives?* Melbourne: Centre for Study of Higher Education, The University of Melbourne.

Kennedy, G. E., Krause, K.-L., Judd, T. S., Churchward, A., & Gray, K. (2008). First year students' experiences with technology: Are they really digital natives? *Australasian Journal of Educational Technology, 24*(1), 108–122.

Margaryan, A., Littlejohn, A., & Vojt, G. (2011). Are digital natives a myth or reality? University students' use of digital technologies. *Computers in Education, 56*(2), 429–440.

McNaught, C., Lam, P., & Ho, A. (2009). The digital divide between university students and teachers in Hong Kong. In *Same places, different spaces*. Proceedings ASCILITE 2009, Auckland, New Zealand. Retrieved January 24, 2011, from http://www.ascilite.org.au/conferences/auckland09/procs/mcnaught.pdf

Oblinger, D. G., & Oblinger, J. (2005). *Educating the Net Generation*. EDUCAUSE Online book. Retrieved August 3, 2011, from http://www.educause.edu/ir/library/pdf/pub7101.pdf

Oliver, B., & Goerke, V. (2007). Australian undergraduates' use and ownership of emerging technologies: Implications and opportunities for creating engaging learning experiences for the net generation. *Australasian Journal of Educational Technology, 23*(2), 171–186.

Palfrey, J., & Gasser, U. (2008). *Born digital: Understanding the first generation of digital natives*. New York: Basic Books.

Pedró, F. (2009). *New millennium learners in higher education: Evidence and policy implications*. Paris: Centre for Educational Research and Innovation (CERI).

Prensky, M. (2001). Digital natives, digital immigrants. *On the Horizon, 9*(5), 1–6.

Prensky, M. (2010). *Teaching digital natives: Partnering for real learning*. London: Sage.

Ryberg, T. (2007). *Patchworking as a metaphor for learning: Understanding youth, learning and technology*. Unpublished PhD thesis, Aalborg University, Aalborg. Retrieved January 24, 2011, from http://www.telearn.org/warehouse/RYBERG-THOMAS-2007_(001783v1).pdf

Ryberg, T., Dirckinck-Holmfeld, L., & Jones, C. (2010). Catering to the needs of the "digital natives" or educating the "Net Generation"? In M. J. W. Lee & C. McLoughlin (Eds.), *Web 2.0-based e-learning: Applying social informatics for tertiary teaching*. Hershey, PA: IGI Global.

Salajan, F. D., Schönwetter, D. J., & Cleghorn, B. M. (2010). Student and faculty inter-generational digital divide: Fact or fiction? *Computers in Education, 55*, 1393–1403.

Salaway, G., Caruso, J. B., & Nelson, M. R. (2008). *The ECAR study of undergraduate students and information technology*. Boulder, CO: EDUCAUSE Center for Applied Research.

Sánchez, J., Salinas, A., Contreras, D., & Meyer, E. (2010). Does the new digital generation of learners exist? A qualitative study. *British Journal of Educational Technology, 42*(4), 543–556. doi:10.1111/j.1467-8535.2010.01069.x.

Schulmeister, R. (2010). Students, Internet, eLearning and Web 2.0. In M. Ebner & M. Schiefner (Eds.), *Looking toward the future of technology-enhanced education: Ubiquitous learning and digital native*. Hershey, PA: IGI Global.

Selwyn, N. (2003). 'Doing IT for the kids': Re-examining children, computers and the 'Information Society'. *Media, Culture and Society, 25*(3), 351–378.

Selwyn, N. (2008). An investigation of differences in undergraduates' academic use of the internet. *Active Learning in Higher Education, 9*(1), 11–22.

Smith, S. D., & Borreson Caruso, J. (2010). *The ECAR study of undergraduate students and information technology, 2010 (Research Study, Vol. 6)*. Boulder, CO: EDUCAUSE Center for Applied Research. Retrieved January 24, 2011, from http://www.educause.edu/ecar

Smith, S., Salaway, G., & Borreson Caruso, J. (2009). *The ECAR study of undergraduate students and information technology, 2009 (Research Study, Vol. 6)*. Boulder, CO: EDUCAUSE Center for Applied Research. Retrieved January 24, 2011, from http://www.educause.edu/ecar

Tapscott, D. (2009). *Grown up digital: How the Net generation is changing your world*. New York: McGraw-Hill.

Tapscott, D., & Williams, A. (2010). Innovating the 21st century university: It's time. *Educause Review, 45*(1), 17–29.

Thinyane, H. (2010). Are digital natives a world-wide phenomenon? An investigation into South African first year students' use and experience with technology. *Computers in Education, 55*, 406–414.

Waycott, J., Bennett, S., Kennedy, G., Dalgarno, B., & Gray, K. (2009). Digital divides? Student and staff perceptions of information and communication technologies. *Computers in Education, 54*(4), 1202–1211.

Wellman, B., Quan-Haase, A., Boase, J., Chen, W., Hampton, K., Isla de Diaz, I., et al. (2003). The social affordances of the internet for networked individualism. *Journal of Computer-Mediated Communication, 8*(3).

Chapter 3
Differences in Understandings of Networked Learning Theory: Connectivity or Collaboration?

Thomas Ryberg, Lillian Buus, and Marianne Georgsen

Introduction

With the popularisation of web 2.0 practices and technologies, we have also witnessed a re-vitalisation or renaissance of terms such as collaboration, sharing, dialogue, participation, student-centred learning, and the need to position students as producers, rather than consumers of knowledge. These are, however, pedagogical ideals, which have been prominent within research areas such as Networked Learning, CSCL and CMC-research well before the emergence of web 2.0. They even pre-date the Internet and World Wide Web (Jones and Dirckinck-Holmfeld 2009). This dialogical, collaborative perspective, which Weller (2007) characterises as the "discussion view," has existed and thrived. However, it seems fair to say that the mainstream and institutional uptake of learning technologies has been primarily oriented towards the "broadcast view," defined by Weller (2007) as delivering content or resources globally, flexibly and on demand to the individual users.

While many of the pedagogical ideals often associated with web 2.0 may not be entirely new, the mainstream adoption of services such as Facebook, Flickr and YouTube seems to have created a stronger platform for ideas such as collaboration, sharing and "user generated content." In relation to these trends the notion of connectivism has been presented as "a learning theory for the twenty-first century," and has been closely linked with the recent technological changes – in particular, the pervasiveness of various "networked technologies" such as email, the web and more recently,

T. Ryberg (✉) • L. Buus • M. Georgsen
e-Learning Lab – Centre for User Driven Innovation, Learning and Design,
Department of Communication and Psychology, Aalborg University, Aalborg, Denmark
e-mail: ryberg@hum.aau.dk

L. Dirckinck-Holmfeld et al. (eds.), *Exploring the Theory, Pedagogy and Practice of Networked Learning*, DOI 10.1007/978-1-4614-0496-5_3,
© Springer Science+Business Media, LLC 2012

social networking, blogs, RSS and various mechanisms for aggregating and filtering information:

> Over the last twenty years, technology has reorganized how we live, how we communicate, and how we learn. Learning needs and theories that describe learning principles and processes, should be reflective of underlying social environments (Siemens 2005, Introduction section, para 1).

The notion of connectivism has been most vividly explored by George Siemens and Stephen Downes, and the authors make some references to the broader heading of networked learning. In an online paper titled "A Brief History of Networked Learning," Siemens (2008) makes references to research projects at Lancaster University and the thesis by de Laat (2006). However, there does not seem to be strong awareness of or references to the understanding of networked learning as it is discussed and developed in the (mainly) European community of networked learning research. There seems to be shared interests amongst the two perspectives in concepts such as "networks," "connections," social learning and learner-centred pedagogies, but also some differences, which are worth exploring.

While learner-centeredness, social learning, participation and collaboration seem to have become the rhetorical mainstay of web 2.0 pedagogy, we argue that there are significantly different interpretations of these terms, and the pedagogies and practices emerging from these diverse understandings. This becomes particularly visible when investigating different conceptual frameworks, such as networked learning, connectivism or more collaboratively oriented pedagogies and theories. In this chapter, we therefore critically discuss and analyse concepts such as networked learning and connectivism. Equally, we briefly present ideas on personal learning environments (PLEs) as a means to identify some broader educational questions, which we believe are important within networked learning research. We draw out some seemingly contradictory concepts, such as personalisation and collaboration, while also providing examples from our own networked learning practices to discuss how we might address or dissolve such dichotomies, and how ideas from networked learning and connectivism can inform each other.

Networked Learning and Different Understandings of Collaboration

In relation to the acclaimed web 2.0 wave of pedagogical transformation there seems to be a slight tendency of overemphasising technological developments as the reason, or vehicle, for pedagogical change. In relation to this we should like to raise the point that we must be careful in ascribing too much power to perceived inert affordances of particular technologies, and focus equally on how the technologies are enacted or taken into use by practitioners (Jones et al. 2006; Suthers 2006).

We are convinced that networked learning theory has much to offer to these ongoing discussions, and in the following we take our point of departure in one of the definitions that has become central within the networked learning community:

> Networked learning is learning in which information and communications (ICT) is used to promote connections: between one learner and other learners, between learners and tutors; between a learning community and its learning resources (Goodyear et al. 2004, p. 2).

Historically, this definition grew out of a series of projects during the late 1990s and an ESRC Research Seminar Series on the implications of the use of networked learning in higher education (Beaty et al. 2010). The seminar series resulted in a manifesto titled "Towards E-Quality in Networked E-Learning in Higher Education" which was presented at the Networked Learning conference 2002 by the "E-Quality Network." As noted by Jones and Dirckinck-Holmfeld (2009), this definition has proved itself to be remarkably robust over the last 10 years, and has developed considerable force especially within European research where it has been developed through a number of publications, and has been associated with the Networked Learning Conference series since 1998 (Jones and Dirckinck-Holmfeld 2009; Goodyear et al. 2004).

Firstly, this definition of networked learning goes beyond merely denoting "online learning" or "e-learning," as it encompasses theoretical assumptions about learning and how to design for learning. The definition stresses the connections *between* people and *between* people and resources, but also points to a certain level of social organisation between learners, tutors and resources, i.e. a learning community. However, the notion of a learning community and the strength of the ties or connections between people can differ in various interpretations. Some have criticised notions such as communities of practice (CoP) (Wenger 1998) and the strong focus on "collaborative learning" within the area of CSCL. They have voiced a concern that these perspectives focus too much on networks composed of strong ties, thus overlooking the value of weak ties between learners (Jones et al. 2006, 2008; Ryberg and Larsen 2008). Simultaneously, proponents of networked learning also argue for learning and collaborative knowledge construction processes organised around focused and intensive negotiations of problems (McConnell 2002; Zenios 2011). Although there are particular values and ideals associated with networked learning, as expressed in the networked learning manifesto (Beaty et al. 2002, 2010), it does not privilege a particular pedagogical model or ideal in terms of uniformly favouring collaboration or unity of purpose in a community of learners (Jones et al. 2008). However, the ideas of relations and connections suggest that learning is not confined to the individual mind or the individual learner. Rather, learning and knowledge construction is located in the connections and interactions between learners, teachers and resources, and seen as emerging from critical dialogues and enquiries. As such, networked learning theory seems to encompass an understanding of learning as a social, relational phenomenon, and a view of knowledge and identity as constructed through interaction and dialogue. Furthermore, as argued by Jones (2008) this aligns well with social practice, socio-cultural or social learning theories that also situate and analyse learning as located in social practice and interaction, rather than as a phenomenon of the individual mind. In addition, prevalent ideas within (some) interpretations of networked learning are associated with more radical pedagogies, where critical reflexivity and dialogue are emphasised as a means to help learners "recognize, critique and move beyond one's taken-for-granted assumptions – about the world, and about one's professional practice and learning" (Goodyear et al. 2004, p. 2). This particular view is also associated with educational values of supporting democratic processes, diversity, inclusion and e-quality drawing on both Paulo Freire's Critical Pedagogy and social constructionists notions of relational dialogue (Beaty et al. 2010).

In relation to the discussions of types of connections (weak or strong) and modes of interaction, such as collaboration or cooperation (which can be said to be strongly tied or more weakly tied respectively), we find the distinction made by McConnell (2002) useful. Building on the work of Roschelle and Teasley (1995) McConnell distinguishes between distributed *collaborative* and *cooperative* learning. Roughly speaking this refers to whether the work on the task or problem and the outcome is shared (collaborative) or whether individuals engage in discussions with others about their reflections on individual assignments (cooperation). This distinction is also similar to what Suthers (2006) refers to as intersubjective vs. individual epistemologies. We believe that there are essential aspects in these distinctions, which can be important to reflect upon. In a recently published book on networked learning (Dirckinck-Holmfeld et al. 2009), Jones and Dirckinck-Holmfeld (2009) discuss the ideas and tensions between strongly tied collaborations vs. more loosely tied cooperative modes of learning (a question also taken up earlier in Jones et al. 2006). They ask whether the internet and broader sociological trends have resulted in a social shift from more cohesive, communal relations towards more dispersed, personalised relations. This they associate with the notion of networked individualism coined by Wellman (2001) and explored by Castells (2001) and they pose the questions:

> Networked individualism might suggest that we need to take a more critical approach to the theories of education and learning that are based on community and collaboration. The term also suggests that we can do this without ruling out the central place of communication and dialogue in education and learning. [...] We argue that a key question for research is whether the Internet will help foster more densely knit communities or alternatively whether it will encourage more sparse, loose knit formations. [...] a significant question is whether designs for networked learning environments should reflect the trend towards networked individualism or serve as a counter balance to this trend, offering opportunities for the development of collaborative dependencies (Jones and Dirckinck-Holmfeld 2009, pp. 6–7).

While we do not view the sociological notion of networked individualism as necessarily opposed to the development of collaborative dependencies within education, we do view an increasing interest in "personalised learning," personal learning environments or networks (PLEs and PLNs) as a challenge to more collaborative organisations of learning (though we also find that these ideas hold developmental potential and can act as a window of opportunity). This concern, we believe, is equally voiced in Beaty et al.'s (2010) recent discussions of the networked learning manifesto where they re-iterate the importance of maintaining a focus on e-quality and explicit educational values:

> We claim that an updated definition of networked learning should not only refer to being a pedagogy based on connectivity and the co-production of knowledge but also one that aspires to support e-quality of opportunity and include reference to the importance of relational dialogue and critical reflexivity in all of this. Following on from the definition of networked learning we reaffirm the point made in the original Manifesto that policy for networked learning should be based on explicit educational values and research (Beaty et al. 2010, p. 585).

We do not mean to argue that "personalised learning" or personal learning environments necessarily preclude e-quality, collaboration or critical reflexive and relational dialogue. However, we feel it is important to discuss some reservations initially voiced by Weller (2007) and re-iterated by Dirckinck-Holmfeld and Jones (2009). They argue that there might be four downsides to PLEs:

- Commonality of experience. PLEs may threaten or loosen the shared experience of studying a course.
- Exposure to different approaches. The educational gain of broadening a local and personal experience may be lost. PLEs may encourage a narrow private view that is resistant to change and encourage a 'customer' focus that relies on consumer choice of a educational goods [sic] that are often not appreciated until after the educational experience has taken place.
- Privacy. Personalisation requires the collection of user data and raises serious concerns in terms of privacy and surveillance. It may also have unintended consequences as once it is known that a system is monitored, user behaviour will adapt to the perceived requirements of the monitoring.
- Content focus. The drive behind PLEs is one that emphasises delivery of personalised content at the expense of communication with others (Dirckinck-Holmfeld and Jones 2009, pp. 264–265).

While some interpretations of PLEs do seem to be exclusively focused on retrieval of personalised content, e.g. through semantic technologies, one can also argue for PLEs as a means to engage in mutual enquiry, reflexive dialogue and self-governed, problem-based and collaborative activities (Dalsgaard 2006).

However, inspired by Dirckinck-Holmfeld and Jones (2009) and Beaty et al. (2010) we wish to raise question such as will learners' (potentially) highly individualised orchestrations of their learning itinerary (or trajectory) across institutional boundaries erode commonality of experiences? Does it lead to a "consumer" view of education? And how may such orchestrations of education impact educational values such as e-quality, inclusion, critical reflexivity and relational dialogue? Our point is not to argue that certain technological tools or orchestrations will uniformly shape the educational use. This is equally shaped by the underlying theoretical perspective and values with which we approach the pedagogical and socio-technical design of networked learning – in particular, how we view and design for the relational interdependencies between learners. Following Beaty et al. (2010), who refer to the "Online Hot Seat Seminar" on connectivism hosted by George Siemens and

Stephen Downes as pre-events for the Networked Learning Conference 2010, we feel that connectivist principles and views of networked learning have something to offer for our current conceptualisations of learning. However, we should also like to explore more critically the notion of connectivism in relation to the notions of networked learning presented above.

Connectivism and Networked Learning

In many ways connectivism seems to align well with networked learning theory, and also challenge ideas around collaboration and tightly knitted communities. The notion of connectivism (Siemens 2005, 2006) has attracted some attention in recent years. As noted by Kop and Hill (2008), it lives a particularly vibrant and dynamic life in the blogosphere around the blogs-spaces and online publications of especially George Siemens (http://elearnspace.org/ and http://connectivism.ca) and Stephen Downes (http://www.downes.ca). But also it is a (seemingly) dynamic object of enquiry and one of the main topics in the open online course "Personal Learning Environments, Networks and Knowledge" (http://ple.elg.ca/course/ moodle/course/view.php?id=3) hosted and organised by Siemens and Downes – and with more than 1,800 "participants." The Massive Open Online Course (MOOC) is/ was according to Mackness et al. (2010, p. 266) (who participated in the course in 2008) "a course and a network about the emergent practices and the theory of Connectivism." Thus, the course is based on the principles and practices of connectivism, which is also (partly) the topic or underlying theoretical perspective of the "learning event" or "un-course."

The reason for mentioning these aspects is that connectivism, in many ways, seems to live and thrive mainly in the outskirts or outside of traditional academic publication and dissemination channels. For one thing, this means that many of the papers on connectivism are not peer-reviewed and published in journals, but are disseminated through the webspaces mentioned. Secondly, the underlying view of knowledge and learning in connectivism does to some extent question or render problematic the discussion of such ideas in more traditional academic outlets: Should one engage in the ongoing, (seemingly) dynamic and volatile conversations in the blogosphere, rather than a monological book chapter? We mention this to acknowledge the fact that the proponents of connectivism also seem to be challenging traditional scholarship and urge the scientific community to think about how knowledge is disseminated and shared. Having said that, we also feel that there is great value and continued need for the admittedly more slow-moving critical dissemination and reflection of academic knowledge represented by the traditional academic outlets. For one thing, peer-review processes force authors to take into account any criticism raised by the reviewers, while authors of blogs may choose not to do so. Secondly, peer-review processes should, in principle, ensure that the reviewers hold expert knowledge within the research area, whereas comments on blogs may be of a more diverse nature. In the following section, we offer a more critical discussion of "connectivism."

Connectivism: A New Learning Theory?

The argument proposed by Siemens (2005, 2006) is that the existing theories or paradigms of learning (behaviourism, cognitivism and constructivism) cannot sufficiently explain or account for the fundamentally changed conditions for learning brought about by the changes in the technological landscape, e.g. the abundance of information, the increasingly shorter half-life of knowledge and the need to continuously stay updated with the newest information and resources. Furthermore, many information processing tasks can be delegated to technology (or social filtering through networks at different levels of scale). Siemens argues that learning rests in the capabilities of forming connections to other people, networks and sources of information and that the capacity to recognize or create useful information patterns are crucial:

> The starting point of connectivism is the individual. Personal knowledge is comprised of a network, which feeds into organizations and institutions, which in turn feed back into the network, and then continue to provide learning to individual [sic]. This cycle of knowledge development (personal to network to organization) allows learners to remain current in their field through the connections they have formed (Siemens 2005, Connectivism section, para 7).

Although, this seems to be very similar to some of the ideas expressed in networked learning theory, it also seems to have a much stronger focus on the individual, and the individual's capacity to sift through, filter, find and utilise various networks to retrieve resources and ideas. These can then enhance the individuals' capacity, and thus the whole network's, in a circular process focusing on and returning to (cognitive, neural) operations of the individual. In this sense other persons (who are themselves personal networks) and networks at different levels of scale seem to become instruments or hubs through which the individual can retrieve updated resources. In our interpretation, it seems that the most fundamental relations are those between an individual and a resource or idea, possibly acquired and filtered through a complex socio-technical network that itself seems to be imbued with a form of (somewhat unexplained or unexplored) agency:

> Currency of knowledge is the function of a network, and raising the value of skills of network-making. The network becomes a separate cognitive element—it processes, filters, evaluates, and validates new information. If content has a short lifespan (as new information is acquired), then it would logically imply that our education and training systems should not be about content in particular—they should specifically be about current content (Siemens 2006, p. 10).

> In a connectivist approach to learning, we create networks of knowledge to assist in replacing outdated content with current content. We off-load many cognitive capabilities onto the network, so that our focus as learners shifts from processing to pattern recognition. When we off-load the processing elements of cognition, we are able to think, reason, and function at a higher level (or navigate more complex knowledge spaces) (Siemens 2006, p. 11).

For one thing, we find it problematic that knowledge is equated with content, albeit this is updated or dynamic content. Although, Siemens argues that knowledge and thinking reside outside the head, it does seem to be a very different perspective when compared to social or socio-cultural theories of learning, also because Siemens relate patterns in external networks with neural networks, thus making a reference to neuroscience:

> Learning is the process of creating networks (see Figure 2) [Authors: see original for the figure]. Nodes are external entities which we can use to form a network. Or nodes may be people, organizations, libraries, web sites, books, journals, databases, or any other source of information. The act of learning (things become a bit tricky here) is one of creating an *external network* of nodes—where we connect and form information and knowledge sources. The learning that happens in our heads is an *internal network (neural)*. Learning networks can then be perceived as structures that we create in order to stay current and continually acquire experience, create, and connect new knowledge (external). And learning networks can be perceived as structures that exist within our minds (internal) in connecting and creating patterns of understanding (Siemens 2006).

Even though the filtering mechanisms are moved outside the individual's head, it is not entirely clear to us, whether this represents a re-location of a basic "cognitivist information processing" metaphor dispersed into a socio-technical network, or a basic "constructivist perspective" where the notion of, e.g. schema is replaced with the metaphor of a network. Also, we are fundamentally concerned with the somewhat unproblematic way in which internal and external networks are equated, and we wonder what the relations are between the two "realms" or if they are the same (without wanting to re-iterate complex discussions around dualism)? We wonder whether the relations or comparisons are meant metaphorically or as a more "realist notion" (that they do functionally compare and interact)? Following from this, we would ask whether it is fruitful (in either sense) to equate basic neuronal transmission or "the connecting" of electrical impulses with the insanely complex landscape of bodies, tables, computers, laws, regulations and the huge number of social and physical artefacts that mediate our engagement with the "world" and others? We wonder whether the metaphor or concept clouds more complex socio-technical and socio-cultural relations that interact with and mediate how knowledge is produced, and regulate our access to and relations with books, journals, web sites and the whole (socio-technical) network where the knowledge content flows and is produced? In relation to this, Siemens (2006) notes that:

> Additionally, it is important to acknowledge that learning is much more than exposure to content. Social, community, and collaborative approaches to learning are important.

However, we wonder whether notions such as "a network becomes a separate (self-organising?) cognitive element" and a strong focus on the flow of (updated) knowledge content renders invisible the processes by which these objects are produced, say through dialogues, negotiation of meaning, regulations, social practices and physical, bodily interaction with digital and analogue resources? And what becomes of notions such as power, voice, access and inclusion? We remain uncertain of whether concepts such as "communities," "negotiation of meaning," "dialogues," "groups," "social practice" and "collaboration" have a more significant role in the notion of "connectivism," or whether they are considered temporary, fleeting, analytically less important hubs or stations in a self-organising knowledge flow of an autonomous network? Likewise, we remain uncertain of the fundamental epistemology of connectivism, and we are unsure of where it is located in terms of other existing theories. We are not sure whether connectivism, as argued by Siemens (2005, 2006), constitutes an entirely new view of relations between world and learner, and ask whether it might fall within or between existing perspectives. This can be fruitfully discussed by highlighting distinctions made between a socio-cultural and socio-constructivist perspective (Dillenbourg et al. 1996). Whereas the socio-constructivist approach understands groups (or collaboration) as consisting of individual and relatively independent cognitive systems, which exchange messages through social interaction, the socio-cultural perspective suggests that groups or collaboration can be understood as a single cognitive system with its own properties. Thus, in a socio-constructivist view (primarily inspired by Piaget) individual cognition is strengthened, matured or catalysed by social interaction, but the cognitive development remains tied to the mental operations of the individual, and has its own logic relative to the existing mental apparatus of the individual. In a socio-cultural view (inspired by Vygotsky), the focus is on social practice, artefacts and how individual cognition and cognitive structures are seen as formed by/forming the social, cultural world. These are also what Suthers (2006) refer to as individual epistemologies vs. intersubjective epistemologies.

In our understanding of Siemens' ideas, it seems that the individual nodes in the network grow by their "own logic" (aka their unique social network or constellation of connections), thus acting as relatively independent nodes, which, however, affect others and the network as a whole (that appears to be an independent cognitive unit). However, we are uncertain whether this indeed represents a novel approach or is an extension of, e.g. a socio-constructivist approach or individualist epistemology with a different vocabulary, and with some additional terms and thinking adopted from the field of "distributed cognition" (Hutchins 1995). It is not clear to us, what is the role of dialogues, collaboration, social practice or mutual construction of knowledge or how well connectivism can account for (or is interested in) such patterns of learning. It seems to be a more individualised or personalised perspective on learning than, e.g. networked learning theory. Although there are many authors who challenge notions of strongly tied communities, concepts such as communication, dialogue and mutual construction of knowledge seem to be more central within networked learning theory. This difference is also reflected in online postings where Siemens expresses a discomfort with the term "collective intelligence," and argues instead for the term "connective intelligence":

> For reasons of motivation, self-confidence, and satisfaction, it is critical that we can retain ourselves and our ideas in our collaboration with others. Connective intelligences permits this. Collective intelligence results in an over-writing of individual identity (Siemens 2008, Collective Intelligence? Nah. Connective Intelligence section, para 3).

As discussed by Mackness et al. (2010) connectivism seems to emphasise and value the autonomy of the learners and cooperative (networked) interdependencies over more strongly tied, collaborative dependencies, such as groups [which Downes (2007) argue are exclusionary vehicles that foster conformity and rule out diversity (potentially resulting in walled-in echo-chambers)]:

> It has been suggested by Downes and Siemens that the whole idea of an educational course needs to be reconceived (Siemens, 2009b) from the traditional, closed group, highly structured course, where students are dependent on tutors, to open networks of self-directed

learners. [...] Downes (2007a, 2008, 2009b) has suggested that the key characteristics of an online course using connectivist principles are autonomy, diversity, openness, and connect-edness and interactivity. 'Autonomy' allows learners maximum choice of where, when, how, with whom and even what to learn. 'Diversity' ensures that learners are from a sufficiently diverse population to avoid group-think and 'echo-chambers' (McRae, 2006) (Mackness et al. 2010, p. 267).

In this sense, the notion of "learner-centeredness" seems to become strongly equated with individual freedom or autonomy over any form of organisation or dependency between learners. We do agree that highly structured courses, where cohorts of students are herded through a predefined set of learning goals and materials provided only by teachers and tutors can be problematic. We also agree that group-thinking and echo-chambers can potentially produce alienation and exclusion (Ferreday and Hodgson 2008). However, we think that the relatively radical individualist focus might be in danger of overlooking positive aspects of collaborative or communal learning processes, and we do not agree that such orchestrations of learning necessarily preclude learner autonomy or diversity. In the following sections, we discuss this through illustrating our own orchestrations and continued development of learning practices at Aalborg University. We do not mean to go into details about any particular setups, systems or courses; rather we try to describe the pathways and lines of thinking we are pursuing and developing.

The Aalborg PBL Model: Our Networked Learning Practice

The foundational pedagogy of Aalborg University (AAU) is a project-based, problem-oriented approach at times referred to as the Aalborg PBL-model (Kolmos et al. 2004) or problem-oriented project pedagogy (POPP) (Dirckinck-Holmfeld 2002). It represents a strongly tied, collaborative organisation of learning, where students are mutually dependent on each other, throughout a whole semester; but also represents a high degree of learner freedom. The POPP was the institutional pedagogical foundation for establishing Aalborg University (1974) and Roskilde University Center (1972) in Denmark. In the late eighties, it also became the basis for open online education programmes and research within online learning (see also other chapters in this book).

At that time the approach represented a radical pedagogical turn where the focus shifted from a model based on delivery of information and knowledge towards a more critical, experientially based pedagogy. The approach emphasises learning as knowledge construction, collaboration in groups and problem-orientation (Dirckinck-Holmfeld 2002). The main pedagogical principles revolve around problem-orientation, project work, interdisciplinarity and participant-controlled learning. The entire learning process is formed around the students' own enquiry into scientific and social problems. Thus, the model emphasises learner freedom and participant control when it comes to defining and working with their problem. However, as students are dependent on each other in their project groups and projects are produced throughout each semester, students cannot individually follow their own pace. To understand and find a solution to the problem, the students go through different stages of systematic investigations: preliminary enquiries, problem formulation, theoretical and methodological considerations, investigations, experimentation and reflection (Dirckinck-Holmfeld). In Aalborg University each semester is therefore organised around approximately 50% course work and 50% project work in groups, where students collaborate on writing their semester project. The students work closely together for an extended period of time (4 months), on formulating, identifying and "solving" their problem, and write a final project report. A continued research effort has been to identify ways in which to support and develop this pedagogical model (for on-campus, as well as for off-campus students) through experimenting with various technologies, learning environments and tools. There has been a strong focus on how to support groups in virtual environments, by providing them with, e.g. shared file spaces, calendars and other tools to support coordination and collaboration. This has drawn specifically on CSCL and CSCW (Computer Supported Cooperative Work) research (Dirckinck-Holmfeld; Tolsby 2009; Tolsby et al. 2002). In these efforts, we have also been inspired and challenged by the notion(s) of networked learning. In particular, we have been inspired by notions of strong and weak ties in learning, the growing educational interest in web 2.0 (e.g. social networks and PLEs), but also ideas expressed in a "connectivist" approach (Ryberg and Larsen 2008; Ryberg et al. 2010). These lines of thinking have particularly raised our awareness about interaction *between* groups, *between* students (and researchers) on the same or across semesters, as well as connections *between* educational programme and the wider world of resources and researchers.

We are affiliated with one of the most student-rich on-campus programmes at Aalborg University (Humanistic Informatics) which recently raised the uptake of students from 90 to 200 students per semester. The doubling has to some degree lessened their experience of interactions with, and knowledge of, "the other" students. Although lectures/workshops and seminars are sometimes organised in "groups" of 30–40 students, teachers and supervisors (particularly those dealing with 1–2 semesters students) were worried that students would only meet each other and their teachers, in either the tightly knitted project groups of 3–5 students, during traditional lectures or in the learning management system (used mainly for announcements, course descriptions and slides). From a pedagogical perspective our concern was (and remains) that the underlying AAU values of active, critical, dialogical and participant-controlled learning become associated almost exclusively with the project work, and where the other half of the students' time and work load will take place in physical and virtual spaces tailored for mass-customised education and management. In addition, we have concerns whether this also affects students' "commonality of experience" and their development of a professional identity or their ongoing processes of "becoming" various types of practitioners of "Humanistic Informatics."

We have therefore become increasingly interested in exploring and designing learning environments that are not only aimed at mutually, dependent collaboration in tightly knitted groups, but also tools and environments that seek to leverage the interaction and transparency *between* groups (Dalsgaard and Paulsen 2009;

Ryberg et al. 2010). Likewise, we are pursuing and experimenting with technologies which can (potentially) leverage and support emerging types of large-scale interactions. We have so far been experimenting with the open source systems Elgg and Mahara (which are PLEs or e-portfolio systems) in combination with other tools. These experiments go beyond small-group interactions and instead attempt to harness the values of larger, diffuse groups (e.g. wiki-writing, twitter-streams, online bookmark-sharing, collective note-taking). In relation to this, we find the ideas and distinctions proposed by Dron and Anderson (2007) valuable. They suggest that we can distinguish between three levels of social aggregations which they term: the group, the network and the collective (Dron and Anderson) – these can, from a network perspective, all be characterised as "networks" although differently tied and at variable levels of scale. Groups are more tightly knit social constellations and often mutually engaged in working with a common problem, project or task (such as a project group at AAU). Networks entails more fleeting membership structures and boundaries, are emergent rather than designed, and do not necessarily revolve around a particular task. Finally, the collective has an even looser and more emergent structure with no sense of conscious membership or belonging. Collectives are aggregations of individuals' uncoordinated actions from which, e.g. tag-clouds, recommendation systems or page-ranking systems emerge. In particular, web 2.0 technologies have amplified and rendered the latter two levels of social aggregation visible. We agree with Dalsgaard (2006) who argues that students' (self-chosen and managed) personal tools can support interaction across these different levels of social aggregation. In this way, we would argue for designs and research which aim to combine or bridge these different social architectures, rather than seeing them as oppositions, dichotomies or internally contradictory. A focus on collaborative work does not preclude a simultaneous focus on facilitating the individual student's gradual development of a personalised (and shared) set of bookmarks or references (e.g. on delicious.com or diigo.com). Their creation of personalised social networks which may include researchers, other students and friends from inside or outside the institution could become valuable resources for other students in their group/semester cohort.

In this way, we aim to offer students' personal tools for construction, presentation, reflection and collaboration, while also facilitating the sharing and exchange of various resources across different levels of social aggregation (the group, the network and the collective). Thus, we want to place the individual learner in the centre, by enabling them to create and maintain a personal presence, so that students, over time, may develop a stronger sense of a professional identity as a student of humanistic informatics – not only through participation in project groups, but also rather through engaging in a variety of settings (inside and outside of the university) and across different levels of social aggregation. Therefore, an aim is to support the individual students' creation of personal learning trajectories, where they can connect to communities, networks and resources of their own interest, while simultaneously belonging to smaller project groups and communities (such as a semester) as places to make sense of the diversity of experiences and resources.

We feel that connectivist principles and lines of thinking are valuable additions to our existing organisations of learning, but we would equally argue that there are some values in more collaborative orchestrations of learning, which we should retain. Connectivism provides an interesting and fresh view on how knowledge artefacts flow in complex social or personalised networks – particularly at levels of aggregation outside the exclusive control of the individual (the collective), and in the intersections between multiple contexts. This is a relatively uncharted area, as many studies within CSCL and networked learning concern, e.g. a particular course or a relatively well-defined network of participants. In this sense the notion of connectivism highlights the value of weak ties, which is also increasingly being explored within networked learning. However, while connectivism provides us with a sense of how updated content might flow in complex variably tied and scaled networks, it leaves us with few, or unclear, analytical and theoretical notions in terms of how people make sense of and use these resources in actual practice. In this regard, the research areas of networked learning and CSCL have much to offer in terms of understanding and analysing how people in variably scaled networks, whether strongly or weakly tied, make sense of, negotiate and critically reflect on "updated content" in order to create knowledge and learning.

In this way, we think that a fruitful avenue for research and networked learning practices lies in exploring diverse orchestrations of learning arrangements, by maintaining an openness and variance in terms of the types of connections, relations and interdependencies we promote.

Concluding Remarks

While the mainstream interpretations of web 2.0 highlight terms such as "social," "learner centred" and "collaborative," our purpose has been to identify and make visible the subtle differences glossed over by such generic terms.

We have argued that there are some underlying theoretical differences in how various perspectives, such as connectivism and networked learning perceive relations between the individual and the social, and how they view cognition and learning. In relation to this, we have raised some critical, more theoretically oriented questions concerning the notion of connectivism, and while we believe there are some valuable insights in connectivism, we also have some reservations or uncertainties in relation to the underlying theoretical perspective. Most importantly we are unsure whether concepts such as "communities," "negotiation of meaning," "dialogues," "groups," "social practice" and "collaboration" are glossed over and forgotten. We are concerned whether notions of networks as separate self-organising cognitive elements, and the strong focus on the flow of (updated) knowledge content renders the processes by which these objects are produced invisible. This, in our view, would severely understate the importance of dialogues, negotiation of meaning, regulations, social practices and physical, bodily interaction with digital and analogue resources. In addition, we ask whether the relatively radical individualist focus is in danger of overlooking positive aspects of collaborative or communal learning processes.

Such underlying differences in perspective can lead to different preferences in terms of interactional dependencies (e.g. collaborative, cooperative or more individualised learning strategies), but also in terms of how various levels of social aggregation (groups, networks and collectives) might be promoted, valued or enacted in particular organisations for networked learning. We believe that the emergence of more dispersed networked technologies and "collective" or "connective" patterns of interaction hold interesting opportunities for expanding existing designs for, e.g. project and problem-oriented pedagogy or collaborative learning – but without excluding the value of more tightly knitted interactional dependencies.

Following from this, networked learning environments can be designed and shaped in different ways depending on the underlying view of cognition, learning and types of interactional dependencies preferred. They can be designed as constellations of technologies where the individuals freely form and control their learning processes by connecting to others for inspiration or resources across the various levels of aggregation. However, learning environments can equally be designed as platforms for strongly tied collaborative work and dependencies with a greater level of transparency between the groups and between the groups and external resources and materials.

In this way, we would not argue that "networked individualism" or notions of PLEs necessarily leads to or encourage more individualised, consumer-oriented provisions of education. However, we feel that we should remain conscious of the more subtle ways in which we understand ideas such as collaboration, participation and connections in our designs for networked learning arrangements. In particular, as different theories and perspectives that (perhaps) underpin our designs might encompass, invoke or promote certain interactional dependencies and underlying views of the relations between individuals.

References

Beaty, L., Cousin, G., & Hodgson, V. (2010). Revisiting the e-quality in networked learning manifesto. In L. Dirckinck-Holmfeld et al., eds. *Proceedings of the 7th International Conference on Networked Learning*. Networked Learning (pp. 585–592). Aalborg: Lancaster University. Retrieved August 3, 2011, from http://www.lancs.ac.uk/fss/organisations/netlc/past/nlc2010/abstracts/PDFs/Beaty.pdf

Beaty, L., Hodgson, V., Mann, S., & McConnell, D. (2002). *Towards e-quality in networked e-learning in higher education*. Retrieved August 3, 2011, from http://csalt.lancs.ac.uk/esrc/manifesto.pdf

Castells, M. (2001). *The Internet galaxy*. New York: Oxford University Express.

Dalsgaard, C. (2006). Social software: E-learning beyond learning management systems. *European Journal of Open, Distance and E-Learning*. Retrieved August 5, 2010, from http://www.eurodl.org/materials/contrib/2006/Christian_Dalsgaard.htm

Dalsgaard, C., & Paulsen, M. (2009). Transparency in cooperative online education. *International Review of Research in Open and Distance Learning, 10*(3), 1492.

de Laat, M. (2006). *Networked learning*. PhD thesis, Politie Acedemie, Apeldoorn. Retrieved August 3, 2011, from http://www.open.ou.nl/rslmlt/Maarten%20De%20Laat_Networked%20Learning_2006.pdf

Dillenbourg, P., Baker, M., Blaye, A., & O'Malley, C. (1996). The evolution of research on collaborative learning. In E. Spada & P. Reiman (Eds.), *Learning in humans and machines: Towards an interdisciplinary learning science* (pp. 189–211). Oxford: Pergamon/Elsevier Science.

Dirckinck-Holmfeld, L. (2002). Designing virtual learning environments based on problem oriented project pedagogy. In L. Dirckinck-Holmfeld & B. Fibiger (Eds.), *Learning in virtual environments* (pp. 31–54). Frederiksberg C: Samfundslitteratur.

Dirckinck-Holmfeld, L., & Jones, C. (2009). Issues and concepts in networked learning – Analysis and the future of networked learning. In L. Dirckinck-Holmfeld, C. Jones, & B. Lindström (Eds.), *Analysing networked learning practices in higher education and continuing professional development. Technology-Enhanced Learning* (pp. 259–285). Rotterdam: Sense Publishers.

Dirckinck-Holmfeld, L., Jones, C., & Lindström, B. (Eds.). (2009). *Analysing networked learning practices in higher education and continuing professional development.* Rotterdam: Sense Publishers.

Downes, S. (2007). Groups vs. networks: The class struggle continues. *Stephen's web*. Retrieved January 24, 2011, from http://www.downes.ca/post/42521

Dron, J., & Anderson, T. (2007). Collectives, networks and groups in social software for e-learning. In G. Richards (Ed.), *World Conference on E-Learning in Corporate, Government, Healthcare, and Higher Education 2007* (pp. 2460–2467). Quebec City, QC: AACE.

Ferreday, D. & Hodgson, V. (2008). The Tyranny of participation and collaboration in networked learning. In V. Hodgson et al. (Eds.), *Proceedings of the 6th International Conference on Networked Learning* (pp. 640–647). Halkidiki: Lancaster University.

Goodyear, P., Banks, S., Hodgson, V., & McConnell, D. (2004). *Advances in research on networked learning.* Dordrecht: Klüwer.

Hutchins, E. (1995). *Cognition in the wild.* Cambridge, MA: MIT.

Jones, C. (2008). Networked learning – A social practice perspective. In V. Hodgson et al. (Eds.), *Proceedings of the 6th International Conference on Networked Learning* (pp. 616–623). Halkidiki: Lancaster University.

Jones, C., & Dirckinck-Holmfeld, L. (2009). Analysing networked learning practices. In L. Dirckinck-Holmfeld, C. Jones, & B. Lindström (Eds.), *Analysing networked learning practices in higher education and continuing professional development. Technology-Enhanced Learning* (pp. 10–27). Rotterdam: Sense Publishers.

Jones, C., Dirckinck-Holmfeld, L., & Lindström, B. (2006). A relational, indirect, meso-level approach to CSCL design in the next decade. *International Journal of Computer-Supported Collaborative Learning, 1*(1), 35–56.

Jones, C., Ferreday, D., & Hodgson, V. (2008). Networked learning a relational approach: Weak and strong ties. *Journal of Computer Assisted Learning, 24*(2), 90–102.

Kolmos, A., Fink, F. K., & Krogh, L. (2004). *The Aalborg PBL model – Progress diversity and challenges.* Aalborg: Aalborg University Press.

Kop, R., & Hill, A. (2008). Connectivism: Learning theory of the future or vestige of the past? *The International Review of Research in Open and Distance Learning.* Retrieved August 3, 2011, from http://www.irrodl.org/index.php/irrodl/article/view/523/1103

Mackness, J., Sui Fai, J. M., & Willams, R. (2010). The ideals and reality of participating in a MOOC. In L. Dirckinck-Holmfeld et al. (Eds.), *Proceedings of the 7th International Conference on Networked Learning.* Networked Learning (pp. 266–274). Aalborg: Lancaster University.

McConnell, D. (2002). Action research and distributed problem-based learning in continuing professional education. *Distance Education, 23*(1), 59–83.

Roschelle, J., & Teasley, S. D. (1995). The construction of shared knowledge in collaborative problem solving. In C. O'Malley (Ed.), *Computer supported collaborative learning* (pp. 69–97). Berlin: Springer.

Ryberg, T., Dirckinck-Holmfeld, L., & Jones, C. (2010). Catering to the needs of the "Digital Natives" or educating the "Net Generation"? In M. J. W. Lee & C. McLoughlin (Eds.), *Web 2.0-based e-learning: Applying social informatics for tertiary teaching* (pp. 301–318). Hershey, PA: IGI Global.

Ryberg, T., & Larsen, M. C. (2008). Networked identities: Understanding relationships between strong and weak ties in networked environments. *Journal of Computer Assisted Learning, 24*(2), 103–115.

Siemens, G. (2005). *Connectivism: A learning theory for the digital age.* Retrieved August 3, 2011, from http://www.elearnspace.org/Articles/connectivism.htm.

Siemens, G. (2006). *Connectivism: Learning and knowledge today.* Education.au. Retrieved August 3, 2011, from http://admin.edna.edu.au/dspace/bitstream/2150/34771/1/gs2006_siemens.pdf.

Siemens, G. (2008). Collective intelligence? Nah. Connective intelligence – elearnspace. *elearnspace – Learning, networks, knowledge, technology, community.* Retrieved November 17, 2009, from http://www.elearnspace.org/blog/2008/02/18/collective-intelligence-nah-connective-intelligence/

Suthers, D. D. (2006). Technology affordances for intersubjective meaning making: A research agenda for CSCL. *International Journal of Computer-Supported Collaborative Learning, 1*(3), 315–337.

Tolsby, H. (2009). Virtual environment for project based collaborative learning. In L. Dirckinck-Holmfeld, C. Jones, & B. Lindström (Eds.), *Analysing networked learning practices in higher education and continuing professional development. Technology-Enhanced Learning* (pp. 241–258). Rotterdam: Sense Publishers.

Tolsby, H., Nyvang, T., & Dirckinck-Holmfeld, L. (2002). A survey of technologies supporting virtual project based learning. In S. Banks et al. (Eds.), *Proceedings of the third international conference on networked learning – A research based conference on e-learning in higher education and lifelong learning* (pp. 572–580). Lancaster: Lancaster University.

Weller, M. (2007). *Virtual learning environments: Effective development and use.* London: Routledge.

Wellman, B. (2001). Physical place and Cyberplace: The rise of personalized networking. *International Journal of Urban and Regional Research, 25*(2), 227–252.

Wenger, E. (1998). *Communities of practice – Learning, meaning, and identity.* New York: Cambridge University Press.

Zenios, M. (2011). Epistemic activities and collaborative learning: Towards an analytical model for studying knowledge construction in networked learning settings. *Journal of Computer Assisted Learning, 27*(3), 259–268.

Part III
New Landscapes and Spaces for Networked Learning

Chapter 4
Mediators of Socio-technical Capital in a Networked Learning Environment

Daniel D. Suthers and Kar-Hai Chu

Introduction

A tradition of discourse in learning communities goes back to the earliest efforts at online education (Feenberg 1993; Hiltz 1986). Following this tradition, asynchronous learning networks were envisioned as "networks" not only in the technological sense, but also in the social sense: networked learners were seen as resources to support each others' learning (Mayadas 1997). Networked learning has several advantages. A feeling of social belonging improves students' online learning experience (Wegerif 1998), and with proper scaffolding, learners can engage together in constructing their knowledge (Aviv et al. 2003; Hansen et al. 1999). Likewise, our approach to university level education values students building on each others' work and seeks to build a sense of community that transcends individual courses. We support overlapping learning communities consisting of graduate level programs in a Department of Information and Computer Sciences, and an interdisciplinary Communication and Information Sciences PhD program. Students and faculty in these programs participate in multiple nested and overlapping groups and are members of a larger community.

Yet, this reality is not well supported by some online learning environments. As they were implemented in our institutional context when this work commenced, systems such as WebCT and Blackboard isolated students from each other. Students encountered materials and each other in individual course contexts, but the software was not designed for group collaboration. This "silo" approach (isolating classes) is

D.D. Suthers (✉)
Information and Computer Sciences, University of Hawai'i at Manoa, Honolulu, HI, USA
e-mail: suthers@Hawaii.edu

K.-H. Chu
Communication and Information Sciences, University of Hawai'i at Manoa, Honolulu, HI, USA

L. Dirckinck-Holmfeld et al. (eds.), *Exploring the Theory, Pedagogy and Practice of Networked Learning*, DOI 10.1007/978-1-4614-0496-5_4, © Springer Science+Business Media, LLC 2012

somewhat intentional: institutions need to restrict access to tuition-paying students, and some pedagogical approaches rely on controlling the order in which information is revealed to the student, viewing building on others' work as a form of "cheating." Unfortunately, the silo approach can inhibit pedagogical approaches that can be conducive to learning, such as collaborative learning (Dillenbourg 1999; Webb and Palincsar 1996), apprenticeships (Lave and Wenger 1991), and interdisciplinary or transdisciplinary collaborations (Derry and Fischer 2005).

In response to this need, we designed a software environment, disCourse, to support individual courses while also allowing for serendipitous discovery of other persons, ideas, and resources in the larger virtual community. We are now studying ways in which participants benefit from persons and resources in contexts other than the original course to which they were assigned, and how the various digital media available in our software support such forms of networked learning. This chapter reports an analysis addressing these questions. We begin with a discussion of the theoretical concept of *bridging socio-technical capital* and its relationship to our software environment. Then we describe a method for empirical estimation of the potential for bridging socio-technical capital by analyzing log files. The rest of the chapter applies this method to one of our learning environments and reports the results of this analysis and its implications.

Background

This section defines the primary theoretical concept of this chapter and describes the software environment that is the source of the data.

Bridging Socio-technical Capital

Long before the recent Web 2.0 explosion of "social networks" as a specific genre of software application, researchers have studied social networks as a phenomenon in face-to-face settings (Freeman 2004), and later in online environments such as scientific collaboratories (Council 1993; Kling et al. 2000) and online learning (Barab et al. 2004; Rekkedal and Paulsen 1989; Renninger and Shumar 2002). Participants often come to such online environments for an instrumental purpose, for example, to participate in a course or professional activities. This instrumental purpose may only require interacting with a prescribed group of people, but the presence of others in the online environment offers further and perhaps unforeseen opportunities.

Bridging (Granovetter 1973; Simmel 1971) or *boundary spanning* (Levina and Vaast 2005) between these instrumental groups can help realize the potential synergy of the larger social network. (Some literatures define "bridging" and "boundary spanning" in terms of membership in two or more groups. In this chapter, we use the terms synonymously for contacts made outside of one's assigned groups, to be explained). Computer-mediated communication enables each person to participate in a much larger number of casual relationships or "weak ties" than is possible through face-to-face interaction (Donath and Boyd 2004). A network of weak ties provides access to more potential collaborators and novel information beyond what is available in one's immediate strong tie circles (Granovetter 1973). Putnam (2000) calls these resources for potential action *bridging social capital*. Properly designed social technologies increase this kind of social capital. Since the capital in socio-technical networks partially resides in how the technology enables the social network, Resnick (2002) refers to it as *socio-technical capital*.

Combining these ideas, we have designed for *bridging socio-technical capital* in two learning-related applications: one for teacher professional development and another for university level education. In these online environments, a number of people who may have something in common are participating in task-specific workspaces that are embedded in a shared virtual space. Our objective is to design this space to offer affordances for the sharing of something of value between participants beyond the specific instrumental objectives that brought them to the workspaces (e.g., professional development activities or taking a course).

Prometheus and disCourse

The software environment studied was first developed in the context of a technology-supported systemic reform effort called Hawai'i Networked Learning Communities (HNLC). Our objective was to improve Science, Math, and Technology education in rural schools of Hawai'i with a program of professional development, supported by a "virtual community center," HNLC.org, that was intended to enable teachers to reach both human and digital resources across geographic and institutional barriers (Suthers et al. 2004; Suthers et al. 2007). As the project matured, we developed a "community of reflective practitioners" approach to professional development (Yukawa et al. 2007). Recognizing that school teams can benefit from the state-wide community, we designed to support "transcendent communities" or the discovery of value in the larger network that forms by embedding smaller groups with well-defined purposes in a common space (Joseph et al. 2007; Suthers et al. 2004). Realizing that the community-oriented nature of HNLC.org also suited our approach to university education, our team generalized the software to a code base called *Prometheus*, and used this to implement the present HNLC.org (teacher community) and disCourse (university community) instances, as well as other instances. Prometheus was written by Sam Joseph in Ruby on Rails, based on designs by Viil Lid. Prometheus is not related to the open source project suppressed by Blackboard.

A Prometheus instance contains the following resources for collaboration and community. (Taken individually, these features are now found in various courseware and social networking environments, but their combination is less common in courseware environments). Any user, without logging in, can access *stories* that are

Fig. 4.1   A disCourse workspace

posted on the home page. When a story is posted, all members receive an email notification. The general public can also access a database of searchable metadata on web-based *resources*. When new resources are created by a community member and made public, they also appear on the home page on a recent resources list. This also helps the public as well as the members become aware of the topics of interest to the community and relevant documents. Logging in, a registered user has additional access to member profiles, discussions, and workspaces. Contributions such as messages, resources, and stories are tagged by a link to the *profile* of the person who posted them, enabling members to learn more about persons who may have similar interests. Member profiles provide contact information and link to each member's workspaces and discussion postings. *Discussions* are web-based threaded discussions, displayed in context to facilitate referencing: one can open up multiple subthreads at the same time on one page and compose one's reply in this context. Discussion postings include a link to the member profile of the author as well as a record of who has read the message. *Workspaces* include many of the other available resources of the environment and add a few features (Fig. 4.1). The intention is to collect in one place everything a workgroup (e.g., class or teacher team) is using to support its work. Each workspace has a main area in which the current object being viewed or edited is displayed, plus various tools and resources listed on the left and right-hand sides. The items accessible on the sides and displayable in the main area include wiki pages, discussions, participant profiles, resources and uploaded files (both in the resource database), a synchronous chat tool, and links to subworkspaces ("sections"). Wiki pages and discussions are paired (center of Fig. 4.1): each wiki page can have a discussion attached to it where participants can discuss the contents of the wiki page as they edit it, and each discussion can have a wiki page at the top for stating the purpose of the discussion, posing questions, summarizing conclusions, etc. In either case, the motivation is "artifact centered discussion": learning and work often require coordinated talk about artifacts (objects or documents) while also modifying them (Suthers 2001).

In summary, the digital mediators by which users may find value in the larger social network include lists of recently contributed resources and recently active workspaces and discussions on the home page; lists and tabs under which one may browse and search available discussions, resources and workspaces; and links from artifacts to contributing and reading members.

Method

The analysis reported in this chapter addressed the following research questions: (1) To what extent do people who come to the online environment find potential value that derives from the presence or products of others outside the workspace in which they pursue their instrumental objectives? That is, do we see evidence that the environment provides bridging socio-technical capital? (2) By what technological mediators do they find this value that we might strengthen and exploit further? What potential mediators are underutilized? A "mediator" can be any digital artifact that is written and read by participants, such as discussions, profiles, resources, and wikis.

Our method is based on automated analysis of log files. Below we discuss how we translate the concept of bridging socio-technical capital into a measurable proxy, namely access to digital artifacts derived from the presence of others.

Operationalizing Potential Value

Our analysis is based on the simplifying assumption that a digital artifact has *potentially* offered someone value if that person has accessed it. Specifically, we consider four kinds of digital artifacts that may be created by one person and accessed by another: discussions, resources (uploaded files and meta-data on external web pages), user profiles, and wiki pages. The normal use of each of these artifacts is to read and post discussion messages, view and post resources, view user profiles, and read and edit wiki pages. If a person does one of these things, then we credit the associated artifact with having potentially provided value. This definition is clearly inadequate with respect to whether the individual involved actually felt that they were gaining value or actually did gain value by some measure, but it is not feasible to interview participants at the scale of this study, nor is it plausible that they would remember every access event let alone provide accurate quantifications of value comparable across participants. For purposes of characterizing the potential of open environments and comparing the relative roles of different media, access events provide an *upper bound* on potential value, as participants could not have gained value directly from artifacts they did not access.

Since we are concerned with *socio*-technical capital, we need to restrict consideration to artifacts that derive from the presence of others in the social environment. Specifically, we consider four kinds of digital artifacts that may be created by one person and accessed by another: discussions, resources, user profiles, and wiki pages. The analysis reported here operationalizes potential value as follows: one potentially gets socially derived value by accessing a discussion if others have posted to the same discussion; accessing a resource that someone else has provided; accessing a wiki if others have edited it; and by accessing someone else's profile.

Capturing Artifact-Mediated Associations in Associograms

A simple yet powerful way to capture, structurally as well as quantitatively, the relationships that derive from participation in a social space is through *sociograms*: graphs in which vertices are persons and edges are "ties" between persons (Scott 1988; Wasserman and Faust 1994). Social network analysis is traditionally concerned with interpersonal ties between persons. Since we are concerned with socio-*technical* capital and with the mediating role of digital artifacts, we treat technological artifacts as "actants" (Latour 2005) that can participate in ties just as persons can. We call these ties "associations" to emphasize that they do not require (and we do not assume) that there is an interpersonal relationship between the persons involved: people can share socio-technical capital via their mutual involvement in an artifact without necessarily knowing each other. For example, when one user accesses a digital resource or artifact provided by another person, the traditional approach might say that there is a tie between the two persons, and create a sociogram that has an edge between vertices representing those persons. However, since we are concerned with socio-technical capital rather than interpersonal relationships, we represent the association between persons as mediated by the artifact, with arcs from person to artifact to person. Networks of such associations are bipartite graphs, a type of affiliation network. The edges are directed arcs to indicate direction of contingency (Suthers et al. 2010): an arc from an artifact to a person indicates that the person has created the artifact; and an arc from a person to an artifact indicates that the person has accessed the artifact. Thus, an association between two persons is represented by a path of two arcs passing via an artifact. We call these actor–artifact graphs "associograms" to distinguish them from sociograms. Figure 4.2 shows a simple example. The two-arc pathway shown represents a mediated association. Resource 13 is contingent on user 14 (its creator), and user 12 is contingent on the resource by virtue of accessing it. The dotted line indicates a spontaneous association, discussed next.

Fig. 4.2 An associogram

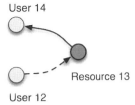

User 14

Resource 13

User 12

Spontaneous Associations

Recall that our first research question asks to what extent participants find potential value *outside* of the contexts in which they pursue their instrumental objectives. Therefore, we want to identify socio-technical capital gained beyond mutual participation in a class or other task-oriented contexts. We make the following distinction. Associations arising between users participating in a workspace to which they were assigned are called *assigned associations*. These associations are very typical and are expected to arise between users because of their assignment to a shared workspace. Associations arising outside such assigned workspaces are called *spontaneous associations*. Spontaneous associations are the primary metric of interest in this study, as they are indicators of what has been gained by placing instrumental workspaces in an open community setting.

Since we are analyzing data from disCourse, in which participation is primarily driven by university courses, we conduct our analysis on a semester basis. Students are assigned to a class workspace at the beginning of the semester. Associations due to interactions between members within these workspaces cannot be considered the basis for bridging socio-technical capital; as such associations could be dictated by classroom requirements. Since subworkspaces of class workspaces are sometimes created throughout the semester, co-membership is inherited from parent workspaces. Our analysis seeks out associations that take place either between two people who were not assigned to the same workspace in the first 2 weeks of the semester, or who were but the mediating artifact is situated outside of their mutual workspace, so potentially involves an association unrelated to their class work. These associations indicate bridging socio-technical capital that would not have been obtained in a silo approach to online learning.

Sample

We analyzed data from four academic semesters (fall 2007, spring 2008, fall 2008, and spring 2009) to search for spontaneous artifact-mediated associations between disCourse users. All users of disCourse and their artifacts were included in the analysis. Users include graduate and undergraduate students, faculty, and a small number of others associated with one of our five degree programs. Workspaces exist for courses, research projects, individual projects, degree program materials, and special interest topics.

Procedure

Prometheus servers log events in a MySQL database. These log entries were transformed and filtered using operations similar to those of exploratory sequential data analysis (Sanderson and Fisher 1994). For a given artifact type (discussion, resource, user profile, or wiki page), the analysis proceeded as follows. First, we selected all events in which any user accessed any instance of the given artifact type at any time. We further constrained these events to the time period in question (the semester being analyzed). Joins with other database tables determined the creator of the artifact and the workspace, if any, that the artifact belonged to. Further computation determined whether the accessing user belonged to that workspace or one of its parent workspaces, and if so, when the user joined that workspace. The accessing and originating users were considered as having an assigned association if they were both members of the workspace or a parent workspace containing the artifact in the first 2 weeks of the semester, and as having a spontaneous association otherwise. The frequency counts reported in the results section are counts of the number of accessor–artifact pairs in the resulting associogram, visualized as the dotted arrow in Fig. 4.2. (There could be multiple accessor–artifact pairs for one artifact–originator pair such as the solid line R13-U14 because many users can access an artifact created by one user). We report both total number of accessor–artifact pairs and the number of those that are due to spontaneous associations. In either case, the resulting set of accessor–artifact–originator triplets were visualized in associograms for our inspection. Finally, we manually examined the artifacts and profiles of users involved in about half the bridging events in order to characterize the apparent nature of the events (i.e., apply our judgment concerning what the users appeared to be doing).

The present analysis improves on and extends a preliminary analysis reported in Suthers et al. (2009) as follows. First, the present analysis includes more recent usage data. Second, the prior analysis included false positives generated when subworkspaces were created after the first 2 weeks of a semester, while the present analysis climbs the workspace containment hierarchy to check for co-membership in a parent workspace. Third, while the prior analysis relied on inspection of network visualizations, the present analysis provides quantitative summaries of the proportion of bridging to overall activity. Fourth, while the prior analysis used ad hoc methods, the present analysis uses prototypes of tools based on an analytic framework we are developing (Suthers et al. 2010; Suthers and Rosen 2011).

Results and Discussion

The quantitative results are summarized in Table 4.1. The "SA" column shows counts for spontaneous associations, enabling a quantitative comparison of bridging activity (access to potential additional value provided by the open learning environment) mediated by each of the artifact types. The "Total" column includes both spontaneous

Table 4.1 Quantitative results of artifact-mediated associations

	Sem.	SA	Total	% S/T	Sem.	SA	Total	% S/T	Avg SA	Avg Total	Avg % S/T
D	F 07	232	4,884	4.8	F 08	218	2,903	7.5	216	3,411	6.3
	S 08	192	3,406	5.6	S 09	221	2,449	9.0			
P	F 07	477	1,103	43.2	F 08	288	924	31.2	305	877	34.8
	S 08	235	788	29.8	S 09	219	692	31.6			
R	F 07	48	139	34.5	F 08	45	273	16.5	54	168	32.1
	S 08	93	139	66.9	S 09	30	122	24.6			
W	F 07	115	8,919	1.3	F 08	32	5,723	0.6	63	6,432	1.0
	S 08	93	5,924	1.6	S 09	10	5,163	0.2			

D discussions, *P* profiles, *R* resources, *W* wiki pages

and assigned associations, providing a measure of overall level of activity for the indicated artifact type. The ratio of the two, "%S/T," indicates what percentage of the total activity constitutes bridging activity. Values are shown for each semester, and the averages across semesters are shown in the right-hand columns.

Comparing the semesters, relative magnitudes of activity are consistent across the semesters, but the overall levels drop off in the spring semester. This may be an artifact of variation in instructor practices across courses, or due to increased activity by new students exploring a novel environment for the first time in the fall. Ranking the artifact types by the total level of activity, wiki pages (average of 6,432 accesses per semester) have the most activity, followed by discussions (3,411), profile views (877), and resource access (168). This provides an indication of the importance, by frequency of access, of each artifact type to the online activity of students in this environment. But the ranking differs according to spontaneous association counts: Profiles (305) account for the most bridging events, followed by discussions (216), wiki pages (63), and resources (54). Those artifact types that receive the most activity have the lowest percentage of bridging events: the ranking by percentages is profiles (34.8%), resources (32.1%), discussions (6.3%), and wiki pages (1.0%). Examination of individual events and their artifacts shows that students are viewing class materials in classes that they are not enrolled in. Many of these spontaneous associations cross between the Information and Computer Sciences and Communication and Information Sciences degree programs. We discuss each artifact type in further detail below.

Discussions and Wiki Pages

The majority of the activity of participants in this environment takes place in discussions and wikis: they are important resources for the work being done. This result can be understood in terms of how the properties of these media are appropriated in practice. Both media are *mutable*: normal use of a discussion and wiki page might involve posting or editing activities, respectively, in contrast to profiles and resources, which are modified infrequently and typically used primarily by reading them. Students are often expected to participate in discussions, and the content of discussions changes over time, motivating repeated access. Wiki pages may be used for dissemination of information to students, in which case only the instructor is expected to edit them, but in this case students may access them regularly for information; and some students edit the wiki pages associated with their project and dissertation work.

Examining the percentage of activity that bridges across instrumental workspaces, we find that discussions and wiki pages have dramatically low percentages (6.3 and 1.0%, respectively). This finding could be dismissed as merely due to these media's effectiveness in supporting task-oriented activity within the workspaces, the high total counts resulting in a large denominator, but from the perspective of bridging socio-technical capital it is clear that there is unrealized potential. The explanation is straightforward: discussions and especially wiki pages exist primarily within workspace contexts, so bridging events would take place only if a user enters a workspace he or she was not a member of. The exception is a small number of discussions that belong to either no workspace or multiple workspaces. (One user with system level privileges had linked discussions to multiple workspaces in an effort to foster continuity of a seminar across semesters). This finding indicates that the potential value of discussions and wiki pages for other users would be better realized if we figured out ways to make them visible and accessible outside of their workspace contexts.

Profiles and Resources

Unlike discussions and wikis, *user profiles and resources* are more accessible outside of workspaces. When new resources are posted and made public, they are listed on a "new resources" list on the home page. There is also a resources page by which one may search for resources. Also, most artifacts have a user name associated (e.g., message poster; last editor of a wiki) that is linked to the user's profile, and one can also use the membership page to search for and view others' profiles. Therefore, even though the total number of accesses to these artifact types was lower, a greater percentage of associations mediated by these two kinds of artifacts bridged instrumental contexts. Some of the profile views are between persons who are in the same class; however, a large portion of the profile views occurs outside of class workspaces. This activity suggests that disCourse users are utilizing profiles, and discovering users from groups that are external to their own. Many resources are not linked to any particular workspace and would not be seen in a user's regular daily navigation, and yet users are viewing these unlinked artifacts. This may be because the home page displays a list of recently added resources. Also, although the site-wide search facility searches all artifact types, profiles resources, and discussions have their own dedicated tabs for browsing and searching.

Summary

Results show that there is appreciable bridging in disCourse across classes and programs, but the types of artifacts studied play different roles in mediating socio-technical capital as measured by bridging or spontaneous associations. While there is much more activity within wikis and discussions, it appears as though little of that activity helps users expand beyond their instrumental contexts. Meanwhile, an appreciable percentage of access to profiles and resources (about a third) are bridging events, but these artifacts support fewer associations, which limits their contribution to bridging socio-technical capital. Discussions and wikis encourage interaction between users that profiles and resources do not. Ideally, we would like to design media that combine the positive attributes of each to have high levels of unsolicited bridging activity. For example, the present results suggest making all artifact types accessible outside of workspaces, and making all of them "discussable" for ubiquitous interaction. Specifically, discussion facilities could be associated with profiles and resources.

Conclusions

The analysis reported in this chapter examined the extent to which people who come to the online environment for instrumental objectives such as taking a course encounter persons or products of others from outside their course workspace. Various digital media available in an online learning environment – discussions, resources, user profiles, and wiki pages – were compared in terms of how they support these encounters. Addressing our first research question, the results indicate that users are accessing potential value (as measured by their initiative in modifying and viewing digital artifacts) outside the workspace context that meets their instrumental objectives in using the environment (taking a class). Since the potential value is mediated by digital artifacts provided by others outside of the class workspace context, we have evidence for *bridging socio-technical capital*. The implication for networked learning is that students can benefit from the presence of others if educational activities are conducted in digital environments that are embedded in a larger community space, rather than isolated from each other.

Yet, not all media are equal and there is room for improvement. Turning to our second research question, we found that in our current design the greatest potential for bridging socio-technical capital in terms of sheer number of bridging events observed is via discussions and profiles, while the greatest potential in terms of percentage of bridging events lies in profiles and resources. To take advantage of these vectors for social capital, we should make profiles and resources visible wherever they are relevant. We should also examine what users are *doing* with the artifacts they encounter, and consider adding more options for activity (e.g., personal messaging) that further realize the potential for socio-technical capital.

It is not surprising that wiki pages did not bridge between class contexts, as these artifacts are created and encountered within workspaces, and one typically must have membership in the workspace to write to or edit these artifacts – e.g. be members of a class. Discussions are also most often encountered via workspaces, although not necessarily: one can enter discussions from the home page or from email notifications of discussion activity. The present results suggest that we need to find ways to make users aware of relevant discussions and especially wikis outside their primary workspaces, and increase opportunities for participation in these media.

A number of simplifications were deliberately made in this analysis to enable us to compute estimates of bridging socio-technical capital from log files. Limitations of the analysis point to several directions for future work. Associations can be measured at multiple granularities. For this initial analysis, we have chosen to count each person's access to a given artifact just once. A more sensitive measure might be obtained by counting each person's access to the artifact every time someone has modified the artifact since the previous access, as there may be new value in the modified artifact. We could also count all access events even if the artifact has not changed under the reasoning that a user returns to artifacts that offer more value. Another direction for future work is to "ground truth" the log file analysis. Interviews could be conducted to obtain participants' retrospective impressions of what they find valuable in this environment and to check our interpretations against these impressions. This would help improve and increase our trust in the results produced computationally from log files. Further work can identify the kinds of associations that are taking place via the technological environment that facilitate generation and spread of ideas, lead to face-to-face relationships, or form the basis for the development of students' professional identities.

Acknowledgments The authors gratefully acknowledge our team members cited as co-authors above for their contributions to these ideas over the years. We especially thank Sam Joseph for design and implementation of the Prometheus code base, and Viil Lid for community interface design. This work was funded by NSF grants #0100393 and #0943147. Authors may be contacted at suthers@hawaii.edu and karhai@hawaii.edu.

References

Aviv, R., Erlich, Z., Ravid, G., & Geva, A. (2003). Network analysis of knowledge construction in asynchronous learning networks. *Journal of Asynchronous Learning Networks, 7*(3). Retrieved August 6, 2011 from http://sloanconsortium.org/system/files/v7n3_aviv.pdf

Barab, S. A., Kling, R., & Gray, J. H. (2004). *Designing for virtual communities in the service of learning*. New York: Cambridge University Press.

Council, N. R. (1993). *National collaboratories: Applying information technology for scientific research*. Washington, DC: National Academy Press.

Derry, S. J., & Fischer, G. (2005). *Transdisciplinary graduate education*. Paper presented at the American Educational Research Association, Montreal, Canada.

Dillenbourg, P. (1999). What do you mean by "collaborative learning"? In P. Dillenbourg (Ed.), *Collaborative learning: Cognitive and computational approaches* (pp. 1–19). Amsterdam: Elsevier.

Donath, J. S., & Boyd, D. (2004). Public displays of connection. *BT Technology Journal, 22,* 71–82.

Feenberg, A. (1993). Building a global network: The WBSI experience. In L. Harasim (Ed.), *Global networks: Computerizing the international community* (pp. 185–197). Cambridge, MA: MIT.

Freeman, L. C. (2004). *The development of social network analysis: A study in the sociology of science.* Vancouver: Empirical Press.

Granovetter, M. S. (1973). The strength of weak ties. *The American Journal of Sociology, 78*(6), 1360–1380.

Hansen, T., Dirckinck-Holmfeld, L., Lewis, R., & Rugelj, J. (1999). Using telematics for collaborative knowledge construction. In P. Dillenbourg (Ed.), *Collaborative learning: Cognitive and computational approaches* (pp. 169–196). Amsterdam: Elsevier.

Hiltz, S. R. (1986). The virtual classroom: Using computer-mediated communication for university teaching. *Journal of Communication, 36*(2), 95–104.

Joseph, S., Lid, V., & Suthers, D. D. (2007). Transcendent communities. In C. Chinn, G. Erkens, & S. Puntambekar (Eds.), *The Computer Supported Collaborative Learning (CSCL) Conference 2007* (pp. 317–319). New Brunswick: International Society of the Learning Sciences.

Kling, R., McKim, G., Fortuna, J., & King, A. (2000). Scientific collaboratories as socio-technical interaction networks: A theoretical approach. arXiv.org. Retrieved August 6, 2011 from http://arxiv.org/pdf/cs.CY/0005007. doi:arXiv:cs/0005007v1 [cs.CY]

Latour, B. (2005). *Reassembing the social: An introduction to actor-network-theory.* New York: Oxford University Press.

Lave, J., & Wenger, E. (1991). *Situated learning: Legitimate peripheral participation.* Cambridge: Cambridge University Press.

Levina, N., & Vaast, E. (2005). The emergence of boundary spanning competence in practice: Implications for implementation and use of information systems. *MIS Quarterly, 29*(2), 335–363.

Mayadas, F. (1997). Asynchronous learning networks: A sloan foundation perspective. *Journal of Asynchronous Learning Networks, 1.* Retrieved August 6, 2011 from http://sloanconsortium. org/system/files/v1n1_mayadas.pdf

Putnam, R. D. (2000). *Bowling alone.* New York: Simon & Schuster.

Rekkedal, T., & Paulsen, M. F. (1989). Computer conferencing in distance education: Status and trends. *European Journal of Education, 24*(1), 61–72.

Renninger, K., & Shumar, W. (2002). *Building virtual communities.* Cambridge: Cambridge University Press.

Resnick, P. (2002). Beyond bowling together: Sociotechnical capital. In J. M. Carroll (Ed.), *Human–computer interaction in the new millennium* (pp. 647–672). Upper Saddle River, NJ: ACM.

Sanderson, P., & Fisher, C. (1994). Exploratory sequential data analysis: Foundations. *Human Computer Interaction, 9*(3–4), 251–318.

Scott, J. (1988). Social network analysis. *Sociology, 22*(1), 109–127.

Simmel, G. (1971). Group expansion and the development of individuality. In D. M. Levine (Ed.), *Georg Simmel on individuality and social forms.* Chicago: University of Chicago Press.

Suthers, D. D. (2001). *Collaborative representations: Supporting face to face and online knowledge-building discourse.* Proceedings of the 34th Hawai'i International Conference on the System Sciences (HICSS-34), January 3–6, 2001, Maui, Hawai'i (CD-ROM). New York: Institute of Electrical and Electronics Engineers, Inc. (IEEE).

Suthers, D. D., Chu, K.-H., & Joseph, S. (2009). *Bridging socio-technical capital in an online learning environment.* Proceedings of the 42nd Hawai'i International Conference on the System

Sciences (HICSS-42), January 5–8, 2009, Waikoloa, Hawai'i (CD-ROM). New Brunswick: Institute of Electrical and Electronics Engineers, Inc. (IEEE).

Suthers, D. D., Dwyer, N., Medina, R., & Vatrapu, R. (2010). A framework for conceptualizing, representing, and analyzing distributed interaction. *International Journal of Computer Supported Collaborative Learning, 5*(1), 5–42.

Suthers, D. D., Harada, V. H., Doane, W. E. J., Yukawa, J., Harris, B., & Lid, V. (2004). *Technology-supported systemic reform: An initial evaluation and reassessment.* Paper presented at the Proceedings of the Sixth International Conference of the Learning Sciences, Santa Monica, CA (pp. 537–544).

Suthers, D. D., & Rosen, D. (2011). *A unified framework for multi-level analysis of distributed learning.* To appear in Proceedings of the First International Conference on Learning Analytics and Knowledge, Banff, AB, February 27–March 1, 2011.

Suthers, D. D., Yukawa, J., & Harada, V. H. (2007). An activity system analysis of a tripartite technology-supported partnership for school reform. *Research and Practice in Technology Enhanced Learning, 2*(2), 1–29.

Wasserman, S., & Faust, K. (1994). *Social network analysis: Methods and applications.* New York: Cambridge University Press.

Webb, N., & Palincsar, A. S. (1996). Group processes in the classroom. In D. Berlmer & R. Calfee (Eds.), *Handbook of educational psychology* (pp. 841–873). New York: Simon & Schuster Macmillan.

Wegerif, R. (1998). The social dimension of asynchronous learning networks. *Journal of Asynchronous Learning Networks, 2*(1). Retrieved August 6, 2011 from http://sloanconsortium. org/system/files/v2n1_wegerif.pdf

Yukawa, J., Harada, V. H., & Suthers, D. D. (2007). Professional development in communities of practice. In S. Hughes-Hassell & V. H. Harada (Eds.), *School reform and the school library media specialist* (pp. 179–192). Westport, CT: Libraries Unlimited.

Chapter 5
Collectivity, Performance and Self-representation: Analysing Cloudworks as a Public Space for Networked Learning and Reflection

Panagiota Alevizou, Rebecca Galley, and Gráinne Conole

Introduction

It has been argued that processes of participatory culture (Jenkins 2006; Bruns 2008), afforded by social media and technologies are beginning to blur the boundaries between creative production and consumption, and open up novel, public spaces for, and styles of, networked learning; social spaces that promote "communities of enquiry", collaborative knowledge building, and shared assets (e.g. interests, goals, contents, ideas, see Alexander 2008; Anderson 2007; Downes 2005). Nonetheless, empirical evidence on the application of such technologies for supporting teaching and learning in higher education contexts is only slowly emerging.

This chapter explores these concepts in the context of analysis of emergent patterns of behaviour and activity in a new social networking site for education: Cloudworks. Cloudworks is a specialised network, and a public space for aggregating and sharing resources and exchanging ideas about the scholarship and practice of teaching and learning. It begins with an overview of the site, and the initial theoretical underpinnings that informed its design, and then briefly describes the activity patterns we are seeing emerge as use of the site evolves. We argue that these patterns of behaviour require further theorising to locate the site in current socio-cultural thinking. We connect the notions of self-representation and collective intelligence that have been used to analyse performance and expression in social media/networked cultures with dimensions of expansive learning, and explore the nuances of mediated networked learning in this open space. We explore not only how connections and interactions are built within Cloudworks (for a given time, or a given purpose, or serendipitously), but also, how the connections and the interactions with materials and resources – and among people and things – are *expressed*, what the

P. Alevizou (✉) • R. Galley • G. Conole
Institute of Educational Technology, The Open University, Milton Keynes, UK
e-mail: p.alevizou@open.ac.uk

L. Dirckinck-Holmfeld et al. (eds.), *Exploring the Theory, Pedagogy and Practice of Networked Learning*, DOI 10.1007/978-1-4614-0496-5_5,
© Springer Science+Business Media, LLC 2012

communicative or discursive dimensions of such expressions might be, and how far they may indicate collective action and community building. We conclude by suggesting that analysis of social, networked media in an educational context can yield new insights into the future of networked learning.

The initial theoretical perspectives on which Cloudworks has been based have been focused around Engeström's (2005) notion of "social objects" in social networking, and Bouman et al. (2007) framework for "sociality". In this chapter, we introduce three additional frameworks and demonstrate how they are helping us with our preliminary analyses of emerging activities on the site, and in particular the insights they provide into the dialogic interchanges and structures of involvement within the site. The first is the notion of collective intelligence (Lévy 1997, 2001; Jenkins 2006). The second framework stems from Ervin Goffman's notions of "face-work" and "ritual performance" (1955, 1963), and the third from a strand of activity theory, relating to expansive learning (Engeström 2001; Griffiths and Guile 2001). For the purpose of this chapter, we present case studies in the form of narrative examples from just two of the many emerging patterns of activity and involvement within the site, namely, "Debates" and "Enquiries and advice".

We argue that these perspectives are useful in studying networked sociality bounded in the context of learning, with wider implications for participation, self-representation, and openness in a higher education context. We contextualise emerging findings through this analytical lens, and aim to offer insights that will shape the agenda for conducting further research on the study of interaction, socialisation and sharing within Cloudworks specifically, and research in networked learning in general. We conclude with the implications such analyses may have for *productive learning in networked environments*" (Jones and Dirckinck-Holmfeld 2009: 1).

Cloudworks Overview

Cloudworks (http://cloudworks.ac.uk) has been developed as part of the Open University Learning Design Initiative (http://ouldi.open.ac.uk). An agile and responsive approach to the development of the site has been adopted across three design phases. Each phase has consisted of a series of design decisions, observation, data analysis and evaluation (Conole and Culver 2009).

Cloudworks is a social networking site, which uses social media to provide a space for education professionals to share, discuss and find learning and teaching ideas. The site combines practices such as sociality, sharing and co-creation common in social networking platforms, wikis and social media, with different forms of dialogue, debate and peer commenting. The site allows for a range of social functions, such as "tagging", "favouriting", RSS feeds, "follow and be followed", and activity streams for different aspects of the site. Collectively, these features provide a range of routes through the site and enable users to collaboratively improve Clouds in a number of ways. Unlike many professional social networking spaces, the site is entirely open and object-centred. We argue that these factors help to enable transient but repeated and focused collaborative activity within, across and between groups

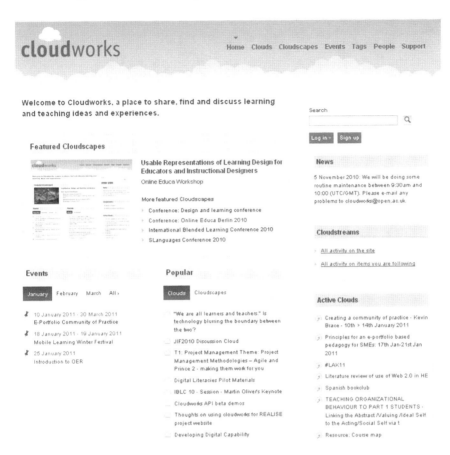

Fig. 5.1 Cloudworks homepage featuring streamed and evolving activity (most active Clouds on the *right*, featured Cloudscapes at the *top*, popular Clouds/Cloudscapes *below*, and events listings *below* and *left*)

from more established Communities of Practice, around events, ideas, designs and questions. The core objects in the site are "Clouds" which provide a space for anything to do with learning and teaching. The functionality of a Cloud is extensive: Clouds can act like blogs, in that material can be added to appear as series of sequential entries; users can post comments as they would in a discussion forum, and Clouds also enable aggregation and embedding of resources such as links, videos, slideshows, images, documents and academic references. The site's inter-connectivity with other channels of Web-communication (particularly Twitter and blogs) has pushed the dimensions of serendipity and association to create opportunities for self-oriented as well as collective aspects of engagement. Indeed, as functionality has been developed to complement blended communicative practices in residential events (such as workshops, seminars and conferences), more examples of activity have emerged, pointing to self-actualisation through archiving of interpretations, citations, and personal reflections (Figs. 5.1 and 5.2).

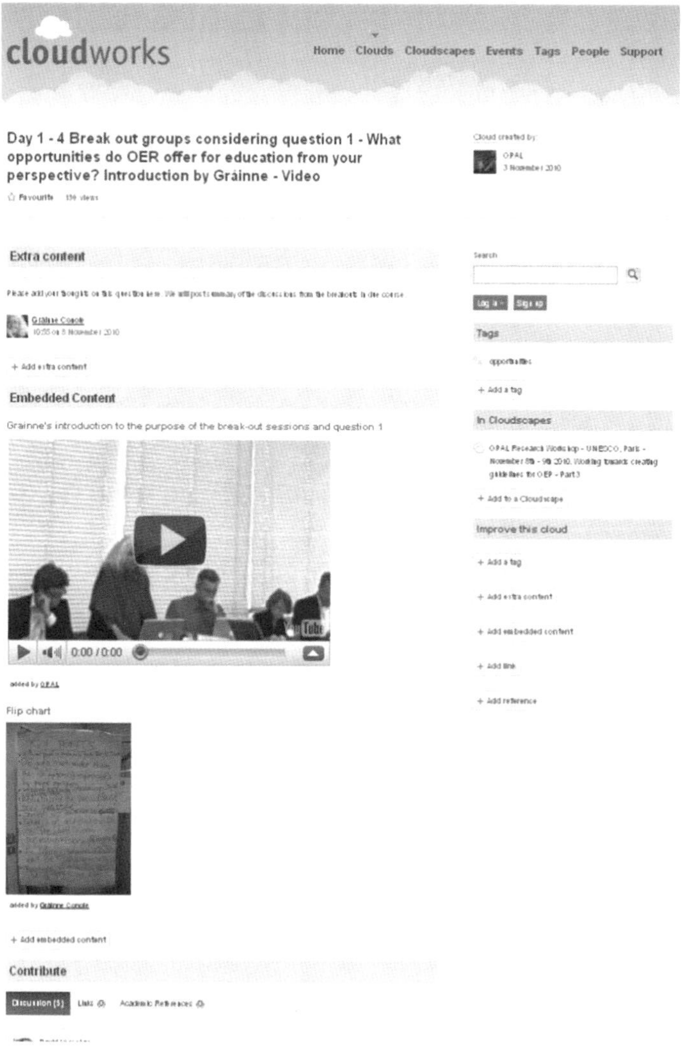

Fig. 5.2 Screen shot of a Cloud aggregating video, images, discussion, links and references

Clouds can be grouped into clusters of interest called Cloudscapes. These might be around a particular event such as a workshop or conference, or a Community of Interest such as a course team or student cohort, or around a topic such as a research theme or project. As of October 2010, the site contained 3,358 registered users, ca. 58,000 "absolute unique" visitors (i.e. distinct IP addresses) from 176 countries. Table 5.1 summarises the patterns of activity pointing to types of uses as they evolved over time and through the added functionalities.

Table 5.1 Core patterns of activity and evolutionary trajectories

Core types of activity	Evolutionary trajectories in use/activity
Events (supported and serendipitous) Workshops Conferences Virtual seminars/conventions	Increased number of requests to the Cloudworks team for setting up pre-designed spaces for events (from Summer 2009) A richer record of events in relation to (a) embedding chapters and presentations; (b) audience responses and dialogic interchanges (back-channels) Increased number of users setting up ad-hoc spaces for back-channel activities (from Autumn 2009)
Audience/interest group targeted Cloudscapes for specific research idea/project or teaching topics and pedagogies	Increased numbers of users outside of the team contributing to the site (71% of Cloudscapes, 79.2% of Clouds and 89.7% of comments in October 2010 were created by users other than the Cloudworks team) Aggregation of topics with more followers; increased personalisation and projected topic-oriented sociality (from Autumn 2009)
Topic/Question oriented sociality	Essentially dialogic in nature – Clouds or Cloudscapes which raise questions and issues, and provide a shared space for users to discuss A new pattern of activity sparking "flash debates" is evident from Summer 2009 Provocative questions and polling style activities – often transferred from the blogs and twitter – generate rich and immediate discussions Aggregation – a record and focal point of discussions in a public space
"Open Research Reviews"	Researchers start posing their research questions and aggregating relevant resources, but also inviting others to contribute and discuss (Autumn, 2009)
Closed community activity in open spaces	Examples of emerging use of the open Cloudworks space for typically closed community activity such as agreeing agenda items and schedules for meetings, development of community targets, etc. (Summer 2010)

Theoretical Perspectives: From Objects to Situations

Having provided a brief description of the evolution of the site, this section describes some of the additional theoretical frameworks that we are exploring to enable us to further analyse the patterns of evident behaviour on the site as a public space for performance of self, and socialisation around shared interests. As outlined above we have deployed socio-cultural perspectives, drawing on ideas of mediation and activity theory for designing object oriented sociality (see Conole and Culver 2009; Bouman et al. 2007; Engeström 2005). Drawing on Wenger (1998) Bouman et al. (2007: 14) argue that "a designer needs to create the mechanisms that allow users to tap into the collective wisdom and experience and use it for their own benefit, learning processes and actualisation". In order to facilitate the building of identity and self-actualisation, the principles of information brokering and participation, or feedback and association, are proposed as core components in the design of sociality. While we adopted this approach to develop the mediating artefacts that structure the interface of the site, Ervin Goffman's notions "facework" and "ritual performance" – used to analyse behaviour in public spaces and widely deployed in the fields of computer meditated communication (CMC) – are useful for exploring the nature of conversational interaction, the networks of feedback and the sharing of guided exploration. These are important design parameters for Bouman et al. and Engeström, and useful to further contextualise behavioural patterns and dialogic interchanges within the site. Essentially, these notions capture and complement the exploration of core *processes* of cultural and semiotic mediation (cf. Hasan 2005), as participants encounter each other in this public space. The idea of collective wisdom or collective intelligence is further discussed to connect patterns of interaction and situated learning practices around shared goals and intersecting discourses. The next three sections introduce these situated theoretical perspectives and are further contextualised through examples from activities and behaviour.

Collective Intelligence

In his seminal book entitled *Collective Intelligence*, Pierre Lévy offers an analysis of the WWW instruments, such as hypertext (1998: 155–157) to articulate a theoretical proposal regarding the ways humans can potentially share, collaborate over, and indeed, produce and reproduce knowledge (1997: 215–216). The idea of a digital networked technology, that makes possible a shared or collective intelligence, originates from Wells (1938) and Bush (1945); it also echoes Engelbart's (1962) ideas and early designs of software that would build organisational capacity to "augment intellect" and enable the sharing of mental associations and collective thought around complex problems. For Lévy, collective intelligence:

> […] is a form of *universally distributed intelligence*, constantly enhanced, coordinated in real time … The basis and goal of collective intelligence is the mutual recognition and enrichment of individuals (1997: 13).

While the cognitive perceptions of the members of a knowledge/discourse community taken individually may be incomplete or inaccurate, together they form a trans-active and transitive memory system that shares domains of knowledge. This can restore the level of organicity that defines oral communities. The idea of collective intelligence as a social pool for mobilising the sharing of resources, perceptions and formal and informal knowledge(s) is also seen as an alternative source to the power of mainstream media; both in terms of interpretation and production (see Alevizou 2006). Inspired by Lévy, Henry Jenkins, the new media and digital literacies scholar, argues that collective intelligence involves "consumption as a collective process" – a process that involves "learning to use that power through our day-to-day interactions with convergent culture" (Jenkins 2006: 4). Most importantly, collective intelligence is part of a new set of critical literacy skills for navigating and participating in digital networked landscapes: participatory culture shifts the focus of literacy from one of individual expression to community involvement. The new literacies involve social skills developed through collaboration and networking, judgment, play, performance (Jenkins et al. 2006; Jenkins 2007).

The idea of cultivating fluency in relation to new forms and spaces of creative representation is a powerful one. For Lévy, collective intelligence can produce a public space that makes possible the representation and dynamic management of knowledge, with the ability to facilitate cognitive transcendence. He uses the *social dispersal of meaning* as a notion that emerges within, and makes possible, the evolution of "cosmopaedia" a space for the dynamic management and representation of knowledge. Unlike earlier visions of global libraries or archives (see Wells 1938; Bush 1945), this space is highly dialogical and transgressive of its own boundaries. While Wikipedia is the ultimate example of volunteer labour mobilisation which collaboratively produces an encyclopaedia, folksonomies and collective annotations of resources (e.g. Delicious, Zotero, etc.) are examples that require minimal participation. This shift to the social notion of knowledge emphasises the *processual* and the expansive, rather than the idea of *"possession"*. The new modalities of social production of knowledge enabled by the combination of social software, digital media and peer collaboration offer new opportunities for encapsulating not the universal (global) ideal of enlightenment, but the local and particular relationships mobilised around networked learning (Alevizou 2006).

Ritual Performances

One can argue that the intersections of self-representation with informational affairs in physical and mediated interaction, depicted in Goffman's televisual insights, are being accentuated in a "Web 2.0" world; a world, where "travel" between the real and virtual, in time and through networks, come to structure domains of social life:

> Every person lives in a world of social encounters, involving him (sic) either in face-to-face or mediated contact with other participants. In each of these contacts, he tends to act out what is sometimes called a line –that is, a pattern of verbal and nonverbal acts by which he (sic) expresses his view of the situation and through this his evaluation of the participants, especially himself (sic) (Goffman 1967: 5).

Goffman's contributions to the study of everyday social life, and in particular the production of the self, and frames of experience, have been widely deployed in the field of computer mediated communication [ranging historically from personal homepages, to blogs and social networking sites (SNS)], and organisational studies. In particular, Goffman's notions of self-representation, ritual performance and analyses of talk in public space are suitable for exploring interactive and dynamic aspects of communication. Recent studies in SNS that adopt Goffman's ideas turn attention to the mediating framework of sites such as Facebook and MySpace and the possibilities that they offer for the presentation of the self. Continuing a tradition of CMC that examines the relationship between offline and online social life, and the frames that shape and regulate it, recent research has explored how social networking sites have been fast established as prominent arenas where university students can become versed in "identity politics" (see Selwyn 2009). Although the concepts of facework and impression management are linked with identity, this research focuses mostly on the dynamic and strategic aspect of communication, namely, sharing information, media artefacts and ideas.

The notion of social life as ritual is particularly relevant for contextualising relations in public spaces, to examine not only community formation within the site but also the random and serendipitous social routines and practices – territories of the self, supportive interchanges, remedial interchanges, tie-ins, and normal appearances – that can be used to instigate a conversation and maintain *coherence* (Goffman 1971 in Branaman 1997: 1xix).

Expansive Learning

Activity theory (AT) provides a useful unit of analysis for enabling a theoretical account of the constitutive elements of an object-oriented, collective, and culturally mediated activity system in all its complex interactions and relationships (Engeström 1987). While the third generation of AT introduced the notions of dialogue, multiple perspectives, historicity and networks of interacting activity systems, Engeström (2001) expanded the framework further to account for *contradiction* as the driving force of change in activity, and expansive cycles as possible forms of transformation. Taking constellations of interacting activity systems as units of analysis to interrogate subjects, motivations, objects and modes of learning, Engeström developed a framework for expansive learning as a mode for researching inter-organisational learning. In the relatively long cycles of expansive learning, therefore, qualitative transformations, questioning and deviation from established norms sometimes escalate into a deliberate collective change effort. According to Engeström (2001: 137), "a full cycle of expansive transformation may be understood as a collaborative journey through zone of proximal development of the activity."

The framework offers a complementary perspective to the theories of learning against vertical processes, aimed at elevating humans towards higher levels of competence. Drawing on the framework of expansive learning, Griffiths and Guile elaborate on one of the main characteristics of boundary crossing as involving a process of *horizontal development*. "Learners have to develop the capability to mediate between different forms of expertise and the demands of different contexts, rather than simply bringing their accumulated vertical knowledge and skill to bear on the new situation" (2003: 61). Griffiths and Guile distinguish between different types of boundary crossing:

(a) Carrying out a known activity in a new context.
(b) "Individuals and groups using the problems which arise while undertaking a task as the basis for developing a new pattern of activity and new knowledge, poly-contextual knowledge, in a new context".

Extending Goodyear, Banks, Hodgson, and McConnell's definition of networked learning (2004: 1), Jones and Dirckinck-Holmfeld (2009: 1) draw out some conceptual developments that they argue help to bridge the gap between the potential of digital networks, and current educational practice, to explore the ways in which "productive learning" may take place in networked environments. Similarly, we seek to address this issue within networked learning and draw on the theoretical instruments and socio-cultural perspectives outlined above to connect notions of identity and performance, as well as expression and collective intelligence, within the site. We do not attempt to analyse the range of collaborative activities or contradictions, conflicts and tensions that are involved in this kind of processual learning; rather, we question how, and how far, access to this specialised platform or public space promotes purposeful and productive social interaction, and facilitates collective intelligence. We argue that these activities can enable zones of proximal development, frameworks for social interaction among individuals who connect not only to the knowledge of other specialists, peers and relational communities but also to their learning resources.

To address these fields we use a combination of methodologies ranging from virtual ethnography (Hine 2000) and reflective logs, to interviews and focus groups, sociolinguistic analysis of multimodal discourse (Bakhtin 1986; Holland et al. 1998; Kress and van Leeuwen 2001) and evaluation data collected in conferences and workshops.

Conceptual and Methodological Frameworks

Recently, we have been seeking to establish conceptual and methodological strategies that while informed by the theoretical frameworks we outlined above, also enable us to more systematically position transactions and emerging patterns of activity on the site so that we can more reliably evaluate these in relation to developing productive communities, professional knowledge and sustained participation (Galley et al. 2010; Alevizou et al. 2010). We have developed a framework to direct our inquiry and empirical investigation in relation to understanding the nature of communication and interaction among groups or individuals that are part of relational networks, and come together to discuss core themes in research and practices. The framework has been informed by a review of the online-communities literature and combines perspectives on CMC and facilitation/mentoring in online learning environments, and consists of four broad aspects or indicators, which appear to influence the development of productive, participatory activity. We argue that the four aspects interlink and have a multiplicative effect on the others, in that if one is missing the others will be significantly reduced; however, it is useful to consider them separately as lenses through which to view activity (Fig. 5.3).

We have deployed perspectives from the upper left and bottom right quadrants to guide our observation logs and the data we analysed: first, *participatory* modes of engagement are evident through repeated contributions and through the surfacing of

Fig. 5.3 Indicators of
community [Galley et al.
(forthcoming)]

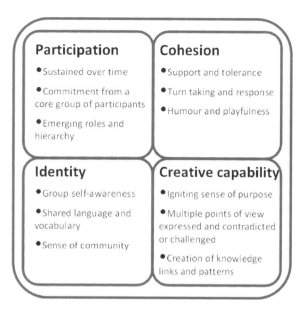

a core group of participants involved particularly in, and surrounding, specific Communities of Practice who develop and perform *identity* through reflection and self-representation. Secondly, the creative capabilities among some of the participants, or facilitators – outside the core Cloudworks team – illustrate and ignite a sense of purpose, and a shared language and understanding of core themes in OER research, scholarship and practice. We have blended *cohesion* and *creative capacity* to view not only whether the ways in which participants interact within a public space such as Cloudworks demonstrates a creative articulation of their respective professional identities, but also if cohesive exchanges exist in the discursive level to illustrate of shared understanding of core themes within educational scholarship or practice and the capacity to creatively discuss – if not necessarily resolve – persistent issues or practical problems.

We connect these three analytical dimensions with communication patterns in popular activities evident in the site, which are grouped according to the following (see Engeström 2007; Gratton 2007; Herring 2004; Rafaeli and Sudweeks 1997; Walzer 1997):

- *Informational* (sharing of resources, links, annotations of presentations, live blogging, etc.).
- *Practical* (sharing of practice or experience, flashpoints of interest).
- *Social* (information modes of address, personal narratives, suggestions to recommendations), that lead or relate to:
  - Discursive (affirmations, welcome notes, supportive interchanges, humour and word plays, etc.)
  - Deliberative (instigating debates, etc.)

Our research attempts to capture the framing effects of different channels of social media, and their intersections in the performance of sharing and talk. Goffman extended notions of symbolic interactionism to account for both the role of frames, occasions and associated semiotic codes and the capabilities of individuals to improvise creatively within these structures. This is particularly relevant to social media environments, where self-actualisation is also located in the ability of users to modify interfaces and re-enact the affordances of these.

The notion of frame, more specifically, could be considered as part of the function of mediation. It refers to the rules and conventions that Goffman perceives as part of the organisation of experience, which helps to define a situation (Goffman 1974). Participants within Cloudworks come to the site through a range of communicative spaces (Twitter, blogs, institutional sites, public and private mailing lists) and interact in several physical and virtual spaces (e.g. workshops and conferences). While examining the detail of the media ecology that promotes "traffic" and supports development within the site is beyond the scope of this chapter, here we would like to draw attention to possible approaches that could be used to analyse the ways in which participants frame their communication based on their perceived audience, contexts of interaction/contribution and the dynamics of specific situations.

In summary, our methodology has been developed to frame our investigations into the ways in which social media tools/technologies might mediate social relations enabling new modes of self- and collective-representation, with respect to communication, inquiry and sharing in the context of education.

Narrative Exploration of Cases

In this section we will introduce three narrative examples of practices that represent the perspectives outlined above ("Debates" and "Enquiry and Expert Advice"), analyse these using the methodology described, deploying data from observation logs informed by virtual ethnographic methods and a surface analysis of linguistic interchanges with regard to reflection and feedback We are conscious that as participants in the network ourselves we will hold intrinsic biases, which are likely to impact on our analysis of activity and remain reflective about this impact.

Debates

Flash points of interest aggregated through a particular question can be seen throughout the site, but are possibly most evident in activities that we have labelled "flash debates". Flash debates began to appear on the site in September 2009, and are sparked from questions that aim to provoke. Most typically a range of comments and activities will erupt almost immediately after initial postings, and will cross a variety of different social networking platforms. The "Is Twitter Killing Blogging?"[1] Cloud is a particularly interesting example. The Cloud has had 1,321 views, 49 rich and detailed comments, 20 links and 6 academic references (November 2010). Initially, a Cloud was set up in response to a tweet on 11th September 2009:

> '[@name] has set up a quick survey to ask people how using Twitter has impacted on how much they blog or not. The results are really interesting. XX is planning to do a more reflective blog on this…'

The Cloud provided a link to the survey, and posed a series of simple questions around the topic. Almost immediately there was traffic to the cloud and a rich discussion soon evolved, involving around 16 different participants. The originator of the Tweet which sparked off the creation of the Cloud acknowledged the value of the Cloud, and proposed that he would follow up with a reflection on his own blog. Cloudworks proved to be a complementary space between the micro-blogging site Twitter (where the debate sparked off) and individual, personal blogs. It provided a collective space to discuss the issues and aggregate resources. Some participants then wrote their own reflective pieces about the debate elsewhere:

> 'This is a reworking of a post in Cloudworks on a Twitter vs Blogging debate'

> 'I guess I should blog this;-)'

Similarly, a flash debate was set up relating to the future of universities: "What will the university of tomorrow look like?"[2] This time the idea for the debate came from a series of videos created for an online conference. Once set up, the location of the debate was Tweeted out and ten individuals quickly began participating in the discussion and aggregation of related materials. To date the Cloud contains 34 comments, 42 links and 8 academic references. It has received 733 visitors (November 2010). Again, there were multiple examples of the discussion moving between blogs, Twitter, Cloudworks, the conference forum and synchronous discussions; these shifts between spaces appearing to facilitate the shifts between discussion, feedback and reflection and back again.

Performance in these flash debates seems to provide a frame that invites critical reflection on communicative processes both in terms of the "bounded events", and in relation to interactions and improvised interpretations of real life situations. Performance also seems dependent on the formal characteristics of the site (combining reflective (micro) blogging with referencing, tagging and networking), or on the degree to which active participants engage in blogging-like activities within the site present themselves strategically, or frame their communication based on the perceived audience and context of interaction to ensure that interactions are successful. For example, the originator of the Cloud can be seen to facilitate the debate in terms

---

[1] http://cloudworks.ac.uk/cloud/view/2266.

[2] http://cloudworks.ac.uk/cloud/view/2586.

of offering supportive comments and encouragement to individuals, value and weight to the discussion itself and, importantly, humour and playfulness:

> "Brilliant thanks for this [@name] - I think this is a really important topic which all institutions need to be considering".

> "Sounds really interesting - have added the wiki as a link. Seems like a lot of people are beginning to think about this…"

> "I know I know it's incredible huh! Lots of good resources and links being added."

> "Great thanks XX - looks like being a great session! Could start a trend of people wearing silly wigs ;)"

Reflective questioning and experiential comments were mixed with references to interpretative accounts of discussions from related conferences and autobiographical or anecdotal remarks, indicating movement between the subjectivity of the academic, the pragmatism of the teacher, the reflexivity of the professional and anxiety of the employee.

Enquiry and Expert Advice

In November 2009 a lecturer from a distance learning university in the UK shared a teaching idea, about creativity and openness for a course relating to new media and ICT: "Integrating multimedia work into assessment".[3] The Cloud has had generated 465 views, and 9 comments and aside from a descriptive node, it also includes an embedded video showcase and a link to a video that provided the inspiration for repurposing. Six months later, the same lecturer repurposed this contribution as an entry for a virtual conference on teaching and learning that was organised by the Open University, and which was supported by Cloudworks. The Cloud: Experimenting with the pedagogy of creativity and openness' has generated 256 views, and contains 9 comments, 3 embedded videos and 6 references and links. The contribution was presented strategically in ways in which illustrate knowledge of the perceived audience; similarly, the context for interaction was structured in such a way so to invite reflection both on the scholarship of teaching surrounding creative open educational resources and the theoretical underpinnings of mediated identities and creativity.

The purpose of both entries has been to share ideas and elicit practical advice, as well as provide feedback on the epistemology of new media and teaching within new media. Interestingly, in the 7-month period that lapsed between the two entries, the core participant (Cloud author/contributor) utilises the reflective comments and points made by other participants in producing the content that was the object of discussion in the second entry. It appears that the initial idea is further developed following feedback. The second entry itself carries over the trajectory of thought and creativity that were initiated in the first entry. Crucially, this trajectory in the use of the space may be considered as positive in the development of professional practice.

---

[3] http://cloudworks.ac.uk/cloud/view/2631.

The core participant demonstrates that she has used sources of technical guidance and support provided by a core member of the Cloudworks team in the first entry, and appears to be more familiar with the interface capabilities of the site.

The majority of other commentators/participants within this particular space come from the same university, and though they hold a variety of roles (e.g. academic faculty and researchers, associate lecturers) they seem to know, and/or have worked with the core contributor – a certain familiar tone in the language used points to this. Three core themes have dominated the discussion: the first relates to student experience and training in using open materials; the second, relates to the pedagogic design and effectiveness of such interventions; the third juxtaposes the role of expertise in teaching in an open environment through the use of open content with the tensions pertaining the relationship among digital identities, exposure and assessment.

There are a number of Clouds and Cloudscapes asking for feedback and answers from expert communities. Some of them are informal and spontaneous (such as the "Using Twitter with students" Cloud[4]), discussed in the previous section. Others are more formal in nature; explicitly eliciting information from a targeted user group. In August 2009, a project group decided to use the site for an "open literature review" with the aim of using the expert elicitation affordances of Cloudworks to identify key themes in the literature relating to the "Positioning of educational technologists"[5] within organisations. The team had originally planned a desk-based literature review, with some online engagement of an established and specific Educational Technology Community of Practice to synthesise the literature (probably through a mailing list). However, it was decided that the project would be modified to encourage the HE community as a whole to identify the literature they judged to be key to the debate, and Cloudworks seemed to them the most appropriate tool to do this.

The methodology chosen by the team was a variation on the Delphi methodology (Linstone and Turoff 1975). This methodology commonly uses a panel of experts who are unknown to each other. Questionnaires are used to elicit the opinions of the experts and each expert communicates only with the lead researcher, rather than directly with the other experts. In the first stage of the process, a set of open questions are asked and the results of these are carefully analysed to identify key themes and a more structured questionnaire produced, the results of which are again analysed and the questions refined. Thus, the process leads to a convergence of findings or a consensus. In the case of this review, the methodology was adapted, using Cloudworks, to promote a divergence of views, and participants were able to communicate with each other. A framework of nine open questions was used to structure the activity. This narrative will focus on the first of these questions "What is the relevance of the student experience to the role of the educational technologist?"[6]

---

[4] http://cloudworks.ac.uk/index.php/cloud/view/2398.

[5] http://cloudworks.ac.uk/cloudscape/view/1872.

[6] http://cloudworks.ac.uk/cloud/view/2039.

Two key themes ran through the discussion, the first about whether the student experience/demand should be of prime importance, or pedagogic effectiveness (and latterly whether the educational technologists' role might be to act as a broker between the two). The second theme was about how far student feedback relating to the educational technologists role was available, and whether there was felt to be a problematic distance, or "disconnect" between students and educational technologists.

Participants appeared to come from a variety of institutions and roles, and expressed multiple points of view as might be expected. There was a level of disagreement about how central students should be in informing the use of technologies and yet the tone of all participants was polite and interested. Generally, language was adjusted to become thoughtful and tentative in tone. Most made reference to other people's points of view, and made links between these and their own experience or knowledge. The discussion was well balanced with a mixture of contributions from project teams and other participants throughout.

Modes of address in discussions like the one cited often turn from the inquisitive to the descriptive and the reflective, discussions often generate more deliberative comments by a large body of participants from a variety of institutions and respective positions, a minority of whom – vocally active in relevant mediated communities – take an evident lead in trying to achieve consensus.

Similar patterns of activity are evident across a range of interactions, particularly around Open Educational Resources (OER) communities, that frequently aggregate within the site to share evidence stemming from practice (see for example the Cloud "Issues in OER research"[7] which is further discussed in Alevizou et al. 2010). What is evident in many such discussions is the sharing of a common discourse facilitated by participation in relevant communities, the members of which meet regularly in similar virtual or physical events.

Discussion and Further Analytical Remarks

Discussions on networked learning and CSCL (computer-supported collaborative learning) often advocate a link between macro-levels of analysis (e.g. in small groups) and the macro-level of analysis including the socio-cultural level in which mediation of learning and activity occurs (see Dillenbourg in Strijbos et al. 2004; Stahl 2006; Jones and Dirckinck-Holmfeld 2009). The frameworks we introduced in the theory section attempted to position Cloudworks within the wider context of social media, which extend a *meso*-level of analysis that is connected to the institutional context of the site's development (Jones and Dirckinck-Holmfeld 2009: 10–12), and the basic conditions that allow object- or resource-based sociality to take place among individuals that connect, share and deliberate within the site (see section "Cloudworks Overview"). In section "Conceptual and Methodological

---

[7] http://cloudworks.ac.uk/cloud/view/980.

Frameworks" we outlined the conceptual and methodological frameworks that have enabled us to direct empirical exploration and evaluation of the site, linking technical affordances with the social and communicative interactions of groups and individuals in particular situations or social practices. We have presented insights that address the micro–meso–micro link focusing on three dimensions that are contingent to this social site that migrate from other cyber-spaces or physical environments, open or private, often blurring the performance of identity and community boundaries, or the flexible negotiation of the private and public, the personal and the collective, where individuals share understandings, resources, and meaning(s) around the practice and scholarship of teaching and learning. In this section, we structure insights that bridge these levels of analysis looking into the three dimensions introduced and discussed in "Conceptual and Methodological Frameworks": participation and collective intelligence; identity and performance; cohesion and creative capacity.

Participation and Collective Intelligence

Engagement is solicited through direct targeting towards individuals, or promoted through cross-media – either targeted (e.g. email) and closed forums (e.g. mailing lists), or open forums (e.g. Twitter, Ning). This is certainly true when an established Cloudworks user uses the site as an informational or discursive hub to aggregate responses to specific enquiries, or launches a debate as we have already outlined in the previous sections. Often, people are enticed to participate serendipitously through encountering popular or featured Clouds within the home page (71.77% of visitors to the home page click through to other pages via home page links) While a small number of participants demonstrate a sustained commitment, and assume the role of ambassador in rebroadcasting several discussions that take place within the site and the participating peripherally (by way of contextualising discussions with resources through embedding links, references or content). The majority of users aggregate to form groups that are often tied to a timed or very specific purpose, or themed activity (for example a conference or debate).

A number of topics have emerged which are pertinent to core debates around the development, uses and reception of Open Educational Resources (OER), for example, or the use of social media as tools to motivate creativity in teaching and learning. Widespread topics can be divided into categories relating to *development* (pertinent to changes practices of teaching and learning wider policies and practices) and *research*. Core Cloudworks participants who use the site in conferences most often use it as a backchannel that complements Twitter, aggregating notes and reflections around particular presentations and discussions. It appears that both structured research community meetings, and projects inviting expert consultations around particular conceptual frameworks, or wider research issues are more vigorous when a proactive facilitator and/or several ambassadors are involved. Workshops and other similar "blended learning spaces" are structured around activities that solicit the sharing of designs, resources and experiences on particular topics. Instructional

Clouds are cross-referenced and linked across a number of aggregated spaces to guide novice participants, but activity usually evaporates after the events are over. For many, participation is often transient and intermittent – creative outbursts of activity illustrate that clear purpose and timely topics ignite engagement among both individuals and relational networks to (re)produce content by expressing a voice that is aligned to interpretative resources, or shared practices surrounding routine or subversive practices, challenges and contradictions on the use of, for example, micro-blogging in higher education:

'[I use it] as a mechanism for students to do short-burst reflection at the end of each taught session (Tweflection!). The idea came from my experience of students finding it difficult to reflect on their learning experiences.'

(Using Twitter with Students Cloud[8])

'Whilst twitter usage is high amongst the 'converted', I wonder how many actually use it within learning and teaching. My use has varied quite a bit (see blog post http://bit.ly/37ASy2), and I think there could be considerable challenges in getting a whole class of active users - anything else would surely raise questions around equality of experiences'.

(Using Twitter with Students Cloud)

'Just started using twitter today for our Web 2.0 and working practices project - see my cloudscapes'

(Using Twitter for teaching and learning Cloud[9])

'I think about half took to it [twitter], those that didn't had the usual reservations. What I think has been interesting is that a few have stayed active beyond the course and twitter is a much better way of maintaining this network than having to commit to using forums say.'

(Using Twitter for teaching and learning Cloud)

These modalities of the social production of "processual knowledge" or collective intelligence is illustrative of the ways in which individuals – to draw from Goffman again – socialise across topics and "orchestrate" their identities in dialogically purposeful and supportive ways, contingent on the socio-cultural- and historically constructed modes of supportive interaction and "crowdsourcing" of resources, experiences and anxieties. Active commentators are often active in posting resources and links – indicating a degree of ownership and belonging, in the "dialogical wrapper" that supports these resources.

Although goals are fluid, and motivations for participation bound around ideas (rather than specific outcomes or collectively produced "products"), the space functions as a pool for mobilising various loosely knit groups or autonomous individuals to share resources, perceptions, experiences, formal and anecdotal knowledge and collective intelligence. This can be seen within various activities that span across related topics and enquiring practices in research-led teaching and learning.

Our observations suggest that there is evidence of participants engaging creatively with each other, and with the resources they interpret to resituate existing knowledge

---

[8] http://cloudworks.ac.uk/cloud/view/980.

[9] http://cloudworks.ac.uk/cloud/view/1946.

and experiences into new intellectual debates on social practices. Yet, certainly not all the activity is public or consensual; instead role conflict exists, and evidence suggests that crossing institutional, professional and personal boundaries and identities within an institutional space like Cloudworks, is productive, but can be "un-easy".

Identity, Self-representation and Performance

As discussed, performance can be seen to be shaped by the formal characteristics and functionality of the site and on the degree to which active participants present themselves strategically or frame their communication. In the data we analysed, and the stories we present here, four main themes of interaction emerge: (a) exchanging practical information and tips, (b) recounting and reflecting on professional experiences and resources, (c) exchanging insights in scholarship and research, (d) getting peer guidance and support (in somewhat more limited occasions).

Positioning of the self is achieved through the consumption of resources and the reflection on practices and experiences, often seeking ad hoc justifications for their own practices or post hoc soliciting of others perspectives on particular situations, and often on reflective consumptions of new media contents and tools. Interestingly, the way in which the "Twitter Killing Blogging" Cloud, for example emerged, evokes Goffman's notions of the ritual theatricality relevant for contextualising relations and serendipitous routines and practices, this time travelling across communicative channels and invoking *co-presence* in networking and virtual spaces (an idea that also emerges in the role of Cloudworks as a conference backchannel). In terms of content, the discussion on the self-referential nature of participation and self-representation is mobilised by the tensions between blogging and microblogging; between the idea of broadcasting and sharing as part of digital identity; in essence the "learning self" is projected in-time and as-time:

> 'Last week, following my quick poll on blogging & tweeting, [@name] started an 'Is Twitter killing Blogging?' discussion on Cloudworks.....I've followed the development of Cloudworks for a while now with some scepticism. However, it's use around the VLE-PLE debate and this blogging-Twitter discussion has really changed my views. I now get it, see a purpose and think it could have a really important role to play as an aggregator, a record and focal point for our discussions.'

('Twitter Killing Blogging' Cloud)

The exchange of comments in the "Integrating multimedia work into assessment" Cloud and associated Clouds reveals a multiplicity of perspectives and yet a consensus on most of the tricky issues discussed. Most participants made reference to each other's point of view, and links were offered to back up experience with evidence from literature and practice on Web 2.0 creativity and mediated learning, while offering personal support and guidance to a known or familiar colleague. The language and tone combines humour and "banter" with a shared vocabulary to express viewpoints, performing respective identities as teachers and researchers in a distant learning institution. Reflective questioning and experiential comments, as well as reference to interpretative accounts on multimodal literacies, creative and personalised learning and tensions of privacy, surveillance and competitiveness that surrounding online expression and collaboration, mediated this and other Clouds, (often at conferences and events since they combine interactions on- and off-line).

Cohesion and Creative Capability

Through each of the narratives above and in the previous section, we can see ways in which the participants lever sociality and mutuality through their dialogue, for example through demonstrations of support, encouragement, tolerance and reciprocity. In the flash debates these supportive exchanges are most often performed by the originator of the Cloud, who will typically use these exchanges to instigate a conversation and maintain coherence (Goffman 1971 in Branaman 1997: 1xix): "thanks for the link", "you are raising an interesting point", "here is a link to…", "I have summarised the discussion above", "thanks to @[name] and @[name] for pointing this out".

These supportive interchanges, remedial interchanges, tie-ins, and normal appearances can be seen to be part of self-and-peer validation; embedded, in the process of sharing and broadcasting experiences and content. This can be seen in the discourse of the open review, where through discussion about the positioning of educational technologist, there were a number of attempts to validate and indeed reposition the community:

"I'm sure most people here will be familiar with that work…"

""Paraprofessionals" - thanks I just learned another great word :)"

"Could XX.'s 'paraprofessional' (a new concept for me too) be viewed as a new assertive attempt at 'positioning'?"

Frameworks for social learning often point to the importance of conflict, disagreement and negotiation in the process of collaborative knowledge creation and developing understanding. However, there is a risk in an open and public space such as Cloudworks that participants do not feel sufficiently secure to enter into disagreement, or that if they do, there are no established social or cultural processes or rules developed over time within the group that enable a conflict to have a positive outcome. Although conflict and playful debate are often present in discussions, the examples given do not – or do not aim to – reach a clear consensus. Again in the "Open review" Cloud given as an example above, there was a level of disagreement about how central students should be in informing the use of technologies and yet the tone of all participants remained polite and encouraging. Similarly, in the enquiry and expert elicitation Cloud "Integrating multimedia work into assessment", the exchange of comments reveals multiplicity of perspectives and yet a consensus on most of the tricky issues was achieved, and links were made to back up experience with evidence from literature and practice. Evidence of a shared vocabulary indicates that most participants express their viewpoints, while performing their respective identities as teachers and researchers in a distant learning institution. At the same time participants are keen to develop more learning and knowledge on the relationship of social media creativity and mediated learning.

While to a certain extent, Cloudworks forms a productive space to mediate object-oriented sociality and interaction, it should be seen as only one node of learning within a networked landscape of practice experienced by its participants. Being a public and eponymous institutionalised space, it often carries forward conversations sparked in private virtual or physical sites; conflicts, productive tensions and resolutions on key issues, and anxieties and more heated disagreements regarding the core debate often occur in private or closed spaces. In many cases, additional personal perspectives are connected via links to personal archives, blogs, conceptual maps, etc., with annotations and context or without. In other occasions additional discussions are intentionally private or are kept invisible. Following our initial observations and our empirical analysis as action researchers, exploring the "traces" that participants leave in Cloudworks, within the landscape of visible and invisible landscapes of personal and networked learning, is at the top of our agenda for future research.

Conclusions

We introduced this chapter with the description of how Cloudworks utilises social media interfaces in an educational context. The variety of ways in which the site has been used has prompted us to revisit aspects of the networked sociality framework and expand this with two additional theoretical frameworks and this has yielded rich new analytical insights into understanding *inscribed* and *actual* use. We aimed to offer examples pointing to the nature of participation, the style of communication and the metaphors of engagement. We argue that Cloudworks is a platform for expressive interactions and collective intelligence, and we consider the wider implications for outcomes for networked learning through more situated research that will explore in further detail the nature of associations, types of roles and connections, and the guided exploration and boundary crossing among participants. We have not only explored how connections and interactions are built within Cloudworks (on a given time, for a given purpose, or randomly and serendipitously) but also offered stories of the ways in which the connections and interactions, actors, activities and resources are expressed, drawing on the communicative and discursive dimensions of expression and sociality. The evidence suggests that Cloudworks is one of the sites blurring formal and informal *cultural* and *networked* learning about being an educationalist, scholar, practitioner or indeed a student (in limited examples) with online interactions and experiences allowing roles to be learned, experiences to be shared, values to be exchanged and – to an extent – identities to be performed and (re)shaped, and communities to gather. The object-oriented nature of the site indeed enables transient, yet repeated and focused collaborative or idea sharing activities to form.

The idea of Cloudworks functioning as one of many productive network spaces or a node within a landscape of professional learning and development is both powerful and visible; we have provided evidence whereby learning can be seen to be both negotiated and improved. But it is too early in our research to generalise such an argument and demonstrate empirically more than glimpses of emerging patterns of what we would like to call "a mediated node in the networked landscape of practice".

We are reflective that we can no longer be described as independent researchers and instead our observations and interventions are those of members of the development and evaluation teams. But while addressing the limitations of this approach, we have now developed a clear idea about research questions that will inform Cloudworks position with this landscape of practice, as well as guide implications for further systematic research.

References

Alevizou, P. (2006). *Encyclopedia or cosmopedia? Collective intelligence for knowledge technospaces*. In 2nd Wikimania Conference, 4–6 August 2006. Cambridge, MA: University of Harvard Law School. Retrieved November 19, 2010, from http://wikimania2006.wikimedia.org/wiki/Proceedings:PA1

Alevizou, P., Conole, G., & Galley, R. (2010). *Using Cloudworks to support OER activities*. Research Report. York: Higher Education Academy. Retrieved November 19, 2010, from http://search3.openobjects.com/kb5/hea/evidencenet/resource.page?record=dSTmZHJ68gg#d STmZHJ68gg

Alexander, B. (2008). Social networking in higher education. In Katz, R. (Ed.), *The tower and the cloud*. Boulder, CO: EDUCAUSE. Retrieved November 19, 2010, from http://www.educause.edu/thetowerandthecloud

Anderson, P. (2007). *What is Web 2.0? Ideas, technologies and implications for education*. Bristol: JISC Technology and Standards Watch. Retrieved November 19, 2010, from http://www.jisc.org.uk/media/documents/techwatch/tsw0701b.pdf

Bakhtin, M. (1986). *Speech genres and other late essays*. Austin, TX: University of Texas Press.

Bouman, W., Hoogenboom, T., Jansen, R., Schoondorp, M., de Bruin, B., & Huizing, A. (2007). *The realm of sociality: Notes on the design of social software*. PrimaVera Working Chapter Series. Amsterdam: Universiteit Van Amsterdam. Retrieved November 19, 2009, from http://choo.fis.utoronto.ca/fis/courses/lis2176/Readings/bouman.pdf

Branaman, A. (1997). Goffman's social theory. In A. Branaman & C. Lemert (Eds.), *The Goffman reader* (pp. xivi–lxxxii). Malden, VA: Blackwell.

Bruns, A. (2008). *Blogs, Wikipedia, second life, and beyond: From production to produsage*. New York: Peter Lang.

Bush, V. (1945). As we may think. *Atlantic Monthly* [online]. Retrieved November 19, 2010, from http://www.ps.unisb.de/~duchier/pub/vbush/vbush.shtml

Conole, C. G., & Culver, J. (2009). Cloudworks: Social networking for learning design. *Australasian Journal of Educational Technology, 25*(5), 763–782. Retrieved November 19, 2010, from http://www.ascilite.org.au/ajet/ajet25/conole.html

Dillenbourg in Strijbos, J.-W., Kirschner, P. A., & Martens, R. L. (Eds.) (2004). *What we know about CSCL – and implementing it in higher education*. Boston: Kluwer.

Downes, S. (2005). E-learning 2.0. *E-learning Magazine, October* 17, 2005. New York: Association for Computing Machinery. Retrieved November 19, 2010, from http://www.elearnmag.org/subpage.cfm?section=articles&article=29-1

Engelbart, C. D. (1962) *Augmenting human intellect: A conceptual framework*. Summary Report. Menlo Park, CA: Stanford Research Institute. Retrieved November 19, 2010, from http://sloan.stanford.edu/mousesite/EngelbartChapters/B5_F18_ConceptFrameworkPT4.html

Engeström, Y. (1987). *Learning by expanding: An activity-theoretical approach to developmental research*. Helsinki: Orienta-Konsultit.

Engeström, Y. (2001). Expansive learning at work. Toward an activity-theoretical reconceptualization. *Journal of Education and Work, 14*(1), 133–156.

Engeström, Y. (2007). From communities of practice to mycorrhizae. In J. Hughes, N. Jewson, &
L. Unwin (Eds.), *Communities of practice: Critical perspectives*. Abingdon: Routledge.

Engeström, J. (2005). *Why some social network services work and others don't – Or: The case for
object-centered sociality*. [Blog] 13 April 2005. Retrieved November 19, 2010, from http://
www.zengestrom.com/blog/2005/04/why_some_social.html

Galley, R., Conole, G., & Alevizou, P. (2010). *Using Cloudworks for an open literature review:
Case study*. York: Higher Education Academy. Retrieved November 19, 2010, from http://
search3.openobjects.com/kb5/hea/evidencenet/resource.page?record=9Fo7dRXy8GM

Galley, R., Conole, G., & Alevizou, P. (forthcoming). Community indicators: A framework for
building and evaluating community on Cloudworks. *Interactive Learning Environments*.

Goodyear, P., Banks, S., Hodgson, V., & McConnell, D. (2004). *Advances in research on
networked learning*. Dordrecht: Kluwer.

Gratton, L. (2007). *Hot spots: Why some companies buzz with energy and innovation – and others
don't*. London: Financial Times Prentice Hall.

Griffiths, T., & Guile, D. (2001). Learning through work experience. *Journal of Education and
Work, 14*(1), 113–131.

Griffiths, T., & Guile, D. (2003). A connective model of learning: the implications for work process knowledge. *European Educational Research Journal, 2*(1), 56–73.

Goffman, E. (1955). On face-work: An analysis of the ritual elements in social interactions.
Psychiatry, 18(3), 213–231.

Goffman, E. (1963). *Behaviour in public places: Notes on the social organization of gatherings*.
New York: Free Press.

Goffman, E. (1967). *Interaction ritual: Essays on face-to-face behaviour*. Garden City, NY:
Doubleday, Anchor Books.

Goffman, E. (1974). *Frame analysis*. Middlesex: Penguin Books.

Hasan, R. (2005). *Language, society and consciousness: Collected works of Ruqaiya Hasan*.
London: Equinox.

Herring, S. (2004). Computer-mediated discourse analysis: An approach to researching online
behaviour. In A. Barab, R. Kling, & H. Gray (Eds.), *Designing for virtual communities in the
service of learning* (pp. 356–357). New York: Cambridge University Press.

Hine, C. (2000). *Virtual ethnography*. London: Sage.

Holland, D., Lachicotte, W., Skinner, D., & Cain, C. (1998). *Identity and agency in cultural worlds*.
Cambridge, MA: Harvard University Press.

Jenkins, H. (2006). *Convergence culture: Where old and new media collide*. New York: New York
University Press.

Jenkins, H. (2007). *What Wikipedia can teach us about new media literacies*. Part I, [Blog].
Retrieved November 19, 2010, from http://www.henryjenkins.org/2007/06/what_wikipedia_
can_teach_us_ab.html and Part II [Blog] http://henryjenkins.org/2007/06/what_wikipedia_
can_teach_us_ab_1.html

Jenkins, H., Clinton, K., Purushotma, R., Robison, A. J., & Weigel, M. (2006). *Confronting the
challenges of participatory culture: Media education for the 21st century*. Chicago: MacArthur
Foundation. Retrieved November 19, 2010, from http://digitallearning.macfound.org/atf/cf/
{7E45C7E0-A3E0-4B89-AC9C-E807E1B0AE4E}/JENKINS_WHITE_CHAPTER.PDF

Jones, C., & Dirckinck-Holmfeld, L. (2009). Analysing networked learning practices: An introduction. In L. Dirckinck-Holmfeld, C. Jones, & B. Lindström (Eds.), *Analysing networked
learning practices in higher education and continuing professional development* (pp. 1–28).
Rotterdam: Sense Publishers.

Kress, G., & van Leeuwen, T. (2001). *Multimodal discourse*. Oxford: Oxford University Press.

Lévy, P. (1997). *Collective intelligence: Mankind's emerging world in cyberspace* (R. Bononno,
Trans.). Cambridge, MA: Perseus Books.

Lévy, P. (2001). *Cyberculture* (R. Bononno, Trans.). Minneapolis and London: University of
Minnesota Press.

Linstone, H. A., & Turoff, M. (1975). *The Delphi method, techniques and applications*. Reading, MA: Addison Wesley.

Rafaeli, S., & Sudweeks, F. (1997). Networked interactivity. *Journal of Computer Mediated Communication, 2*(4) [online]. Retrieved November 19, 2010, from http://jcmc.indiana.edu/vol2/issue4/rafaeli.sudweeks.html

Selwyn, N. (2009). Faceworking: Exploring students' education-related use of Facebook. *Learning, Media and Technology, 34*(2), 157–174.

Stahl, G. (2006). *Collaborating with technology: Mediation of group cognition*. Boston: MIT. Retrieved November 19, 2010, from http://www.cis.drexel.edu/faculty/gerry/mit/

Walzer, M. (1997). *On toleration*. New Haven, CT: Yale University Press.

Wenger, E. (1998). *Communities of practice: Learning, meaning and identity*. Cambridge and New York: Cambridge University Press.

Wells, H. G. (1938). *World brain*. London: Methuen.

Chapter 6
A Classroom with a *View*: Networked Learning Strategies to Promote Intercultural Education

Juliana E. Raffaghelli and Cristina Richieri

Introduction: A Foreshadowed Problem

This chapter explores the intercultural dimension of networked learning processes between communities from different language and cultural backgrounds. On the basis of our results it is possible to affirm that, thanks to networked learning, the above-mentioned communities are able to build new cultural spaces on the Net, thus enlarging their own cultural perspective. This may happen because networked learning can provide new strategies to work with and on diversity, which is such a widespread phenomenon in contemporary global, society. The title is to be linked to a metaphor we deliberately wanted to use: A Room with a View is a 1908 novel by the English writer E.M. Forster, about a young woman in the repressed culture of Edwardian England. Set in Italy and England, the story is both a romance and a critique of English society at the beginning of the twentieth century, when the protagonist discovers Florence and the possibilities of "looking beyond" her own culture. In the novel, the view is provided by the window. In our work, the play on words relates to the Internet, which is conceived of as a way of going beyond the walls of the classroom and the curriculum in search of other cultures, thereby helping individuals to explore otherness and reflect on one's own cultural values. This metaphor is also linked to an important concept introduced in this chapter, namely the *enlarged cultural context of learning* (Raffaghelli 2008).

Furthermore, these concepts are applied to the practical field of teacher education, since the case study is focused on teachers' key competences in dealing with diversity and new complex educational environments.

J.E. Raffaghelli (✉) • C. Richieri
Interuniversity Center of Educational Research and Advanced Training (CIRDFA),
Ca' Foscari University, Venice, Italy
e-mail: j.raffaghelli@unive.it; richieri.c@libero.it

L. Dirckinck-Holmfeld et al. (eds.), *Exploring the Theory, Pedagogy and Practice of Networked Learning*, DOI 10.1007/978-1-4614-0496-5_6,
© Springer Science+Business Media, LLC 2012

Compared to other social contexts, multiculturalism has entered the classroom as a really complex phenomenon that genuinely challenges school systems (Banks 2001; Gundara 2000). The nature of the cultural "*software of mind*" (Hofstede and Hofstede 2005), through which kids, parents, and teachers read facts and practices, challenges the well-founded beliefs of traditional education: academic success, intelligence, learning performance, didactics, teaching (Banks 2001). The discussion is not new at all: in most European countries with relatively high immigration (France, Germany, Belgium, and The Netherlands) multiculturalism has been an issue since the 1950s, and since the mid-1980s the Council of Europe has promoted a number of dedicated educational projects. In these projects, education is no longer conceived of as multicultural (referring to different cultures living in the same place without any mutual interaction), rather as intercultural, with strong emphasis on reciprocity and mutual modification (Leclerq 2003). This is a strategy aimed at drawing attention to democracy, pluralism, and dialogue among different cultures. In Coulby's words: *If education is not intercultural, it is probably not education, but rather the inculcation of nationalist or religious fundamentalism* (2006: 246). The point here seems to be about the relationship with otherness for mutual respect, together with what this interaction implies, i.e., *cultural change*. To grasp this idea, which is the kernel of the discussion about a new concept of intercultural education, we should now recall the definition of *culture*. In anthropology it has two meanings (1) the different ways in which people living in different parts of the world classify and represent their experiences, and act creatively and (2) the evolved human capacity to classify and represent experiences through symbols, and to act imaginatively and creatively according to those shared meanings (Geertz 1973). The first definition leads us to think of culture as something rather static, like a finished, already completed entity, whereas the second, allows us to think of it as something alive, created through symbolic interaction, in a continuous meaning-making process. Indeed, while the former definition comes from anthropologists interested in defining and describing different cultures, the latter, which represents the contemporary perspective based on postmodern thinking, sees culture as an evolving entity that we can interpret. Similarly, in the educational field, the positions taken have been (a) multiculturalism, which implies a wide-spread, "normal," general culture, and minorities which exist at the same time in the same place; (b) interculturalism, which implies several cultures living together and interacting peacefully (Coulby 2006).

In the last few years, the focus has been put on new meaning-making processes and the cultural change which is taking place in the global, liquid-networked society. In fact, the Internet is becoming one of the most important places where learning occurs, no matter what educational policies are decided or what experts, headmasters, teachers, and trainers actually do (Carneiro 2007).

Nevertheless, it is only recently, that the idea that intercultural learning may also take place on the Net has been highlighted (Dunn and Marinetti 2002; Edmundson 2007; McConnell et al. 2007; Rollin and Harrap 2005; Rutheford and Kerr 2008). In this literature, the definition "culturally sensitive eLearning environments" seems to be controversial, encompassing the whole discussion about "cultural interaction/change" mentioned before. In fact, on one hand, research supports the idea of intercultural learning through the Net, considering diversity management and instructional design in order to facilitate participation and adaptation of foreigners into eLearning courses (Edmundson 2007; Liu 2007; McLoughlin 2007; Rutheford and Kerr 2008). On the other, researchers criticize the idea of assimilation of "cultures" to national stereotypes, promoting the notion of construction of "learning cultures" on the Net (Goodfellow 2008), with its implications for the representation of learning and teaching in building shared learning design principles (McConnell 2008), the individual's construction of identity and power relations (Macfadyen 2008; Reynolds 2008).

In any case, the cultural embeddedness of the Internet needs to be disclosed from an intercultural perspective, bearing in mind that this perspective will need to be deeply revisited on the basis of those cultural spaces already existing on the Web. Moreover, we still think of education for this complex society as intercultural but our concern leads us to pose this question: will networked society change the definition of *intercultural* education, since it brings new ways of building relations and hence of *creating culture*?

The Net as a Place to Meet Equal-But-Diverse People

All people taking part in Web interaction, such as the *Screenagers* generation (Rushkof 2006), are exposed to an amazing quantity of stimuli coming from the Net and, as a result, participate in several *virtual environments* and *communities*, sharing new cultural values and behavioral patterns. If, in some cases, these patterns have been declared as foreign and extraneous to the participants, the main cyberculture studies emphasize that a new culture of cybernauts is emerging (Rheingold 1993) producing multi-identities in relation to which real life is only one of the possible sceneries where the self is forged (Turkle 1996). According to Maistrello's beautiful metaphor, these young people are citizens in new territories on the Net (Maistrello 2007). Indeed, in cyberculture studies, this problem has been considered in terms of virtual communities (Paloff and Pratt 1999), online identities (Turkle 1996), online interactions (Rovai 2002; Hewling 2006), digital discourses, access to and denial of the Internet, and the design of virtual interfaces (McLoughlin 2001; 2007). According to cyber-anthropologists' definitions, cyberspace becomes a social space in which people still meet face-to-face, even though new definitions for both "meet" and "face" are needed. In David Silver's words (2000), *while cyberspace may lack for the most part the physical geography found in, say, a neighbourhood, city, or country, it offers users very real opportunities for collective communities and individual identities*. It is worth remembering, at this point, the classical concept of *agorá*. The Greek word *agorá* comes from the verb *ageirein* meaning "to gather" and, initially, it designated the assembly of the whole people, as opposed to the council of chiefs (*boulé*). Subsequently, it came to designate the location of that assembly and what occurred there, hence its later meaning of "market-place." In Greek society, the *agorá* became an important place which represented mainly democracy. Moreover, it was the place which offered the possibility of communicating, learning, and exchanging not only goods but also ideas. In fact, in Aristotle's ideal city, the *agorá* represents the life of the city as it is separated into two domains: the vulgar, for business and commerce, and the free *agorá* for more serious political, intellectual, and religious activities (*Politics, 13331a31*). Thus, it seems clear that the *agorá* is what people build through intense participation, rather than, a simple localized, architectonic place.

We could conclude that meeting people from several cultural backgrounds and experiences on the Net is possible through the new contextualization of interaction in the symbolic place provided by virtual learning environments and networks.

If people are given the opportunity of creating meaning through engagement and participation in group activities, then a cultural manifestation takes place, introducing the prospect of cultural change. Based on this assumption, we could affirm that the possibility of establishing interactions which might lead to the creation of a virtual space on the Net – like an *agorá* – could promote more than *intercultural* learning (as a relation between two separated entelechies). In fact, this kind of new space could be culturally inclusive through the process of cultural change, emphasizing the dimension of the Web as a *third space*, a dimension, it could be argued, that gives people the opportunity of practicing dialogue, discovering the relativity of one's own cultural position, and being engaged in new hybrid culture creation.

Our point here is that, even if *possible*, the above result is not necessarily automatic. Indeed, it requires a critical position and awareness of what is happening while the subject is involved in intercultural relations on the Net. In that sense, there is shared construction but also reflective deconstruction of one's own cultural values and personal positions, as well as otherness recognition. In our view, these elements are necessary in order to bring about an intercultural dimension within global networked learning.

Reconceptualizing the Intercultural Dimension Within the Framework of Networked Learning

The notion of networked learning encompasses the idea of connection between learning communities and resources, by enhancing information and communication technologies (Goodyear et al. 2004). This concept goes far beyond the access to virtual learning spaces, resources, or facilities provided by technologies to improve communication. Based on the belief that learning is a social practice, this concept implies participation and transformation of reality (Jones 2008). It can be assumed that Networked learning is not an individual process, but a joint activity carried out through *connectedness* (Zenios and Goodyear 2008). In global society, it necessarily introduces the concept of difference as an element embedded in every single interaction, creating situations where difference could be recognized or not. In global multicultural networks, Networked learning should emphasize Bruner's idea about education as *forum* where culture is not transmitted but generated through interaction (Bruner 2005). In other words, difference leads to the creation of *new learning cultures* (Goodfellow 2008).

This is not an automatic result: participating in such interconnected, creative learning cultures encompasses a specific attitude to be put on by the individual in order to let learning take place, namely being aware of the necessity of otherness to carry out one's own lifelong learning project (Bowskill et al. 2008). This implies that new educational contexts have the not easy task of helping the individual to acknowledge the limits of oneness and the crucial value of differences which distinguish each individual, as *"a pedagogy which makes difference invisible is poor training for engaging with 'global world'"* (Asmar 2005). In fact, it is through the very process of differentiation from as well as of identification with others that individuals are able to grow up, develop, and form their own identity (Koole 2010). This construction of the self takes place in a *"continual cycle of reciprocity between self and community"* (Koole 2010: 242) by means of relational dialogue which brings about a constant mutual transformational process, which is the ground where learning takes place.

Being aware of the need for otherness is only the first step toward this idea of learning. What educational contexts should provide for the individual to develop is a learning environment in which he/she can discover and practice how to take part effectively in a learning community. This implies the development of specific competences: being able to listen to the others actively (Gordon 1977), being able to reflect on the gains produced by interaction, and being able to acknowledge the role of otherness in one's own learning process (Mezirow 1991). Thus, it is a matter of training the individual to look for authentic communication with otherness and implementing educational strategies aimed at establishing wefts of positive interdependence between individuals.

These considerations about how to take part in learning communities have been central when disclosing diversity as intrinsic to every human group, in a critical, postcolonial and feminist approach. They may well be applied to Networked learning, hence avoiding a too far extended vision of *intrinsic goodness of international/global communities on the Net* (Reynolds 2008).

Research in the field of Networked learning has considered the issue of intercultural embededdness of learning processes within international groups (Macfadyen et al. 2004; Goodfellow and Lamy 2009). From one hand some works introduce empirical evidence which shows that online interaction, when carried out through written posts/texts/messages, offers the opportunity to pondering over what is being communicated since the posts/texts/messages can be re-read, both before sending them and after receiving them (Hewling 2006; Macfadyen 2008), thus fostering true mutual understanding, especially when the use of a foreign language is involved. Moreover, according to this research line, being exposed to contexts which are different from one's own (otherwise, why should online interaction be used to promote international exchanges?), encourages the assumption of different perspectives toward reality and helps understand one's own existential postures by detecting in other individuals' culture what is different from and what is similar to one's own (Macfadyen 2008).

On the other hand, some authors have focused on the need to understand inter-cultural relations in global networked learning experiences from a critical point of view, since elements such as learning design (McConnell 2008; Morse 2003) and pedagogical conceptions of teaching and learning (McConnell 2008; Zhang and Huang 2008) could influence the sense of engagement and genuine interaction with otherness. In fact, social status and power lies behind every human group, and online environments are not exceptions (Hodgson and Reynolds 2005).

In any case, research covering international networked learning processes, emphasizes the fact that, by being exposed to other individuals' experiences of the world, everyone enacts his/her learning, and this is much more evident in Net-based multicultural interactions where networked learning is produced by the encounter of macroscopically different cultures. However, authors in this research tradition point out, consistently with the above conception of culture on the Net as a dynamic pro-cess, that identifying culture with nationality (Hofstede 2001; Hall 1959, 1960; Hampden-Turner and Trompenaars 2000) is not of great use since "*Characterising individuals culturally as homogeneous microcosms of particular (different) nation states belies the complexity and significance of individual difference and experience in the social process of being human and of learning*" (Hewling 2008: 570).

So, what takes place in intercultural networked learning processes implies much more than simply thinking of instructional design needs or diversity management. With the growing phenomenon of hybrid cultures on the Net, like "*Screenagers*," we should think of a new pedagogical approach, where critical deconstruction of symbols and cultural positions would lead to equity, expression of diversity, and participation in the construction of new meaning.

A Case Study

The experience discussed in this chapter was part of an international cooperation project called PERMIT. The research was based on a participant/constructivist approach. This meant that the research team took part in the process of developing e-learning strategies and designing an online platform that allowed 24 teachers from Italy, Turkey, and Slovenia to interact in order to carry out the piloting of the activi-ties developed within the PERMIT project during a school year. The experimenta-tion consisted in creating learning activities that would allow an intercultural perspective within the topics tackled with the students.

The underlying assumption was that networked learning which emphasized the exploration of diversity and engagement in creating new *shared learning cultures* through international peer support and joint collaboration, would reshape teaching practices toward the development of intercultural sensitivity. In this sense, we drew on Bennet's definition (1993), where intercultural sensitivity is supposed to evolve from more ethnocentric positions to ethnorelative ones, envisioning the importance of networked learning as an opportunity to experiencing otherness. Furthermore, if we consider the key role played by a teacher's professional and existential identity in effective teaching (Beijaard et al. 2004; OECD-TALIS 2009), it seems reasonable to assume that his/her own intercultural sensitivity would lead to opportunities for his/her students to enrich their learning processes with intercultural sensitivity.

Based on such a constructivist, mixed-methods approach, the key stages of the above-mentioned approach were

- *Learning design and training process.* One of the researchers (who played the role of a participant researcher) took part in the process of developing e-learning strategies and designing the international online platform where teachers and students interacted.
- *Follow-up.* The community made up of twenty four teachers worked online for 6 months, participating in three international residential workshops (three days each) and sharing the Virtual Working/Learning Space every day (*).
- *Questionnaires* were administered to the whole group, while some of the members of the group were *interviewed* during the actual learning process.
- *Participation in Italian monitoring.* Focus group with students.
- *Participation in students VWLS.* Teachers' implementation of a VWLS to be used by their own students.
  (*) The VLE consisted of three areas – International Teachers Community; National – Italian, Turkish, Slovenian – Teachers' Community; Students' Community – divided by subjects, with an interdisciplinary approach, "Languages Community (LC)," "Humanities Community (HC)," "Sciences Community (SC)." Inside these communities, the following activities were analyzed: Italian Teachers' Community (nine online forum and one activity of geolocalization); International Teachers' Community: seven online forum; Students' Community: eight online forum (HC); seven online forum (LC); three online forum (SC). Analysis of online discourse and structure of online learning spaces was made considering the semantic categories (codes) emerging from those materials, which is the most superficial level of qualitative analysis.

An initial data set, relating to the contextualization of intervention and justification of the strategies adopted in introducing a virtual learning space, was collected through questionnaires and analyzed using very simple descriptive statistics. A second set of data, relating to the process of creation, implementation and impact of virtual working/learning space for PERMIT teachers and students, required mostly qualitative analysis: free and axial codification of interview transcriptions, focus group interaction, open written answers in the questionnaires and excerpts from the online forum. The aim was to create a conceptual map of the processes of meaning creation emerging from the learning community. The resulting codification guided us toward further conceptualization and confrontation with the initial project goals and suppositions made by the group about research questions: *What actually happens when people from different cultural backgrounds are engaged in networked learning processes? Is it possible to influence learners' cultural identities and sense of belonging, thereby opening possibilities to new learning cultures?* These initial general questions would lead to a more specific question about the focus of the case, which would help explore the impact of this global networked learning model on local practices: *Is it possible to influence teachers' practices toward an intercultural perspective of teaching through this model?*

PERMIT Online Learning Space: What Can We Do to Get Teachers Involved in an Intercultural Vision of Their Own Practice?

The PERMIT project aimed at promoting the Civil Society Dialogue between the European Union and Turkey with a specific focus on ensuring better knowledge and understanding of Turkey within the European Union. From the beginning, this goal was transformed by the Scientific Committee into a more significant and representative one, aimed at promoting a process of mutual learning from practice and reflection upon partners' cultural identities in the context of inducing the development of intercultural sensibility. As a result, the following working hypothesis was designed: *Intercultural awareness among researchers, teachers and students involved in the project (samples 10, 100, 800) is presumed to be low. The innovation in teaching methodologies and materials is expected to enhance researchers, teachers and students' awareness of cultural diversity and its understanding, as a dimension of intercultural sensitivity.* An important issue was raised in carrying out the project, namely the need to work out a successful teacher training program which would have an impact on the intercultural dimension, based on the latest conceptions on continuing teacher training. The idea had been expressed from the very first discussions about training methodology, as interweaving formal learning (seminars and e-learning) with teachers' expertise, i.e., linking their practical knowledge (non-formal learning), considered as a process of reflection, to practice recognized on an academic level. Discussions and processes of mutual understanding between teachers from several cultures were then fundamental to generate individual teaching projects for subsequent classroom implementation. The training strategy was based on the implementation of three international collaborative seminars followed by online activities that were designed to accompany experimental teaching activities. The process started from the negotiation of content and the training approach by the three teams of trainers from Slovenia, Turkey, and Italy. From the beginning, the need to take responsibility was emphasized by the Research/ Training group. Consequently, every teacher was asked to produce learning units to be implemented in their classes, making use of common strategies (belonging to the large PERMIT framework) in order to implement intercultural dialogue. Discussions between teachers generated individual learning units. Furthermore, the groups of teachers were supported in their decision-taking process by academics who brought research trends in intercultural education developed in the three countries involved. It was assumed that only through collaboration in both international plenary sessions and broad subject groups could the teachers create learning units deriving from both their best practices and innovation. Hence, intercultural strategies within pedagogical practices were going to emerge from existing strengths and the extension of the vision of what was feasible. It was assumed that only through collaboration, in both plenary sessions and in broad subject groups of teachers from different countries and from different kinds of school, could new approaches and lesson schemes be forged out of their combined best practices. Intercultural strategies within pedagogical practices would therefore emerge from existing strengths and extensions of the vision of what was possible. The need to give continuity to the process launched through the workshops was immediately evident. How could participants from several different countries and realities give continuity to their collaboration? The teachers and their materials needed to *go virtual*.

Creating the Virtual Working/Learning Space: What Kind of Place Do We Need on the Net to Give Continuity to Teachers' Cross-border Debates?

According to the initial discussion above, and considering the further training hypothesis implied in the project, the VWLS (also called *The Space*) had been given significant attention from the very first seminar. *The Space* was set up to keep the aims and objectives of the project at the forefront, and to store the information the teachers might need in addition to their teaching materials. *The Space* was also conceived as a way of giving supportive empathy to those teachers looking for colleagues' help with their creative process.

Within *The Space* (inspired by the above mentioned idea of Agorà) the teachers were not seen simply as downloaders of information. Instead, they were perceived of as *uploaders*, considering Web 2.0 philosophy, since artifacts, tools, and spaces were progressively going to be shaped by teacher-led intervention and published in *The Space*. Coherently with this, teacher's professionalism was envisaged as a process of critical deconstruction of one's own practices/knowledge, whereby the teacher becomes a reflective practitioner (Schön 1983), who obtains a deep understanding of the discipline through teaching (Margiotta 2007; Whitehead and McNiff 2006). So, he/she becomes the author of his/her own teaching resources and strategies. This active and reflective approach was supported by both the possibility of publishing contributions on the Net very easily, and the subsequent collaboration with colleagues and students made possible by Web tools. This process of cross-border collaboration and critical deconstruction with peers from several different cultures would induce the development of intercultural sensitivity through (a) one's own and other people's cultural awareness; (b) decentralization of the conception of one's own subject and practices, toward a more ethnorelative position (implying the

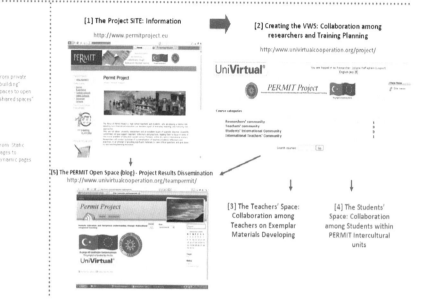

Fig. 6.1 Original idea of *The Space*

acceptance of self as part of a broader picture, moving beyond local practice). *The Space* was designed to reflect this idea of professional development and to adhere to the above mentioned training strategies. Figure 6.1 explains the structure and areas in *The Space*.

In this figure, the several spaces making up the general "geography" of "The Space" (the virtual Agorà) are shown. The figure also makes it clear how these virtual working areas are linked to each other for several purposes: information, communication, and learning.

According to the principles of Web 2.0, extremely simple software was used to provide the users with several user-interface, software and storage facilities, all through their browser, thereby using the web as a "platform" (O'Reilly 2005). These characteristics were supposed to make the users' experience on the Net more direct and spontaneous. The VWLS was built by integrating Drupal (release 6.0) and Moodle (release 1.9). While the news and the project site ran on Drupal, discussions and learning activities were placed on Moodle. A blog on WordPress was eventually used to contain the final version of work, while videos and photos were embedded into an e-learning platform Moodle by using You Tube, Flickr, and Picasa Web Albums.

Implementing the VWLS

Figure 6.2 shows the development of the project throughout its various phases. A set of online modules was proposed to the teachers as part of their training, but the main activity was to upload their own materials and to collaborate in the implementation of pilot classroom experiences.

The online modules were connected to the project development phases as follows:

The First Phase was devoted to the understanding of the guiding principles of the PERMIT Project in order to start the developing of PERMIT Learning Units. The online modules were connected to (a) in-depth understanding of the problem of intercultural pedagogy (Cultural Values influencing Schooling System); (b) teachers' skills in enacting reflection and collaboration across frontiers (use of Portfolio to develop reflection on intercultural teaching practice; use of tools to participate within a virtual learning environment).

The Second Phase was devoted to the implementation of PERMIT Units in class. Online modules were focused on (a) Presentation and Analysis of PERMIT units Learning Design through self assessment and peer discussion; (b) Web tools to

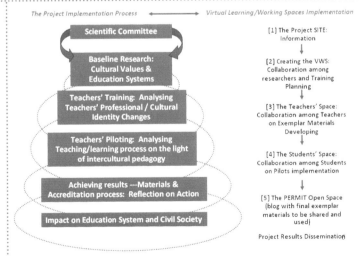

Fig. 6.2 The coherence between project development and the construction of *The Space*

let students interact across frontiers; (c) the Use of Portfolio to introduce intercultural competence self assessment (understanding the level of intercultural
sensitivity development).
The Third Phase was focused on the evaluation of the results achieved by the
students in class. Online modules were to deal with Reflections on Effective
Intercultural Teaching ("My best Lesson").
The Fourth and closing phase was dedicated to the dissemination of results in wider
teachers' communities.

Consequently, implementation was progressive and organic in a context of
bottom-up logic, as the spaces were shaped in accordance with the groups' needs.
The analysis of the training phases, FTF and the online learning activities (from the
first to the third residential seminar) allows us to understand how *The Space* became
something more than an e-learning platform in the sense of being merely a structured space for formal learning activities, without any connection with experimental
practice and emotional engagement. In fact, it evolved into a space for experimentation and the sharing of reflection on the *meanings* emerging from practice, prior to
discussion in residential meetings.
The red dotted lines indicate the progressive process of building the third cultural
space on the Web. The cultural space starts from interaction and continues to impact
on other social/cultural dimensions.

Outcomes I: The VWLS as the Matrix of Shared Knowledge

The teachers piloted ideas, developed through a networked learning process, in their
own classes. The following data comes from 19 questionnaires delivered through an
online form at the end of each working session ("After Training Questionnaires");
the respondents were the teachers from the three countries involved in the project.
The main result to emerge from the above mentioned questionnaire was that 92% of
the respondents thought the VWLS was a useful tool for developing an intercultural
professional identity, mainly because:

> [...] It gave us the opportunity to see other colleagues' didactic approaches, compare teach-
> ing perspectives, spark ideas, give help to other teachers, sharing materials [...] (Slovenian
> teacher).

> [...] The platform was generally considered useful for giving teachers the idea of a working
> group "across frontiers", eliminating national barriers and borders; as it means a lot to stu-
> dents too, especially when they see that in so many schools their peers do the same pilots,
> and come up with similar or very original questions! [...] (Italian teacher).

> [...] Because for cancelling the contours and the borders of the bodies and the brains, it is
> more necessary and usefull to come together than the other technologic methods in opinion
> me [...] (Turkish teacher).

Participating in an international community of teachers and students had an
impact on personal practice, because it was an opportunity to work with people

from different educational contexts, bound together by certain ideas and beliefs. The PERMIT international teachers' community was made possible by *The Space*, whose virtual representation could be considered a semiotic representation of a meeting place (where iconicity and symbolism of shared words become "things" of common use). The platform could be therefore considered as an instrument supporting some of the crucial processes of the PERMIT approach: the sharing of experiences and working models, the opening of a window on communication between students and teachers from the many contexts involved in the project. Nevertheless, the potential of this kind of tool is still to be developed. Some teachers reported:

> [...] The Space was somehow the "storage space" [...] and its proper value and the purpose is about to come; The Space was important and it can become more important if it becomes a means of communication amongst students and teachers; [I] think it should be implemented for the relation between students [...] (Turkish teacher).

> [...] Technical barriers as equipments and teachers' skills are a problem to face if this kind of instrument is to be used [...] (Italian teacher).

Outcomes II: The Sense-Making Process – Building Metaphors for Intercultural Dialogue

Metaphors are forms of language expressing shared sense-making processes, since they stimulate a "double process of semantic mapping," through the operation of linking one category to another, and thus condensing meaning (Lakoff and Jonhson 1980; Mercer 2000). Metaphoric thinking is also deeply rooted by images (Lakoff and Jonhson 1980). This cognitive assumption could make the use of metaphors frequent in intercultural conversation. Between the second and third phase of teacher training and experimentation, metaphors started to circulate among the teachers and their classes (while communicating across frontiers), as part of the process of negotiating meaning, and in the effort to come to an understanding with otherness, but also as a way of generating a common context for intervention. A first metaphor, "The PERMIT Coffee House" (see Fig. 6.3), which identified the online forum, was conceived in order to meet the international group's need to create a "meeting point" where to have free, informal interactions. This metaphor was launched through an image which illustrated the students' area and the diversity which it could contain. The teachers discussed the pros and cons of this proposal at the International Teachers Community (Plenary Discussions Forum, from Interaction 11 to Interaction 18: six participants). The main problem faced by the teachers was the perception of the risks involved in (a) allowing *The Space* too loose a connection with planned learning activities; (b) keeping a check on students' behavior even in this place – which is both in and out of school. The teachers decided to allow free contact among the students. This decision had a positive impact, since the Coffee House allowed the students to get to know some aspects of their foreign peers' everyday life, and supported their reflection on lifestyles and identities in different cultures. Feedback activities revealed the strong impact on some Italian students:

Fig. 6.3 A metaphor for an informal place of meeting

[…] We would never imagine that a Turkish girl could be a Physician's daughter, and that she could have travelled the world more than we did […] (Vocational Training School, Mestre, 14 May 2009).

[…] Reading about the life of these kids, I realized that their likes, their thoughts, their fears, are very similar to those of mine […] (Vocational Training School, Mestre, 14 May 2009).

[…] The insertion of the piece in the puzzle is a good example of the relationship that has emerged between the Italian students and the foreign students, Turkish and Slovenian, of PERMIT project. In fact, this project is a puzzle that has been completed, and that established an important and constructive link among three very different cultures, that at the same time are together in wishing to know each other and wanting to understand each other. To me, Permit Project has been an important springboard to a deeper knowledge of cultures different from mine […] (Art School, Padova, 28 May 2009).

The Humanities group produced another significant metaphor, that of the "Skyline" (the shape of a city seen against the skyline at sunset). The "Skyline" was used by the teachers and the students to represent themselves to the others. Linked to this idea, the Skyline was the first metaphorical image easily shared despite the communication difficulties linked to trying to use English as a "lingua franca" (the Humanities group, being formed by people with very different disciplinary and experiential backgrounds, suffered intensely from this difficulty in negotiating sense within a common project). At first, the teachers agreed to exchange their own photos of their home city. They subsequently began to ask their students to take pictures, reflect on the "shapes and shadows," as visible and invisible parts of their own city, and therefore reflect on the "shapes and shadows" of other PERMIT cities. This phase was followed by the introduction of the theme "The cities" in the Lesson Plan of very different subjects, such as Design (as a *mood board* for fashion design), Literature (as a starting point for producing literary texts and introducing Italo Calvino's work *Invisible Cities*), Art (as a starting point for the study the works of art in the cities involved in the program), History (as a means of stimulating the study of the historical context of certain buildings acting as a link between cities in different countries).

The cognitive mapping process produced by this metaphor was also extended to other categories to represent intercultural dialogue, for example, the metaphor of the iceberg, which suggests the idea of what is visible of one's own intercultural identity, and what is invisible, hidden under water.

This impregnation of common images through the students' production and the teachers' reflection on their students' work, was a clear representation of the cognitive and emotional effort made in building a common narrative of cross-border and disciplinary practice. Thanks to free negotiation and consensus as opposed to the constraints of curricula or external coordination, an intercultural context for common practice was created.

This is the introducing page to the PERMIT Coffee House created by a teacher.

Conclusions

The aim of this research was to explore three different points:

- The results of the process of networked learning which takes place between people from different cultural backgrounds having to interact for work purposes (hence generating concrete outcomes for their respective professional contexts).
- To what extent it is possible to conceive the idea of influencing teachers' original cultural identity with the aim of bringing about a sense of belonging to an enlarged learning culture – a community of teachers across frontiers connected by the Web.
- The possibility of developing and fostering teachers' practices toward an intercultural perspective of teaching as an extension and impact of the two previous points.

From the results we obtained, it emerged that the networked learning process generated a perception among the teachers (and later among the students, too) of the centrality of *The Space* as a tool and a place of communication which supported a sense of cross-border community. In fact, the chance of knowing other *glocal* realities, and communicating with them through the use of a virtual space was considered by the participants not only relevant, but also crucial from the perspective of dialogue with otherness and *disclosing and exploring diversity*. All the teachers emphasized the motivation and curiosity showed by their students about the different realities taking part in the PERMIT experience, seeing *The Space* as a window to look "*outside the walls of the classroom/curriculum*" (Teachers internal meeting, Venice, 15 May 2009). After a while, this produced a local effect, as reflection affected *praxis*: teachers stressed the need to enhance this motivation for educational innovation in class and at school, by introducing common activities across frontiers, and the students themselves asked to carry on taking part in *The Space* in order to communicate with peers from other countries. This interest shows how narrow the space offered by the classroom (physically delimited) and the curriculum (symbolic delimitation) is becoming: in fact, what the students and the teachers were asking for was a new *territory (in the sense of symbolic spaces for a connected self)*, the only frontiers of which are the limits of *imagination* (in the sense of a multimodal representation of sense-making processes) This is where the Web can play a role, not as a technological device, but as a semiotic space capable of creating the coordinates of an *enlarged cultural context*.

Networked learning – as part of a wider training vision – seems to offer the possibility of featuring symbols and iconicity in a significant way. As a result, the recognition and the resignification of cultural symbols and metaphors belonging to other cultures create *new contexts which allow new narratives*, as emphasized by Sharples et al. (2007: 231):

> […] learning not only occurs in a context, it also creates context through continual interaction. The context can be temporarily solidified, by deploying or modifying objects to create supportive work space, or forming an ad hoc social network out of people with shared interests, or arriving at a shared understanding of a problem […].

This could match our attempt to raise awareness of the need for a critical approach of the potential of networked learning for introducing an intercultural dimension into teaching/learning processes. The evidence about the construction, use and impact of VWLS collected within the PERMIT experience, shows a process of creation of a semiotic space, a place where re-interpretation of one's own experience occurs, followed by new common narrative. This process seems to motivate people to participate in international online communities aimed at achieving a vision of otherness, as they seem to perceive themselves as outside a specific cultural context: a new symbolic representation that goes beyond *my place* – with my own cultural rules – or *yours*. By means of *electronic conversation* this place becomes a third, new place. Furthermore, the fact that the process is crystallized in electronic texts and icons, we are allowed to believe that diversity is discovered, explored and kept in the memory before reaching *thirdness*. We could conclude that networked learning is a kind of learning that takes place in *enlarged cultural contexts*, thus causing the reformulation of the concept of *inter* cultural learning. This implies the creation of a context by several cultural identities, rather than by fixed entities that exchange meaning. This new context generates a sense of belonging to a wider project, a territory where virtual/planetary citizenship can be implemented. Of course, this is rather utopian, even because cyberspace can house symbolic violence as well as real places do. Consequently, we are aware that participation based on a bottom-up logic is not enough to produce new learning cultures, since thoughtful and critical guidance to a participatory approach is necessary to support the processes of deconstruction and reconstruction of cultural meaning.

Will these encounters in online spaces have an impact on local spaces? This question, the kernel of new education (comprehensive of networked learning as well as intercultural education) certainly requires further research. The metaphors emerged and shared by the teachers and the students about their common teaching and learning activities were supported by *The Space*; they were hence transferred into local classrooms, promoting continuity in the sense-making process from virtual (global) to FTF (face-to-face or local). In fact, connections among teachers and students supported by technologies led the participants to achieve emotional engagement, confrontation and concrete experience that allowed them to build new discourses about diversity. *The Space* in the PERMIT project, suggesting the idea of a *place* where to meet (an *agorá*), generated the perception of a room where people introduced their diversity to the others, shared activities and goals, and recognized otherness. Perhaps this gave the participants the idea of a classroom without walls, an enlarged cultural context where intercultural dialogue, and further cultural construction could take place: *a classroom with a view*.

In the light of these conclusions, we can highlight further questions that could shape future practice:

- From the perspective of networked learning, how can teachers work with their colleagues to help them develop their understanding of intercultural education in all their different subject areas?
- Are teachers likely to want to give time to building new discourses about diversity when they are often overworked and when they have to "cram" so much into the curriculum?
- How can teachers be helped to achieve this much-needed perspective on intercultural learning and teaching?

Teachers need to become aware of the importance of managing complexity induced by diversity at any level of learning experience. Teachers' effectiveness depends on this awareness, which can generate appropriate educational actions.

Considering the positive impact on intercultural sensitivity generated by the PERMIT project by spreading international residential seminars blended with networked learning over lengthy periods of time, similar experiences should be shared and disseminated, in order to let new teachers know the educational gains brought about by meeting otherness on the Net, and promote their participation in similar activities. Furthermore, academics, researchers and teacher trainers should help them investigate their own discipline's epistemology in international networked learning activities, both as pre-service and in-service training opportunities in which teachers can reflect on those dimensions of their discipline that can be affected by intercultural sensitivity and competence.

For example, the European Commission is providing a policy context to promote teachers' professional mobility (Comenius Projects: Lifelong Learning Programme, Strategic Priorities, 2010). Thus, introducing a perspective of the type explored in this chapter can certainly improve outcomes in terms of teachers' professionalism.

Further Implications for Research

Our empirical work represents an attempt to collect evidence about networked learning as a process of culture construction, where otherness can be effectively represented, explored, and deconstructed in order to generate new meaning.

In our view, the need to think of networked learning as an opportunity to expand one's own cultural context through active participation in its construction opens up the possibility of research on new modes of using connections (with people and with multimodal resources on the Net). The aim is to produce learning cultures as a further result of learning processes.

Research in this field supports this perspective by elaborating on the evolution of the concept of "intercultural" learning on the Net. For example, Goodfellow (2008) explores a mosaic of positions, like "providing culturally appropriate instruction on virtual learning environments"; the role of language and intercultural communication in foreign languages in building understanding, especially where cultural backgrounds are supported only by reduced cues within electronic medium; studies that emphasize the emergence of new cultural and social identities in virtual learning communities which draw on contemporary cybercultures and their role in shaping individual cultural identities. He concludes that, even when these studies draw on broader, interdisciplinary approaches, such as cultural theory, language and semiotics, and instructional design, they seem focused on *"problems of designing and implementing e-learning for non-western consumers, with the majority of accounts coming from the US and other Anglophone contexts"* (Goodfellow 2008: 555).

It is clear that future research on cultural embededdness of networked learning experiences needs to go beyond instructional design (tailored courses for foreigners), even if this perspective cannot be abandoned completely (Banks et al. 2008).

The balance among "new learning culture" discourses and the representation of multiple voices in a network is delicate and difficult. Further research might investigate how emerging new learning cultures represent diversity effectively, in an attempt to answer the questions: what has been lost in adopting some of the new cultures and why? Connections and nodes (people or resources) that can superficially give the idea of a "smooth" learning experience need to be deconstructed in order to understand both the individual's intercultural sensitivity, as well as power and dominant discourses which may neglect the expression of diversity.

It seems that reflections and theoretical research have explored the question to some extent. Nevertheless, we are today observing an impressive use of virtual environments to cross national/local frontiers, not only in higher education (on which the majority of studies seem to have focused) but also at other levels of formal education, such as our own experience, and in other informal and nonformal learning contexts.

As a consequence, we believe there is a clear need for more empirical evidence and reflection on networked learning in the *enlarged cultural context.*

References

Asmar, C. (2005). Internationalising students: Reassessing diasporic and local student difference. *Studies in Higher Education, 30* (3), 291–309; quoted by Reynolds, Perspectives… 2008, p. 732.

Banks, J. A. (2001). *Cultural diversity and education: Foundations, curriculum, and teaching* (4th ed.). Boston: Allyn & Bacon.

Banks, Sh., McConnell, D., Bowskill, N. (2008). A feeling or a practice? Achieving interculturality in an elearning course. *Proceedings of the 6th International Conference on Networked Learning* (pp. 712–719). ISBN 978-1-86220-206-1. Retrieved September 10, 2010, from http://www.networkedlearningconference.org.uk/past/nlc2008/abstracts/PDFs/Banks_712-719.pdf

Beijaard, D., Meijer, P. C., & Verloop, N. (2004). *Reconsidering research on teachers' professional identity*. Leiden: Institutional Repository Leiden University, Leiden University. Retrieved December 23, 2010, from https://openaccess.leidenuniv.nl/handle/1887/11190

Bennet, M. J. (1993). Towards a developmental model of intercultural sensitivity. In R. Michael Paige (Ed.), *Education for the intercultural experience*. Yarmouth, ME: Intercultural Press.

Bowskill, N., McConnell, D., & Banks, S. B. (2008). Reflective practices in intercultural e-tutor teams: A UK-Sino case study. *Proceedings of the 6th International Conference on Networked Learning* (pp. 707–711). ISBN 978-1-86220-206-1. Retrieved September 10, 2010, from http://www.networkedlearningconference.org.uk/abstracts/PDFs/Bowskill_707-711.pdf

Bruner, J. S. (2005). *La mente a più dimensioni*. Bari: Editori Laterza [Original title *Actual Minds, Possible Words*, 1986]. Cambridge, MA: Harvard University Press.

Carneiro, R. (2007). The big picture: Understanding learning and meta-learning challenges. *European Journal of Education, 42* (2), 151–172.

Coulby, D. (2006). Intercultural education: Theory and practice. *International Education, 17* (3), 245–257.

Dunn, P., & Marinetti, A. (2002). *Cultural adaptation: Necessity for eLearning*. Retrieved September 10, 2010, from http://www.linezine.com/7.2/articles/pdamca.htm

Edmundson, A. (Ed.). (2007). *Globalized e-learning cultural challenges*. Hershey: Information Science Publishing.

Geertz, C. (1973 [2000]). *The interpretation of cultures*, New York: Basic Books.

Goodfellow, R. (2008). New directions in research into learning cultures in online education. *Proceedings of the 6th International Conference on Networked Learning* (pp. 553–559). ISBN 978-1-86220-206-1. Retrieved September 10, 2010, from http://www.networkedlearningconference.org.uk/past/nlc2008/abstracts/PDFs/Goodfellow_553-559.pdf

Goodfellow, R., & Lamy, M. N. (2009). *Learning cultures in online education*. London: Continuum.

Goodyear, P., Avgeriou, P., Baggetun, R., Bartoluzzi, S., Retalis, S., Ronteltap, F. et al. (2004). Towards a pattern language for networked learning. In S. Banks, P. Goodyear, V. Hodgson, C. Jones, V. Lally, D. McConnell, & C. Steeples (Eds.), *Proceedings of the Fourth International Networked Learning Conference*. Retrieved September 4, 2010, from http://networkedlearningconference.org.uk/past/nlc2004/proceedings/individual_papers/goodyear_et_al.htm

Gordon, T. (1977). *Leader effectiveness training*. New York: Wyden.

Gundara, J. (2000). *Interculturalism, education and inclusion*. London: Paul Chapman.

Hall, E. T. (1959). *The silent language*. Garden City, NY: Anchor Press.

Hall, E. T. (1960). *The hidden dimension*. Garden City, NY: Anchor Press.

Hampden-Turner, C., & Trompenaars, F. (2000). *Building cross cultural competence: How to create wealth from conflicting values*. Chichester: Wiley.

Hewling, A. (2006). Culture in the online class: Using message analysis to look beyond nationality-based frames of reference. *Journal of Computer-Mediated Communication, 11*, 337–356.

Hewling, A. (2008). Culture ecologies in online education. *Proceedings of the 6th International Conference on Networked Learning* (pp. 569–573). ISBN 978-1-86220-206-1. Retrieved September 10, 2010 from http://www.lancs.ac.uk/fss/organisations/netlc/past/nlc2008/abstracts/PDFs/Hewling_569-573.pdf

Hodgson, V., & Reynolds, M. (2005). Community, difference and networked learning designs. In V. Hodgson, L. Perriton, & M. Reynolds (Eds.), *Community and networked learning (Studies in Higher Education), 30(1)*, 11–24.

Hofstede, G. (2001). *Culture's consequences: Comparing values, behaviors, institutions, and organizations across nations* (2nd ed.). Thousand Oaks, CA: Sage.

Hofstede, G., & Hofstede, G. J. (2005). *Cultures and organizations: Software of the mind (Revised and expanded 2nd)*. New York: McGraw-Hill.

Jones, C. (2008). Networked learning – A social practice perspective. *Proceedings of the 6th International Conference on Networked Learning* (pp. 616–623). ISBN 978-1-86220-206-1. Retrieved September 4, 2010, from http://www.networkedlearningconference.org.uk/past/nlc2008/abstracts/PDFs/Jones_616-623.pdf

Koole, M. (2010). The web of identity: Selfhood and belonging in online learning networks. *Proceedings of the 7th International Conference on Networked Learning 2010* (pp. 241–248). ISBN 978-1-86220-225-2. Retrieved September 4, 2010, from http://www.lancs.ac.uk/fss/organisations/netlc/past/nlc2010/abstracts/PDFs/Koole.pdf

Lakoff, G., & Jonhson, M. (1980). *Metaphors we live by*. Chicago: University Chicago Press.

Leclerq, J. (2003). *Facets of interculturality in education*. Strasbourg: The Council of Europe Publishing.

Liu, Y. (2007). Designing quality online education to promote cross-cultural understanding. In A. Edmundson (Ed.), *Globalized e-learning cultural challenges* (pp. 35–39). London: Information Science Publishing.

Macfadyen, L. P., Roche, J., & Doff, S. (2004). *Communicating across cultures in cyberspace: A bibliographical review of online intercultural communication*. Hamburg: Lit-Verlag.

Macfadyen, L. P. (2008). Constructing ethnicity and identity in the online classroom: Linguistic practices and ritual text acts. *Proceedings of the 6th International Conference on Networked Learning* (pp. 560–568). ISBN 978-1-86220-206-1. Retrieved September 10, 2010, from http://www.networkedlearningconference.org.uk/past/nlc2008/abstracts/PDFs/Macfadyen_560-568.pdf

Maistrello, S. (2007). *La parte abitata della Rete*. Milano: Tecnologie Nuove.

Margiotta, U. (2007). *Insegnare nella Società della Conoscenza*. Lecce: Pensa.

McConnell, D. (2008). Examining conceptions of e-learning in an intercultural Sino-UK context. *Proceedings of the 6th International Conference on Networked Learning* (pp. 720–726). ISBN 978-1-86220-206-1. Retrieved September 10, 2010, from http://www.networkedlearning-conference.org.uk/abstracts/PDFs/McConnell_720-726.pdf

McConnell, D., Banks, S., & Lally, V. (2007). Developing a collaborative approach to e-learning design in an intercultural (Sino-UK) context. In H. Spencer-Oatey (Ed.), *e-Learning initiatives in China: Pedagogy, policy and culture* (pp. 175–187). Hong Kong: Hong Kong University Press.

McLoughlin, C. (2001). Inclusivity and alignment: Principles of pedagogy, task and assessment design for effective cross-cultural online learning. *Distance Education, 22* (1), 7–29.

McLoughlin, C. (2007). Adapting e-learning across cultural boundaries: A framework for quality learning, pedagogy and interaction. In A. Edmundson (Ed.), *Globalized e-learning cultural challenges* (pp. 223–238). London: Information Sciences Publishing.

Mercer, N. (2000). *Words and minds: How we use language to think together*. London: Routledge.

Mezirow, J. (1991). *Transformative dimension of adult learning*. San Francisco: Jossey-Bass.

Morse, K. (2003). Does one size fit all? Exploring asynchronous learning in a multicultural environment. *Journal of Asynchronous Learning Networks, 7* (1), 37–55.

O'Reilly, T. (2005). *What's web 2.0? Design patterns and business models for the next generation of software*. Retrieved December 23, 2010, from http://oreilly.com/web2/archive/what-is-web-20.html

OECD (2009). *Creating effective teaching and learning environments: First results from TALIS (Teaching and Learning International Survey)*. Paris: OECD. Retrieved December 22, 2010, from http://www.oecd.org/dataoecd/17/51/43023606.pdf

Paloff, R., & Pratt, K. (1999). *Building learning communities in cyberspace.* San Francisco: Jossey-Bass.

Raffaghelli, J. (2008). *Project Alfa-MIFORCAL: A global e-learning model to develop social and professional teachers' identity.* Poster Presentation at the European Distance E-Learning Network – Research Workshops – Promoting Access and Social Inclusion through E-learning, UNESCO, Paris, France.

Reynolds, M. (2008). Perspectives on the International student experience: A review. *Proceedings of the 6th International Conference on Networked Learning* (pp. 727–735). ISBN 978-1-86220-206-1. Retrieved September, 10, 2010, from http://www.networkedlearningconference. org.uk/past/nlc2008/abstracts/PDFs/Reynolds_727-735.pdf

Rheingold, H. (1993). *The virtual community, homesteading on the electronic frontier.* Cambridge: MIT.

Rollin, I., & Harrap, A. (2005). Can e-learning foster intercultural competence? *Brookes eJournal of Learning and Teaching, 1* (3). Retrieved November 11, 2009, from http://bejlt.brookes.ac. uk/vol1/volume1issue3/practice/rollin_harrap.html

Rovai, A. P. (2002). Building sense of community at a distance. *International Review of Research in Open and Distance Learning, 3* (1), 1–16. ERIC Document Reproduction Service No. EJ646664.

Rushkof, D. (2006). *Screen-agers: Lessons in chaos from digital kids.* New York: Hampton Press Communication.

Rutheford, A., & Kerr, B. (2008). An inclusive approach to online learning environments: Models and Resources. *Turkish Online Journal of Distance Education, 9* (2). Retrieved May 21, 2009, from http://tojde.anadolu.edu.tr/tojde30/pdf/article_2.pdf

Schön, D. (1983). *The reflective practitioner: How professionals think in action.* London: Temple Smith.

Sharples, M., Taylor, J., & Valvoula, G. (2007). A theory of learning for the mobile age. In *The Sage Handbook of e-learning research* (pp. 221–245). London: Sage.

Silver, D. (2000). Looking backwards, looking forward: Cyberculture studies 1990–2000. Retrieved May 15, 2008, from http://rccs.usfca.edu/intro.asp. [Original work published on *Web.studies: Rewiring media studies for the digital age* (pp. 19–30), edited by D. Gauntlett. Oxford: Oxford University Press, 2000].

Turkle, S. (1996). *Life on the screen* [Italian Ed., 1997, *La vita sullo schermo. Nuove Identità e relazioni sociali nell'epoca di Internet*]. Milano: Apogeo.

Whitehead, J., & McNiff, J. (2006). *Action research: Living theory.* London: Sage.

Zenios, M., & Goodyear, P. (2008). Where is learning in networked learning construction? *Proceedings of the 6th International Conference on Networked Learning* (pp. 607–615). ISBN 978-1-86220-206-1. Retrieved September 4, 2010, from http://networkedlearningconference. org.uk/past/nlc2008/abstracts/PDFs/Zenios_607-615.pdf

Zhang, Z., & Huang, R. (2008). Challenges for Chinese learners in Sino-UK intercultural online interactions – Case study of an eChina–UK Project. *Proceedings of the 6th International Conference on Networked Learning* (pp. 743–748). ISBN 978-1-86220-206-1. Retrieved September 10, 2010, from http://www.lancs.ac.uk/fss/organisations/netlc/past/nlc2008/abstracts/ PDFs/Zhang_743-748.pdf

Part IV
Dynamics of Changing Tools
and Infrastructures

Chapter 7
The Challenge of Introducing "One More Tool": A Community of Practice Perspective on Networked Learning

Patricia Arnold, John David Smith, and Beverly Trayner

Introduction: Communities and Technologies

It has become commonplace for many communities of various kinds to support their communication and mutual learning with Internet technologies (e.g., Barab et al. 2004). Creating this "digital habitat" (cf. Wenger et al. 2009) often starts with a need to find a "home" for documents that are made easily accessible for all members of a community. It can grow with the need to bridge communication between face-to-face meetings or to create a shared memory of face-to-face events. Communities often consider tools and technologies that will support emerging goals and suit their evolving context. The questions about what technologies to use and how to introduce them into the community have always been complex. Research has been carried out into the sorts of designs most conducive to producing and nurturing online communities (e.g., Bielaczy and Collins 1999; Paloff and Pratt 1999; Preece 2000). Other research has focused on what happens when a community's communication is transferred into the online space due to changing organizational structures (e.g., Kimble et al. 2001).

With a proliferation of communities in so many diverse contexts the opportunities and challenges presented by new tools and technologies become significant ones for people involved in community leadership, design, and support. Internet technologies seem ever more accessible and easy-to-use. For example, preparing and publishing video on the Internet is now in reach for anyone interested in these freely available technologies, whereas it used to require complex software tools and expert

P. Arnold (✉)
Faculty of Applied Social Sciences, University of Applied Sciences, Munich, Germany
e-mail: patricia.arnold@hm.edu

J.D. Smith
Learning Alliances, Portland, OR, USA

B. Trayner
Independent, Setúbal, Portugal

L. Dirckinck-Holmfeld et al. (eds.), *Exploring the Theory, Pedagogy and Practice of Networked Learning*, DOI 10.1007/978-1-4614-0496-5_7,
© Springer Science+Business Media, LLC 2012

competencies. Moving to a new, improved platform is not such an expensive or complicated business as it once was. "One more tool" becomes an apparently easier option for facilitators, technology stewards, and community members.

As community consultants, designers, and facilitators, we face the questions that result from the proliferation of tools on a daily basis. As people who are also engaged in research we try to unpack the intricate relationship between communities and technologies at a fine-grained level (cf. Arnold et al. 2006, 2007). In this chapter, we investigate the implications of (just) "one more tool" in communities and networks we are working with. We use the idea of "communities of practice" (Lave and Wenger 1991; Wenger 1998) as a broader conceptual framework for reflecting on our work, thus offering a distinct, nonmainstream perspective on networked learning.

The notion of "networked learning" has been elaborated in many publications and international conferences (cf. Beaty et al. 2010; Dirckinck-Holmfeld et al. 2009; Goodyear et al. 2004a). It shares similar roots with the notion of "communities of practice". Both concepts provide a framework to reflect on learning in its social dimensions but there are relevant differences as well. Networked learning fundamentally is concerned with enhancing formal educational settings and the *teaching* enterprise (Beaty et al. 2010), with a focus on higher education, attending to the complex interplay of pedagogy, institution, subject, technology, and infrastructure (Jones and Dirckinck-Holmfeld 2009, p. 7). The concept of "communities of practice" has been taken up in many different sectors and sheds light particularly on *learning* in informal settings and the processes of peer-to-peer learning (Wenger 2010). Networked learning research thus often operates at a more aggregated level such as looking at policies to be introduced in an institution. This is different from communities of practice research that takes place at a smaller scale, such as investigating various processes and their interdependence within a learning community.

Generally, we argue that communities and networks are two aspects of the social fabric of learning and that both communities and networks enhance social learning processes (Wenger et al. 2011). Our lens in this chapter is to look at the social processes within two cases as regards technology, especially how a new tool might both blur boundaries and create new ones at the same time. One of our "one more tool" cases describes the introduction of video as a way of bringing in absent voices to a face-to-face meeting of a global community of international agricultural researchers and practitioners. The other case describes the use of a specialized, practitioner-oriented platform in a higher education course where students take one step outside the teaching institution.

The question that guides our inquiry is: what are the design considerations for supporting and extending a community's learning when introducing one more tool? Rather than analyze the cases in hindsight, we share our reasoning about the introduction of a new tool at the same time as we are facing the challenge ourselves. Thus, we change the classic case study approach from analyzing a "completed" case that happened in the past to analyzing and "reflecting in action" upon a case that presents a design challenge in networked learning right now. We invite the reader backstage to engage with our considerations as they evolve in an iterative cycle of action and research.

Our descriptions elaborate a highly aggregated pattern (cf. Kohls 2009) rather than focusing on any of these particular technologies. In other words, we are describing the introduction of one more tool to a community as opposed to the pattern of "introducing video" or "introducing a new platform". Our result is not a complete pattern for introducing "one more tool" but a more reflexive rethinking of our roles as technology stewards when introducing one more tool into the learning in a community setting.

The structure of this chapter is as follows: in the next section we elaborate on a community of practice perspective on networked learning and what this implies for supporting a community with technologies. Following that, we describe our research method, the two cases and our perception of the design challenges they represent. We then discuss and analyze both cases, concluding with some reflections on what we learned in the process of our investigations and in what ways it contributes to the conversation about networked learning.

Networked Learning and New Tools: A Community of Practice Perspective

Networked Learning and Communities of Practice

Our perspective on networked learning is greatly influenced by social theories of learning in general and by communities of practice in particular. Networked learning theories and community of practice theories have a lot in common with a community of practice perspective offering a different view and lens of analysis for networked learning.

The most important shared ground consists of a social theory of learning at the core of all theoretical and practical considerations as opposed to cognitive individualist stances on learning. Such a social understanding of learning is characterized by the following properties of learning as described by some of the leading researchers on networked learning (Jones and Dirckinck-Holmfeld 2009, p. 8):

> Learning is mediated by tools, both symbolic tools such as language and physical artefacts.
> Learning is social and language and artefacts are both cultural and social products rather
> than learning being the products of individual minds. Learning is historic because we
> "inherit" cultural tools we need to understand the history of their development.

From a community of practice perspective knowledge is embedded in social practice. Communities that develop, share, and refine a specific practice are called communities of practice (Lave and Wenger 1991; Wenger 1998). Communities of practice are a key element of learning. The boundaries between communities of practice are also central to learning. It is at these boundaries where there can be misunderstandings as well as possibilities for negotiating new meanings.

Networked learning, however, can be defined as:

> learning in which information and communication technology ... is used to promote con-
> nections: between one learner and other learners; between learners and tutors; between a
> learning community and its learning resources. (Goodyear et al. 2004b, p. 1)

The conversations, examples, and advances in practice regarding networked learning in the past decade are a response to the impact new tools and technologies are having on educational settings, primarily in higher education.

Both the networked learning body of work and the efforts to understand and cultivate communities of practice are the result of a larger "social turn" in literacy studies, new media studies, learning theory, and childhood studies (Ito et al. 2009). A communities of practice perspective on networked learning puts community processes and their contribution to learning at its center. Whereas in networked learning the focus is on education that leverages social networks and connectivity (Jones and Dirckinck-Holmfeld 2009, p. 5), the focus in communities of practice is on the development of a shared identity – or collective intention – around a set of challenges (Wenger 2010). To take a community of practice perspective on networked learning also implies to take into account the manifold social settings where learning occurs whether or not they are tied to educational settings.

Conversations in communities of practice are guided by the question of what works *in practice*. A shared identification with a domain of interest brings people together who share a common concern with this *domain* of knowledge. They engage in a joint enterprise, commit themselves pursuing activities around this domain, and develop relationships of trust that make an inquiry into their practice possible. In their interactions around the domain of knowledge the *community* creates a shared repertoire of language, concepts and communication tools that make practice discussable (Wenger 2009). These three structural elements *community*, *domain*, and *practice* are mutually constitutive. All three evolve in response to changes in each of the others. In earlier work on communities of practice (Wenger 1998), the key elements of a community of practice were described as "joint enterprise, mutual engagement, and shared repertoire". Later on, the structural dimensions of "community, domain, and practice" proved more useful in analyzing and reflecting on communities of practice (Wenger 2009; Wenger et al. 2002, etc).

The dimension of *community* includes the people, their relationships, mutual trust, and their trajectories toward knowledgeabilty and competence at an individual and collective level. The *domain* is the issue the community cares about; the knowledge area around which the community gathers and which the community constantly refines with their practice. By *practice* we refer to the activities, language, and tools that form the enterprise the community and its members engage in. The practice both means applying the knowledge domain and constantly refining it. The shared repertoire of language, tools, methods, and patterns of thought plays an important part in any community's practice. Practice also entails the learning that occurs in a community, changing and transforming member's identity and at the same time being transformed and changed as members manifest their identity within the community. Communities that interact using technology must regard the use of technology as part of their practice of being together (Wenger et al. 2009).

Boundaries are another important concept within communities of practice. A practice with any depth reflects a sustained history of social learning, which creates a boundary with those who do not share that history. At the same time there are new insights that come from mixing perspectives between contexts and seeing things in new ways. Clearly defined boundaries are important for a community's sense of identity and the meaning that the practices produce. At the same time permeable boundaries are important for fresh ideas and practices and for negotiating how practices produced by one community are relevant to the other. For many communities, technologies are one of the ways boundaries are expressed, created, or removed, whether intentionally or not.

Using such a community of practice lens for analyzing networked learning settings raises a question about *which communities* and *which case studies* are emblematic, serving as the basis for generalizations: should we study learning communities in formalized educational settings or look more closely at communities that are independent of "school instruction and ... the pedagogical intentions of teachers and other caregivers" (to quote Lave and Wenger 1991, p. 61)? We suggest that it is particularly useful to investigate these latter communities where an educational agenda does not play a major role (cf. as well Arnold 2003). Our line of argument follows Lave and Wenger's (1991, pp. 61–62) as to why comprehensive theories of learning should be based on learning settings other than those in the formalized school sector. Lave and Wenger argue:

> Because the theory and the institution have common historical roots (Lave, 1988), school-forged theories are inescapably specialized. They are unlikely to afford us the historical-cultural breadth to which we aspire. It seems useful, given these concerns, to investigate learning-in-practice in situations that do not draw us in unreflective ways into the school milieu, and to look for "educational" occasions whose structure is not obscured quite so profoundly as those founded on didactic structuring. (Lave and Wenger 1991, pp. 61–62)

In addition to seeking communities and learning activities that are outside formal educational settings, we are drawn to cases that involve new tools and technologies. New tools and technologies create yet different settings where learning takes place and often blur boundaries: boundaries between learning in formal and informal settings, boundaries around a community or educational institution, etc. At the same time tools and technologies can create new boundaries when access, handling or usage of these tools constitutes an obstacle for participating. The cases we are engaged in and which we present in this chapter extend the range and breadth of learning settings in a way we hope is as fruitful for others as they have been for ourselves.

Networked Learning and New Tools and Technologies

Supporting a community's practice with technologies is increasingly common for dispersed communities as well as for those who meet face-to-face regularly, within or outside educational settings. We have a growing number of choices for creating "digital habitats" (Wenger et al. 2009) using tools such as groupware, learning or content management systems, social network platforms, wiki software, weblogs, and chat rooms. New technologies open new possibilities for creating "places" for people to meet and hold conversations. They also change the cues for context and the boundaries that determine who belongs and who does not. These become key issues when facilitating learning in communities.

A situation that arises frequently for community facilitators is the need to select a new tool to add to the repertoire of tools used by the community. For historical reasons, a community may support its practice with a set of tools and establish the main technologies to use. An increasing number of tool options and successful examples of new technology practices lead to the potential for a more developed digital habitat and a more efficient way of reaching the community's goals, raising the issues of whether and how to introduce "one more tool". A community facilitator, acting as "technology steward" (Wenger et al. 2009, 131ff.) often takes a leading role in considering other available tools that could meet the needs of a community.

What should be the design considerations for introducing this one more tool into a community? It is easy to see that a new tool will influence a community's practice, if it is adopted, but what about the other constitutional elements of a community of practice? What are the considerations for domain and community? We argue that introducing a new tool and the practices around using that tool will change the landscape for building relationships and trust among community members that in turn shape the domain. Thus, when we are introducing one more tool we need to consider how a change in practices around that tool will affect community formation and struggles around the domain as much as we need to consider tool features or the process of implementation of that tool.

Designing for Community Learning: Our Workbench Cases

To ground our theoretical reflections in the *practice* of introducing new tools for enriching the learning of distributed communities, we present two design challenges that we are facing in our work. These "workbench cases" are not classic case studies that we analyze retrospectively but cases that are "in progress" – where we analyze and reflect upon our own practice in terms that can be shared with a wider audience. Even though both cases are different in their "one more tool" challenge and in the roles and mandate we have in relationship to the community, we present the cases under the same rubrics.[1]

Our research method lies between action research and autoethnography (cf. Ellis 2004) and is explained in more detail in Arnold et al. (2006, 2007). It has some similarity with action research in that we intervene and engage actively in the field we are investigating. In contrast to classic action research designs, however, the research decisions are not reached in a participatory process with the learners involved in the cases. Here we rather adopt an autoethnographic design in that we use our anxieties, observations, and reflections as community facilitators and technology stewards as a starting point for the investigation. Our roles in the given communities provide us with enough insight and contextual knowledge about the community, i.e., we belong enough to use participant observation. For a critical reflection on our relative positions in the communities we observe, we use a community of practice perspective as an analytical framework. Additionally, our simultaneous involvement and facilitating roles in many other communities sharpens our awareness of the issues at

---

[1] These are inspired by the rubrics suggested for e-learning pattern development (Kohls 2009).

Fig. 7.1 Our workbench
cases in relation to
educational contexts

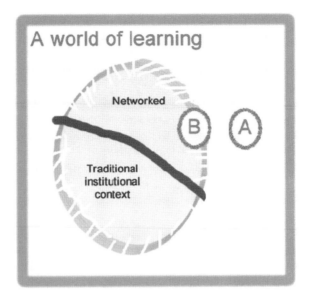

stake as does our mutual reporting and shared reflection among ourselves as both researchers and practitioners. In short, our data consists of extensive notes from joint planning, reporting and reflection sessions, individual participant observation as well as artifacts from the communities on which we report.

Case A is located completely outside of an educational context, whereas Case B is located on the boundary between an institution and the ongoing professional lives of practitioners in the field (Fig. 7.1).

In the case descriptions that follow we change voice from "we" (referring to all three authors who have jointly thought through these issues, "worked the cases" and written the text) to "I" (indicating participant observation and involvement in community facilitation and technology stewardship). "Voices of the community" refers to the perspectives presented by different people in the community.

Workbench Case A: Global Community of Practice in the Agricultural Development Arena[2]

Context

Members of a global community of practice are coming together to discuss their shared vital concerns.

The community consists of agricultural researchers, institutions, governments, and nongovernmental organizations concerned with advancing agricultural

---

[2]Some details of this case have been modified to respect the privacy concerns of the community.

knowledge and practice internationally. Current communication practice is mostly email, telephone, and regional face-to-face meetings. An international face-to-face meeting is planned in Africa when 20 key people will come together to reflect on how they are learning from and with each other and to think of how to do it better. I am looking at which tools can be introduced to enrich and extend the conversations outside the *same time/same place* of a face-to-face meeting. I have decided to integrate video and audio recording to the repertoire of communication tools. I can use the recordings for bringing the voices of physically absent people to the table at the face-to-face meeting.

Design Challenge

Many members of this group do not have straightforward access to the Internet or to broadband. Trust is an important issue on several levels. Members come from neighboring countries with sensitive diplomatic relations. Within countries there are clearly defined hierarchical positions. Some members need to be cautious about who shows up where and with whom. Tools that support transparent processes or leave digital traces can easily be viewed as breaches of protocol or political maneuvres rather than as opportunities for dialogue. Another design problem is that people are very busy. Their focus is on the immediate pressures of their day-to-day concerns. There is a tension between responding individually to immediate, local problems and contributing to a community's response to those issues on a larger scale.

Added Value

Recordings can help extend the event beyond "same time same place" and let more people participate actively regardless of their physical location. Another advantage of video and audio recordings is that a person can contribute content while I manage the tool. In other words, someone does not have to be adept at the tool in order to have his or her voice heard. This is in contrast to other tools such as Google docs, wikis, and blogs where someone's voice may not be heard if people are not digitally literate.

Potential Pitfalls

A first video that I recorded in a Skype interview brought up a number of potential pitfalls. Although I have seen some uses of Skype for telephony, the interviewee's webcam produced a poor quality black and white image. Watching a Skype video with a poor image added nothing to the content. This seemed relevant given the social sensitivities of many members of the group. Editing the video to increase its quality was time-consuming and required a kind of know-how that is not widely enough available in the community. At a certain point the time spent editing videos did not add anything to connecting people and developing the community. Another potential pitfall given the sensitivities of the group are those of privacy and confidentiality. Just one perceived breach of confidentiality could be seen as a serious breach of trust.

Forces at Work (Behind the Scenes)

In the community there is rhetoric of openness to new tools but people do not have time to invest in learning how to use or integrate them into their day-to-day work. Until now new tools have been dismissed for one reason or another: Google docs was too hard, Twitter was too politically sensitive, Skype was not practical. I know that I have to do something that will show the value of new tools without creating a lot of work for members.

Workbench Case B: Community of Distance Learners in Higher Education

Context

This community is situated in an online study program that is especially designed for students who are working in different parts of the country as they study. To offer greater flexibility in time and location, only 25% of the study modules are taught face-to-face and 75% of the modules are taught completely online. A standard commercial learning platform is used for online modules. Current communication practice in the online modules include discussion forums, chats, and file management functions such as the assignments/drop box, etc. Students have been using this mix of technologies for 2 years and generally enjoy collaborating and sharing their work and study challenges. A sense of community has evolved rapidly. For the second half of their study program a new online module lasting four semesters is being designed. It will introduce students to peer counseling techniques and is meant to bridge theoretical concepts and their actual work situations. Students are expected to discuss cases from their work in small subgroups in a systematic way that has been developed especially for the social sector where funds for external supervision often are not available. Another focus will be on their changing professional roles as many prepare with the study program for a management position in their field of work.

Design Challenge

Existing tools only support online peer counseling techniques while they are enrolled as students so I am considering moving to another platform that they will be able to use when their study program ends. The new platform is designed to enable online peer counseling in the social sector and supports practicing social workers. However, moving to another platform requires that the students give up established routines and time to get to know the new platform. Also, the special peer counseling platform is still under development and students would be exposed to platform development bugs. Learning a new platform in beta may be daunting for working students with time constraints

Added Value

Students will get to know a peer counseling platform that they can use now and after their studies for their work. Experience in online peer-counseling will be useful for people hoping to become experts in social work and related management positions. Using the specialized platform, they join a larger community of social work professionals who explore, apply, and refine online peer counseling. Being involved in the feedback and ongoing development of the platform could be an interesting experience as they also help shape the design of software to support social work.

Potential Pitfalls

Changing from one communication platform to another always runs several risks. The new platform requires a new set of access credentials (ID/password), a particularly daunting prospect for students working from different locations and computers. Other course modules will continue using the standard learning management system, requiring them to access two platforms. In addition, shortcomings of the existing platform are familiar to students whereas they will have to develop new work-arounds for the new platform. They may even feel mistreated as experimental subjects in a software development process.

Forces at Work (Behind the Scenes)

The colleague with whom I run this module is an expert on peer counseling and one of the founders of the peer counseling platform that is being considered. He cannot be expected to invest a lot of energy to map counseling features onto the functionalities of a standard learning platform. In addition, partnership with a university is a good test bed for the platform and an opportunity to get future professionals already familiar and using it. I wonder if we are misusing the students in this process. On the other hand, study programs should enable students to acquire "real world" competences. Using the counseling platform is a chance for students to practice peer counseling techniques under authentic conditions and to go beyond the boundaries of a higher education context.

"One More Tool" Interacts with the Entire Community: Discussion

The workbench cases are quite different from each other. The higher education learning community, studying together in its digital habitat, has routines for communicating and co-operating that are quite different from those of a community looking to bridge between face-to-face meetings. In our discussion of the cases, the aim is not to compare the different communities or their different communication designs. Our aim is to look at the design considerations for introducing "one more tool" and the potential changes that technology stewards and other community leaders should consider. It may be easy to see that the introduction of a new tool, recorded video in workbench case A and a specialized platform in workbench case B, will affect a community's sense of "being together". However, by looking at it more closely through the community–domain–practice lens we see that a new tool not only influences practice but also interacts with the community and the domain.

Analysis Workbench Case A: Global Community of Practice in the Agricultural Development Arena

The "one more tool" being introduced is that of video conversations with people who cannot be at the event but who have something to say. "One more tool" in this practice refers to a cluster of tools that will be used for recording, editing and publishing, and watching the video conversations.

Interaction with Practice

- As we introduce a tool for recording people who cannot attend we start developing practices for opening a face-to-face event to people who are not physically present. This changes the dynamics of whose voices are at the table and changes the shape of the community.
- The recordings lead to practices of publishing and archiving conversations that stay around longer than face-to-face conversations. This could eventually influence the domain as people consider differently what issues are important and what issues have been discussed previously.
- The practice of creating artifacts that are different from traditional meeting outputs normally concerned with capturing conclusions and decisions made will call for different types of skills and leadership roles from within the community.
- Issues around privacy will lead to developing ethical and other practices as we consider where the video is stored. The decision about who has access to the videos will change the community and how members perceive their roles.

Interaction with Community

- We are using the tool as a way to involve people even if they cannot be present. Community development will help build trust; additional voices as a result of trust will help shape the domain.
- Holding controversial voices in the broader discussion, rather than letting them be silent, will have implications for the practice of listening while also changing the issues of domain.
- Through developing ways of holding informal conversations in a setting where formality and status can hinder the deepening of conversations could change a range of practices related to formality.
- Nurturing a sense of horizontal accountability to fellow-practitioners who are not present could lead to more practices that support peer-to-peer conversations.

Interaction with Domain

- Additional voices will change the framing of the issues facing the community. The (virtual) presence of a controversial voice will affect the way the community views their domain issues.
- As video is introduced, there are many decisions that will have a bearing on domain: who to interview, what questions to ask, what editing if any, control over video recordings, etc. All these decisions will also affect the relations between people as they develop the practices around interviewing, editing, and publishing the recordings.

Analysis Workbench Case B: Community of Distance Learners in Higher Education

The "one more tool" being introduced is that of a specialized peer counseling platform that is used by a variety of social professionals to organize peer counseling. Until now this specialized platform has not been linked to any higher education context.

Interaction with Practice

- Counseling each other on cases consists largely of communication through various means: The specialized platform offers communication features (a non-threaded forum, a wiki, a file repository – all with personalized notification and geared to the different phases of peer-counseling). These features will change the established routines of communicating at a fine grained-level, including whose voice is being heard.

- Students will gain more control over the community's practice: Immediately after registration, they can create their own counseling rooms on the new platform and decide who they allow in, whereas the standard platform keeps that kind of control in the hands of the instructor.
- Students can see other peer-counseling groups (outside the higher education context) and could join them if interested. The work of these neighboring groups will eventually change the domain of this student group.

Interaction with Community

- On the standard learning management system, the community is clearly defined and confined to students in the program. With the new platform boundaries blur immediately: students can allow people outside the study program in, for example, other users of the specialized platform or their own colleagues at work. Communication across student cohorts will now be effortless. With the consent of the group, they can also join other counseling groups, visible on the platform, and thus potentially collaborate with other social professionals who use the platform. This will lead to a range of new practices and a reframing of the domain in many ways.
- Students will have to decide whether they want their counseling group to be visible to any platform user or not. In case they opt for visibility, these other users might ask permission to join them. Practices related to permissions will have to be developed.
- Unlike on the standard platform, the default would be that the counseling groups are not open for the instructors. Therefore, the role of the instructor changes because now they can easily be "left out". In general, the whole set-up of who is "in the classroom" changes and the roles of students and instructors are much less certain than they were traditionally.

Interaction with Domain

- The community's principal domain in this module is peer counseling. By using the specialized platform that is still under development, a socio-informatics dimension is added to the domain: does the platform support the online peer-techniques well enough? Platform organizers ask users for feedback on the platform's design and functionality. This will be the first time student perspectives form part of the joint reflection and evaluation.
- As the cases that student peers discuss can now come from a wider variety of settings and sources, the scope of the domain will change. This will redefine which cases are seen as relevant and the formation of the community around this changing domain.
- The instructor's view of domain is now contestable because other voices are potentially in the conversation. This changing power relationship over the domain will shape who knows and who does not know and the practices for bringing other voices in to talk about the domain (Table 7.1).

Table 7.1 Synopsis of "one more tool" interacting with the structural elements of a community

Workbench case	Practice Language, concepts, and tools	Community Membership, relationships, history	Domain Shared concern or inquiry
A: recorded conversations	Brings in different communication patterns Triggers question of expanding tool repertoire (e.g., for the storage of videos)	Changes whose voice is heard and whose is not Contests the boundaries of the community Influences power politics within the community	Extends domain issues and intensifies domain negotiation as previously marginal voices come into focus
B: peer counseling platform	Connects "secluded" study practice with mainstream professional practice Shifts control of practice from instructor to students Introduces an add-on practice: evaluating software	Allows community relationships to extend beyond an academic time-frame Extends participation boundaries: connects with professionals outside higher education	Extends the domain from "study" to "ongoing professional practice". Proposes adding "evaluating technology" to the domain of social work

Looking Back and Ahead: Conclusions

In this chapter, we looked closely at two different "one more tool" situations. From positions of facilitators and technology stewards for two different communities we shared the design considerations and analyzed the interplay between domain, community, and practice in the introduction of a new tool. What might appear as the introduction of a tool that would merely change a community's practice now seems to be more complex. The introduction of a tool will change whose voice is being heard, which voices can be legitimately brought to the table, how competence is negotiated, and, indeed, what matters to the community. Introducing the tool will influence the practices that are developed, shared, and refined by the community that cares about the domain. Just one more tool potentially transforms our participation and our sense of identification with the community and the world. It represents a different way of engaging with each other and therefore a different way of learning.

Meanwhile, and all too often, we get frustrated that a community does not accept a new tool. As facilitators or leaders, we explain or provide training in how to use that tool, we use incentives, cajole and chastise our communities as we try to encourage innovation and new ways of communicating. However, it turns out that introducing one more tool has larger implications related to engagement in the community, the practice, and the domain. Engagement goes beyond the mastery of a tool or even of a practice. Dealing with one more tool involves testing, contesting, and negotiating the boundaries of a community. And in negotiating who is at the table, we are negotiating the issues that concern us. In other words, we are contesting the domain.

In offering two cases that may seem outside the mainstream arena of networked learning we wanted to contribute to the conversation on networked learning in a complementary way. Our focus has been on a learning partnership that creates an identity around a common area for learning as distinct from a networked learning approach that focuses on optimizing the connectivity between people.

How does our reflection on the introduction of one more tool help us in our practice of designing for communities? How does it help us introduce a new tool or technology into a learning community? And how does it contribute to the conversations on networked learning? In the process of writing this chapter we came to the conclusion that in introducing a new tool the following questions are worth consideration: How will this tool influence the voices at the table? How will it affect who is a party to the conversations and who is not? How will it affect who decides? And what does that mean to this community? These are the questions we intend to pursue, investigating with greater detail how a new tool or technology impacts boundaries.

We see three contrasts between communities inside and outside educational settings that bear on the "one more tool situation":

- *Structuring social interaction.* An educational context typically includes a privileged person such as a tutor, who has a mandate and learning outcomes in mind and whose participation is constrained by an academic calendar. The role and privileges of leaders in communities outside educational settings are generally more contestable, leaders are more easily replaced, and time is structured less by an academic calendar and more by external community or organizational constraints.

- *Institutional support and resources.* Educational institutions, like other organizations, typically build up support structures, including technological support, in a systematic, structured, and procedural process over long periods of time. Technology and tools have to comply with existing policies and traditions and they have to fit into longer term plans and world-views. Creative experimentation with new tools and technologies often needs to take place outside the institutional mind-set. Depending on their membership, communities outside educational or organizational contexts might be able to look for support and resources in a more ad hoc fashion. They can be more experimental or improvisational, even if they have to look for "free" tools, for funding or sponsorship of the tools they use. A new tool for communities thus must be compatible with the relevant mode of organizing support and resources.
- *Domain boundaries.* The domain boundaries in a world of networked learning are more flexible than in an environment where the boundaries are defined by academic or organizational traditions and decision-making bodies. However, domain boundaries are even more fluid in a community outside an educational institution where the relevance of a topic can be driven by current practice, not curricular or disciplinary concerns. Introducing a new tool, with its effect on the voices in the community might therefore have an even bigger influence on the evolution of the domain.

Summing up, through writing this chapter we have gone from seeing ourselves as people who advocate for the introduction of one more tool to viewing ourselves as convenors of new and different combinations of voices in a community. We started writing this chapter with the intention of proposing design considerations for facilitators and technology stewards who are introducing "one more tool" to expand and enrich a community's learning. We ended our inquiry by seeing ourselves as convenors of new and different voices that might change and contest the domain and practices of a community through the introduction of just one more tool. It is with that sensitivity and responsibility with respect to boundaries that we take on the introduction of new tools into the practices of a community. And we advise to take up that stance – possibly with adaptations – for the more mainstream cases of networked learning.

References

Arnold, P. (2003). *Kooperatives Lernen im Internet: Qualitative Analyse einer Community of Practice im Fernstudium.* Münster u.a: Waxmann 2 (Medien in der Wissenschaft, Bd. 23) (also Doctoral Dissertation at the Institute of vocational learning, professional development and telematics of the Helmut-Schmidt University Hamburg 2002).

Arnold, P., Smith, J. D., & Trayner, B. (2006). Using narrative to generate and reveal context in virtual settings. In A. de Figueiredo & A. Afonso (Eds.), *Managing learning in virtual settings: The role of context* (pp. 197–218). London: Idea Group Publishing.

Arnold, P., Smith, J. D., & Trayner, B. (2007). Narrative, community memory and technologies – or writing a literature review in high modernity. In L. Stillmann & G. Johanson (Eds.), *Constructing and sharing memory: Community informatics, identity and empowerment* (pp. 18–29). Cambridge: Cambridge Scholars Publishing.

Barab, S. A., Kling, R., & Gray, J. H. (2004). *Designing for virtual communities in the service of learning.* Cambridge [u.a.]: Cambridge University Press.

Beaty, L., Cousin, G., & Hodgson, V. (2010). Revisiting the E-quality in networked learning manifesto. In L. Dirckinck-Holmfeld, C. Jones, M. de Laat, D. McConnell, & T. Ryberg (Eds.), *Proceedings of the 7th International Conference on Networked Learning 2010* (pp 585–592). Aalborg, Denmark: Aalborg University.

Bielaczy, K., & Collins, A. (1999). Learning communities in classrooms: A reconceptualization of educational practice. In C. Reigeluth (Ed.), *Instructional-design theories and models. Volume II. A new paradigm for instructional theory* (pp. 269–292). Mahwah, NJ: Lawrence Erlbaum.

Dirckinck-Holmfeld, L., Jones, C., & Lindström, B. (Eds.). (2009). *Analysing networked learning practices in higher education and continuing professional development.* Rotterdam: Sense Publishers.

Ellis, C. (2004). *The ethnographic I: A methodological novel about autoethnography.* Walnut Creek: Alta Mira.

Goodyear, P., Banks, S., Hodgson, V., & McConnell, D. (2004a). *Advances in research on networked learning.* Dordrecht: Kluwer.

Goodyear, P., Banks, S., Hodgson, V., & McConnell, D. (2004b). Research on networked learning: An overview. In P. Goodyear, S. Banks, V. Hodgson, & D. McConnell (Eds.), *Advances in research on networked learning* (pp. 1–10). Dordrecht: Kluwer.

Ito, M., Baumer, S., Bittanti, M., boyd, D., Cody, R., Herr-Stephenson, B., et al. (2009). *Hanging out, messing around, and geeking out: Kids living and learning with new media.* Cambridge, MA: MIT Press.

Jones, C., & Dirckinck-Holmfeld, L. (2009). Analyzing networked learning practices. In L. Dirckinck-Holmfeld, C. Jones, & B. Lindström (Eds.), *Analysing networked learning practices in higher education and continuing professional development* (pp. 1–27). Rotterdam: Sense Publishers.

Kimble, C., Hildreth, P., & Wright, P. (2001). Communities of practice: Going virtual. In Y. Malhotra (Ed.), *Knowledge management and business model innovation* (pp. 220–234). Hershey, London: Idea Group Publishing.

Kohls, C. (2009). E-Learning Patterns – Nutzen und Hürden des Entwurfsmuster-Ansatzes. In N. Apostulopoulos, H. Hoffmann, V. Mansmann, & A. Schwill (Eds.), *E-Learning 2009. Lernen im digitalen Zeitalter* (pp. 61–72). Waxmann: Münster.

Lave, J., & Wenger, E. (1991). *Situated learning: Legitimate peripheral participation.* Cambridge: Cambridge University Press.

Paloff, R., & Pratt, K. (1999). *Building learning communities in cyberspace. Effective strategies for the online classroom.* San Francisco: Jossey-Bass.

Preece, J. (2000). *Online communities: Designing usability, supporting sociability.* Chichester [u.a.]: Wiley.

Wenger, E. (1998). *Communities of practice; learning, meaning and identity.* New York: Cambridge University Press.

Wenger, E. (2009). Social learning capability: Four essays on learning and innovation in social systems. In *Social innovation sociedade e trabalho* booklets, 12, separate supplement. Portugal: MTSS/GEP & EQUAL.

Wenger, E. (2010). Communities of practice and social learning systems: The career of a concept. In C. Blackmore (Ed.), *Social learning systems and communities of practice, Part III,* DOI: 10.1007/978-1-84996-133-2_11, the Open University 2010. Published in Association with Springer-Verlag London Limited.

Wenger, E., McDermott, R., & Snyder, W. (2002). *Cultivating communities of practice: a guide to managing knowledge.* Cambridge, MA: Harvard Business School Press.

Wenger, E., Trayner, B., & De Laat, M. F. (2011). *Promoting and assessing value creation in communities and networks: A conceptual framework.* Heerlen: Ruud de Moor Centrum, Open University.

Wenger, E., White, N., & Smith, J. D. (2009). *Digital habitats: Stewarding technology for communities.* Portland, OR: CPsquare.

Chapter 8
Implementation of an Infrastructure for Networked Learning

Tom Nyvang and Ann Bygholm

Introduction

Information and Communication Technology (ICT)-supported learning, understood as the use of ICT to support and enhance learning practices, has become an integrate part of university education. This is, however, only a small part of the full story. Institutions, departments, and individual members of faculty utilize ICT in quite different ways depending on the kind of ICT and assumptions about which designs for learning are the most productive. Problem-based learning (PBL), computer-supported collaborative learning (CSCL), and networked learning are examples of (overlapping) genres in learning design that offer different ways of thinking about ICT support for learning and many more could be mentioned. PBL stresses the importance of working with authentic real world problems and projects as an integral part of (university) education (Kolmos et al. 2004). PBL has spread in universities since the 1970s which of course is before ICT developed into a significant part of educational processes, but is today often associated with ICT support for collaboration and project management (Dirckinck-Holmfeld 2002; Dirckinck-Holmfeld et al. 2009; Ryberg and Dirckinck-Holmfeld 2010; Haakon Tolsby et al. 2002). PBL has its theoretical roots in the very early constructivists Dewey (1910), Vygotsky (1978), and Piaget (1999). The problem with the PBL genre is that it tend to say little about all the aspects of education that is not problem solving and it has only to a smaller extent been developed in the light of ICT. CSCL is born with the personal computer in the 1980s and stresses the learning outcomes of close collaboration between learners in a computer-supported environment (Koschmann 1996). CSCL has its theoretical roots in the social constructivism and some of the same early works that underpin PBL (Koschmann 1996). Today CSCL has developed its own

T. Nyvang (✉) • A. Bygholm
Department of Communication and Psychology, Aalborg University, Aalborg, Denmark
e-mail: nyvang@hum.aau.dk

L. Dirckinck-Holmfeld et al. (eds.), *Exploring the Theory, Pedagogy and Practice of Networked Learning*, DOI 10.1007/978-1-4614-0496-5_8,
© Springer Science+Business Media, LLC 2012

theoretical foundation in works by Koschmann, Stahl, and others (Stahl et al. 2006). In the case of CSCL, the focus on close collaboration is its strength and weakness at the same time; we regard it a strength that the genre is very focused, but a weakness that it cannot be applied above the microlevel since no or very limited perspectives on the relation between close collaboration in the organization is offered (although Jones et al. (2006) suggested more work on meso-level design in CSCL and networked learning). Networked learning has a broader definition:

> Learning in which information and communication technology (ICT) is used to promote connections: between one learner and other learners; between learners and tutors; between a learning community and its learning resources.
>
> (Goodyear et al. 2004, p. 1)

The concept networked learning has developed over the past 10 years along with the increased use of networked personal computers for learning support in universities and other educational institutions. Networked learning draws on the early constructivists (Dewey 1910; Piaget 1999; Vygotsky 1978) just as PBL and CSCL. Networked learning has similarities with the views on networks presented by Castells (2000) and Siemens (2005) and they have to some extent influenced the development of networked learning (Bell 2010; Jones and Dirckinck-Holmfeld 2009; Jones et al. 2008). Castells do not focus specifically on learning, but on the network society and the concept of networked individualism describing the interdependence between individual and network (Castells 2001). Siemens (2005) does, however, focus on learning and argues that ICT is a core driver for learning by supporting connection of nodes and sense making.

With networked learning ICT support for learning has developed from being an isolated and uncoordinated endeavor of individual technology interested teachers to being an institutional commitment. If there is no institutional or managerial commitment the network for learning is not likely to have many nodes or stretch across an institution. With few nodes it is also not likely to foster the kind of connections needed for networked learning to take place. If the network stretches beyond the class of the individual teacher it is, however, also evident that the network of learners becomes quite complex. Actors (teachers, students, managers, others) will have to develop their own contributions and yet make sure they fit into the network of other actors and resources.

Jones et al. (2006) suggest that for CSCL and networked learning to be developed further research and practice should focus on the meso-level of collaborative learning:

> On how to design for collaborative learning at the institutional level, in organizations, school settings, and in networked learning environments,
> On what the basic conditions are that allow for collaborative learning in these settings,
> On how the technology and infrastructure affords, and mediates the learning taking place.
>
> (Jones et al. 2006, p. 37)

The meso-level is in other words the level that lies between the overall societal or institutional macrolevel in large institutions and the very local microlevel teaching and learning practices.

With this chapter we aim to uncover the meso-level conditions under which institutional actors decide upon ICT strategies for networked learning purposes. We chose to do so because we suspect that the meso-level is where networked learning is made possible, but also where different rationales, priorities, and values may clash in an unproductive manner and hinder the implementation of a networked learning environment that helps the learner to learn something useful to her. We know from earlier research that decisions are often made in an ecology of multiple actors, tools, and intentions (Bygholm and Nyvang 2009). To develop leadership and change strategies in and around networked learning we thus experience a need to develop insights that are qualitative in nature.

In the following sections, we present our case study methodology, our analysis, and discuss our findings.

Human Centered Informatics: Case Study Design

The case study focuses on implementation of ICT in the program Human Centered Informatics, a program within the humanities at Aalborg University. The program offers bachelor and master level educations and has approximately 700 students distributed across two campuses, one in Aalborg and another in Ballerup (in the Copenhagen area). The program combines studies in communication, organization, esthetics, learning, and ICT.

This case study is a follow-up to another case study committed 4–8 years ago when Human Centered Informatics went through a development process ending with the implementation of Lotus Quickplace (later renamed Lotus Quickr), an information and communication system to be used by administration, students, and teachers. According to Nyvang (2008), the early stages of the project aimed to uncover the existing ICT-related practice in the organization. The project also aimed to identify the goals to be pursued by using ICT in the organization. In the end, the goals were transparency, coherence, flexibility, and quality in teaching and learning – these were however also at a high level and open for interpretation. At a more concrete level, the new ICT were supposed to support PBL approaches to teaching and learning (Nyvang and Tolsby 2004; Tolsby et al. 2002). The latter had a significant influence on the choice of Lotus Quickplace because it supported group collaboration. Lotus Quickplace was, however, also chosen for its flexibility as a content management system which meant that it could be rearranged to manage course-related communication too. The case study conducted 4–8 years ago also focused very much on the implementation process – on the change from a myriad of different systems and ways of communicating to one common system and way of communicating across the organization (Bygholm and Nyvang 2009; Nyvang 2006; Nyvang and Poulsen 2007): What were the needs of the different members of the organization? How were ICT adopted and adapted? What were the main influences on the many decisions made on different levels and by different actors in the organization? The main influences were ICT already used in the organization, ICT known from other contexts, culture and pedagogical model, and the existing division of labor between teachers, students, and administration (Nyvang 2008). Members of the organization discussed whether one common tool for all students, teachers, and administrators would be the most productive way to proceed. Those discussions never came to any concrete conclusion. Lotus Quickplace was chosen as a common framework, but many teachers and students chose other ways to communicate and collaborate, and discussions and negotiations kept bringing the technology to the forefront of attention in the organization.

This case study investigates under which conditions actors in institutions decide upon which ICT to use for networked learning purposes? The occasion is when Human Centered Informatics has decided to discard Lotus Quickplace and implement a suite of tools with Moodle at the center instead. From an overall perspective, it seems unclear what the organization has learned about networked learning so far and how it affects the decision to implement Moodle and the day-to-day decisions on how to use Moodle. With the research behind this chapter we aim to uncover the so-far invisible or unspoken rationales developed and used by different actors in the decision and implementation process. Our working hypothesis is that the tools, infrastructures, and technologies we use will never permanently step into the background. From time to time, they will require attention for one reason or another and it is when they spring into attention we have a special opportunity to gain a deeper insight in the practices and challenges of networked learning in the organization. Tyre and Orlikowski (1994) support the hypothesis that times of change are relatively short when new systems are implemented in organizations and that the windows of opportunity for studying change are equally small. Research by Flores et al. (1988) supports the hypothesis from a different perspective – namely, by suggesting that the situations when tools or practices fail and thus come to the forefront of attention offer access to information that is usually invisible or resembles silent knowledge.

The case study methodology and analysis used in the Human Centered Informatics case is rooted in the theoretical frame of activity theory. Activity theory derives from Russian psychology where psychologist like Vygotsky (1978) and Leont'ev (1978) developed a cultural historical social psychology during the twentieth century. Over the past 20–25 years activity theory has been subject to growing attention in the Western Europe and in the USA and across a diverse set of research and practice fields. Yrjö Engeström (1987), a major contemporary contributor to activity theory and others have developed the use of activity theory in education and learning. Kari Kuuti has also taken part in the development of activity theory for use in human computer interaction and defines it as:

> a philosophical and cross-disciplinary framework for studying different forms of human practices as development processes, with both individual and social levels interlinked at the same time.

> (Kuutti 1996, p. 41)

Vygotsky originally founded activity theory based on a criticism of the behaviorist stimulus–response (S–R) model of human behavior – a theoretical model that explained human response to stimuli with prior positive or negative experience of a similar stimulus and response (Vygotsky 1978, pp. 39–40). He found the S–R model too simple to explain human reasoning in a socio-cultural context and argued that human action internally (in the mind) and externally (in the world) is mediated by some sort of mediator. Language is one such mediator that shapes the way we think. Tools are another kind of mediator – a hammer in hand mediates the way we think about and approach a task. Vygotsky also stressed that human action is goal-oriented. Leontjev moved on to add that human goal-directed action is subordinate to a motive and takes place under certain contextual conditions. Engeström (1987) took activity theory a step further by developing the understanding of the relation between individual and collective.

Early works by Vygotsky (1978) used case studies to develop activity theory, but from these works, we cannot learn much about the methodology. One of the major contributors to activity theory-based methodology, Engeström (1987, 2009) did, however, take his developmental research a step further by claiming that research based on activity theory should involve the researcher in action research like developmental cycles to fully uncover the nature of development. Kaptelinin et al. (1999) went on to suggest an activity check-list aimed at studies of human computer interaction – not specifically calling it case studies, but from their description of the check-list they were obviously a tool for organizing studies of cases of human computer interaction. Later on, Kaptelinin and Nardi (2006) and Spinuzzi (2003) have developed more comprehensive methods for organizing analysis and design processes aimed at different instances of human computer interaction. These methods thus fall into the expansive developmental research tradition of Engeström, but they also contribute to the body of methodological knowledge by developing tools with a specific domain in mind – and by developing tools aimed at both practitioners and researchers.

For the research reported in this chapter, we draw on the analytical tools provided by Kaptelinin et al. (1999). Our choice is based on the simple and yet knowledge generating nature of the methodology. This means that we have the following foci when designing data collection and analysis:

- Means/ends: Deals with the hierarchical nature of an activity – conditions, goals, and motives for activities in the organization.
- Environment: Deals with the objects in the context of an activity – tools and technologies used in the organization and by its members.
- Learning/cognition/articulation: Deals with the exchange between internal mental processes and external processes – ways of thinking and how they interact with technological potential for representation in the world.
- Development: Factors influencing change in the organization – the history of core activities and how they shape present changes.

In our data collection, we have focused on all of the four major issues of the activity check-list when asking questions in interviews, reading documents, and examining ICT that are in use in the organization. For data collection, we have conducted qualitative interviews with key members of staff. In our search for key members of staff we look for what von Hippel (1986) defines as lead users. Lead users are users with the special quality that they can identify the needs of a larger population before the rest of the population does so. In our search for lead users we have also focused on finding the influential members of staff. We ended up with a teacher who is a networked learning expert, two from the division responsible for the design and support of networked learning systems, and the head of the study program Human Centered Informatics. We have also met 80 third semester students in a workshop-like situation where the students were asked questions, discussed these, and returned short answers in writing. Finally, we have studied existing documents (research mentioned earlier in this section) and the primary system used so far: Lotus Quickplace.

We have chosen not to focus on the interaction with higher levels in the organization and stick to actors very close to the technological infrastructure even though our interest in meso-level design might suggest a broader scope. We have done so because the head of studies and the study board behind him at the time of the data collection had the resources and power to make this kind of decisions without involving higher levels in the organization. It is, however, important that higher levels in the organizations allowed this kind of local decisions and that it was possible to buy technical support for it in the organization. We thus plan to broaden to scope further in future research.

Analysis

The activity of interest is networked learning at Human Centered Informatics at Aalborg University and the aim of the analysis is to reveal practices and problems with the existing system, and also ideas and positions to the new system. The data analysis has been organized in two steps – first we identified different groups involved in realizing networked learning at Human Centered Informatics and then we read and coded our data with the activity checklist in mind. The major groups identified were management, support, and key users, i.e., students and teachers. They are all important but of course they engage very differently and play different roles in realizing networked learning. In our report of the analysis, we go through the groups with focus on means and ends – the hierarchical structure of the activity. The hierarchical structure, that is the distinction between conditions, goals, and motives, opens for an understanding of different aspect of the use of technology, i.e., physical/technical interactions, conceptual interactions, and contextual interactions (Kuutti and Bannon 1993). Focus on means and ends imply furthermore that you start with identifying the goals of the various actions and then extend the scope of analysis both "up" to activity level and "down" to operations (Kaptelinin et al. 1999).

Management

The first theme, management, was informed by all interviews and by the students, but primarily by the interview with the manager of the program. This excerpt from the interview transcription (our translation) gives an impression of the statements of the head of program:

My only opinion is that we need to have a system that is super useful and super efficient for the students […] but we also need a system that matches the ambitions we have […] we need something that match these and I am told and can see myself that Moodle perhaps meets this requirement better than Quickplace. And also it may be argued that Moodle, which we agreed on relatively fast, is more scalable and easy to handle in terms of implementing supplementary systems as ELG or Mahara […] which we also have ambitions to do.

(Head of programme)

The motives directly or implicitly expressed by the head of program stress branding by use of state-of-the-art systems for networked learning. Since state-of-the-art shifts, he implicitly expresses a positive attitude toward change and implementation of a new technology. The head of program also emphasizes the students whom we interpret as his major concerns in the excerpt and in the interview in general. Emphasis on students is perhaps not surprising, but he could, however, also have chosen a more indirect approach to the students by bringing the working conditions of his administrative or teaching staff to the forefront of attention.

Lower in the hierarchical structure, we find the more concrete activity and goals of the management. He admits that he has only used the existing platform very little. He has, however, experienced some of the problems with the platform reported by others: Often response times are rather slow (and worse if you use the wrong browsers and operating systems) and from an esthetic point of view he regards the platform as a disaster. In relation to the change of infrastructure for networked learning he has put together an expert group of researchers and support staff to help him choose a new platform for networked learning. What the head of program wants from the new platform in terms of actual use is, however, unclear and, based on the interview, it is our impression that he likes it that way. He wants the experts to tell him and the teachers how to proceed.

When managing Human Centered Informatics, the research done by the teachers in the program is a prominent condition. It is so in more ways; firstly a relatively large research center in the department researches networked e-learning; secondly another research center in the department researches media and esthetics, and thirdly, research-based programs have to develop content (and form) as time goes by and research develops new insights. These conditions altogether pose a context that influences the management toward choosing state-of-the-art networked learning environments – and perhaps also to put more emphasis on the esthetics of the networked learning environments. Other prominent conditions are the pedagogical culture and the organizational readiness to implement new systems. These conditions are further discussed in the following sections.

Operation and Support

The operation and support of the learning platform are divided into two different tasks, the operation of the server and the support of users, that is students, teachers, and administrative staff, using the platform. The support task is taken care of by a special section and the following is primarily informed by our interview with two people from this section. The people working in the section have the overall responsibility for organizing the support task and they use a group of (hired) students to take care of much of the actual support. The following excerpt from the interview transcription (our translation) gives an impression on the issues that are emphasized by the support section.

> Our role has been to organize the support. What kind of support and how should we deliver it? Who is going to do what? And so on. We have a group of student employees, how do we divide tasks, coordinate the duty roster, etc. [...] we use mail lists and similar to communicate internally [...] part of the support is to document procedures, we have produced a manual on how to handle support, shift in semesters and so on, on e.g. Human Centered Informatics.

(ICT supporters)

The original design/appropriation of Lotus Quickplace was based on a questionnaire to students which revealed a wish for a flat structure with relatively immediate access to the particular places in the platform. Principles of immediate access and relevant overview have also guided the further appropriation of the platform, thus a major reorganization gave the users from Human Centered Informatics their own Lotus Quickplace with a common notice board and a room for each semester, recently a SMS service has been added in order to provide users with relevant information.

The ongoing support "peaks" every time a new semester is beginning and a major task for the support section is to make sure that all the semester forums/rooms on Lotus Quickplace are allocated with the right students, teachers, and courses. In the interview, the support people mention that they often hear students complain about the very different ways in which the system is used by the teachers. In other words, there are huge differences in the way the courses are organized, several teachers do not use it at all, etc., and that the students would like the teachers to follow a more uniform pattern of use. The support section have tried to accommodate these needs by developing a course forum template indicating the basic demands for content and offering support to teachers in setting up the courses. Without much success though as the teachers have shown no interest.

Much effort in the support section has been done to systematize and standardize the support task. Thus, a help list has been implemented to take care of the day-to-day support, FAQ-lists, list of general rules for use, formulas for requesting rooms for project groups, and a task-divisions list for internal use in the support section. Also, documentation of the various practices has been developed.

The target actions of the support section are the ongoing day-to-day support of the users and also an appropriation of the system. The main concern is on the day-to-day support and they try to organize this as effectively as possible. The overall goal or motive is to deliver effective, useful, and prompt support and, in order to do so; they have developed tools and procedures to follow both for the users and for themselves. Questions concerning how to use the systems, e.g., the dissatisfactions expressed by students about the teachers' use of the system and the teachers' lack of interest are of less concern.

Teachers and Students

The third theme, teachers and students, was informed by all interviews, by input from the students and by our reading of the Lotus Quickplace platform. The primary insights did, however, emerge from the teacher interview and from the inputs from the students. This excerpt from the interview transcription (our translation) gives an impression of the statements of the teacher:

> I would have liked to have more dialogue in Quickplace – I believed that I would have been able to make the students more active and thus I had planned to make a café […] for infor-mal talks […]. My experience from other settings is that if you add some fun elements it may motivate students to log in just from curiosity to see what is going on […]. Some of them did not want to blog, just out of principle because they were forced to do so […]. But as the course was about basic ICT we have also used other tools […].

> (Teacher).

The motives directly or implicitly expressed by the teacher points toward the peda-gogical model of the program (PBL) as a core motivation. She stresses the importance of student involvement and active participation in the learning processes. The motive of the teacher is, however, challenged by students that repeatedly argue for more standardized teacher-generated input – e.g., lectures and readings. We interpret this as the students strive for a reduction of the uncertainty and stress that may follow when teachers hand over the responsibility for tasks and problem solving to the students.

At the activity and goal-oriented level of the activity, much attention from both teachers and students seemed to be given to day-to-day planning and accomplishment of teaching and learning activities. The teacher structured activities and published information to students. Sometimes she also searched for information about the con-tent of other courses, but was often unsuccessful. The students spent time on finding out which activities they were expected to take part in and on preparing for the activi-ties by reading or meeting with other students to work on tasks or projects. The busy lives on both the teacher side as well as on the student side might lead to a contradic-tion founded in the division of labor: The teacher pushed tasks to the students and the students pushed tasks to teachers and administration. The input from students and from the interview with the support staff told us that a lot of students used the virtual group rooms in Lotus Quickplace to support collaboration in the project group work. Apparently, this practice was invisible to the management since a new facility for group collaboration was given less priority in the Moodle implementation (in spite of the emphasis on collaborative PBL) than the course management.

The conditions for teaching and learning practices indeed include the official pedagogical model of the organization: PBL in different shapes and forms is very difficult to avoid. The platform for networked learning offered is another important condition – today, it is Lotus Quickplace and, in the future, it will be Moodle.

Platforms of different kinds that teachers and students use in other contexts also influence the way they interpret the needs of Human Centered Informatics. The teacher we interviewed know the platform First class from another program and likes the way it supports dialogue – and the students point toward Facebook for a well-functioning platform for communication and collaboration.

Discussion

It appears from the analysis that a multitude of issues, practices, and opinions forms the experience of the system in use and the decision to implement a new one. Different kinds of dissatisfaction have been expressed. A prevalent issue echoed in almost all interviews is that the existing system is inflexible meaning that there are too many levels to go through in order to get the desired information in, e.g., a specific course room. Also in general, the users find the system slow in use, response time being too long and, too many operations are required in order to perform relatively simple actions as posting a piece of information. This experience forms a contrast to the intention of support staff to ease the user's access and overview. This point to the fact that overview is highly sensitive to the actual context, but perhaps also that reproducing the structure from the physical context, e.g., semesters and courses, might not be the best solution. Another issue of dissatisfaction is expressed in the students' request for a more consistent and homogeneous use of the system on the teachers' part. Differences in use span from rather sparsely information, like a link to another system or perhaps a course plan to comprehensive use from some teachers with lots of material, interactions, and dialogue opportunities distributed in several subrooms. Hence, there is a contradiction between the students' needs for uniformity and a clear line of direction in where to find what is expected on the one hand, and, on the other hand, the teachers' need for doing things in their own way. This contradiction, that exists on the organizational level will of course not be solved by implementing a new system. Instead, it points to a basic discussion of what kind of role the "official" system should have. Different systems and different use practices in educational activities are tolerated, which on the one hand gives the opportunity to experiment, to innovate or to do next to nothing, on the other hand this also means that the students have to tolerate a wide variety of systems and use practices. Although the meso-level design and use of networked learning are mature in the sense that they are integrated, supported and have the attention of management, it is not at all clear how networked learning more specifically is supposed to be practiced.

If Tyre and Orlikowski (1994) are right, then Human Centered Informatics only have a small window of opportunity in which the existing unsatisfactory practices can be changed. This case study compared to earlier case studies in the same organization also suggests that Tyre and Orlikowski are right – very few changes have actually happened since the early days of the implementation of Lotus Quickplace. This suggests a need to work systematically with the development of new practices around the implementation of Moodle. What a suitable approach to development of practices looks like depends on which perspective on change the organization adopts. De Freitas and Oliver (2005) list five different perspectives represented by five models: the fordist model, the evolutionary model, the ecological model, the community of practice model, and the discourse-oriented model. The fordist model implies a strong management and emphasis on division of labor, whereas the evolutionary, ecological, community of practice, and discourse models imply a focus on learning (e.g., through a series of smaller developmental steps over time) and the importance of communication in the organization. In this case, one could argue that the evolutionary learning-oriented model has failed so far since the pre-dominantly bottom-up approach to development by means of Lotus Quickplace has failed. This is, however, not to argue that the fordist model would be a better approach to change management in the organization. The evolutionary learning-oriented models still have something to offer, but management and other parties involved need to accept that the evolutionary models also call for active participation, intervention, evaluation, and dissemination in the organization for the learning to take place and inform future practice. This implies that some sort of management intervention is desirable if the organization is to secure an implementation of Moodle that helps to develop teaching and learning practice in Human Centered Informatics. Drawing on the inspiration from Stein et al. (2011), it seems reasonable to aim for a process model that integrates different kinds of support for teachers (and students) with different attitudes and approaches to ICT. Drawing on the inspiration from the activity checklist (Kaptelinin et al. 1999) and keeping in mind the critique expressed by management, teacher(s), and students regarding the lack of shared visions for the use of networked learning, it becomes increasingly evident that Human Centered Informatics needs to work on both the why (why networked learning?) and the how (how are we going to use networked learning?).

Conclusion

We set out to uncover the meso-level conditions under which institutional actors decide upon ICT strategies for networked learning purposes. Moreover, we have drawn on a definition stating that networked learning is learning in which ICT is used to promote connections between actors in the learning ecology. Just as we suspected actors in the organization have quite different reasons for suggesting strategies for change that are also quite different in nature. Based on our literature study, case study, and discussion there is no reason to conclude that one strategy is better or for that matter more correct than another. Each strategy and its associated goals suggested that change should focus on issues that are important to different kinds of actors. Instead of searching for *one* correct strategy, we suggest that organizations aim for a multitude of interacting change strategies. A multitude of strategies that interact would build on the multitude of perspectives we have observed in our case and be in concurrence with the idea that nodes in the network are different

Table 8.1 Dilemmas in implementation of networked learning

	Goals certain	Goals uncertain
Technology certain	(a) A well-known situation: technology as well as goals are certain	(b) Need for negation: technologies are known but goals are uncertain
Technology uncertain	(c) Need for experiments: overall goals are certain but how goals are best pursued is uncertain	(d) Need for inspiration: goals and technologies are both uncertain

and connects differently. There will, however, still be a need to balance common overall development goals and local private goals of individual teachers.

In Table 8.1, we generalize these findings in a Matrix inspired by Thompson and Tuden (1959). The purpose of the table is not to identify the situation as one of the four prototypical situations mentioned. On the contrary, it is an attempt to display the complexity in working with ICT strategies for networked learning purposes. In the case of Human Centered Informatics some actors and tasks are in one situation, whereas other actors and task are in another situation, and at the same time. There is also no indication that the organization should aim for a situation with complete agreement on goals and technology since it would hinder the dynamics of the developing learning network. On the contrary, the infrastructure should support both the ordinary services defined by agreement of goal and technology and leave room for trying out new ideas. And the point is that in order to develop networked learning practices in the organization there should also be incentives to experiment with different technologies (how) and to take part in discussion on the reasons for and values of networked learning (why).

References

Bell, F. (2010). Network theories for technology-enabled learning and social change: Connectivism and actor network theory. In *Proceedings of the Seventh International Conference on Networked Learning 2010*. Networked Learning 2010. Aalborg.

Bygholm, A., & Nyvang, T. (2009). An infrastructural perspective on implementing new educational technology. In L. Dirckinck-Holmfeld, C. Jones, & B. Lindström (Eds.), *Analysing networked learning practices in higher education and continuing professional development*. Rotterdam/Boston/Taipei: Sense Publishers.

Castells, M. (2000). *The rise of the network society* (IIth ed.). Malden, Oxford, Carlton: Blackwell Publishing.

Castells, M. (2001). *The internet galaxy: Reflections on the internet, business, and society*. Oxford: Oxford University Press.

de Freitas, S., & Oliver, M. (2005). Does E-learning policy drive change in higher education? A case study relating models of organisational change to e-learning implementation. *Journal of Higher Education Policy & Management, 27*(1), 81.

Dewey, J. (1910). *How we think*. Boston, New York, Chicago: D.C. Heath & Co.

Dirckinck-Holmfeld, L., Nielsen, J., Fibiger, B., Danielsen, O., Riis, M., & Sorensen, K. E. (2002). Designing virtual learning environments based problem oriented project pedagogy. In L. Dirckinck-Holmfeld & B. Fibiger (Eds.), *Learning in virtual environments*. Fredriksberg: Samfundslitteratur.

Dirckinck-Holmfeld, L., et al. (2009). Problem and project based networked learning: The MIL case. In L. Dirckinck-Holmfeld, C. Jones, & B. Lindström (Eds.), *Analysing networked learning practices in higher education and continuing professional development* (pp. 155–175). Rotterdam: Sense Publishers.

Engeström, Y. (1987). *Learning by expanding*. Helsinki: Orienta.

Engeström, Y. (2009). The future of activity theory: A rough draft. In A. Sannino, H. Daniels, & K. D. Gutiérrez (Eds.), *Learning and expanding with activity theory*. Cambridge: Cambridge University Press.

Flores, F., Graves, M., Hartfield, B., & Winograd, T. (1988). Computer systems and the design of organizational interaction. *ACM Transactions on Office Information Systems, 6*(2), 153–172.

Goodyear, P., Banks, S., Hodgson, V., & Mcconnell, D. (2004). Research on networked learning: an overview. In P. Goodyear et al. (Eds.), *Advances in research on networked learning*. Massachusetts: Kluwer Academic Publishers.

Jones, C., & Dirckinck-Holmfeld, L. (2009). Analysing networked learning practices. In L. Dirckinck-Holmfeld, C. Jones, & B. Lindström (Eds.), *Analysing networked learning practices in higher education and continuing professional development*. Rotterdam: Sense Publishers.

Jones, C., Dirckinck-Holmfeld, L., & Lindström, B. (2006). A relational, indirect, meso-level approach to CSCL design in the next decade. *International Journal of Computer-Supported Collaborative Learning, 1*(1), 35–56.

Jones, C. R., Ferreday, D., & Hodgson, V. (2008). Networked learning a relational approach: Weak and strong ties. *Journal of Computer Assisted Learning, 24*(2), 90–102.

Kaptelinin, V., & Nardi, B. (2006). *Activity theory and interaction design*. London, England: MIT Press.

Kaptelinin, V., Nardi, B., & Macaulay, C. (1999). Methods & tools: The activity checklist: A tool for representing the "space" of context. *Interactions, 6*(4), 27–39.

Kolmos, A., Fink, F., & Krogh, L. (2004). *The Aalborg PBL model – progress, diversity and challenges*. Aalborg: Aalborg University Press.

Koschmann, T. (1996). *CSCL: Theory and practice of an emerging paradigm*. Mahwah, NJ: Lawrence Erlbaum Associates.

Kuutti, K. (1996). Activity theory as a potential framework for human-computer interaction research. In B. Nardi (Ed.), *Context and consciousness: Activity theory and human-computer interaction* (pp. 17–44). Cambridge, MA: The MIT Press.

Kuutti, K., & Bannon, L. (1993). Searching for unity among diversity: Exploring the "interface" concept (Using the approach of activity theory). In *Proceedings of INTERCHI '93*. INTERCHI '93. Amsterdam: IOS Press.

Leont'ev, A. (1978). *Activity, consciousness, and personality*. Englewood Cliffs: Prentice-Hall.

Nyvang, T. (2006). Implementation of ICT in Higher Education. Proceedings of the Fifth International Conference on Networked Learning 2006. Lancaster: Lancaster. http://www.lancs.ac.uk/fss/organisations/netlc/past/nlc2006/abstracts/nyvang.htmUniversity. Accessed September 24th, 2011.

Nyvang, T. (2008). *Ibrugtagning af ikt i universitetsuddannelse (implementation of ICT in higher education)*. Aalborg: Aalborg University, Institut for Kommunikation.

Nyvang, T., & Tolsby, H. (2004). Students Designing ICT Support for Collaborative Learning in Practice. Proceedings of the Networked Learning Conference 2004. Lancaster: Lancaster University. Accesssed 24th September, 2011.

Nyvang, T. & Poulsen, C. R. (2007). Implementation of ICT in Government Organizations - User Driven or Management Driven? In A. M. Kanstrup, T. Nyvang, & E. M. Sørensen (Red.), Perspectives on e-Government: Technology & Infrastructure, Politics & Organization, and Interaction & Communication. Aalborg: Aalborg University Press.

Piaget, J. (1999). *The construction of reality in the child*. London: Routledge.

Ryberg, T., & Dirckinck-Holmfeld, L. (2010). Analysing digital literacy in action: A case study of a problem-oriented learning process. In R. Sharpe, H. Beetham, & S. De Freitas (Eds.), *Rethinking learning for a digital age* (pp. 170–183). New York: Routhledge.

Siemens, G. (2005). Connectivism: A learning theory for the digital age. *International Journal of Instructional Technology and Distance Learning, 2*(10), 3–10.

Spinuzzi, C. (2003). Tracing genres through organizations: A sociocultural approach to information design. In B. Nardi, V. Kaptelinin, & K. Foot (Eds.), *Acting with technology*. Cambridge, Massachusetts: The MIT Press.

Stahl, G., Koschmann, T., & Suthers, D. D. (2006). Computer-supported collaborative learning. In R. K. Sawyer (Ed.), *The Cambridge handbook of the learning sciences*. New York: Cambridge University Press.

Stein, S. J., Shephard, K., & Harris, I. (2011). Conceptions of e-learning and professional development for e-learning held by tertiary educators in New Zealand. *British Journal of Educational Technology, 42*(1), 145–165.

Thompson, J. D., & Tuden, A. (1959). Strategies, structures and processes of organizational decision. In J. D. Thompsom et al. (Eds.), *Comparative studies in administration*. Pittsburgh: University of Pittsburgh Press.

Tolsby, H., Nyvang, T., & Dirckinck-Holmfeld, L. (2002). A survey of technologies supporting virtual project based learning. In S. Banks (Ed.), *The third international conference on networked learning* (pp. 572–581). Sheffield, England: University of Sheffield.

Tyre, M., & Orlikowski, W. (1994). Windows of opportunity: Temporal patterns of technological adaptation in organizations. *Organization Science, 5*(198–118).

von Hippel, E. (1986). Lead users: A source of novel product concepts. *Management Science, 32*(7), 791–805.

Vygotsky, L. (1978). *Mind in society: The development of higher psychological processes*. Cambridge: Harvard University Press.

Part V
Understanding the Social Material
in Networked Learning

Chapter 9
Who's Taming Who? Tensions Between People and Technologies in Cyberspace Communities

Terrie Lynn Thompson

Introduction

> We routinely live at different scales, in different contexts, and at different settings – Default, Phone-only, Avatar On, Everything Off – on a number of screens, each with its own size, interface, and resolution, and across several time zones. We change pace often, make contact with diverse groups and individuals, sometimes for hours, other times for minutes, using means of communication ranging from the most encrypted and syncopated to the most discursive and old-fashioned, such as talking face-to-face ... We isolate ourselves in the middle of crowds within individual bubbles of technology, or sit alone at our computers to tune into communities of like-minded souls or to access information about esoteric topics (Antonelli 2008, 15–16).

The scale of the collective on the Internet astounds. Yahoo reports over 115 million members in its 10 million groups (Preimesberger 2010). Technorati (2008) reports 900,000 blog posts made every 24 h. In 2011, more than 500 million active users were on Facebook spending more than 700 billion minutes each month interacting with 900 million objects (i.e. pages, groups) (Facebook, 2011). According to YouTube (2011), 24 h of videos are uploaded to their site every minute, the equivalent of over 150,000 full-length movies each week. Although these statistics are in flux, they suggest that for many people, spaces and places on the Web have become an integral part of their lives. This may include seeking out learning opportunities in online communities. But how does one come to be connected with others for learning? How do people negotiate the materiality of screens and settings; discussion boards, RSS feeds and avatars; passwords and Facebook profiles?

To explore the implications of people and objects intertwined in materially imbued learning activities, this research study asks: "How do the interactions between Web technologies and self-employed workers shape work-related learning

T.L. Thompson (✉)
Athabasca University, Athabasca, AB, Canada
e-mail: terrie@ualberta.ca

L. Dirckinck-Holmfeld et al. (eds.), *Exploring the Theory, Pedagogy and Practice of Networked Learning*, DOI 10.1007/978-1-4614-0496-5_9,
© Springer Science+Business Media, LLC 2012

practices of self-employed workers in online communities?" Non-standard workers (including the self-employed) are a significant part of the labour force, often left on their own to create spaces for learning activities. Increasingly, workspaces are hybrid spaces – temporally, spatially and relationally – with this workforce perched precariously on the edge of such changes. Many people, including self-employed workers, are venturing into an array of online communities. The online communities of interest in this study were spaces *outside* the auspices of formal courses: gatherings of people online which are more organic and formed because people are interested in exploring a topic with others. Professional associations, workplaces and commercial enterprises may also nurture such spaces.

These digital terrains are replete with complex relational and material practices. In this chapter, I delve into the sociomaterial nature of informal work-related learning practices in such spaces. Because connectivity in cyberspace entails a mishmash of entanglements, alliances, resistances and willing partnerships between technology objects and (non)human actants, presencing of materiality is important. By bringing them out of the background, Web technologies and their politics in learning processes can be examined. This chapter also illustrates how Actor Network Theory (ANT) can be used to address such research questions, offering some additional theoretical resources to networked learning researchers.

Taking a relational view of learning, networked learning focuses on connections among learners, other people, learning resources and technologies (Goodyear et al. 2004). Learning is thus a connected, interactive and fluid process. Emphasized in the Networked Learning Manifesto (E-Quality Network 2002) is the need to attend to the connectivity between these diverse network elements as well as the processes, generated by such connectivity, which support learning. Although networked learning analysis does not necessarily privilege human–human relations (Jones et al. 2008), it is clear that appropriate conceptual and theoretical tools are required to explore other types of relations, particularly human–non-human associations. ANT is one perspective that enables both relational and material exploration of heterogeneous networks. Latour (2002, 250) muses, "We never tame technologies, not because we lack sufficiently powerful masters, not because technologies, once they have become 'autonomous', function according to their own impulse … but because they are a true form of mediation". We are never "in ourselves" but rather co-constituted with the objects around us. The nature of the co-constitutive and performative relationship between people and Web-computer technologies complicates work-learning practices online and encourages researchers to bring these Web technologies to critical inquiry.

ANT is a unique collection of *sociomaterial* understandings, concerned with associations between human and non-human actants in day-to-day practices. ANT creates an opening for regarding "technology" as one entity entwined in relation with other entities – human or non-human. Thus, objects, such as grass, can do things in the world, just as atoms and Popeye do (Harman 2009). The *principle of symmetry* emphasizes heterogeneous networks composed of people (humans) and objects (materials), both of which are treated analytically in the same way. ANT is a philosophical orientation, not a learning theory *per se*. Nevertheless, ANT emphasizes how learning (and other practices) emerges as the effect of a network of relations.

By studying particular webs of relations, researchers can better understand the sociomateriality of learning practices. As Fenwick (2010) explains, ANT challenges the overt focus on human processes in learning by foregrounding the material world and treating it as continuous with the human. This chapter draws on ANT to explore human–non-human connections and entanglements in an effort to deepen the understanding of different configurations of relationships possible within a networked learning perspective. Such an analysis does not reify objects, such as Web technologies, making them more important than human actors. Nor does it privilege or diminish the role of technology vis a vis pedagogy. Rather, ANT's contribution is to explore the associations that ensue when technologies become actants within networks and the effect of these entanglements on learning practices and processes, including pedagogy.

The chapter begins with how relationships between technologies and humans are positioned in the literature. I, then, explain how ANT was used to guide the analytic work in this research project. Data is presented to explore the sociomaterial nature of online work-related learning practices. The chapter concludes with a discussion of the political implications of such extensive entanglements between people and objects (namely, Web technologies).

Attending to Materiality

There is much said about how technology is framing new ways of knowing. Labelled the participatory Web, Web2.0 ostensibly offers openness, user control, dynamic participatory bottom-up construction of knowledge, sharing and collective intelligence. However, it is an amorphous term. Alexander (2006) explains that Web2.0 is often applied to a mix of familiar and emergent Web services. Others argue that Web2.0 is not just a set of technologies, but is a set of new *practices* (Bonderup Dohn 2008). Ryberg's (2008, 664) assertion is fitting: "It is not only a matter of adopting new technologies, but equally concerns the interaction between technological, pedagogical and organizational understandings of practice and knowledge".

The promise of online communities is wrapped up in the Web2.0 rhetoric and thus constructed by the media, developers of "community" software, the research literature and even educators. One assertion is that ways of knowing are changing because of the shift in how people use and create knowledge: a shift facilitated by Web-based technologies. In the more "socially connected Web, people can contribute as much as they consume" (Anderson 2007, 4). In this sense, knowledge becomes "decentred, multiple and less hierarchical" (Edwards and Usher 2008, 120). As relationships between people and technologies change, we are witnessing a change in our relationship with knowledge, what is meant by learning, and how learning progresses (Haythornthwaite 2008).

Bryant (2005, para. 4) explains that the shift in the way we communicate and collaborate "is not the technology itself – there is remarkably little that we can do now that wasn't possible 5 years ago – but rather the critical mass of connectivity between people that we are finally reaching". It would seem that it is the practices or, to use Young's (2006, 257) phrase, the "sociality" *around* Web2.0, not the properties of the technology itself, which drives this reconfiguration of ways of knowing. Access to social media applications does not automatically transform someone into a producer of knowledge. It is only when these new technology objects link to other objects and people – *creating new socialities* – that there is potential for these networks to generate new ways of knowledge creation: knowledge with its own social-material life. As this chapter illustrates, this is an uncertain, fractious and fluid process.

Overlooked, But Not Forgotten

Several issues become apparent in the Web2.0 literature: (a) despite cautionary voices, much rhetoric is generated by technology enthusiasts and commercial agendas; (b) empirical work on how Web technologies address pedagogical needs is a nascent area of research, with a strong focus on incorporation into formal classrooms and (c) technologies are often backgrounded or treated in an overly deterministic way. This chapter addresses the third critique by foregrounding relevant Web technologies and objects that knit together with human actants to form a sense of online community and the enactment of work-related learning practices.

Because objects "require new ways of interacting with them even as they find new ways to interact with us" (Waltz 2006, 56), it is vital to untangle the alliances between technologies and human actors. Objects are sidelined in many educational studies and theorizing. Yet, Web technologies are significant, given how they are enmeshed in changing ways of knowing, learning and working. Latour (2002, 248) argues that technologies belong to the human world in modalities other than "instrumentality, efficiency or materiality". He adds that instead, it is best to speak about technologies "in the mode of the *detour*". In other words, the mediation of technology experiments with *being-as-another* or *alterity*: without these technological detours, the "properly human cannot exist" (251). And so, hybrid subject–objects "emerge" within networks. Introna (2007, 14) uses the example of a consultant using a mobile phone. In using the mobile phone, the phone and the consultant are reconstituted. The phone "is no longer 'merely' an object and the consultant becomes a human that embodies the possibility to contact and be contacted at a distance". Thus, technologies and people fold into each other. Human and non-human actants are in a co-constitutive relationship.

ANT brings relevant objects to the forefront along with human actants and offers a different way to examine work-learning practices in online communities. ANT advocates that actants – human or non-human – are co-constituted in webs of relations with other actants. An actor-network exists only because of ties between entities. Callon (1987, 93) explains that "an actor-network is simultaneously an *actor* whose activity is networking heterogeneous elements and a *network* that is able to redefine and transform what it is made of" (emphasis added). It is through interactions between actants in networks that learning, ways of knowing and knowledge are performed. When actants are joined together, "stuff" (ideas, practices, actions, intentions, inscriptions, innovations) circulates in the conduits. ANT is interested in the work that goes on to build, maintain and disassemble these configurations and questions how actants end up juxtaposed and enacted with others.

Distinctions are often made between ANT and after-ANT. Law (2009) suggests that the new material semiotics is caught up in sensibilities, such as enactment, multiplicities, fluidity and ontological politics. Notions of obligatory passage points, centralized control and rigid actor-networks feature more prominently in early ANT studies. In this chapter, I draw on four ANT concepts, primarily from after-ANT theorizing as these best fit the nature of the phenomena explored: passages, translation, socio-technical constructions and black boxes. These concepts are explained throughout the chapter.

Exploring Actor-Networks

In an effort to bring Web technologies to critical inquiry, they are treated as key participants in this study. The participant list, therefore, included postings; avatars; tool bars; emoticons; archives; community member profiles; viruses; hyperlinks; the delete button; passwords and the technology that delivers postings, such as e-mail, discussion forum or RSS feed. Human actants included "newbies", "wannabes", colleagues, "big names", celebrities, competitors, posers, lurkers, employment recruiters, clients, friends, strangers and the online paparazzi.

Human participants in this study were own-account self-employed workers (contractors and consultants who do not have staffs). Semi-structured interviews, which varied in length from 1 to 2 h, were conducted with 11 self-employed workers to explore how they engaged with others online and how the online spaces and interactions described provided (or did not provide) a sense of online community. They ranged in age from 35 to 51. These workers had been self-employed for 6 months to 21 years and worked in a variety of fields: consultants (in international development, organizational change, leadership development or occupational health); the learning field (e-learning designer, corporate trainer, sessional university instructor); one was a sport psychologist, another was a graphic artist and another a day-care provider; two were entrepreneurs in the midst of (re)defining their business.

Regarding the non-human participants, Michael (2004, 20) argues that entities should not be "spoken 'about', 'for', or 'of'". Instead, the researcher "speaks 'with', 'by', 'through' and 'as' these entities". Therefore, my task as researcher was to collect data *with* these objects. I developed several heuristics for "interviewing" objects: follow the actors, study breakdowns and accidents, untangle tensions and construct co(a)gents (see Adams and Thompson 2011; Thompson 2010). Briefly, Latour (2005) advocates "following the actors", noticing what an actor – either human or material – is compelling other entities to do. Another strategy for catching glimpses of objects in motion is to study accidents and breakdowns. Michael (2000, 24) comments that when intermediaries break down, "we suddenly become aware of their mediating role: all the work … [and] arrangements that enable them to be ordinary, invisible, become spectacularly apparent". The third heuristic highlights how both stabilizations and disruptions are a necessary tension. Paying attention to efforts to stabilize *and* disrupt is another way to catch a glimpse of objects in interaction and helps to map many contradictions. Finally, Michael (2004) describes a *co(a)gent* as human and non-human operating together to produce patterns of connection. Using this concept, researchers can then trace the patterns of connections that comprise different co(a)agents.

Latour (2005) advises against starting with a pre-defined group and instead to follow the actors. In this spirit, I articulated the actor-networks implicated in the practices described by these self-employed workers and then started to unravel these. A list of 30 incidents was developed into 11 anecdotes. Each of these anecdotes served as an entry point for analysis. In Latour's terminology, these anecdotes enabled me to create conduits into the rest of my data and became layered as new associations and connections with other data came into focus. I was prompted to pull in other participants' experiences and continue to unravel networks. Choosing which entities to follow and networks to untangle is political decision made by the researcher. Following actors became an overwhelming task at times as more interactions and actants emerged. It is comforting to realize that the point is not to create an exhaustive list of all possible entities or to describe everything going on but rather to look for "mediators making other mediators do things" (Latour 2005, 217). Consistent with this focus, two anecdotes are presented and explored in this chapter. Each reflects a layering of other participants' experiences as well as inclusion of both human and non-human "voices". Readers interested in exploring other data from this study may refer to Thompson (2010).

In this study, online communities were not *containers* for online activities but rather *networks* of relations in flux: sociomaterial specificities constantly being enacted. These enactments led to different ways of knowing and different work-related learning practices. To examine how evolving inter-relationships between technologies and people shaped work-learning practices, one of my first realizations was that participating "in" an online community (which is itself constantly being performed) was a series of journeys and passages. It also became apparent that these passages or moves towards stabilizing tenuous actor-networks were countered by unpredictable disruptions, creating ongoing (dis)orderings that transformed networks. I begin with these explorations. A deeper examination of the entanglements between human and non-human actants led to questions about "who's taming who". The chapter concludes with an exploration of the politics of technology invoked by such extensive connectivity.

Passages and Journeys

Actants move. Networks shift. Relations stretch and sometimes rupture. Work-related learning in online communities is not a seamless or singular experience, as this data anecdote illustrates:

> Liz is part of a close online group that has recently moved from communicating via group e-mails to a "proper" discussion forum. The discussions are lively, people check in throughout the day, and they are learning. Their group has become popular and new people are asking to join. But these new people do not seem to participate. "We ask them to introduce themselves. Invite them to share their questions and opinions. Nothing". Behind the scenes, the original nine are disgruntled and e-mail each other back and forth. "This is not a community for lurkers", they say. With no public announcement they make a sudden move back to dialoguing by e-mail. Several years later, they are still e-mailing and a few of them get together. They have moved on in their careers, their work changed, the conversations different, but the relationships continue to grow stronger. Liz has no idea what happened to the discussion forum.

Even though this network is constantly mutating, it is searching for a workable configuration of technologies and people to keep them connected in the way they want. The sense of an ongoing journey suggests a "nomadic" actor-network. Moser and Law's (1999) exploration of dis/ability as the performance of specific passages between specific material arrays is helpful here. Brought into focus are the "character of the materials which en/able those passages and the arrays which secure or do not secure them" (201). Moser and Law explore "necessary passages" which order relations. "Good" passages are described as "moving smoothly between different specificities and their materialities. 'Bad' passages are about awkward displacements, movements that are difficult or impossible" (205). The notion of *passages* as fluid, multiple and performative changes to relations is a helpful ANT concept to explore how actor-networks shift. It does not presuppose, as in earlier ANT work, a centering obligatory passage point.

The assembly of actants described by Liz shifts several times, evoking a number of passages. The move from a small group connected by e-mail to a larger group with many new people in an online discussion forum is one passage. But this move transforms their daily exchanges into a fishbowl: a few people discussing and the rest looking on anonymously. This passage is not welcome. Instead of colleagues, they become performers and audience. The closing of ranks and movement back to e-mail – and enrolling other objects, such as birthday cards, telephone and dinner invitations – is a necessary passage for this small group to keep the collegial exchange in circulation. *Enrolment* is an ANT way of examining the way entities are brought into, or kept in, a network. Thus, birthday cards sent from one person to another help knit these people together. It seems that each passage brings about a different enactment of online community and a different enactment of work learning. Despite changes in the shape of these different configurations – or different specificities (in Moser and Law's (1999) terminology) – they are surprisingly fluid passages.

With each passage, there is a possibility that the actor-network might break apart. But there is something about the fluidity of the passages and objects in these networks that keep the enactment of the most important relations and conduits intact for over 12 years. Mol and Law (1994, 643) suggest that social space may behave like a fluid: "sometimes boundaries come and go, allow leakages or disappear altogether, while relations transform themselves without fracture". The series of configurations outlined by Liz suggest a series of passages, one version of a network gently morphing into another version. The core group of people, conversations and camaraderie stays intact, withstanding the disruptions of new people, the fishbowl configuration and the discussion forum technologies. Law (2002, 99) suggests that fluid objects help to enact a fluid form of space in part due to mobile boundaries. He is careful to point out that sometimes things and relations can change so much that they become unrecognizable. Liz's actor-networks do not change beyond recognition. Although each passage brings about a different enactment of online community, these *necessary* passages, abetted by fluid objects, serve to maintain the connections and circulations that are most valued.

Stabilizations and Upsets

Liz's collective is looking for a home, trying out configurations and moving on until it feels right. Despite ongoing (dis)assembly, this actor-network seeks stability. The data highlights how both the self-employed workers and Web technologies act to stabilize enactments of an online community. However, such networks are unpredictable and fraught with resistances. ANT theorists attend to both the stable and the fluid. Latour (2005) argues the importance of attending to what network elements have been stabilized, given that a "normal" state of any network is one of flux and unpredictability. Establishing and maintaining durable networks is a move to stability. However, small refusals and disconnections were evident in this study. As Moser and Law (1999) explain, not everything is as it seems. Passages may be presupposed or normatively prescribed and public smoothnesses often conceal both work and private disruptions.

These tensions are explored in this section, drawing on the key ANT tenet of *translation*. Translation describes the actions and alliances working to keep an actor-network functioning and stabilized. It is a way of arranging. Through a series of translations, entities interface with others, change and become linked. Fenwick and Edwards (2010, 12) explain: "ANT's notion of translation helps to unpick practices, processes and precepts to trace how things come to be".

In Liz's nomadic community, the sense of being infiltrated by outsiders has ripple effects throughout the network and leads to a stabilization. Purposefully excluding some cuts the network and shapes a new configuration which draws a tighter circle around a smaller group. A heightened sense of inclusion results. By excluding the new people who merely lurk, a new circulation is mobilized: a reaffirmation that, "*We* are all equally committed to this group and participate accordingly. *We* don't lurk". Enrolling objects to help the group close ranks is done purposefully. For example, as Liz explained, e-mail addresses are made available only to select people. They are not shared with all. When the group reverts back to e-mail, this bundle of technologies (objects) re-establishes boundaries. New actants, such as birthday cards and dinner invitations, are then enrolled and help stabilize this new configuration.

Upsets and refusals can also lead to stabilizations through a reordering of elements. Changing media is a resistance by Liz's group to the upset of "infiltration" by outsiders. Reordering leads to a new and stable configuration. However, stabilizations are ongoing negotiations. As Nespor (1994, 12) writes, "networks expand, contract, and shift configuration over time, and even the most stable and predictable of them are constantly being reappropriated and redefined by the nature of the flows that animate them".

At times, networks are too porous. Entities are easily hijacked and moved into different configurations, creating upsets. For example, in order to make an online space conducive to learning, people share. Making postings, sharing attachments, sending and reading private messages and disclosing personal information are common. In the following anecdote, these kinds of texts flowed freely until an incident:

> Lee feels very comfortable in his online community. It is a close knit group and they are online almost every day. One day he opens an attachment from a new community member only to discover it is loaded with viruses that proceed to attack his hard drive. It also contains personal and private information about him. He spends the next year trying to erase all records of his identity on the Internet.

This is an upset. This is not supposed to happen. Lee becomes more cautious. His relationship to other Web-based technologies changes. Artefacts strewn over the Web now seem to reveal rather than just share – they have become things that need to be hidden, destroyed or managed. Information is translated from something that is shared, in order to build a connection and learn with others, into something that reveals. Lee's online practices change as he resists this intrusion and tries to prevent future incidents by making his Internet presence less ephemeral so he can better control it.

This is a passage about digital trails and online security. It is not an easy journey. One's Internet presence – the places you have been and the things you said and did – is amalgamated and translated into a *digital trail*, which is public and not easy to alter. Attending to online security and its related technologies (objects) has become a necessary passage. There are ongoing negotiations of boundaries as Lee wrestles with how much public exposure he can tolerate. For Lee, these ongoing negotiations to be protected, unexposed and virus-free have become more onerous. The perception of connection to others with just a click of a key knits together all sorts of assumptions and alliances. Lee's experience reveals that there can be a price for a sense of connection online.

Who's Taming Who?

Instability is inherent in stable relations between actants. Actants juxtaposed in an actor-network come and go, change and want different things. For most of these self-employed workers, there was a sense of wanting to be able to control the interactions in their online communities enough to reap the benefits efficiently while at the same time being open to the serendipitous way of learning offered by the Web. The actants' stories are rife with attempts to tame or discipline; attempts to order. As human actants attempt to tame the technology, the technologies in use are doing their part to tame other actants. Participants want to control their online inter-actions and work hard to make them efficient and predictable. They are well-aware that time online can get out of control resulting in billable time lost and unproductive distractions. They enrol numerous objects in this quest: filters, the delete button, subject lines, the clock, clicking on "unsubscribe" and opting for digest versions of online conversations. At the same time, the technologies in use in this research study are doing their part to discipline other actants. One such strategy is to make things (appear to be) easy to do. Reliance on default settings and delegating tasks to the technologies (objects) is apparent. Some people stay in an online community simply because by default the technology continues to keep them connected: messages just keep coming into an inbox. Digest versions of online conversations are a delegation to technology to amalgamate and forward – daily or weekly – a compilation of all the contributions to the discussion forums.

Socio-Technical Constructions

Both technologies and human actants are busy taming each other in attempts to (dis)order passages. But not in a deterministic way, as ANT moves past that thinking. The data describes entanglements between humans and non-humans that make it very difficult to separate the two. Rather, these self-employed workers and the Web technologies in use are *co-constituted* in the work-learning practices described. Introna (2007, 14) states that technologies "fold into us as much as we fold into them". Think about a consultant with a cell phone, a chef and his knives, the doctor and her stethoscope. Suchman (2007, 286) concludes that it is not about "assigning agency either to persons or to things but to identify the materialization of subjects, objects, and the relations between them as an effect … of ongoing sociomaterial practices".

The ANT notion of co-constitution is important here. Michael (2000) suggests that rather than speaking of humans and objects as two distinct entities, perhaps both are *socio-technical constructions*: hybrid human and object entanglements. In this study, a prominent entanglement is one's digital trail, a hybrid of text/images + the screen + hyperlinks + the person. As Lee discovers, his Internet presence is translated into a *digital trail* over which he has limited control. Yet, one's digital presence is often important professionally. Boyd (2006, 14) states that "from the flow of text in chatrooms to the creation of Profiles, people are regularly projecting themselves into the Internet so that others may view their presence and interact directly with them". As these self-employed workers explained, it is logical to expect that others, such as potential clients or partners, Google you. The socio-technical construction of one's digital trail mediates boundaries between private and public worlds, ability to manage one's professional image and perceptions of control and ownership. The complexity and sophistication of the hybrids in circulation, such as one's digital trail, raises questions, which I explore in the next section.

The Politics of Technology

This chapter has explored sociomaterial interactions between Web technologies and self-employed workers. I employ one of the classic and productive ANT approaches to further untangle the co-constitutive nature of online work-learning practices: opening *black boxes*. Latour (1987) explains that when many elements are made to act as one, a black box is created. By patiently tracing threads between human and non-human actants that appear to be unified and/or foolproof, ANT researchers unpack networks of alliances, often reawakening controversies (Harman 2009).

The relational and material dimensions of learning practices has implications. Introna (2007, 15) writes that folded into the "nexus of human and technology relationships are (un)intentions, (im)possibilities, (dis)functions, affordances/prohibitions that renders possible some ways of being and not others, that serves the (il) legitimate interests of some and not others". ANT contributions to this debate come from Latour's insistence on acknowledging the place of non-human actants within a political remit (making things public) and Law and Mol's work on ontological politics which recognizes multiple, overlapping and contested networks and realities. Three issues were highlighted by the data in this study and critical to work-learning practices in online communities: delegation, invisible practices and necessary literacies. Each presents opportunities for further study.

Delegation

In this study, when a person participates in an online collective, objects offer – or are chosen – to distribute a person's commentary. These technologies take on the role of archiving, indexing and amalgamating this content. Some of these delegations are more visible than others and a person may be given some options. Nevertheless, bits and pieces of one's activities often become black boxed by technologies into something more opaque than transparent. Indeed, ubiquitous computing is designed with the premise that technologies will fade into the background (van Dijk 2010).

Introna (2007) states that although decisions and actions are often delegated to technology because it is convenient or necessary, we are often unaware of what we have delegated and always delegate more than we realize. While we can appreciate gains in usefulness, efficiency or convenience, awareness of the subtle changes in our way of being emerges over longer periods of time. For example, Chesher (2002, 7) declares that when learning new software, "I have tied myself to an upgrade path. The tasks become habitual and I can no longer perform them without this software". Think about the ubiquity of e-mail and how many of us have tied ourselves to being an e-mailer. Juxtaposed with Web-computer technologies, our way of communicating and being has changed over time.

It is the arrival of the virus that sparks Lee's realization of how revealing his digital trail is. Yet, *not* engaging with an array of objects and Web technologies makes it impossible to be someone who is connected online or to engage in learning online. There is much discussion around privacy, security and ownership of Web and e-mail data. Anderson (2007, 52) speculates that if some of the more negative aspects of Web2.0 persist, "it is quite possible to envisage … 'Web 3.0' as a backlash to Web2.0: where software that 'cleans up' after you, erasing your digital path through the information space, and identity management services, are at a premium". Diligently opening black boxes is crucial to managing the potential negative implications of delegating done in the cause of "online presence". Latour (2005) maintains that ANT's distinctive politics can highlight how relations come to be stabilized so that "matters of concern" are not quietly and prematurely turned into "matters of fact".

Invisible Work

By opening black boxes, the invisible is made momentarily visible. After a strong focus for a decade on actants *in* the network, there is a noticeable shift among ANT theorists to explore the "stuff" not present – the invisible. Attending to the *not so visible* is a political move. Law (2004) advocates more ontological radicalism to attend to difference and to reach the elusive, absent and other. Because the Internet has become an everyday technology – mundane and accessible – we often do not think twice about the complex work that goes into being engaged online. In her research on a public health initiative, Singleton (2005, 782) concludes that "the practices that construct the mundanity and accessibility [of the program] also serve to make the complexity and heterogeneity of the work of practice invisible". Considering online learning, Haythornthwaite (2008, 599) draws attention to how the hype over online communities ignores the efforts and techniques embedded in roles which are "now swept away as every individual is [her/his] own teacher, journalist, librarian, writer, and publisher".

The work that Lee now takes on daily to ensure a safe online presence is not something that most self-employed workers can include as billable time. The work that Liz's group did over the years to build a connected and collegial space conducive to learning was largely invisible to, and perhaps not appreciated by, the new people who entered *en masse*. The efforts that go into finding and joining an online space are likewise sidelined. The works done by all the participants in this study to build appropriate online literacies are expected and unremarkable, despite the significant outlay of time, money and effort reported.

Information and Media Literacies

Despite the wide-open nature of the Web, there are differences in the way people are able to access and leverage learning opportunities. Data suggests that discontinuities in this study included uneven distributions of: pre-existing knowledge and networks, ease grasping and working within community norms, capacity to connect with the right people, skill in framing questions and ability to participate online (and take it offline) in ways that enhance learning. Although the technology for the most part is not overly complex, it did create complex situations for some participants around online safety, anonymity and privacy. Being disciplined and strategic is an essential aspect of informal learning practices in an online context. This seemed to be easier for some than others. Singleton (2005) maintains that when access and competence are unevenly distributed, different capacities to negotiate specific technologies become evident: a political issue.

In this study, configurations did not always successfully align to achieve the sense of community most conducive to these workers' purposes. The notion of "community" is well-known (albeit often problematic) and the technology in many instances is little more complicated than e-mail. Yet, as this study has shown, the enactment of learning comprised new objects, relations and mobilization of practices. Adult educators risk underestimating the literacies required to participate in these online spaces if these spaces are seen as little different than e-mail or doing a Google search. These literacies encompass more than being able to use technology. They include ethical and responsible use of the Internet, attending to safety on the Internet and ability to navigate complex intellectual property, privacy, data security and authenticity issues (Oblinger 2008).

Conclusion

This chapter explores the sociomaterial interactions between Web technologies and self-employed workers engaged in work-related learning in online communities in order to gain insight into the politics of technology and the implications of such profound intertwining of people and objects in everyday learning practices. Although networked learning acknowledges the significance of technology in the co-construction of knowledge (see Beaty et al. 2010), trying to understand human–technology entanglements is a complex undertaking and a relatively new area of educational research. In this chapter, I have drawn on ANT in an effort to explore such juxtapositions. I drew on four ANT concepts to guide data analysis: passages, translation, socio-technical constructions and black boxes. As Fox (2009) explains, applying ANT to such questions entails seeing the learner and the learning process in a distinctive way: as network effects.

Networked learning researchers and practitioners seem to be interested in more radical pedagogies, often taking a critical stance towards the role of technology. ANT provides useful conceptual tools for trying to get at the particular and everyday, especially practices which have become taken for granted or opaque. Law (2007, 126) writes that if practices do cohere as learning practices, this is only temporary, and paradoxically if practices look streamlined, then it is because the bits that do not fit and the choreography that holds it all together are not visible or understood. ANT can be used to explore this work of choreography, especially the networked relationships between human and non-human actants. Through such analysis, ANT provides another way networked learning can explore the politics of technologies used in learning processes.

Web2.0 (and whatever comes next) offers fascinating ways to rethink how we experience learning, knowing, connecting and working with others. To sort through the rhetoric that accompanies technology advances, examining the specificities of material entanglements is paramount for understanding the experience of work-related learning online. Pels et al. (2002, 1) proclaim that objects are back in strength: "Talking to intelligent machines … being glued to mobile phones, roving around in cyberspace … is to mingle our humanity with not-so-mute, active, performative objects in a way which we find equally fascinating as disconcerting". The objects that were part of this research study were at times fluid, approachable, elastic, prickly or opaque. Nevertheless, these are the objects that interact with human actants to co-create learning environments. As this chapter highlighted, such entanglements raise questions about delegation, invisible work and necessary information and media literacies.

References

Adams, C., & Thompson, T. L. (2011). Interviewing objects: Including educational technologies as qualitative research participants. *International Journal of Qualitative Studies in Education*, 1–18. http://www.tandfonline.com/action/showAxaArticles?journalCode=tqse20

Alexander, B. (2006). Web 2.0: A new wave of innovation for teaching and learning? *EDUCAUSE Review, 41*(2), 33–44.

Anderson, P. (2007). *What is Web 2.0? Ideas, technologies and implications for education* (JISC Technology and Standards Watch). Retrieved from JISC website: http://www.jisc.ac.uk/media/documents/techwatch/tsw0701b.pdf

Antonelli, P. (2008). Design and the elastic mind. In L. Hruska & R. Roberts (Eds.), *Design and the elastic mind* (pp. 14–27). New York, NY: The Museum of Modern Art.

Beaty, L., Cousin, G., & Hodgson, V. (2010). Revisting the e-quality in networked learning manifesto. In L. Dirckinck-Holmfeld, V. Hodgson, C. Jones, M. de Laat, D. McConnell, & T. Ryberg (Eds.), *Proceedings of the 7th International Conference on Networked Learning 2010*. Available from http://www.lancs.ac.uk/fss/organisations/netlc/past/nlc2010/index.htm

Bonderup Dohn, N. (2008). Knowledge 2.0 – tensions and challenges for education. *Proceedings of the 6th International Conference on Networked Learning* (pp. 650–657). Retrieved from http://www.networkedlearningconference.org.uk/past/nlc2008/Info/confpapers.htm#Top

Boyd, D. (2006). G/localization: When global information and local interaction collide. Paper presented at the O'Reilly Emerging Technology Conference. Retrieved from http://www.danad.org/papers.Etech2006.html

Bryant, L. (2005, January 6). Blogs are not the only fruit [Web log message]. Retrieved from http://headshift.com/blog/2005/01/blogs-are-not-the-only-fruit.php

Callon, M. (1987). Society in the making: The study of technology as a tool for sociological analysis. In W. E. Bijker, T. P. Hughes, & T. J. Pinch (Eds.), *The social construction of technological systems: New directions in the sociology and history of technology* (pp. 83–103). Cambridge, MA: MIT Press.

Chesher, C. (2002). Why the digital computer is dead. *CTheory*, a106. Retrieved from http://www.ctheory.net/printer.aspx?id=334

Edwards, R., & Usher, R. (2008). *Globalisation and pedagogy: Space, place and identity* (2nd ed.). Milton Park, England: Routledge. doi:10.1080/158037042000225191.

E-Quality Network. (2002). *E-quality in e-learning Manifesto.* Presented at the Networked Learning 2002 conference, Sheffield, available at http://csalt.lancs.ac.uk/esrc/

Facebook. (2011). *Statistics.* Retrieved from http://www.facebook.com/press/info.php?statistics

Fenwick, T. (2010). Re-thinking the "thing": Sociomaterial approaches to understanding and researching learning in work. *Journal of Workplace Learning, 22*(1/2), 104–116. doi:10.1108/13665621011012898.

Fenwick, T., & Edwards, R. (2010). *Actor-network theory in education.* Abingdon, UK: Routledge.

Fox, S. (2009). Contexts of teaching and learning: An actor-network view of the classroom. In R. Edwards, G. Biesta, & M. Thorpe (Eds.), *Rethinking contexts for learning and teaching: Community, activities, and networks* (pp. 31–43). New York, NY: Routledge.

Goodyear, P., Banks, S., Hodgson, V., & McConnell, D. (2004). Research on networked learning: An overview. In P. Goodyear, S. Banks, V. Hodgson, & D. McConnell (Eds.), *Advances in research on networked learning* (pp. 1–11). Dordrecht: Kluwer Academic Publishers.

Harman, G. (2009). *Prince of networks: Bruno Latour and metaphysics.* Melbourne, Australia: Repress.

Haythornthwaite, C. (2008). Ubiquitous transformations. *Proceedings of the 6th International Conference on Networked Learning* (pp. 598–605). Retrieved from http://www.networkedlearningconference.org.uk/past/nlc2008/Info/confpapers.htm#Top

Introna, L. (2007). Maintaining the reversibility of foldings: Making the ethics (politics) of information technology visible. *Ethics and Information Technology, 9*(1), 11–25. doi:10.1007/s10676-006-9133-z.

Jones, C. R., Ferreday, D., & Hodgson, V. (2008). Networked learning a relational approach: Weak and strong ties. *Journal of Computer Assisted Learning, 24*(2), 90–102. doi:10.1111/j.1365-2729.2007.00271x.

Latour, B. (1987). *Science in action: How to follow scientists and engineers through society.* Cambridge, MA: Harvard University Press.

Latour, B. (2002). Morality and technology: The ends of the means. (C. Venn, Trans.). *Theory, Culture & Society, 19*(5/6), 247–260.

Latour, B. (2005). *Reassembling the social: An introduction to actor-network theory.* Oxford, England: Oxford University Press.

Law, J. (2002). Objects and spaces. *Theory, Culture & Society, 19*(5/6), 91–105.

Law, J. (2004). *After method: Mess in social science research.* Milton Park, England: Routledge.

Law, J. (2007). Pinboards and books: Juxtaposing, learning, and materiality. In D. W. Kritt & L. T. Winegar (Eds.), *Education and technology: Critical perspectives, possible futures* (pp. 125–149). Lanham, MD: Lexington Books.

Law, J. (2009). Actor network theory and material semiotics. In B. S. Turner (Ed.), *The new Blackwell companion to social theory* (pp. 141–158). Chichester, England: Wiley-Blackwell.

Michael, M. (2000). *Reconnecting culture, technology and nature: From society to heterogeneity.* London, England: Routledge.

Michael, M. (2004). On making data social: Heterogeneity in sociological practice. *Qualitative Research, 4*(1), 5–23. doi:10.1177/1468794104041105.

Mol, A., & Law, J. (1994). Regions, networks and fluids: Anaemia and social topology. *Social Studies of Science, 24*(4), 642–671.

Moser, I., & Law, J. (1999). Good passages, bad passages. In J. Law & J. Hassard (Eds.), *Actor network theory and after* (pp. 196–219). Oxford, England: Blackwell Publishers.

Nespor, J. (1994). *Knowledge in motion: Space, time and curriculum in undergraduate physics and management.* London, England: The Falmer Press.

Oblinger, D. G. (2008). Growing up with Google: What it means to education. In *Emerging technologies for learning* (Vol. 3, pp. 11–29). Retrieved from http://www.becta.org.uk/research/reports/emergingtechnologies

Pels, D., Hetherington, K., & Vandenberghe, F. (2002). The status of the object: Performances, mediations, and techniques. *Theory, Culture & Society, 19*(5/6), 1–21.

Preimesberger, C. (2010). *Yahoo refreshes, upgrades some products.* Retrieved from http://www.eweek.com/c/a/Search-Engines/Yahoo-Refreshes-Upgrades-Some-Products-775120/

Ryberg, T. (2008). Challenges and potentials for institutional and technological infrastructures in adopting social media. In *Proceedings of the 6th International Conference on Networked Learning* (pp. 658–665). Retrieved from http://www.networkedlearningconference.org.uk/past/nlc2008/Info/confpapers.htm#Top

Singleton, V. (2005). The promise of public health: Vulnerable policy and lazy citizens. *Environment and Planning D: Space and Society, 23*(5), 771–786. doi:10.1068/d355t.

Suchman, L. A. (2007). *Human-machine reconfigurations: Plans and situated actions* (2nd ed.). Cambridge, England: Cambridge University Press.

Technorati. (2008). *State of the blogosphere 2008.* Retrieved from http://technorati.com/blogging/state-of-the-blogosphere/

Thompson, T. L. (2010). *Assembly required: Self-employed workers' informal work-learning in online communities.* PhD dissertation, University of Alberta.

Van Dijk, N. (2010). Property, privacy and personhood in a world of ambient intelligence. *Ethics and Information Technology, 12*(1), 57–69. doi:10.1007/s10676-009-9211-0.

Waltz, S. B. (2006). Nonhumans unbound: Actor-network theory and the reconsideration of "things" in educational foundations. *Educational Foundations, 20*(3/4), 51–68.

Young, N. (2006). Distance as a hybrid actor in rural economies. *Journal of Rural Studies, 22*(3), 253–266. doi:10.1016/j.jrurstud.2005.11.007.

YouTube. (2011). *Statistics.* Retrieved from (2011). *Statistics.* Retrieved from http://www.youtube.com/t/press_statistics

Chapter 10
Learning Technology in Context: A Case for the Sociotechnical Interaction Framework as an Analytical Lens for Networked Learning Research

Linda Creanor and Steve Walker

Introduction

In this chapter, we argue that there have been limitations in the learning technology literature related to a widespread implicit technological determinism. While the concept of networked learning goes some way to redress this, a more systematic use of sociotechnical findings theories developed in the fields of technology studies and information systems can help us to avoid mechanistic accounts. This has frequently contributed to gaps between the claims made for learning technologies and the reality of their use. The study of networked learning as a distinctive aspect of learning technology practice has countered this to some extent by placing the emphasis on communication and connections (Goodyear et al. 2004; McConnell 2006) and their relationship to learning (Dirckinck-Holmfeld 2010). Indeed our critique is underpinned by the definition of networked learning proposed by Jones and Steeples (2002) who describe it as:

> …learning in which information and communication technology (C&IT) is used to promote connections: between one learner and other learners; between learners and tutors; between a learning community and its learning resources (2002, p. 2).

This understanding of the relationship between learning and technology does not necessarily require a new theory of *learning* (Mayes and de Freitas 2007). Rather, it emphasises the social, rather than individual or knowledge-process aspects of learning (Goodyear 2002). This socio-cultural perspective is particularly relevant in the evolving landscape of networked learning where learners are

L. Creanor (✉)
Caledonian Academy, Glasgow Caledonian University, Glasgow, UK
e-mail; l.creanor@gcu.ac.uk

S. Walker
Department of Communications and Systems, The Open University, Milton Keynes, UK

L. Dirckinck-Holmfeld et al. (eds.), *Exploring the Theory, Pedagogy and Practice of Networked Learning*, DOI 10.1007/978-1-4614-0496-5_10,
© Springer Science+Business Media, LLC 2012

appropriating mobile, Web 2.0 and social media technologies and educators are seeking to use them to enrich the learning experience. It also resonates strongly with the democratic and inclusive nature of the trade union education context within which much of our own research has been conducted (e.g. Creanor and Walker 2005; Walker and Creanor 2009).

In the networked learning domain the focus has often been on the impact of asynchronous discussion forums, in the main within carefully designed formal learning contexts (e.g. Kear 2004; Ellis and Calvo 2004), and often problematising the issue of communication in terms of "best fit" for the technology platform (McAteer et al. 2002; Hammond 1999).

> ... engaging in online textual discourse, attenuated over time and space, or packed densely into a realtime chat, is a central practice of much networked learning and teaching (Goodyear 2009, p. viii).

Recent research has begun to recognise the social elements of technology use more explicitly with its emphasis on the learner perspective (Hardy and Bates 2009; Sharpe et al. 2010), providing an important, though incomplete, corrective to technology-centred views of the learning experience. This leads to a consideration of learning at levels beyond the individual and also opens the door to consideration of a stratified model of learning taking account for example, of learning at the group, organisational or community levels (e.g. Pawlowsky 2001).

Going further, there are traditions of studying technology generally, and information and communications technology in particular, which view its use as the outcome, rather than the instigator, of complex interactions between people and the material world (Law and Hassard 1999). These traditions include social informatics (Kling 2000), social shaping of technology (Mackenzie and Wacjman 1999), soft systems (Checkland and Holwell 1998), sociotechnical systems (Trist and Bamforth 1951) and others. They have yielded a collection of "mid-range" theories and concepts which, we suggest, have been under-utilised in studies of networked learning. Further, this lack of consideration of the interaction between social agency and learning artefacts has frequently resulted in stark discrepancies between the claims made about the potential of particular technologies and the subsequent realities of their use in a learning context (Selwyn 2007; Laurillard 2005).

A distinguishing feature of networked learning research is its focus on socio-cultural theories (Jones and Dirckinck-Holmfeld 2009), including those of Lave and Wenger (1991), Wenger (1998) and Engeström (1999), which often look beyond formal learning to informal communities of practice and learning within organisations. In this context, shared goals and the co-construction of knowledge are key aspects. Elsewhere, learning technology research has drawn primarily on educational theories of learning, which place the emphasis on the cognitive or socio-cognitive processes of developing personal knowledge and understanding (Mayes and De Freitas 2007; Jonassen and Land 2000).

In this chapter, we contend that sociotechnical approaches developed in technology studies, and in particular the study of information systems (IS) and information and communication technologies (ICT) can also provide a rich source of concepts which are under-used in the networked learning literature. We illustrate this with a brief summary of our own use of one of these, Kling et al. (2003) "sociotechnical interaction network (STIN)." We conclude by arguing that these approaches in general, and the STIN concept in particular, are important conceptual tools in dealing with issues currently confronting contemporary networked learning research, such as the spread of Web 2.0 and mobile technologies, the increasingly complex social and technological contexts of many learners, and the increasingly blurred distinction between abstract and formal learning, and situated informal learning.

Limitations in the Literature

We have asserted previously that understanding the complex relationship between learning and technology requires a theoretical framework which takes into account a diverse range of sociotechnical and environmental factors (Walker and Creanor 2009). Historically, attempts to interpret this relationship through a purely mechanistic lens have displayed significant weaknesses, most notably in the dissonance between claims made for the effectiveness of technology for learning and empirical evidence. Indeed as Selwyn points out there is,

> ...a growing need for the education community to account for the distinct 'digital disconnect' between the enthusiastic rhetoric and rather more mundane reality of university ICT use (2007, p. 84).

The literature reveals an uneasy relationship between pedagogy, technology and agency, with a persistent technological determinism limiting a more careful analysis of the nature of this interplay. The implementation and use of technology in education often appear resistant to repeated pleas for evidence-informed pedagogy (Laurillard 2009; Conole and Oliver 2007) and are frequently driven by political agendas and tactical funding opportunities (Hughes 2008; Conole et al. 2007; Clegg et al. 2003). Most recently, this can be seen in responses to the spread of collaborative technologies such as mobile devices and Web 2.0 applications which, while not designed primarily for learning, are being embraced by educators in a *"creative explosion of new ideas"* (Laurillard 2009, p. 5) in a context where social networking is a well-established presence in the lives of many learners (Jones and Ramanau 2009; Creanor et al. 2008). Indeed we are warned of *"a crisis looming and a paradox emerging"* (Traxler 2009, p. 70) over issues of agency, ownership and control in light of the rapid evolution of these devices and applications and their adoption by learners. It can be seen too in the attention commanded by immersive 3D virtual worlds as claims about their educational potential become more widespread (Bayne 2008; Bronack et al. 2008). Here again many accounts default to technologically determinist, with rapid technological and social changes leading developments in education, often at the expense of pedagogy and theory.

It is becoming increasingly challenging for educators to keep pace with, and make sense of, the speed of technological change, while simultaneously responding to demands for learning experiences which develop the capacity for the collaborative, as well as independent, learning skills now increasingly demanded of graduates in the workplace (e.g. Nielsen 2009). It is against this background that a shift in emphasis appears to be taking place, from a predominantly evaluative approach to an increasingly theoretical analysis of the educational potential of these constantly evolving collaborative technologies (e.g. Code and Zaparyniuk 2009; Savin-Baden 2008).

While the need for an inter-disciplinary approach to theory is recognised (Oliver et al. 2007; Jones and Steeples 2002), the epistemological foundation for learning technology research derives predominately from traditional theories of learning, with social constructivism continuing to lead the field (e.g. Jones and Bronack 2008; Parker and Chao 2007; Felix 2005). Nonetheless, it is clear that the boundaries between education systems and the wider sociotechnical environment are becoming increasingly blurred. Recognising this, research into networked learning has placed the emphasis on *"epistemic fluency"* (Goodyear 2009, p. x), invoking a broader range of theoretical frameworks, including, among others, network theory (e.g. Jones 2004), actor network theory (e.g. Fox 2002), complexity and chaos theory (e.g. Barnett 2000) as well as the concept of communities of practice (e.g. Ryberg and Larson 2008). With the exception perhaps of Lave and Wenger's (1991) communities of practice or Wenger's (1998) learning communities model, there is little evidence in the literature of widespread adoption of these frameworks within "mainstream" learning technology research or practice where the networked learning metaphor may not appear immediately relevant, for example in a campus-based, blended learning context (e.g. Bonk and Graham 2006; Oliver and Trigwell 2005). As attention shifts increasingly towards the affordances of collaborative and social networking, however, new perspectives are relating learning technology and social practices more closely by harnessing the concepts of "the collective" (Dron and Anderson 2009) and "connectivism" (Siemens 2004). These emerging theories, while still relatively untested, claim to provide alternative lenses through which learning in the Web 2.0 world may be examined. A potential danger in this approach, however, is in tipping the balance towards social agency at the expense of individual autonomy.

The learner experience debate of recent years, again given added momentum by the availability of strategic funding and the "popularised" interest in the net generation, has helped to shift the focus from the relatively narrow confines of formal education to the wider consequences of technology use in the everyday lives of learners (Sharpe et al. 2009; De Freitas and Conole 2010). Studies of the agency of individual learners in the appropriation of social media and personal mobile devices for learning purposes have shed new light on previously hidden attitudes and behaviours (Creanor and Trinder 2010; Czerniewicz et al. 2009). Nevertheless there is a growing recognition that a focus on the individual and their personal networks often fails to take fully into account the impact of context (Jones and Healing 2010). Here, theoretical approaches have drawn on activity theory (Engeström et al. 1999) and more recently critical realism's concepts of morphogenesis/morphostatis (Archer 1995). It would appear then, that alongside a growing recognition of the multiplicity of factors which can influence learning in a technology-rich context, there is a greater appreciation of the need for appropriate sociotechnical frameworks which can make sense of these new interactions and analyse their consequences. Although more established traditions have been explored to some extent, particularly in the study of networked learning, there remains a limited understanding of how the increasingly connected learning context can benefit from a closer inspection of existing sociotechnical understandings of technology.

Sociotechnical Approaches

An often implicit assumption in much learning technology research is that technology itself is conceptually straightforward. In its strong, explicitly deterministic, form this asserts that a particular technology largely determines the kind of use that happens once it is introduced. A weaker version, closer to what Kling (2000) has termed the "standard tool" model of ICT, may emphasise the fit between a technology and a pedagogy, either choosing/developing a pedagogy to fit the technology or choosing the technology to fit a pedagogy. Such views often oversimplify the processes involved in ICT design and use; a wide range of cultural, organisational, social, political (and Political), economic, technical, gender and other processes are at play in the real-world introduction of technologies, in ways which are often contingent and indeterminate.

There is a wide range of approaches to studying technology which attempt to capture this complexity for differing purposes, in different ways and at different levels. These include sociotechnical systems (Emery and Trist 1960), soft systems (Checkland 1984), social informatics (Kling 2000), social shaping of technology (Williams and Edge 1996) and social construction of technology (Bijker and Law 1992). Perhaps the best known of these in the learning technology literature are actor network theory (Law and Hassard 1999; Latour 2005) and activity theory (Engeström 1999). We cannot introduce and consider these variously complementary and competing approaches here but merely highlight their range and note that they have generated valuable ways of thinking about the complexity of human–technology relationships. While these approaches differ quite radically from each other, a common concern is to avoid technologically determinist accounts of technology. They share a number of recurring features:

- The social and the artefactual are closely related in the production and use of technologies, such that it is rarely, if ever, helpful to try to consider them separately.
- The ways technologies are designed and used are substantively context-dependent.
- The distinction between technology design and use is frequently blurred. Indeed, the term "user" is often a problematic and inadequate term to describe relationships to technology.
- The focus of research is typically on the design/and or use of technology "in the wild" rather than on controlled laboratory-style tests.
- They frequently claim to be "critical" theories either in the sense of questioning many of the assertions made about technologies by enthusiasts, manufacturers, policy makers and others, and/or in the sense of being emancipatory, for example by highlighting the need for user and stakeholder participation in effective designs.

In the following section, we illustrate the value of a particular sociotechnical approach to studying the interaction of learners and technology through an example from our own research, in which we apply the concept of a "sociotechnical interaction network" (STIN) (Kling et al. 2003) to a case study of computer-mediated distance learning[1] from the world of transnational trade union education.

Thinking Sociotechnically: The Example of the Sociotechnical Interaction Network

In a recent article journal paper we have used Kling et al's in our own collaborations (Creanor and Walker 2005; Walker and Creanor 2005, 2009), we have particularly drawn on the "social informatics" perspective on technology closely associated with the work of Rob Kling (e.g. Kling 2000). The term has two broad meanings. Firstly, according to Kling, social informatics is a "body of research that examines the design, uses, and consequences of information and communication technologies in ways that take into account their interaction with institutional and cultural contexts" (Kling 2000, p. 217). It is a "field that is defined by its topic (and fundamental questions about it) rather than by a family of methods, much like the fields of urban studies, or gerontology" (Kling 2000, p. 218). Understood in this way SI effectively defines the topic of analysis as ICT in its social and organisational contexts, in effect as a critique of technologically determinist or "standard tool" models of technology. The second meaning refers to the concepts and theories generated by such approaches. Horton et al. (2005) have pointed out, from a European perspective, that this is a rather broader field with a richer range of research traditions than Kling himself appears to credit in his summaries of archetypal SI research (e.g. Kling 2000). As well as defining the field, Kling and colleagues have made substantive contributions to the understanding of technology, as outlined below.

In a recent article journal paper we have used Kling et al.'s (2003) concept of the STIN to analyse a case of cross-border networked learning in trade union education (Walker and Creanor 2009). The STIN takes a network view of the relations between the material and the social, in which the technological is seen as co-constitutive with the social, such that the technological elements cannot sensibly be discussed independently of the social aspects. Behaviour is not simply a consequence of the affordances of a particular technology or artefact. Rather, it emerges from participants' interactions with other people, with institutions and with artefacts.

---

[1] Computer-mediated distance learning (CMDL) was the term used in the original project. We have reinstated it here in response to a reviewer's comment that our original use of the term "technology-enhanced learning" itself reflects a degree of technological determinism.

The STIN embodies several conceptual differences from the "standard model" of technology use (Kling et al. 2003). Firstly, the analytic focus is ecological, deliberately looking beyond the affordances of the technology or the narrow relationships between participants and artefacts in a particular network. Secondly, a limited view of the "user" is replaced with a wider view of participants as social actors who have multiple roles and relationships which can affect behaviour in a STIN under analysis by linking that STIN to others in multiple ways. It is understood therefore, that participants will share the benefits of their shared knowledge, artefacts and expertise across the various networks to which they belong. This reconception of the user as a social actor better reflects the typical situation, in which a technology is not at the centre of the "user's" world but is one thing among many human and non-human elements with which they interact in the process of accomplishing something. These interactions, rather than any inherent properties of the technology, are identified by Orlikowski (2000) as the ultimate determinants of network structure. Thirdly, technology is viewed as open to local adaptation and social influence (it is "configurational"), rather than simply offering a limited set of functions.[2] The STIN traces and represents the key interactions between people and technologies, allowing us to consider the impact of these interactions on informal and formal learning

To sketch our case study very briefly (for more detail, see Walker and Creanor 2009), learner-participants were trade union members and officers from unions in two or more European countries who took part in transnational blended online/face-to-face learning episodes addressing a range of trade union-related topics. These took place as part of a large-scale project with 16 partners, supported by the European Social Fund, which aimed to increase capacity for social dialogue across a range of European trade union organisations. In particular, the learning interventions were aimed at preparing trade unionists to respond better to the increasing workplace regulation originating at the European Union, rather than the national, level. In all, the project developed 32 courses, involving a total of 471 trade union officers and representatives along with 27 tutors and facilitators. The courses were designed and delivered by experienced trade union educators with knowledge of online learning from their own national practices, with academic support. In various ways the courses all involved some extended elements of online collaboration, using the First Class conferencing system, complementing the classroom-based seminars. Our analysis focussed on the human/technology relationships in these networked learning events which were rendered even more complex by their multicultural and multilingual aspects.

A mixed-mode methodology incorporating online observation, questionnaires, interviews and video-recording of an evaluation workshop produced a rich dataset.

---

[2] The sociotechnical interaction network has a number of similarities with actor network theory in the way it conceives of technology. There are, though some important differences. Most notably, STINs do not assume a symmetry between the human and the material as in the ANT concept of the actant, and they highlight interactions both within and across networks.

In order to render the data collection manageable, the various groupings of participants were conceived of as a series of case studies (Yin 2003), thus enabling an in-depth examination of their outcomes. Following are two[3] examples of how thinking in terms of STINs directed our attention beyond the immediate online activities to examine aspects of the learners' environments and the organisation of the learning event.

Firstly, we considered how learners integrated technologies into their pre-existing technology-related environments and practices. As is common with adult part-time learners, this frequently involved complex domestic or organisational arrangements which influenced their ability to engage fully in the learning intervention. In our case study, a particular set of issues arose around the use of the conferencing system's client software which required to be downloaded to each participant's PC to allow them to access the online learning environment either from home or from their workplace. Instructions on how to do this were given at the first face-to-face session, with the offer of additional support by phone or email. Although not strictly speaking a networked learning activity, any delay in doing this would have meant a late start for participants which could have had a detrimental impact on their initial enthusiasm for learning and their ongoing motivation.

It soon became clear that what had not been fully considered were the issues participants might face in accessing the learning environment from their workplace. The client software did not use standard internet protocols, leading it to being blocked by some organisations' firewalls. While the project's own technical support could give guidance on how to configure firewalls to allow the client to access the server, the actual process for many learners centred on the negotiation with their local organisations' technical staff to open the firewall to the client. While some network managers were happy to allow access others were not, forcing participants to revert to the less flexible web interface. In other cases, firewall settings were changed informally and would be lost when the firewall was subsequently reset or upgraded. For participants in these situations, access to the learning environment disappeared in apparently arbitrary ways, rendering them disempowered as learners.

For participants from work premises, then, accessing the online learning environment required a set of social/organisational as well as technical arrangements to be established. Perhaps ironically, learners who accessed the servers from home (in many cases, precisely because they did not have organisational "support") generally experienced less difficulty; the STINs in these cases were considerably simpler. Where domestic firewalls did exist, learners who were unsure could be guided directly through the process of opening the appropriate channels by the project's support staff.

We characterised the sociotechnical networks through which individual participants gained access to the online environment as "ego-STINs" (analogous to the ego-networks of social network analysis). Elsewhere in the literature (Greene and Kirton 2003), issues such as negotiating access to a family computer in order to participate in online learning, are highlighted and might be considered to be

---

[3]Space does not allow discussion of a third aspect here – the evolution of STINs over the life of a networked learning event.

elements of these ego-STINs. Personal networks may also include the use of social media and mobile technology to connect to family, friends and work colleagues. The complexity of relationships, both social and technical, within these ego-STINs is often invisible to tutors, yet can have a significant impact on the engagement with, and outcome of, networked learning.

Secondly, and following on from our consideration of aspects of learners' local environments as STINs, we viewed the networked learning event itself as a form of STIN which was designed to knit together these diverse local networks for the purpose of enabling learning. The courses were designed to bring trade unionists from different countries together to examine the changing workplace skills required by their union members. Face-to-face sessions were conducted with simultaneous translation, but the online working was designed to be carried out by national groups linked together by (bilingual) tutors.

Illustrating this, the effectiveness of the online learning episode in a second case study was significantly disrupted when a training session in the use of the conferencing system planned for an initial face-to-face workshop was missed because the tutor experienced unforeseen travel problems. The course brought together two national groups of participants, each of which had distinct socio-cultural profiles in their trade union context, their approaches to learning and their familiarity with learning technologies. One national group of learners was already familiar with the system since it was the same one used by their own union, therefore they subsequently used it broadly as the tutors had planned. The other was unfamiliar with the system and instead these learners carried out their online collaboration using their normal email application. This rendered their online activities invisible both to the other group and to the tutors, and the subsequent evolution of the online phase of the learning event was very different from the way the tutors had originally envisaged it (Fig. 10.1). The tutors meanwhile, drew on their own tutor network for guidance and support. Although both groups completed the learning activities successfully and reported positive experiences despite using different technologies, the transnational element of the online course, originally a key focus, was lacking. Nevertheless, the fact that each group interpreted and implemented the learning activities correctly is testament to the validity and clarity of the pedagogical design which proved to be independent of a particular technology.

Again, it is difficult to explain these observations without noting the very close relationship between context, planned pedagogy and technology. That the planned learning outcomes were still achieved by both groups might be taken as further evidence of the capacity of "users" to work around technologies which don't address their needs. We likened the conduct online to a (sociotechnical interaction) network of (sociotechnical interaction) networks, designed to link up the ego-STINS in ways which would allow learning.

These examples illustrate the close, and in practice inseparable, relationships between the technological, the social and the pedagogical, in networked learning. The sociotechnical interaction approach to modelling a networked learning event allowed us to draw out and interpret the complexity of the processes at play in networked learning episodes which may otherwise have remained hidden. This is not unusual in

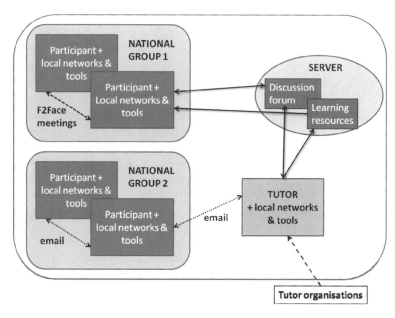

Fig. 10.1 Diagram showing the complexity of interactions during online course

social studies of technology, where a concern with actual practice draws out the way in which rather mundane issues, and responses to them, are essential to allowing technologies to function. The approach provides a framework for identifying key aspects of the context of networked learners and learning which goes beyond the obvious. It also illustrates findings common in wider studies of information systems.

Firstly, it illustrates that patterns of design and use of technologies are highly context-dependent. The ability of learners to participate effectively in the former case was influenced strongly by whether they tried to take part from home or from work, and in the latter case on their ability to negotiate with other learners. Secondly, it demonstrates the path-dependence of technology use: differing groups of participants' patterns of use were heavily influenced by prior exposures to technologies once the planned training failed. There was nothing inevitable about the way learners used particular technologies. The apparently small, local contingency of a missed training event can have significant consequences for the conduct of a 3-month learning event.

Discussion: The Value of Sociotechnical Approaches to Networked Learning

We have argued that sociotechnical approaches to conceptualising technology design and use go beyond the mechanistic and the technological determinism of much current research in the learning technology field. We have illustrated this through our application of one these approaches, the STIN, to two case studies of networked learning, demonstrating that achieving access and maintaining engagement with learning can be as much a social as technical accomplishment for learners (as well as tutors, administrators and others) who may be working in very different social and technological settings. When confronted with difficulties in using a particular technology to collaborate online, learners improvised their own way of working, drawing on their prior knowledge of communications technologies. Simply looking at technology, the learning design or indeed the learning outcomes, would tell us very little about the conduct of this event.

A stronger research focus on the contexts and specificities of networked learning events and applications will help us to avoid over-generalisations based on particular successes (or, indeed, failures). It is likely that claims made on behalf of technologies in support of networked learning would be rather more modest than is often the case currently.

Beyond these general arguments, sociotechnical approaches to learning technology in general, and the concept of the STIN in particular, have very particular value in contemporary learning technology research. Firstly, this is because many of the Web 2.0 technologies that are currently the focus of practice and research are examples of technologies which are particularly "malleable," "configurational" or "highly intertwined" with the social. The social elements of many social media technologies are particularly obvious and the technologies cannot usefully be studied independently of the social arrangements that accompany them. For example, what is remarkable and interesting about the success of Wikipedia derives at least as much from the changing social arrangements and practices and their "embodiment" in software as it does from the underlying programmes and infrastructure of a wiki.

Secondly, these technologies are being introduced in a period when higher education is undergoing profound environmental change. There is, for example, increasing pressure to develop "work-ready" graduates who have the independent learning skills so sought after by employers (Archer and Davison 2008), leading to a greater emphasis on authentic work-related learning activities and a growing interest in sociotechnical models of learning which derive from organisational and workplace studies (e.g. Littlejohn et al. 2009). While making the final revisions to this chapter, indeed, recommendations for radically changing the entire nature of higher education funding in England from the state to the student have been proposed and appear likely to form the basis of future policy.

Thirdly, recent learner experience studies have highlighted the complex and often subversive nature of technology use among learners (i.e. the diversity and complexity of STINs with which learning technologies and practices interact). Many learners have emphasised the importance of using technology to connect their learning to their wider social environments and personal networks in order to gain the support they needed for their ultimate success (Sharpe et al. 2009; Trinder et al. 2008). Applying a sociotechnical interaction framework to these diverse learner situations and behaviours may provide a more holistic and detailed view of both formal and informal aspects of learning which goes beyond that captured by current networked learning research.

Conclusion

In this chapter, we have highlighted the need for an inclusive and encompassing range of theoretical perspectives in networked learning research if we are to continue to interpret the complex social, pedagogical and technological landscape in which networked learning resides. We have recognised the distinct character of networked learning research where "epistemic fluency" is encouraged. We have also noted weaknesses in some aspects of learning technology research based on technologically determinist assumptions and argued that there exist bodies of research from technology studies and information systems which can help us better to conceptualise the relationship of people, technology and pedagogy in learning technology environments. We have illustrated this by developing a concept from the social informatics tradition to a case study of trade union education, and suggested how such an approach can contribute to a more grounded and detailed understanding of how learners interact with systems designed to support their learning. Research based on sociotechnical strategies will, we suggest, complement accepted socio-cultural theories in networked learning and enrich our ability to interpret the complex interactions at play.

References

Archer, M. (1995). *Realist social theory: the morphogenetic approach*. Cambridge: Cambridge University Press.

Archer, W., & Davison, J. (2008). *Graduate employability: the view of employers*. London: The Council for Industry and Higher Education.

Barnett, R. (2000). *Realizing the university in an age of supercomplexity*. Buckingham: SRHE/OpenUniversity Press.

Bayne, S. (2008). Uncanny spaces for higher education: teaching and learning in virtual worlds. *ALT-J: Research in Learning Technology, 16*(3), 197–205.

Beasley, N., & Smyth, K. (2004). Expected and actual student use of an online learning environment: a critical analysis. *Electronic Journal of e-Learning, 2*(1).

Beetham, H., & Sharpe, R. (Eds.). (2007). *Rethinking pedagogy for a digital age. Designing and delivering e-learning*. London: Routledge.

Bijker, W. B., & Law, J. (Eds.). (1992). *Shaping technology/building society: studies in sociotechnical change*. London: MIT.

Bonk, C. J., & Graham, C. R. (2006). *The handbook of blended learning: global perspectives, local designs*. San Francisco: Pfeiffer.

Bronack, S., Sanders, R., Cheney, A., Riedl, R., Tashner, J., & Matzen, N. (2008). Presence Pedagogy: Teaching and Learning in a 3D Virtual Immersive World. *International Journal of Teaching and Learning in Higher Education, 20*(1), 59–69.

Checkland, P. (1984). *Systems thinking, systems practice*. Chichester: Wiley.

Checkland, P., & Holwell, S. (1998). *Information, systems and information systems: making sense of the field*. Chichester: Wiley.

Clegg, S., Hudson, A., & Steel, J. (2003). The Emperor's New Clothes: Globalisation and e-Learning in Higher Education. *British Journal of Sociology of Education, 24*(1), 39–53.

Code, J. R., & Zaparyniuk, N. E. (2009). The emergence of agency in online social networks. In S. Hatzipanagos & S. Warburton (Eds.), *Handbook of research on social software and developing ontologies* (pp. 102–118). London: IGI Global.

Conole, G., & Oliver, M. (Eds.). (2007). *Contemporary perspectives in e-learning research: themes, methods and impact on practice*. London: Routledge.

Conole, G., Smith, J., & White, S. (2007). A critique of the impact of policy and funding. In G. Conole & M. Oliver (Eds.), *Contemporary perspectives in e-learning research: themes, methods and impact on practice* (pp. 38–54). London: Routledge.

Creanor, L., & Trinder, K. (2010). Managing study and life with technology. In R. Sharpe, H. Beetham, & S. De Freitas (Eds.), *Rethinking learning for a digital age* (pp. 43–55). London: Routledge.

Creanor, L., Trinder, K., Gowan, D., & Howells, C. (2008). Life. *Learning and Technology: views from the learners, Journal for Learning and Teaching in Higher Education, 2*, 26–41.

Creanor, L., & Walker, S. (2005). Learning architectures and the negotiation of meaning in European trade unions. *ALT-J, 13*, 109–124.

Czerniewicz, L., Williams, K., et al. (2009). Students make a plan: understanding student agency in constraining conditions. ALT-J Research in Learning Technology, 17(2), 75–88.

De Freitas, S., & Conole, G. (2010). The influence of pervasive and integrative tools on learners' experiences and expectations of study. In R. Sharpe, H. Beetham, & S. De Freitas (Eds.), *Rethinking learning for a digital age* (pp. 15–30). London: Routledge.

Dirckinck-Holmfeld, L. (2010). Design of a Networked learning master environment for professionals – using the approach of problem based learning to establish a community of practice. In Dirckinck-Holmfeld, L., Hodgson, V., Jones, C., De Laat, M., McConnell, D., and Ryberg, T. (Eds), *Proceedings of the 7th International Conference on Networked Learning 2010* (pp. 551–557) http://www.lancs.ac.uk/fss/organisations/netlc/past/nlc2010/abstracts/PDFs/Dirckinck_Holmfeld_2.pdf. Accessed 19 Oct 2010.

Dirckink-Holmfeld, L., Jones, C., & Lindström, B. (Eds.). (2009). *Analysing networked learning practices in higher education and continuing professional development*. Rotterdam: Sense.

Dron, J., & Anderson, T. (2009). How the crowd can teach. In S. Hatzipanagos & S. Warburton (Eds.), *Handbook of research on social software and developing ontologies* (pp. 1–17). London: IGI Global.

Ellis, R. A., & Calvo, R. A. (2004). Learning through discussion in blended learning environments. *Educational Media International, 41*(3), 263–274.

Emery, F. E., & Trist, E. L. (1960). Socio-technical systems. In C. W. Churchman & M. Verhurst (Eds.), *Management science, models and techniques* (Vol. 2, pp. 83–97). London: Pergamon.

Engeström, Y. (1999). Activity theory and individual and social transformation. In Y. Engeström, R. Miettinnen, & R.-L. Punamäki-Gitai (Eds.), *Perspectives on activity theory* (pp. 19–39). Cambridge: Cambridge University Press.

Engeström, Y., Miettinnen, R., & Punamäki-Gitai, R.-L. (Eds.). (1999). *Perspectives on activity theory*. Cambridge: Cambridge University Press.

Felix, U. (2005). E-learning pedagogy in the third millennium: the need for combining social and cognitive constructivist approaches. *ReCALL, 17*(1), 85–100.

Fox, S. (2002). Studying networked learning: some implications from socially situated learning theory and actor–network theory. In C. Steeples & C. Jones (Eds.), *Networked learning: perspectives and issues* (pp. 77–93). London: Springer.

Goodyear, P. (2002). Psychological foundations for networked learning. In C. Steeples & C. Jones (Eds.), *Networked learning: perspectives and issues* (pp. 49–75). London: Springer.

Goodyear, P. (2009). Foreward. In L. Dirckink-Holmfeld, C. Jones, & B. Lindström (Eds.), *Analysing networked learning practices in higher education and continuing professional development* (pp. vii–x). Rotterdam: Sense.

Goodyear, P., Banks, S., Hodgson, V., & McConnell, D. (2004). Research on networked learning: an overview. In P. Goodyear, S. Banks, V. Hodgson, & D. McConnell (Eds.), *Advances in research on networked learning* (pp. 1–11). Dordrecht: Kluwer.

Greene, A.-M., & Kirton, G. (2003). Possibilities for remote participation in trade unions: mobilising women activists. *Industrial Relations Journal, 34*, 319–333.

Hammond, M. (1999). Issues associated with participation in on line forums - the case of the communicative learner. *Education and Information Technologies, 4*(4), 353–367.

Hardy, J., and Bates, S. (2009). Taking the lead: learners' experiences across the disciplines. In Davis, H. and Creanor, L. (Eds), *In dreams begins responsibility' – choice, evidence and change*. Proceedings of the Association for Learning Technology conference, 8–10 September (ALT-C), Manchester, UK, pp. 1–9.

Horton, K., Davenport, E., & Wood-Harper, T. (2005). Exploring sociotechnical interaction with Rob Kling: five "big" ideas. *Information Technology & People, 18*, 50–67.

Hughes, J. (2008). Letting in the Trojan mouse: using an eportfolio system to re-think pedagogy. In *Hello! Where are you in the landscape of educational technology?* Proceedings of Ascilite, Melbourne. http://www.ascilite.org.au/conferences/melbourne08/procs/hughes.pdf. Accessed 24 Jan 2011.

Jonassen, D. H., & Land, S. M. (Eds.). (2000). *Theoretical foundations of learning environments*. NJ: Lawrence Erlbaum.

Jones, C. (2004). Networks and learning: communities, practices and the metaphor of networks. *ALT-J: Research in Learning Technology, 12*(1), 81–93.

Jones, J., & Bronack, S. (2008). Rethinking cognition, representation and processes in 3D online social environments. In P. C. Rivoltella (Ed.), *Digital literacy: tools and methodologies for the information society* (pp. 176–206). London: IGI.

Jones, C., & Dirckinck-Holmfeld, L. (2009). Analysing networked learning practices. In L. Dirckinck-Holmfeld, C. Jones, & B. Lindström (Eds.), Analysing networked learning practices in higher education and continuing professional development. Rotterdam.

Jones, C., & Healing, G. (2010). Net Generation Students: agency and choice and the new technologies. *Journal of Computer Assisted Learning, 26*, 344–356.

Jones, C., and Ramanau, R. (2009). Collaboration and the net generation: the changing characteristics of first year university students. In O'Malley, C., Suthers, D., Reimann, P., and Dimitracopoulou, A. (Eds.). *Proceedings of the 8th International Conference on Computer Supported Collaborative Learning, CSCL2009: CSCL practices*. 237–241 June 8–13, Rhodes, Greece

Jones, C., & Steeples, C. (2002). Perspectives and issues in networked learning. In C. Steeples & C. Jones (Eds.), *Networked learning: perspectives and issues* (pp. 1–12). London: Springer.

Kear, K. (2004). Peer learning using asynchronous discussion systems in distance education. *Open Learning, 19*(2), 151–164.

Kling, R. (2000). Learning about information technologies and social change: The contribution of social informatics. *Information Society, 16*, 217–232.

Kling, R., Mckim, G., & King, A. (2003). A bit more to it: Scholarly communication forums as socio- technical interaction networks. *Journal of the American Society for Information Science and Technology, 54*, 47–67.

Latour, B. (2005). *Reassembling the social: an introduction to actor network theory*. Oxford: Oxford University Press.

Laurillard, D. (2005). E-learning in higher education. In P. Ashwin (Ed.), *Changing higher education: the development of learning and teaching* (pp. 71–84). Oxford: Routledge.

Laurillard, D. (2009). The pedagogical challenges to collaborative technologies. *The International Journal of Computer-Supported Collaborative Learning, 4*(1), 5–20.

Lave, J., & Wenger, E. (1991). Situated learning: legitimate peripheral participation. Cambridge: Cambridge University Press.

Law, J., & Hassard, J. (1999). *Actor network theory and after*. Oxford and Malden, MA: Blackwell.

Littlejohn, A., Margaryan, A., and Milligan, C. (2009). Charting collective knowledge: Supporting self-regulated learning in the workplace. In *Proceedings of the 9th IEEE International Conference on Advanced Learning Technologies (ICALT)*

Mackenzie, D., & Wacjman, J. (Eds.). (1999). *The social shaping of technology*. Milton Keynes, UK: Open University Press.

Mayes, T., & de Freitas, S. (2007). Learning and e-learning: the role of theory. In H. Beetham & R. Sharpe (Eds.), *Rethinking pedagogy for a digital age: designing and delivering e-learning* (pp. 13–25). London: Routledge.

McAteer, E., Tolmie, A., Crook, C., MacLeod, H., & Musselbrook, K. (2002). Learning networks and the issue of communication skills. In C. Steeples & C. Jones (Eds.), *Networked learning: perspectives and issues* (pp. 309–322). London: Springer.

McConnell, D. (2006). *E-learning groups and communities*. Maidenhead: SRHE/Open University Press.

Nielsen, K. (2009). A collaborative perspective on learning transfer. *Journal of Workplace Learning, 21*(1), 58–70.

Oliver, M., Roberts, G., Beetham, H., Ingraham, B., Dykes, M., & Levy, P. (2007). Knowledge, society and perspectives on learning technology. In G. Conole & M. Oliver (Eds.), *Contemporary perspectives in e-learning research: themes, methods and impact on practice* (pp. 21–38). London: Routledge.

Oliver, M., & Trigwell, K. (2005). Can 'blended learning' be redeemed? *E-Learning and Digital Media, 2*(1), 17–26.

Orlikowski, W. J. (2000). Using technology and constituting structures: a practice lens for studying technology in organizations. *Organizations Science, 11*(4), 404–428.

Parker, K., & Chao, J. (2007). Wiki as a teaching tool. *Interdisciplinary Journal of Knowledge and Learning Objects, 3*, 57–72.

Pawlowsky, P. (2001). The treatment of organizational learning in management science. In M. Dierkes, B. Bethoinantal, J. Child, & I. Nonaka (Eds.), *Handbook of organizational learning and knowledge*. Oxford: Oxford University Press.

Sharpe, R., Beetham, H., & De Freitas, S. (Eds.). (2010). *Rethinking learning for a digital age: how learners are shaping their own experiences*. New York: Routledge.

Ryberg, T., & Larson, M. C. (2008). Networked identities: understanding relationships between strong and weak ties in networked environments. *Journal of Computer Assisted Learning, 24*, 103–115.

Savin-Baden, M. (2008). From cognitive capability to social reform? Shifting perceptions of learning in immersive virtual worlds. *ALT-J: Research in Learning Technology, 16*(3), 151–161.

Selwyn, N. (2007). The use of computer technology in university teaching and learning: a critical perspective. *Journal of Computer Assisted Learning, 23*(2), 83–94.

Sharpe, R., Beetham, H., Benfield, G., DeCicco, E., and Lessner, E. (2009). *Learners Experiences of E-learning Synthesis Report: Explaining Learner Differences*, https://mw.brookes.ac.uk/display/JISCle2f/Findings. Accessed 24 Jan 2011.

Siemens, G. (2004). *Connectivism: a learning theory for the digital age*. http://www.elearnspace.org/Articles/connectivism.htm. Accessed 24 Jan 2011.

Traxler, J. (2009). Students and mobile devices: choosing which dream. In Davis, H., and Creanor, L. (Eds). *"In dreams begins responsibility" – choice, evidence and change. Proceedings of the Association for Learning Technology conference* (pp. 8–10) September (ALT-C), Manchester, UK, pp. 70–81.

Trinder, K., Guiller, J., Margaryan, A., Littlejohn, A., and Nicol, D. (2008) *Learning from digital natives: integrating formal and informal learning: final project report*, Higher Education Academy, UK. http://www.academy.gcal.ac.uk/ldn/LDNFinalReport.pdf. Accessed 24 Jan 2011.

Trist, E. L., & Bamforth, K. W. (1951). Some Social and Psychological Consequences of the Longwall Method of Coal-getting. *Human Relations, 4*(1), 3–38.

Walker, S., & Creanor, L. (2005). Crossing complex boundaries: transnational online education in European trade unions. *Journal of Computer Assisted Learning, 21*, 343–354.

Walker, S., & Creanor, L. (2009). The STIN in the tale: a sociotechnical interaction perspective on networked learning. *Journal of Educational Technology and Society, 12*, 305–316.

Wenger, E. (1998). Communities of practice: Learning, meaning and identity. Cambridge and New York: Cambridge University Press.

Williams, R., & Edge, D. (1996). The Social Shaping of Technology. *Research Policy, 25*, 865–899.

Yin, R. K. (2003). *Case study research: design & methods*. London: Sage.

Part VI
Identity, Cultural Capital and Networked Learning

Chapter 11
Just What Is Being Reflected in Online Reflection? New Literacies for New Media Learning Practices

Jen Ross

Introduction

In this chapter I argue that new literacies are required when reflective practices in higher education move online. Online reflective writing in education, whether publicly visible, limited to small groups of learners, or restricted to just a student and their teacher, is profoundly influenced by wider cultural understandings of blogging and personal disclosure and risk online. Addressing this demands understanding spaces for formal online reflection (primarily weblogs and e-portfolios at the time of writing) as a new site of practice which takes its meaning from a specific and complex set of social and technical relations (Goodfellow and Lea 2007).

Reflective writing and practices are an important element of teaching and learning (and, increasingly, assessment) in many disciplines, particularly those with a professional or vocational focus. Reflection in education is generally grounded in a humanist discourse of a "true" or "central" self which can be revealed, understood, recorded, improved or liberated through the process of writing about thoughts and experiences. This discourse underpins the various projects of reflective writing in higher education as described by (for example) Boud et al. (1985), Brockbank and McGill (1998) and Moon (1999). However, it is problematic for two main reasons: it masks the increasingly invasive character of educational practices which demand confession and self-surveillance as evidence of progress and learning, and it assumes a knowable, malleable yet autonomous self at its centre. These problems are greatly exacerbated by the increasingly common use of online environments for reflection.

Despite this, the literature dealing with educational blogs and e-portfolios mostly uncritically accepts these tools and practices as beneficial above and beyond offline practices, in terms of efficiency, accessibility, relevance, the enhancement of technical skills, and in terms of the ease of finding an audience and fostering community and dialogue.

J. Ross (✉)
Institute for Education, Community and Society, University of Edinburgh, Edinburgh, UK
e-mail: jen.ross@ed.ac.uk

L. Dirckinck-Holmfeld et al. (eds.), *Exploring the Theory, Pedagogy and Practice of Networked Learning*, DOI 10.1007/978-1-4614-0496-5_11,
© Springer Science+Business Media, LLC 2012

Where drawbacks are identified, these are usually attributed to lack of motivation, understanding or technical proficiency on the part of students or teachers, lack of institutional understanding or support, concerns about privacy and safety in the online environment, or sometimes a lack of time or resource to properly implement these otherwise promising technologies.

There is also very little in the way of engagement with the online subject in this literature. Online reflective accounts are assumed to have a straightforward relationship with the offline selves of students, and few authors writing about online reflection ask what it means to create digital-textual selves or what impact reflecting online has on the subjectivity of students and teachers. Where digital difference is acknowledged in online reflective practices, it is seen to be technological rather than conceptual, and beneficial rather than problematic (Butler 2006, p. 12).

In this chapter, I challenge this technicist perspective. I argue that online reflective practices are conceptually different from their offline counterparts, by showing one way that they are affected by their digitality: by their association with blogging as a cultural phenomenon.

Blogging is a genre which privileges individual voice, addressivity, and a blurred distinction between public and private spheres (Walker Rettberg 2008). We can see in current blogging practices a convergence of the rise of the concept of personal branding (Peters 1997; Lair et al. 2005), and what Scott describes as the "cultural tendency to seek out confessional narratives of self-disclosure" (2004, p. 92). This convergence exposes a number of tensions: between self-promotion and authenticity, between accusations of narcissism and pressures to confess, and between moral panics around privacy and safety and a growing sense that online invisibility equates to personal and professional negligence, and that the more presence the better. As students negotiate the management of personal, academic and sometimes also professional voices in blogs and reflective e-portfolios, they must bring in to play literacies which are new not in their substance but in their modality. Literacies are socially situated and multiple practices (Barton et al. 2000; Lea and Street 2009; Lillis 2003), and writing both reflects and constructs identities (Ivanič 1998). The context of writing reflectively *online* is different from other forms of reflective writing, with different sorts of implications for the identities and practices of the student-writers.

In what follows, I propose a set of (often conflicting) norms and expectations widely associated with blogging. These cluster around themes of authenticity, risk, pretence, othering, narcissism and commodification. I explore how these are reflected in the assumptions and practices of students and teachers, and go on to argue for greater attention to be given to the nature of *online* reflective writing, and a more explicit and critical engagement with the tensions it embodies.

This Chapter in the Context of Networked Learning

This chapter defines "networked learning" in two senses. First: as learning that involves students being purposefully digitally connected with other people and with electronic resources. In 2002, the E-quality for E-learning manifesto declared that in "quality" networked e-learning, "connectivity and process is as valuable as the substance and focus of the connection" (E-Quality Network 2002). The manifesto proposes a balance between content and conversation, and attempts to redress what the authors saw as a harmful fixation on information, at the cost of connection. The manifesto was prescient in its insistence on this: a trend towards connectivity is apparent in the rise of Web 2.0, in subsequent writing about e-learning, and in more recent popular writing about the Web. Goodyear, Banks, Hodgson, and McConnell, for example, warn that "use of online *materials* is not a *sufficient* characteristic to define networked learning" (2004, p. 2), and Doctorow has provocatively reversed the maxim that "content is king", claiming that: "conversation is king. Content is just something to talk about" (2006). Online reflective practices in higher education are complex in their connectivity – they can cover the continuum from private to public, from intensely networked to one-to-one. Nevertheless, the foundational notion is one of personal engagement in a digital environment for the gaze of another or others (see McKenna's 2005 work on addressivity for an exploration of the effects of writing for a "superaddressee" or unknowable potential audiences in digital environments) and the concept of networked learning in this sense most certainly applies to online reflection.

The second notion of "networked learning" I am working with here is of learning that is immersed in networks and digital flows of information and culture. In emphasising the value of the network, quality e-learning is proposed by the manifesto as social, communicative and, by extension, cultural. However, the culture in which all learning, but especially e-learning, is immersed extends beyond the walls of the institution, as Carpenter contends: "[electronic] environments allow for and even encourage active integration and dynamic interaction, resulting in a mixing of genres and literacy practices that does not respect conventional categories, divisions, or dichotomies, including the border that separates…the popular from the academic" (2009, p. 144). Jones and Dirckinck-Holmfeld (2009) make a similar claim, that computer networks have a tendency to "disrupt and disturb traditional boundaries in education" (p.13), including the boundaries of public and private which are of great relevance here. I would argue that this is due not primarily to the homogenising power of digital interfaces, as Carpenter claims, or to the extent to which tools "fundamentally mediate both higher mental functioning and human action", as Jones and Dirckinck-Holmfeld (2009) put it. Instead, as Castells has argued, organisations (including educational institutions) may trigger, but ultimately cannot control, flows of information and communication in digital space:

> A structural logic dominated by largely uncontrollable flows within and between networks creates the conditions for the unpredictability of the consequences of human action through the reflection of such action in an unseen, uncharted space of flows (Castells 1999, p. 59).

Online reflection is highly attuned to its cultural context – sometimes deliberately, as for example with pedagogical designs which aim to "harness" what Duffy and Bruns call "a growing impetus towards personal expression and reflection, and also the sharing of personal 'spaces'" (2006, p. 34). However, even when not intentional, online reflection is perceived by students and teachers in my research as part of a wider cultural move towards digital disclosure. The issues of privacy, authenticity and risk that attend blogging, social networking and the social and digital practices of popular culture are also to be found in the educational practices which reflect them. Students react to this momentum towards disclosure with varying degrees of alarm, resistance and performativity – and in ways which can be significantly at odds with the stated aims of the reflective practices they are engaged in. Rehabilitating online reflection requires attention to be paid to the appropriateness of those aims in a digital context, and to the literacy requirements of practices which are multivocal, personal and "drenched in social factors" (Holquist 2002, p. 61).

Research Context

This chapter emerges from my research exploring how students and teachers negotiate issues of identity, authenticity, ownership, privacy and performativity in high-stakes online reflection in higher education. By high-stakes, I mean reflection which is summatively assessed or has a direct impact on access to a profession or professional body. The chapter draws on data from 31 semi-structured interviews with students and lecturers from across 8 university programmes in the UK which have a high-stakes reflective component. The programmes span face-to-face, online, undergraduate and postgraduate contexts, and subject areas including education, social work, built environment, health and law. Four of the universities involved in my study are based in England, and the other four in Scotland. I spoke with 14 female and 6 male students, and 9 female and 3 male teachers. The cultural background of participants was mainly English or Scottish, but I also interviewed students from Germany, Italy, Australia, Canada and Ukraine. The interview extracts cited in this chapter have been anonymised and pseudonyms used in place of real names.

Participating teachers defined themselves as doing high-stakes online reflection on programmes or courses. I worked with constellations of students, teachers and reflective artefacts, to situate the data in specific contexts of practice. Participants took part in one interview and were also asked for documentary data – relevant documentation about their high-stakes reflective practices in the case of teachers, and access to their reflective artefacts in the case of students.

Interview transcripts were produced by me in some cases and by an external transcriber in others, reviewed in detail, and coded according to emerging themes from the interviews and the parallel theoretical work being done to analyse reflective practices as masks (Ross 2011). The data that are presented in this chapter are drawn from work around a broader theme of the "trace" – focusing on the cultural practices which make their way into academic practices (as discussed here), but also on the concepts of ownership, subjectivity and the archive.

Having described the context in which this data was generated, I now move on to describe six "stories" associated with blogging, and show how these are reflected in the assumptions and practices of teachers and students. The chapter concludes by proposing engaging more creatively and critically with the digital, and with matters of subjectivity and authenticity, in online reflective practices.

Six Stories of Blogging

In the past decade, blogging has become emblematic of the social or read-write web, and its influence has been felt in social, political, cultural and professional spheres (Bruns and Jacobs 2007). Before Facebook and Twitter emerged to attract the indignation of commentators dismayed by the narcissism, pointlessness and disregard for privacy that apparently characterises social media, blogging was the prime target of such speculations (Nardi et al. 2004). At the same time, bloggers themselves, along with some social media and business scholars position blogging practice as one of authentic self-development, personal branding, or both (Reed 2005; Dutta 2010). These discourses are now part of the digital cultural landscape, and both students and teachers in my research are influenced by them when they come to engage in online reflection.

Lillis describes the writing "voices" of students as being informed by their multiple identities and experiences. So, the meanings that students attribute to the writing practices of online reflection are influenced the social and cultural context they are in. She goes on to point out that student writing is also shaped "by the voices they are attempting to respond to" (2001, p. 46). Where teachers have their own tacit understandings of being online, students must feel their way through a minefield of overlapping, conflicting discourses to arrive at a mode of writing which meets the explicit criteria, but also the implicit expectations that are being shaped by a broader digital cultural context.

Poster calls the online domain a "new speech situation" (2006, p. 156). He frames this in terms of subjectivity, but it can also be framed as a literacies issue – it is a new "system of authoring, owning and appropriating texts" (Goodfellow and Lea 2007, p. 52). Despite the academic setting of online reflection, and regardless of the specific tools being used (institutional or commercial weblogs, e-portfolios, or virtual learning environments), the structures employed are those of the blog as cultural product, and teachers and students "read and construe meaning from cultural products in complex, nuanced ways" (Carpenter 2009, p. 139). These six stories of blogging are an attempt at capturing different facets of this broader context and aligning them with what teachers and students say about their online reflective practices. In doing so, the stories tease out conflicts and tensions which need to be addressed in developing and deploying these practices.

Authenticity: Blogs Should Be Authentic and Honest

Reflective educational practices have always demanded confession and certain kinds of stories about the self (Devas 2004; Hargreaves 2004; Macfarlane and Gourlay 2009; Ross 2011). Online reflective practices, like their offline counterparts, often continue to be framed in terms of authenticity, integrity, purposefulness and autonomous selfhood (Barrett and Carney 2005; Stefani et al. 2007). However, to move online is to tap in to new modes of representing the self in what can feel like an especially public or surveilled space. Authenticity is surfaced in online practices, for students and teachers, more explicitly than in an offline mode. This is echoed in the blogging literature.

Bloggers outside educational contexts often appear to see their practice as not only necessarily authentic, but visibly so, and reflective of a knowable self (Holbrook 2006). As Reed comments, "[bloggers] treat weblogs as straightforward indexes of self; they commonly assert that 'my blog is me'" (2005, p. 227). The perception is that audiences expect and assess the authenticity of a blogger's voice: "aware of the constant possibility that a fictional text may be posing as non-fiction, readers online have been exhaustive in investigating suspicious texts" (Freidrich 2007, pp. 62–63).

Students in my research were insistent that they are both honest and authentic in their online writing. For some, this is described as natural or intrinsic. Megan acknowledged a degree of formality that may be associated with the assessed nature of the writing she does in her online reflection, but insists on a "voice" that is uniquely her own, that bridges her online and offline life, and that she makes no attempt to "cover up":

> I'm not going to make no effort online, but I'm not going to make any effort to cover up, you know…maybe it's slightly more formal in the blog because I know it's going to be assessed, but it's the same, there's definitely a voice in there that I think if you had a look at my personal blog you you could see a definite, you'd go 'okay I can tell these are the same person' (Megan, PG student).

For others, authenticity is perceived as a requirement of their course:

> I can't remember whether they said you know 'make sure you're creative and honest and free' but I felt like that was part of the criteria somehow, whether explicit or implicit (Alex, PG student).

Alex expressed no particular discomfort with the idea of being required to be authentic in his online reflective space (which was structured as a blog), but notably the assessment criteria for his online reflection did *not* explicitly include such a requirement. He was not clear himself where the idea of being "creative and honest and free" had come from – it was a "feeling" that he associated with the activity, rather than an instruction given by his teachers or in his course material.

The distancing or anonymising effects of the online environment was seen by some interviewees to be associated with an increasing comfort with self-disclosure. Several lecturers on distance programmes saw a benefit to reflecting at a distance because students will not have to face or deal socially with the lecturers who see their reflections, and can, therefore, be more open and honest:

> some of them are very very honest and up front in their weblogs in a way which I really doubt that they would be if, if the pedagogy was a, a face to face you know course with a, a written diary or something (Jane, lecturer, PG).

> because they never meet us, they can in fact open their hearts and give very personal views about their difficulties, their hopes, their fears, you know, what, what's going on in a way that they do admit, some of them, that they have never opened up to with their partners even….it's cathartic (Jess, lecturer, PG).

This openness may relate, as Dyson (1998) predicted, to the way that being online is reconfiguring what privacy and display mean, and how they are experienced:

> As people feel more secure in general on the Net, they will become accustomed to seeing their words recorded and replayed. They will no longer feel uncomfortable being on display, since everyone around them is on display too…Everyone has personal preferences for privacy, but they are influenced by the surrounding culture and by the surrounding economy (p. 275).

This shift towards digital disclosure may produce quite personal reflections in the digital domain, and this can align well with the desire for authentic reflection that underpins reflective practice in many disciplines. Peter picked up on this point, and thought that the solitary, asynchronous context of online reflection provoked a degree of honesty and uninhibitedness even on programmes where teachers and students meet face to face:

> some of them were reporting some quite you know personal stuff about feeling afraid and,…there's something about the, I don't know whether it's the fact it's people, you know enter their, you know enter their details and write these things in the wee small hours of the morning when, you know, they've had a few beers or something…and and it's almost like a a confession, like people write in their diaries about (Peter, lecturer, UG).

Teachers are often worried about the implications of "oversharing" online, though, and this produces a problematic tension for students when they are not clear about the line between authentic reflection and dangerous disclosure.

Risk: Sharing Too Much Information Is Dangerous

Recent work on youth social media practices has revealed that, as boyd has pointed out, privacy remains important, but its meaning is different in mediated spaces, where it denotes the ability to "limit access through social conventions" (boyd 2008, p. 131), and where tactics such as "security through obscurity" replace structural boundaries (p. 133). Despite these tactics, the erosion of privacy online is viewed as highly "risky" in cultural discourses around blogging, and the dangers of too much disclosure are disturbing for students and teachers. Many experienced online disclosure as risky in the sense that it is or has the potential to become public, and to be misused:

> I had a guy come to see me yesterday with a [public web] portfolio…and I just said to him 'look, you've given up enough information here if someone really wants to, to claim your identity' and he said to me 'what do you mean?' and I said 'name, address, date of birth, family name' and he went 'oooh my god' and [I] said 'so can you take that down off your [portfolio] now, can you sort it out', and I and we went through various documents that were on there to do with his portfolio and I said 'I'd like that off, I'd like that off, I'd like that off and I'd' and it was 'no no you'll mark me down' and I said 'no I won't. I won't mark you down' (Sam, lecturer, UG).

Sam's students are allowed (though not required) to create their portfolios on a public web site, but she worries about the implications of what she sees as a lack of common sense in their approach to personal disclosure – both factually and in terms of what she calls the "darker parts" of reflection. At the same time, the student she discusses here clearly believes that he is required to make these disclosures, and fears being penalised when it comes to assessment if he does not. Like Alex's perception of "honesty" as an assessment criterion, this student interprets the task of reflection as a task of disclosure, and this creates problems for some teachers who fear the risks and consequences.

Some students have the same fears and respond by withdrawing from or removing what is seen as personal from their online reflection:

> Jen: how come you didn't put, be more sort of explicit about the kind of the depths of your soul or however you put it?

> Dave (UG student): Um, because, I mean, again because you're not quite sure who's going to be reading it, or because [pause] and what I was writing in the blog was honest I just, you know I just wasn't going to you know go in to the depths.

Similarly, Beth, an undergraduate student on a campus-based programme, explained that she would not communicate unhappiness about a course or lecturer in her (non-public) e-portfolio because it would then be "floating around in this virtual, you know, this void somewhere [laughs]". This use of language is revealing: a dangerous void is perceived by some even in the safety of digital walled gardens.

Much has been written about the moral panics surrounding internet safety and risk, especially in relation to young people (Carrington 2007; Hope 2008), and as Efimova and Grudin (2007) argue, "people are not careful". The result is an undercurrent of fear, danger and caution which is certainly affecting how students and teachers approach their online reflective practices. This is at odds with many of the foundations of reflective practice; where what is personal becomes, through the process of reflective writing, fused with other materials of learning in ways which allow for independence and creative exploration (Creme 2005, p. 289). It is difficult (though perhaps not impossible) to square risk and fear with creative exploration, and negotiating that process requires more sensitivity on the part of teachers to the complex rhetorical strategies that online reflection demands. These strategies are not routinely discussed with or taught to students, and this is a serious gap in an increasingly common digital practice. At present, the gap is filled in part by an intense concern on the part of students about a discourse of "pretence" – they equate strategic performance with dishonesty. The cultural context of blogging positions the Web as a medium for deception, and students energetically distance themselves from such a possibility.

Pretence: No One Is Really Themselves Online

A key narrative around blogging and online presence in general is that, in contrast to the notion of authenticity and the associated riskiness of online disclosure, the Web is a medium which facilitates deception. Research into online dating (Ellison et al. 2006) and teenagers' self-presentation in social networking (Bortree 2005), for example, emphasises the careful and self-conscious crafting of identity which goes on in spaces which are, for one reason or another, high-stakes. This is a delicate operation, however, as the appearance of authenticity remains extremely important.

I have previously suggested that in educational contexts students may commit with extra intensity to "authenticating" the self they perform in reflection online, to regain or maintain a sense of control in a digital space which invites them, as Bayne (2005) has argued, towards a dangerous fluidity (Ross 2011). Adele had quite a sophisticated understanding of identity itself as performance:

> you're always performing somehow I mean...[pause] you know I think identity is made up of so many shades and it's, you can't really say the one is your true identity and the other one isn't (Adele, PG student).

She was, nonetheless, adamant about her authenticity within her reflective space: "I don't have the feeling that it's, that I put on a different identity for it. [pause]...I never had the feeling that I was making this up". Identity may be fluid, in other words, but it is still under her control.

One lecturer in my research explained how her students embraced and even demanded their tutors' presence in their reflective space:

> I've been able to log on and see what they've they've been doing, literally on a daily basis if I wanted to. We did give the students the option to not have me do that and to take me off that facility. What was interesting was, the students were all unanimous in that, no no no, they wanted that...what they were actually saying was that made them think about how to use it and how to behave in terms of recording their reflective journal (Maria, lecturer, UG).

For these students, having their behaviour monitored was preferable to the doubt over their engagement, or of getting it wrong, that *not* being monitored opened up. I think this is partly about being seen to be a "real" reflective person who is observable at any time because they are doing what they are supposed to do. Alex was quite explicit about this, describing his choice not to edit his blog before submitting it for assessment because, he explained, he thought it would demonstrate his "journey" better:

> I didn't think that assessment wise it would benefit from [editing] cause I thought that it, that the assessment would probably include whether there was a journey as well, well maybe not directly but I think, it wasn't being assessed as a finished work, it was being assessed as a diary, my reflective work, so it doesn't really make sense to edit what you thought at the time cause that's still valid (Alex, PG student).

The "othering" of the blogger in the press and other popular media produces a range of ambivalent positions on the part of teachers and students. Alex's orientation towards assessment is also interesting because it suggests a response to the problem of blogging being seen as an illegitimate or narcissistic activity – to stress the extent to which it is being done as a requirement, externally imposed, rather than as a result of a desire on the part of the student.

Othering: What Kind of Person Would Share that with the Whole World?

An important aspect of popular narratives of blogging is that they are very often constructed by outsiders who examine blogging culture and practices from a conspicuous distance. There is a discourse of othering running through many if not most media reports, editorials and even some academic literature (for example, Nardi et al. 2004) on the subject, where blogging is very often represented as the sort of thing that *other kinds of people* would do. Sometimes blogging behaviour is even pathologised, as in Buffardi and Campbell (2008) and Jacobs (2003), who claims that "the very interactive nature of blogging makes it innately supportive of both exhibitionistic and voyeuristic behaviours" (p. 2).

This tendency to view bloggers as strange or "other" extends to some of the teachers I spoke with:

> I [pause] I don't know why people blog. I, I'm not, it doesn't appeal particularly. [pause] I can see having a public voice on the web would be nice, but it assumes that people are interested in what you've got to say and it means that you know that you have to have interesting things to say every week or twice a week, and that's not really a pressure that I particularly want but, a lot of people obviously do, so (Jane, lecturer, PG).

Students, too, make comments which emphatically demonstrate their non-blogger status:

> Jen: do you think at all about what you do, were doing in [the e-portfolio] as being like a weblog?
>
> Beth (UG student): No, not really. No, I just, I just see it as a means of me getting, you know, getting my work done, really.
>
> Jen: Yeah, okay. Um, and what do you think about kind of blogging, in the world, more generally?
>
> Beth: ...I can't see me doing it. Maybe I feel like I, I honestly haven't got anything interesting to say, but I just think I haven't really got time and I don't... And what I think I just kind of kind of keep it to myself, I'm not really bothered about spreading it internationally! It's not a, not a great urge of mine, and I just, well, who'd read it, who'd really care, you know?

In order to stake a claim of not being like the people described above, students and teachers have to distance themselves from their own practices to some extent. They do not want to be seen as one of the strange, narcissistic people who *choose* to engage in blogging practices (writing or reading):

> I don't read other blogs really. I'm just not that interested. If people have got something to tell me they'll come and tell me. And I'm not in to the big brother idea. I've never watched that programme. I just, um I don't see the fascination that some people have with knowing everything about certain people's moves (Theresa, UG student).

For students, who generally have not had a choice about whether to engage in online reflection, the claim is that they are just doing what is required of them, that it is nothing to do with who they are; arguably not a very conducive starting position from which to develop reflective habits: "a lot of students will start by saying 'oh my god I hate blogging, why are you, why are you asking me to do this?'" (Jane, lecturer, PG). For teachers, who in many cases design these practices, or at least are responsible for promoting them to students, the claim would seem to be more subtle: that their practices are different, are not of the risky, self-absorbed, problematic sort that they can critique as well as anyone:

> I think there's a big psychological risk to being online too much. You know why do we want to go out and, I don't know ... I'll tell you what I think it is, I think it's this celebrity, cult of celebrity thing (Sam, lecturer, UG).

For both students and teachers, there is a shadow hanging over their online reflective practice, one that illustrates the extent to which discourses of blogging leak into educational settings.

Narcissism: Bloggers Are Shallow and Self-Obsessed

As we see above, most discourses of blogging "other" the blogger in ways that are problematic for educational uses of online reflection. The most common charge is that only narcissistic, self-involved people blog. Guadagno et al. (2008) claim that bloggers are predisposed towards neuroticism, while Curtain characterises the primary emotion of the blogger as one of anxiety:

> Anxiety may be the primary emotion associated with giving accounts of blogging, and perhaps of blogging itself – Do I update enough? Why don't I write? Who is reading me? Why aren't there more? What do they think about what I say? Have I said enough about enough... (2004, online).

The discourse of the self-obsessed blogger is pervasive and problematic for the use of online reflection in educational contexts. Some students may be happy to claim and perhaps subvert these less flattering descriptions:

> I'm a show off and loudmouth by nature … So, I kind of feel like I'm happy for anybody to see sort of anything about me, I'm the sort of person who has a public profile on Facebook. [laughter] (Megan, PG student).

Megan's confident construction of herself as naturally "showing off" indicates both a clear understanding of the discourse, and a certain degree of powerlessness in the face of an intrinsic character trait. Other students are more susceptible to anxieties when they are reflecting online, especially when they are aware that their teachers can see their work at any time, and may be looking. It is notable, I think, how closely Charles' questions here echo Curtain's above:

> this kind of kind of dependency like one gets hooked on cigarettes or something [laughter], one kind of gets hooked on the tutor and thought, you know, 'oh, why is she taking so long to mark this?', you know 'why aren't I getting any feedback now?', and it wasn't long at all!…'oh, she's forgotten about me, oh that's a real shame'. 'Oh, didn't I make more impression than that?' [laugh] (Charles, PG student).

Charles believes that his task is to make an impression on his teacher – and that the mark of his success will be if he provokes her feedback. He sees himself as having been addicted, "like one gets hooked on cigarettes or something", to her response, and both desperate and helpless in the face of her silence. Mallan argues that, rather than implying mental health issues on the part of the blogger, these sorts of fears of invisibility are a fundamental aspect of the construction of "shifting subject positions" online:

> These subject positions are not just ontological states, but inevitably entail a politics of visibility, both at the personal level and at the level of technological infrastructure. It is this "visibility" which gives rise to epithets of narcissism and susceptibility (2009, pp. 51–52).

Another possible response to this charge of narcissism is to view blogging in a very pragmatic, commodified way, tapping into discourses of employability and personal branding. The online context intensifies questions of what should not be said, as we have seen, and also about how to put a "best face forward", how to leverage online presence as "personal brand" to best effect.

Commodification: Your Online Presence
Is Your Personal Brand

Within the framing of the Web as medium for deliberate self-presentation, there is increasingly the notion that it is essential for success in today's world to nurture and manage a highly visible "personal brand" online. This discourse is managerial and market-driven:

> A strong personal brand identity ideally can endure for decades... To be successful, aspirants must adapt to the growing maturity of the marketplace, competitive threats, changes in social mores and values, proliferation of communication channels, and other factors that serve to challenge brand resilience (Rein et al. 2005, p. 349).

The personal brand which lasts for decades is cast as not only a benefit but one which can and must be harnessed and controlled by the "aspirant". Cultivating a personal brand requires a strategic and calculating posture towards online disclosure and identity, and just the right combination of authenticity and marketing prowess. Some students, taking this to heart, are very concerned about getting their online reflections "right" in the first instance and wary of losing control of their message online:

> It felt safer writing it in a Word document first. There's something about writing directly you know into an online format whatever that is more [pause] live I suppose... I need to be absolutely sure that what I'm writing is what I want to write because it might it might disappear onto the internet at any time, you know? [laugh] ...maybe it's something to do with um what you, sort of preconceptions of what a blog is and what the internet is ...you know, that blogs are very public things (Lynne, PG student).

Because it felt risky, public and "live", Lynne put off her engagement with the online reflective space so that she entered it only when she was sure of what she wanted to say. Lynne's cautious approach would seem to bear out Kimball's concern that the persistent nature of digital archives may cause students to back away from a more spontaneous, authentic process of reflection (2005, p. 454). The fear of losing something in the Web – something which can never be retrieved, but that will forever follow and mark its author – is where the risk of disclosure meets the promise of the personal brand, and it is extremely problematic for traditional notions of what reflective practice should be about.

Personal branding also goes hand in hand with a stated need to stand out in what is often referred to as an "attention economy" (Lanham 2007). Here again, students are aware of and engaged with the possibilities for their reflective online spaces, even if it is not immediately intended for a wider audience:

> there's something quite motivating and engaging about just publishing something even if it's only to one person... if I wanted to I could share it publicly and I could promote it and I could get people to look at it. And even though I'm not doing that I kind of know that I could (Alex, PG student).

The rhetoric of empowerment and professionalisation that blogging carries with it depends to a large extent on a belief in the control of the individual over their brand, and the harnessing of the Web for the individual's goals and purposes. However, even if bloggers manage only to release aspects of themselves which are professionally appropriate, the archive constitutes a form of compulsory memory over which individuals have little control: "we do not produce our databased selves, the databased selves produce us" (Simon 2005, p. 16). Database-driven technologies for *storing* the data produced in online reflection may, in the case of public or potentially public reflection, produce a radical recontextualisation, as "digital archives allow situational context to collapse with ease. ...search engines can collapse any data at any period of time" (boyd 2001, p. 33). A remixed, recontextualised version of yourself may bear little resemblance to the identity you are trying to project. The carefully crafted online personal brand is, therefore, an illusion, and a constraining one at that.

Conclusion

There is a growing openness in higher education to an e-learning agenda which positions new digital "tools" as the answer to market needs, globalisation, and a new generation of so-called digital native consumer-students, without an accompanying critical stance which would support students and teachers to engage creatively and carefully with digital practices and cultures (Clegg et al. 2003; Goodfellow and Lea 2007; Bayne and Ross 2011). These tools and environments are neither innocent nor culturally neutral, though as they are "inscribed with social meaning, power relations, possibilities for and restrictions on the expression of personal identity" (Goodfellow and Lea 2007, p. 128), and their use in higher education can produce many points of tension.

As we see in the previous section, new pressures and problems are produced when reflection moves online. Cultural constructions of the blog as a space of confession, the reconfiguration of privacy online, and a perceived need to "prove" one's authenticity in the face of a web which facilitates deception sit uneasily with the riskiness and danger associated with too much disclosure. Too much disclosure also carries with it the possible charge of narcissism, and the construction of a "bad" personal brand, archived forever. It is clear that new rhetorical strategies are needed to make the best use of online reflective spaces, and that more explicit engagement with the "webness" of these practices is urgently required. In particular, online reflection in higher education requires a new orientation towards authenticity that takes account of issues of power, identity and disclosure in the online context.

Lillis describes a dominant "practice of mystery" (2001, p. 74) surrounding academic writing in higher education. In her research context, teachers know what they want and expect students to know how to deliver it. In online reflective practices, teachers are in a new and complex space in which they do not always know what they want. This is partly, as Carpenter claims, because online literacy practices are at odds with notions of boundary crossing, joining the club, or "insiderdom" (Russell et al. 2009, p. 413) that characterise traditional academic practices (Carpenter 2009, p. 142). It is also because a discourse of replication is so prevalent in the sphere of e-learning, claiming that online practices can be imported wholesale from their offline counterparts. This is, quite simply, not so.

As teachers, we need to review and revise how we induct students into the practice of online reflective writing, and what we expect of their online reflections. This could mean, for instance, being more definite in welcoming students' fictions, and their experiments with voice and subjectivity, whether cautious or playful. At present, students feel they must, at all costs, be seen to be authentic in their online reflections, and this, paradoxically, is hampering their understanding of and engagement with a challenging mode of writing. If explicitly offered the online reflective space as a space of construction, experimentation and refinement – as a challenge to situate themselves as academic and professional actors within a particular disciplinary framework – the need for a strategic approach could be less confusing and more rewarding for students.

The values of authenticity and personal development need to be reviewed for networked learning contexts which are social in complex ways, and enmeshed in webs which do not respect boundaries separating vernacular and academic discourses or spaces. Some university teachers are actively exploring these kinds of new perspectives, and are both excited and challenged by what they are finding. For example, Hughes and Purnell (2008) have been working with e-portfolios, and are concluding that:

> the new landscapes may offer exciting 'openings' (Stronach & MacLure, 1997) for learning and teaching that support the shift from traditional anxious academic literacy practices of monologic addressivity to a more fluid and exciting literacy 'infidelity' allowing for increasing dialogue and exchange within student groups (p. 151).

More broadly, as researchers into networked learning, we should always be attending to networks in both senses described in the early part of this chapter: purposeful digital connections and inevitable digital flows. In their networked learning practices, students and teachers are working at the boundaries of the deliberate and the unruly, and this is a difficult and fascinating space which would benefit from more exploration and creative and critical attention.

References

Barrett, H., & Carney, J. (2005). *Conflicting paradigms and competing purposes in electronic portfolio development*. Retrieved 22 September, 2011, from: http://www.electronicportfolios.com/portfolios/LEAJournal-BarrettCarney.pdf

Barton, D., Hamilton, M., & Ivanič, R. (2000). *Situated literacies: Reading and writing in context*. London: Routledge.

Bayne, S. (2005). Deceit, desire and control: The identities of learners and teachers in cyberspace. In Land R. & Bayne, S. (Eds.), *Education in Cyberspace*. London: RoutledgeFalmer.

Bayne, S., & Ross, J. (2011). 'Digital Native' and 'Digital Immigrant' Discourses: A Critique. In R. Land, & S. Bayne (Eds.), *Digital difference: perspectives on online learning* (pp. 159–170). Rotterdam: Sense.

Bortree, D. (2005). Presentation of self on the Web: An ethnographic study of teenage girls' Weblogs. *Education, Communication & Information, 5*(1), 25–39.

Boud, D., Keogh, R., & Walker, D. (1985). *Reflection: Turning experience into learning*. London: Kogan Page.

boyd, D. (2001). *Faceted Id/entity: Managing representation in a digital world*. Cambridge: MIT.

boyd, D. (2008). Why youth (heart) social network sites: The role of networked publics in teenage social life. In D. Buckingham (Ed.), *Youth, identity, and digital media* (pp. 119–142). Cambridge: MIT.

Brockbank, A., & McGill, I. (1998). *Facilitating reflective learning in higher education*. Buckingham: SRHE/Open University Press.

Bruns, A., & Jacobs, J. (2007). *Uses of blogs*. New York: Peter Lang.

Buffardi, L., & Campbell, W. K. (2008). Narcissism and social networking web sites. *Personality and Social Psychology Bulletin, 34*(10), 1303–1314.

Butler, P. (2006). *A review of the literature on portfolios and electronic portfolios*. Palmerston North: Massey University College of Education. Retrieved 22 September, 2011, from: http://akoaotearoa.ac.nz/download/ng/file/group-996/n2620-eportfolio-research-report.pdf

Carpenter, R. (2009). Boundary negotiations: Electronic environments as interface. *Computers and Composition, 26*, 138–148.

Carrington, V. (2007). 'I'm Dylan and I'm not going to say my last name': Some thoughts on childhood, text and new technologies. *British Educational Research Journal, 34*(2), 151–166.

Castells, M. (1999). *Critical education in the new information age*. Oxford: Rowman & Littlefield.

Clegg, S., Hudson, A., & Steel, J. (2003). The emperor's new clothes: Globalisation and e-learning in higher education. *British Journal of Sociology of Education, 24*(1), 39–53.

Creme, P. (2005). Should student learning journals be assessed? *Assessment & Evaluation in Higher Education, 30*(3), 287–296.

Curtain, T. (2004). Promiscuous fictions. In Gurak, L. J. Antonijevic, S., Johnson, L., Ratliff, C., & Reyman, J. (Eds.), *Into the blogosphere: Rhetoric, community, and culture of weblogs*. Retrieved 22 September, 2001, from: http://blog.lib.umn.edu/blogosphere/promiscuous_fictions.html

Devas, A. (2004). Reflection as confession: Discipline and docility in/on the student body. *Art Design and Communication in Higher Education, 3*(1), 33–46.

Doctorow, C. (2006). Disney exec: Piracy is just a business model. *Boing Boing*. Retrieved 22 September, 2001, from: http://www.boingboing.net/2006/10/10/disney-exec-piracy-i.html

Duffy, P., & Bruns, A. (2006). *The use of blogs, wikis and RSS in education: A conversation of possibilities*. Presented at the Online Learning and Teaching Conference 2006, Brisbane.

Dutta, S. (2010). Managing yourself: What's your personal social media strategy? *Harvard Business Review, 2010*, 1–5.

Dyson, E. (1998). *Release 2.1: A design for living in the digital age*. New York: Broadway Books.

Efimova, L., & Grudin, J. (2007). Crossing boundaries: A case study of employee blogging. *Proceedings of the Fortieth Hawaii International Conference on System Sciences (HICSS-40)*. Los Alamitos: IEEE Press.

Ellison, N., Heino, R., & Gibbs, J. (2006). Managing impressions online: Self-presentation processes in the online dating environment. *Journal of Computer-Mediated Communication, 11*(2). Retrieved 22 September, 2001, from: http://jcmc.indiana.edu/vol11/issue2/ellison.html

E-Quality Network (2002). *E-quality in e-learning manifesto*. Presented at the Networked Learning 2002 Conference, Sheffield. Retrieved 22 September, 2001, from: http://csalt.lancs.ac.uk/esrc/

Freidrich, B. (2007). *Fictional blogs: How digital narratives are changing the way we read and write*. Cedar Rapids, IA: Coe College.

Goodfellow, R., & Lea, M. (2007). *Challenging E-learning in the university: A literacies approach*. Maidenhead: Open University Press.

Goodyear, P., Banks, S., Hodgson, V., & McConnell, D. (2004). *Advances in research on networked learning*. Dordrecht: Kluwer.

Guadagno, R., Okdie, B., & Eno, C. (2008). Who blogs? Personality predictors of blogging. *Computers in Human Behavior, 24*, 1993–2004.

Hargreaves, J. (2004). So how do you feel about that? Assessing reflective practice. *Nurse Education Today, 24*, 196–201.

Holbrook, D. (2006). *Theorizing the diary weblog*. Chicago: University of Chicago.

Holquist, M. (2002). *Dialogism*. London: Routledge.

Hope, A. (2008). Internet pollution discourses, exclusionary practices and the 'culture of over-blocking' within UK schools. *Technology, Pedagogy and Education, 17*(2), 102–113.

Hughes, J., & Purnell, E. (2008). Blogging for beginners? Using blogs and eportfolios in teacher education. *Proceedings of the 6th International Conference on Networked Learning*. Lancaster: Lancaster University.

Ivanič, R. (1998). *Writing and identity: The discoursal construction of identity in academic writing*. Amsterdam: Benjamins.

Jacobs, J. (2003). *Communication over exposure: The rise of blogs as a product of cyber-voyeurism*. Paper presented at ANZCA03 Conference, Brisbane.

Jones, C., & Dirckinck-Holmfeld, L. (2009). Analysing networked learning practices. In L. Dirckinck-Holmfeld, C. Jones, & B. Lindström (Eds.), *Analysing networked learning practices in higher education and continuing professional development*. Rotterdam: Sense Publishers.

Kimball, M. (2005). Database e-portfolio systems: A critical appraisal. *Computers and Composition, 22*, 434–458.

Lair, D. J., Sullivan, K., & Cheney, G. (2005). Marketization and the recasting of the professional self. *Management Communication Quarterly, 18*(3), 307–343.

Lanham, R. (2007). *The economics of attention*. Chicago: University of Chicago Press.

Lea, M., & Street, B. (2009). Student writing in higher education: An academic literacies approach. In F. Fletcher-Campbell, G. Reid, & J. Soler (Eds.), *Approaching difficulties in literacy development: Assessment, pedagogy and programmes*. London: Sage.

Lillis, T. (2001). *Student writing: Access, regulation, desire*. London: Routledge.

Lillis, T. (2003). Student writing as 'Academic Literacies': Drawing on Bakhtin to move from critique to design. *Language and Education, 17*(3), 192–207.

Macfarlane, B., & Gourlay, L. (2009). The reflection game: Enacting the penitent self. *Studies in Higher Education, 14*, 455–459.

Mallan, K. (2009). Look at me! Look at me! Self-representation and self-exposure through online networks. *Digital Culture and Education, 1*(1), 51–66.

McKenna, C. (2005). Words, bridges and dialogue: Issues of audience and addressivity in online communication. In R. Land & S. Bayne (Eds.), *Education in cyberspace* (pp. 91–104). London: RoutledgeFalmer.

Moon, J. (1999). *Reflection in learning and professional development: Theory and practice*. London: Routledge.

Nardi, B., Schiano, D., & Gumbrecht, M. (2004). *Blogging as social activity, or, would you let 900 million people read your diary?* Computer Supported Cooperative Work '04, Chicago, IL.

Peters, T. (1997). The brand called you. *Fast Company*, 10. Retrieved 22 September, 2001, from: http://www.fastcompany.com/magazine/10/brandyou.html

Poster, M. (2006). *Information please: Culture and politics in the age of digital machines*. Durham: Duke University Press.

Reed, A. (2005). 'My blog is me': Texts and persons in UK online journal culture (and anthropology). *Ethnos, 70*(2), 220–242.

Rein, I., Kotler, P., Hamlin, M., & Stoller, M. (2005). *High visibility: Transforming your personal and professional brand*. New York: McGraw-Hill.

Ross, J. (2011). Traces of self: Online reflective practices and performances in higher education. *Teaching in Higher Education, 16*(1), 113–126.

Russell, D., Lea, M., Parker, J., Street, B., & Donahue, T. (2009). Exploring notions of genre in 'academic literacies' and 'writing across the curriculum': Approaches across countries and contexts. In C. Bazerman, A. Bonini, & D. Figueiredo (Eds.), *Genre in a changing world. Perspectives on writing* (pp. 459–491). Colorado: WAC Clearinghouse/Parlor Press.

Scott, S. (2004). Researching shyness: A contradiction in terms? *Qualitative Research, 4*(1), 91–105.

Simon, B. (2005). The return of panopticism: Supervision, subjection and the new surveillance. *Surveillance and Society, 3*(1), 1–20.

Stefani, L., Mason, R., & Pegler, C. (2007). *The educational potential of e-portfolios: Supporting personal development and reflective learning.* Abingdon: Routledge.

Walker Rettberg, J. (2008). Blogs, literacies and the collapse of private and public. *Leonardo Electronic Almanac, 16*(2–3), 1–10. Retrieved 22 September, 2001, from: http://jilltxt.net/txt/Blogs--Literacy%20-and-the-Collapse-of-Private-and-Public.pdf

Chapter 12
Objectified Cultural Capital and the Tale of Two Students

Laura Czerniewicz and Cheryl Brown

Introduction

Almost a decade has passed since the participants of the ESRC seminar series on the Implications of Networked Learning for Higher Education in the UK expressed a vision for a higher education, where access and connection were championed. This chapter considers those issues of access and connection, through the lens of Bourdieu's theoretical concepts, and argues that specific types of objectified capital can change students' technological habitus, opening up the possibilities of increased access to higher education practices.

In this chapter, we report on the role of the objectified forms of cultural capital (specifically cell phones) and the ways these forms of capital inter-relate with other forms of cultural capital, shifting power relations and opening up access to the field of higher education. This is particularly pertinent in the South African context, where increased demand and participation by a diverse range of students have resulted in massification of the sector: both student numbers overall and the number of black students in particular have grown substantially since the apartheid regime ended in 1994 (Council on Higher Education 2009, p. 5). Indeed, the proportion of African students in the public higher education system as a whole increased from 49% in 1995 to 61% in the 10 years post the apartheid government. And by 2007, African students made up 63% of the total enrolment in public higher education (Council on Higher Education 2009).

At the same time, the sector is resource constrained. While there has been a steady increase in state funding for higher education since 2004, both in absolute terms and when inflation is taken into account, the proportion of the national budget going to higher education has declined (Council on Higher Education 2009).

L. Czerniewicz (✉) • C. Brown
University of Cape Town, Cape Town, South Africa
e-mail: laura.czerniewicz@uct.ac.za

L. Dirckinck-Holmfeld et al. (eds.), *Exploring the Theory, Pedagogy and Practice of Networked Learning*, DOI 10.1007/978-1-4614-0496-5_12, © Springer Science+Business Media, LLC 2012

Equally, state spending on computer equipment has declined, leaving technological provision dependent on the ability of individual institutions to raise additional funding. In South Africa, universities increasingly rely on other sources of funding; on average, a third of their income is from non-state sources. But the capacity of institutions to generate other funding streams differs, and the proportion of funds coming from other sources differs across institutional types with universities of technology most dependent on state funding (Council on Higher Education 2009).

This is especially problematic in a country characterised by a severe digital divide and a higher education sector, where students from particular groups are disadvantaged in terms of their ICT access particularly with regard to ability and support (Czerniewicz and Brown 2009). The type of university they have access to, with that institution's concomitant ability to raise funds for learning technology, thus becomes yet another factor which can advantage or disadvantage individual students.

The cases reported in this chapter arise from long-term research on South African university students' access to and use of information and communication technologies (ICTs) principally for learning (Brown and Czerniewicz 2010; Czerniewicz and Brown 2006; Czerniewicz et al. 2009). Here, we present case studies of two students who can be regarded as exemplars of the two clusters of students we identified in a large-scale study (described later), clusters we categorised as the "digital elite" and "digital strangers". The digital elite formed 11% of our total sample – they were characterised by having more than 10 years experience using ICTs, had grown up with access to ICTs, indicated they had learnt to use a computer by teaching themselves or through social networks of family and friends and were able to solve current ICT problems themselves. We found in the South African context that this elite matched the characteristics of the "digital native" as espoused by Prensky (2001a, b), but differed in one important aspect – it was not about age, but about experience. The group identified as digital strangers was significantly larger – 22% of our sample. They had not had access to computers before coming to university, had less than 2 years experience using computers and relied most often on formal channels to acquire this knowledge.

Discussions about access to ICTs in the scholarly literature and the policy discourses usually refer directly to computers – hence, the more common references to computer literacy. Even the later term ICT literacy tends to mean computers rather than other types of technology. Yet, we found that while the group of "digital strangers" in our research were indeed strangers to computer-based technology, they were not strangers to all digital technology. Importantly, they all had access to and experience of cell phones.

This is especially relevant in the South African context, where growing up digital applies to only a small proportion of the population; only 14.8% of households have a personal computer (compared – a few years ago – to 75% in the UK and 70% in the USA) (International Telecommunication Union 2007). There is also a marked connectivity divide between provinces within the country, with only two of the provinces (Western Cape and Gauteng) having a positive ratio in terms of the proportion of Internet users in a province compared with the proportion of the total population (Goldstuck 2008). Furthermore, there is a marked rural/urban divide. One illustrative case study undertaken in the KwaZulu Natal Province involved a spatial analysis of the rural–urban divide and concluded that ICT access correlates with higher incomes and urban investment (Odendaal et al. 2008).

Yet 67% of the South African population owns a cell phone (AMPS 2010), and the number of unique South African users accessing the mobile Internet using WAP is already just about double the size of the number of users accessing the fixed Internet (Joubert 2009). Among the students we had surveyed previously, cell phone ownership was ubiquitous (98.5% in 2007) and not socially differentiated. In addition, cell phones were the main means of access to the Internet off campus by students from low socio-economic groups (SEGs) (Brown and Czerniewicz 2010).

Given that all students inhabit digitally mediated worlds, that the digital forms part of their identities and that in the South African context this is facilitated by cell phone technologies, we were keen to consider what access to such ubiquitous technology might mean in terms of accessing and contributing to higher education. We found Bourdieu's theoretical concepts a useful way to do so.

Bourdieu's Theoretical Framework

Bourdieu's framework provides a way of describing students' practices through the key concepts of "field", "habitus" and "capital". The field explains and defines the structures or systems within which individuals attempt to achieve their outcomes. It is "a structured system of social positions … the nature of which defines the situation for their occupants" (Jenkins 2002). Higher education is one of a series of relatively autonomous worlds or fields whose complex interactions constitute society. Like all social fields, higher education is a site of struggle over resources of all kinds, as it is "a system of forces which exist between these positions ….structured internally in terms of power relations" (ibid).

Access to forms of capital is central, as "positions [in the field] stand in relationships of domination, subordination or equivalence (homology) to each other by virtue of the access they afford to the goods or resources (capital) which are at stake in the field. … The nature of positions, their 'objective definition', is to be found in their relationship to the relevant form of capital" (ibid). Bourdieu explains that " … the structure of the distribution of the different types and subtypes of capital at a given moment in time represents the immanent structure of the social world, i.e., the set of constraints, inscribed in the very reality of that world, which govern its functioning in a durable way, determining the chances of success for practices" (Bourdieu 1986, p. 241).

Capital presents itself in four fundamental forms: economic, social, cultural and symbolic. Economic capital refers to assets either in the form of or convertible to cash. Social capital is about connections, social obligation and networks, i.e. who you know (or do not know) and advantages or disadvantages of a person. Cultural capital occurs in three states; embodied cultural capital refers to "long-lasting dispositions of the mind and body" (ibid), expressed commonly as skills, competencies, knowledge and representation of self-image. Objectified cultural capital refers to physical objects as "cultural goods which are the trace or realization of theories or critiques of these theories" (Bourdieu mentions pictures, books, dictionaries, instruments, machines, ibid). Institutional cultural capital is the formal recognition of knowledge usually in the form of educational qualifications. Symbolic capital is appropriated when one of the other capitals is converted to prestige, honour, reputation and fame – it is about recognition, value and status.

Importantly, one form of capital can be converted into another. The different forms of capital are different forms of *power*, but the relative importance of the different forms varies according to the field.

Habitus is the way that all the different constructs come together, the dynamic and shifting relationship between particular field and capitals. Bourdieu explains that habitus is a system of durable and transposable dispositions, developed in response to determining structures. An individual's habitus is both involuntary (outside of their control) and voluntary (changeable). Habitus is about identity, about being in the world and is the intersection between structure and agency.

It is, therefore, clear that while individuals are able to exercise agency, that agency is socially constrained and is exercised within the existing social conventions, rules, values and sanctions, negotiated specifically within the rules of the fields in which they operate.

The Project

The Overall Study

This research is based on a research project that has been ongoing since 2003. The project, which comprised three phases to date, investigates various aspects of students' access to and use of ICTs. Phases 1 and 2 involved surveys of 6,577 students from 6 universities in the Western Cape region of South Africa in 2004, and 3,533 students in 6 different universities located in other regions of South Africa in 2007. Phase 3 (on which this chapter is based) is a qualitative study which adopts a nested case study approach (Lieberman 2005). Initially, we conducted a brief survey of 513 students across 4 universities as background. This survey was undertaken on students doing computer literacy training and information literacy/library courses on the one hand and those studying courses where ICT competencies were a required professional component on the other hand.

From this, we selected students with contrasting levels of access to ICTs and a range of degrees of use and then followed this up with 114 first-level telephone interviews. We then conducted 38 second-level interviews with a subset of this group culminating in 6 focus groups.

The Case Studies

The research reported here draws on data from the Phase 3 research, in particular, two illustrative cases of students who participated in all four levels of data collection. We selected these as they represented the two extremes of digital literacy that we had encountered in the earlier phases of our research. These two cases are an example of how students exposed to different technologies at different stages of their lives used cell phones and computers for learning. The students Sipho and Nhlanhla (not their real names) are both similar (they are young, black males, live away from home and attend universities within the same province) and different (one grew up in a rural context and the other in an urban context, and they attend different kinds of institutions). Sipho attends a medium-sized, previously disadvantaged, comprehensive[1] university while Nhlanhla attends a small, traditional, previously advantaged university. Neither speaks English as a first language with isiXhosa being Sipho's home language and isiZulu, Nhlanhla's. Sipho's interviews were conducted in both English and isiXhosa and the focus group in which he participated was largely conducted in isiXhosa. Nhlanhla's interviews and focus group were all conducted in English.

Findings

Nhlanhla: The Digital Elite

Nhlanhla arrived at university part of the digital elite having "grown up digital" with his first digital experience through the family computer at age 7. He had access to a multiple range of ICTs and was a frequent user of technology socially. His advantage is manifest in his economic and social capital, especially with regards to the ability to persuade his parents to buy him new kinds of technology, as this snippet of family history indicates:

> [With regards technology in the family] I was in the driver's seat, … and my brother would be on the passenger seat and my parents would be behind us, … my brother and I were the only people that actually really cared about technology, so it has always been us who've been in charge of, lets get this, lets do that, they don't really mind what, ja, we just tell them we need to get this and if we convince them enough then they would … buy it

Nhlanhla lives in residence and uses three different university laboratories on campus, one of which is open 24 h a day. He has access to *"pretty much all the things that any post-teen/young adult has access to … cell phone, the walkman,*

---

[1]Comprehensive universities are a new category of higher education institution in South Africa which involved a merger between a university and a former "technikon" in the restructuring of the higher education system which occurred post 2000.

the iPod, laptop, computer and the internet". He has a smart phone, not even a year old, and has Internet access and Wi-Fi so if he can find a hotspot he can use his phone for downloads. He would prefer to have Internet on his laptop, but his *"mother complained about the bill so she disconnected it"*.

Nhlanhla remembers first starting to use the family computer at age 7. His formative experiences were with computers. He acquired his first cell phone when he was 12 years old. He was motivated to start using technology by interest *"since my father was also into it, and we enjoy doing the same things, we both got into it"*. As he was growing up, he *"would read about technology in magazines, etc"*. Nhlanhla is extremely confident with using technology saying that he finds pretty much everything easy because *"I've grown up with computers so I can do all the basics and quite a lot of the advanced stuff"*.

His activities and interests are sometimes curriculum driven *"I do information systems and I'd love to go into the programming section of my work. Right now we're doing databases and word documentation and we haven't got to the programming part yet"*.

Nhlanhla has a wide range of options in terms of access to technology and as a result he makes his choices about his technology practices in order of preference. He uses his phone to access the Internet as his first preference. *"At the beginning of the month yes a lot because that's when my contract has just been recharged so I can afford to but towards the end of the month my contract is nearly exhausted so I use the computers on campus"*. Once he runs out of cell time, if *"I don't feel like walking out at night so I ask my friends if I can use their internet"* and *"If I need to use the internet desperately and my friends are busy I would primarily go to the jet labs or the union labs"*.

He values both cell phone and a laptop but would prioritise the cell phone: *"Right now it's the cell phone, sometimes it's hard to lug around a laptop everywhere so I'd say a cell phone is important, with internet access. My cell phone has wifi so if there's a wifi spot I can use my phone to download something"*. Although the cell phone came later in his overall ICT experience and is part of a myriad of technological devices, it is his first preference in terms of Internet access and if he could buy any new technology in the next 6 months, it would be a cell phone with more highly developed capabilities.

Sipho: The Digital Stranger

When Sipho arrived at university, he was a digital stranger having only just been exposed to computers for the first time in his final year of school, not having had access to ICTs while he was growing up.

On campus, Sipho's choices are limited: the general university labs require booking and have a time limit on use and his department labs which *"we have to share ... with the first years, second years, all those guys"*. He lives away from campus and has an old desktop computer for university that he describes as *"not that good, the thing is old. It has Windows 2000. So it lacks some things, anything that requires javascript it can't accommodate"*. His father and brother do use a computer at work and when he goes back home he takes his computer with him and *"we only use it to play music and fun and games, that kind of thing, so nothing serious that we do"*. In addition, he has a cell phone with WAPs well as a flash drive.

It was through his cell phone that Sipho had his first exposure to ICTs, the Internet and indeed was able to teach himself how to use a computer, and it is through the cell phone that he has the majority of his ICT-based social engagement. His earliest digital experiences were acquired first through his cell phone which his parents bought him in his final year of school. While he was also introduced to computers around this time, his first experience of the Internet was through his cell phone. He taught himself how to use the cell phone via the manual and how to use a computer by downloading computer tutorials through the Internet on his cell phone and then working through them on his desktop. He did not do a computer literacy course when he started university as he was confident using ICTs, but he has had training through his degree programme as he is studying computer science.

Sipho is passionate about technology and about using it to access information, *"Yes, you must always search so that you remain up to date – so that you avoid being outdated. In other words in order to be up dated you must subscribe to those development sites, so that you often get newsletters – so that you know what is happening currently – what is happening just around"*. He continues to teach himself new skills, *"I was learning about creating html pages, and we don't do that in school. And also the linux stuff, how to work on the linux 08"*.

While Sipho's access to technology is more limited in terms of what technology he can use off campus, it appears that his choices are more strategic and driven by activity. In contrast to Nhlanhla, he has to make choices about which tasks to do in the light of what technology he has available to him. When Sipho is at university, he uses the "school" computers, but these have limitations because *"they are some things you seem to be unable to be done on the internet for instance because the administration and all that kind of stuff because ... there are so many restrictions"*. He uses his home computer for studying and storing things. He finds *"doing assignments and such things more easy on the computer because the computer has the keyboard and mouse and when it comes to a cell phone it would be difficult to do it"*. He uses his cell-based Internet to solve problems, *"When I am studying at home or when there something that I think of doing, maybe I come across that particular topic that I am not good at, I then use internet – in other words it's some bit of research"*. But he is conscious of the limitations of mobile Internet *"because in most times a cell phone produces different results from those of a computer – it's a bit limited, so if I want to do a thorough research I then use a computer or when I realize that its something that I must go deeper into it – but if I just want it to introduce something for me, then I use it (a cell phone), --I think it assists me but if I want to understand something that is difficult or if I am also looking for the other sites because the other sites are not compatible with my cell phone, so then a computer accommodate those"*.

Overall, while Sipho considers computers important, he says he cannot live without his cell phone.

Discussion

With access to capital of all kinds shifting in different conditions, and varying at their respective universities, the two students use a range of technologies in a range of locations to facilitate their learning activities. In previous studies, we found that on-campus access was the key mechanism for ensuring equality of access for all students given that off-campus access has been so varied and unequal (Czerniewicz and Brown 2009). Certainly, that is still true in these cases, as both students do have and use on-campus access. Yet, off campus, despite obvious differences, there are important similarities between these two students, with the central leveller being the cell phone. The increasingly complicated relationships users have with the different types of technology have led researchers Donner and Gitau (2009) to suggest that "mobile-centric Internet use" can occur in different ways. They created a typology of mobile-only Internet users and mobile-primary Internet users, with subcategories for those who had and those who had not used a PC prior to mobile Internet.

How are these students similar and how are they different? What can be observed about their individual habitus? Does the appropriation of a particular form of objectified cultural capital change the power relations between students usually regarded as advantaged and those traditionally regarded as disadvantaged? Does access to the field of higher education shift for particular individuals?

We see in these accounts the different ways that two students have converted their embodied cultural capital into an integral part of their person, i.e. their habitus. We are able to observe their "ways of acting, feeling, thinking and being. It captures how [they] carry within [their] history, how [they] bring this history into [their] present circumstances, and how [they] then make choices to act in certain ways and then not others" (Maton 2008).

Both students have appropriated a specific type of cultural capital in its objectified form. They both acquired the economic capital to appropriate the material object and have attained the embodied cultural capital in the form of appropriate knowledge and skills to use ICTs for their cultural capital, in terms of "the digital", to be recognised or represented, thus acquiring important symbolic capital.

However, although each student acquired the symbolic capital of digital literacy, they have not done so the same way nor have they had the same choices. This is not unexpected, as the process of choice is influenced by an individual's cultural and social capital and material constraints (Ball et al. 2002).This resonates with other interpretations of Bourdieu's conceptualisation of the differences between people's choices as "the opposition between the tastes of luxury (or freedom) and the tastes for necessity" (Bourdieu, 1986, p. 177–178; Ball et al. 2002). Nhlanhla can make choices around what he prefers in terms of technology as he has access to multiple technologies in multiple locations. However, Sipho has to make his choices out of economic necessity because he does not have the same freedom of choice and must use the technology that is available to him either on or off campus.

For our two students, both the age at which the "work of transmission and accumulation of embodied capital" (Bourdieu 1990) began and the way in which occurred are markedly different. This is important because, as Bourdieu (1986) reminds us, cultural capital "always remains marked by its earliest conditions of acquisition …". The process through which our students appropriated the objectified cultural capital and the time necessary for this to take place have also had a marked influence on their attitudes. As a "digital elite", Nhlanhla is comfortable with what he knows and feels confident that the opportunity to learn presents itself. Having grown up in a family endowed with strong cultural capital in terms of ICTs, he has always had the opportunity to accumulate his embodied capital and he can continue to assume that when he needs to acquire new digital skills he will be able to. He has no reason to suspect that the opportunity does not present itself and therefore no need to ensure that he grabs the chance when he can.

On the other hand, Sipho having started off as a "digital stranger" has had to acquire his embodied cultural capital in a much shorter time frame. His agency is expressed through motivation in learning new things and advancing his digital literacy. Sipho's demonstration of agency is not unique; we have previously examined the "inventive capacity" students show to "circumvent the constraints imposed by structures" in earlier research (Czerniewicz et al. 2008).

However, what is relevant in this discussion is that the cell phone has been integral in enabling Sipho's agency – his habitus has been "reconfigured" by access to embodied cultural capital in the form of a ubiquitous technology. The opportunity afforded by the cell phone for Sipho to fast track the appropriation of the embodied capital to be able to successfully use ICTs for his learning in a way that has reconfigured his identity as the "digital stranger" he was when he entered university.

Bourdieu's theoretical approach has been criticised for being determinist, and indeed the difficulties of change are illustrated in his comment that "the precondition for the fast easy accumulation of every kind of useful cultural capital, starts at the outset, without delay, without wasted time only for the offspring of families endowed with strong cultural capital" (1986).

On the contrary, Sipho's story provides evidence that the structures of habitus are not "set", "but evolve – they are durable and transposable but *not immutable*" (Maton 2008). Thus, these two stories indicate that habitus can change and that access to specific forms of objectified cultural capital can have far-reaching effects.

Conclusion

It is through habitus that individuals are able to appropriate and maximise different forms of cultural capital. In order to do so, they need an understanding of the field, its required activities and its legitimate discourses. Thus, capitals exist in terms of field, and may have different values in different constellations in different fields. The field of higher education is especially rule bound, both explicitly and implicitly. South African universities have mixed responses to the use of cell phones with few utilising them proactively for educational ends; indeed, some academics even ban their use in lecture theatres. Even so, students are using this technology to access the practices of higher education, often without the knowledge and buy-in of the institutional authorities. In these two cases, both students are seen to be using cell phones for learning, with the more disadvantaged student benefiting particularly. This study opens up questions regarding the relative importance of how capitals vary, and in particular the relationship of the different forms of cultural capital to one another and to the field of higher education is of special interest given that cell phones have great legitimacy in other fields.

The question also arises as to how one form of cultural capital is converted to another. The assumption is always that it is embodied capital which is required for the objectified state of cultural capital to have any meaning, but this study suggests that the acquisition of a particular form of objectified capital (i.e. the cell phone) has an influence on – indeed transfers to – the embodied capital itself. It also raises the question of how social capital inter-relates with cultural capital, especially in the light of the requirements of the field. While both students access social capital, this is variable and assists them differentially. Thus, social positions can be changed and shifted by increased access to different forms of objectified cultural capital.

Bourdieu's framework had provided a useful tool for the exploration of the complex and multi faceted concept of access to higher education as mediated by ICTs, expanding the notion beyond the simpler one of mere access to the technology itself.

References

All Media and Products Survey (AMPS) (2010). "Trended media data: Cell phone trends." undertaken by South African Advertising Research Forum (SAARF) accessed 8 November, 2010, from http://www.saarf.co.za/

Ball, S., Davis, J., et al. (2002). Classification and judgement: social class and the cognitive structures of choice of higher education. *British Journal of Sociology of Education, 23*(1), 51–72.

Bourdieu, P. (1986). The forms of capital. In J. Richardson(Ed.), Handbook of theory and research for the sociology of education (pp. 241,258). New York: Greewood.

Bourdieu, P. (1990). *The logic of practice.* Cambridge: Polity.

Brown, C., & Czerniewicz, L. (2010). Debunking the digital native: beyond digital apartheid, towards digital democracy. *Journal of Computer Assisted Learning, 26*(5), 357–369.

Czerniewicz, L., and Brown, C. (2006). The virtual Möbius strip. *Research Report Series 1.* University of Cape Town. Cape Town, Centre for Educational Technology.

Czerniewicz, L., & Brown, C. (2009). A virtual wheel of fortune? Enablers and constraints of ICTs in higher education in South Africa. In S. Marshall, W. Kinuthia, & W. Taylor (Eds.), *Bridging the knowledge divide: educational technology for development.* Colorado: Information Age Publishing.

Czerniewicz, L., Williams, K., et al. (2008). *Students make a plan: understanding student agency in constraining conditions.* ALT-C 2008: Rethinking the digital divide. Leeds, UK.

Czerniewicz, L., Williams, K., et al. (2009). Students make a plan: understanding student agency in constraining conditions. *ALT-J Research in Learning Technology, 17*(2), 75–88.

Donner, J., & Gitau, S. (2009). *New paths: exploring mobile centric internet use in South Africa.* Chicago: International Communication Association (ICS).

Goldstuck, A. (2008). Internet access in South Africa 2008. Johannesburg, World Wide Worx, from.

Council on Higher Education (2009). "The state of higher education in South Africa." Higher Education Monitor 8, CHE, Johannesburg.

International Telecommunication Union (2007). "ICT Statistics database." Accessed 9 November, 2010, from http://www.itu.int/ITU-D/icteye/Indicators/Indicators.aspx#

Jenkins, R. (2002). *Pierre bourdieu*. London: Routledge.

Joubert, R. (2009). "The mobile web: an untapped opportunity for publishers." Accessed 25 January 2011, from http://www.bizcommunity.com/Article/196/15/30508.html

Lieberman, E. (2005). Nested analysis as a mixed method strategy for comparative research. *American Political Science Review, 99*(3), 435–452.

Maton, K. (2008). Habitus. In M. Grenfell (Ed.), *Pierre Bourdieu: key concepts* (pp. 49–65). London: Acumen.

Odendaal, N., Duminy, J., et al. (2008). *Is digital technology urban: Understanding inter-metropolitan digital divides in South Africa*. Proceedings of the Conference of the Computer-Human Interaction Special Interest Group (CHISIG) of Australia on Computer-Human Interfaction, Cairns.

Prensky, M. (2001a). Digital natives, digital immigrants. *On the Horizon, 9*(5).

Prensky, M. (2001b). Digital natives, Digital immigrants, Part 2: Do they really think differently? *On the Horizon, 9*(6), 1–6.

Chapter 13
How Do Small Business Owner-Managers Learn Leadership Through Networked Learning?

Susan M. Smith

Introduction

This chapter shows how learning within networked learning can be understood through the lens of situated learning theory (SLT) through the concept of legitimate peripheral participation (Lave and Wenger 1991) and the situated curriculum (Gherardi et al. 1998). The focus of the study is a 10-month leadership programme called LEAD for owner-managers of small- to medium-sized enterprises (SMEs). Specifically, it asks, "How do SME owner-managers learn to become leaders through networked learning?" The chapter reports key findings from an ethnographic study, including a virtual ethnography of one cohort of 25 delegates. It shows how delegates co-construct the situated curriculum and, through gaining fuller participation as a delegate in the networked learning community, identify more fully with the identity of leader. The facilitators within this networked learning experience are conceived of as enablers of the social construction of the delegates' LEAD identity. Given the importance of the enablers' roles, it is argued that critical reflexivity is essential within a networked learning programme like the one under investigation.

The chapter begins by contextualising LEAD, describing what the programme is and the pedagogy which underpins it as a networked learning programme.

S.M. Smith (✉)
Lancaster University Management School, Lancaster University, Lancaster, UK
e-mail: sue.smith@lancaster.ac.uk

L. Dirckinck-Holmfeld et al. (eds.), *Exploring the Theory, Pedagogy and Practice of Networked Learning*, DOI 10.1007/978-1-4614-0496-5_13,
© Springer Science+Business Media, LLC 2012

LEAD: A Networked Learning Programme for SME Owner-Managers

LEAD is a networked learning programme based on a social theory of learning and is influenced largely by SLT, whereby learning is situated or embedded within activity. In terms of networked learning, this chapter specifically refers to the definition of networked (management) learning as drawing mostly on theories supporting social learning and social constructionism in relation to technology-supported management education. In the "E-quality in e-learning Manifesto", networked learning refers to:

> those learning situations and contexts which, through the use of ICT, allow learners to be connected with other people (for example, learners, teachers/tutors, mentors, librarians, technical assistants) and with shared, information rich resources. Networked e-learning also views learners as contributing to the development of these learning resources and information of various kinds and types (E-Quality Network 2002, p. 5).

Recently, these authors have called for a revisit to this manifesto and definition (Beaty et al. 2010), but the definition is used here to show the perspective used in relation to LEAD as a networked learning programme. The relationship between facilitators and learners within LEAD is based on collaboration and co-construction of knowledge rather than on that of expert and acolyte (E-Quality Network 2002, p. 6). Such a collaborative and participative approach to learning relies on the dialogical creation of meaning and construction of knowledge as discussed by Hodgson and Watland (2004, p. 126). LEAD is rooted in a pedagogy which aims to support participative approaches to learning as proposed by Hodgson and Reynolds (2005, p. 11). The programme is designed to encourage the delegates to learn from each other, relying less on the tutor(s) as the "sage on the stage" but as the "guide on the side" (Jones and Steeples 2002, p. 9). Sharing knowledge of running small businesses is integral to the delegates' learning of how to develop their leadership capabilities.

The programme adopts an integrated learning approach (see Fig. 13.1) starting with an induction day and an overnight experiential followed by masterclasses, coaching, action learning, business shadowing and business exchanges over a 10-month period. An online discussion space supports communication and peer-to-peer interaction between everyone involved in LEAD (delegates and facilitators) when not physically together. Smith and Peters' (2006) paper gives a detailed overview of how LEAD was designed. In brief, the following key learning processes underpinned the programme:

- Taught learning – to heighten the salience of leadership to stimulate greater identification with the social role as leader
- Observational learning – to provide opportunities for owner-managers to observe a number of leadership styles
- Enacted learning – to refine the observed learning in action
- Situated learning – to ensure that the enactment is context relevant and not artificial (ensuring relevance and applicability)

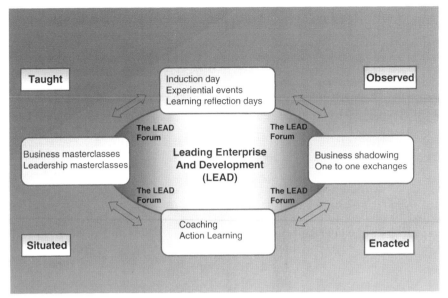

Fig. 13.1 The LEAD-integrated learning model

Typically, SME owner-managers do not see themselves as leaders and often have no one to talk to about their business issues and little opportunities to learn leadership. The pedagogy of LEAD is designed to provide opportunities to alleviate the feelings of isolation experienced by owner-managers of SMEs (see Smith and Peters 2006). Together, the learning interventions result in knowledge that is socially constructed, largely through a dialogical process through peer-to-peer learning emerging from relational dialogue (see Ferreday et al. 2006). The salience of the conversations the delegates have lies at the heart of this. The delegates engage with the ideas that come from the different elements of LEAD and develop skills and capabilities relevant to their own situations back in their businesses. This enables them to address problems and share knowledge (see Wenger 2004) and the peer-to-peer learning is designed to help them make sense of the taught, situated, observed and enacted learning.

Learning arises from participation in a community and gaining recognised membership within that community (see Lave and Wenger 1991). The activity for the delegates on the programme is their own work practice as owner-managers of SMEs. In other words, the learning they experience as a result of LEAD is situated back into their own contexts. Hodgson (2009, p. 131) makes the link between SLT and management education arguing that becoming a member of a community can be interpreted as:

> learning through participation in the pedagogy and curriculum of a given educational programme. Through this participation "students" learn how to be a participant or member of a given knowledge community and acquire the language and an identity that is recognised by that community.

This chapter presents the key findings from a qualitative piece of research which explored the learning processes within LEAD. The methodology is discussed next followed by the key findings.

Methodology

This is an interpretive study that draws on empirical qualitative research gathered over a period of four years. The main method of enquiry has been through an ethnography both online and offline with one cohort of 25 owner-managers who were on LEAD. As discussed, LEAD is rooted in a pedagogic assumption that peer-to-peer learning is beneficial to the SMEs. The aim of the study was to explore how the delegates learn leadership through networked learning. The author was also the director of LEAD and for this cohort also took on the role and identity of researcher undertaking an ethnography of the cohort under investigation. As such, she immersed herself as fully as possible in LEAD, trying to experience LEAD when and where the delegates experienced it. Ethnographic research is based on observational work in a particular setting (Silverman 2005, p. 37) and allows qualitative researchers to get "inside the minds" of those being studied (Curran and Blackburn 2001, p. 113). Ethnographies are typically carried out in a physical space, a tendency which is exacerbated by the historical roots of anthropology in the study of relatively isolated communities (Hine 2000). Certainly, there is a tendency to treat the field site as a physical place, where one goes and writers stress the importance of face-to-face presence in events and interactions (Van Maanen 1998).

In addition to a "traditional" ethnography including observations and interviews, a virtual ethnography was conducted online on the LEAD forum. Hine (2000, p. 59) proposes that it could be useful to treat the Internet as a separate cultural sphere in order to understand how it is articulated into, and transforms off-line relationships. She continues, "This would enable a much richer sense of the uses of the Internet and the ways in which local relationships shape its use as a technology and as a cultural context" (ibid, p. 60). Networked learning seeks to connect learners to resources and although technology is a prominent feature, the connections can be to physical resources also (see Hodgson and Reynolds 2005). This study combines online and off-line observations and the connectivity between the two.

Having an off-line relationship with the delegates also gave the researcher what Tapscott et al. (2000) termed "digital capital" during discussions with the delegates online. Combining the off-line and virtual ethnography allowed the researcher to follow the delegates into different areas and elements of LEAD, although as with any ethnography the research cannot be "everywhere at once" or record everything that happens within a particular group or context. Data partiality is a topic of discussion within qualitative research. Drawing on Silverman (2005, p. 52), a claim is not made to "give the whole picture" and the inevitable partiality is celebrated through the validity and reliability of the analysis and interpretation.

The data were analyzed using the theoretical frameworks of SLT and Communities of Practice theory. In the context of networked learning, other authors have also drawn upon these frameworks to inform the design of networked learning (Cousin and Deepwell 2005); to provide a context for understanding practices within communities that can be applied to networked learning (Fox 2005) and to critique the collaborative approach advocated by networked learning (Hodgson 2009). This study focused on the learning processes within the networked learning community. The following discussion presents the key findings in relation to identity and learning from this study. It should be noted that the pseudonyms are used for the delegates' names when presenting the data.

Key Findings

The key findings are presented to show how small business owner-managers learn leadership within networked learning. They are: the situated curriculum, challenging the situated curriculum, identity and legitimate peripheral participation, enablers and reflexivity in networked learning.

The Situated Curriculum

Social theories of learning are concerned with the practices within learning communities. In seeking to understand the learning processes, the study explores how the learning community develops a situated curriculum which is co-constructed between the delegates and facilitators.

To show how delegates learn to engage with the integrated learning model, the idea of a curriculum is invoked. Curriculum is often equated to a syllabus or a body of knowledge content and/or subjects with education being the process by which these are transmitted or "delivered" to students by the most effective methods that can be devised (Blenkin et al. 1992, p. 23). Lave and Wenger (1991) argue that a teaching curriculum is constructed for the instruction of newcomers into a community. As a leadership programme, LEAD has a teaching curriculum, but learning to be a member in this community (and therefore a LEAD delegate) goes further than being exposed to or learning through the teaching curriculum. It is proposed that Gherardi et al.'s (1998) notion of the situated curriculum can be used to show how the owner-managers learn the craft of being a delegate. Gherardi et al. (1998, p. 275) use the concept of the situated curriculum understood as "the pattern of activities that instruct the process socialization of novices in a context of ongoing work activities". Gherardi et al. use it to describe how workplace learning takes place on a construction site in Italy through researching how practical expertise and tacit skills are passed from senior workers to novices. It is proposed that LEAD has its own situated curriculum and the delegates learn to "behave" in the different learning interventions through learning, developing and enacting the situated curriculum. In doing so, they gain the identity as a LEAD delegate.

In addition to the situated curriculum, LEAD can also be considered to have what Wenger (1998) terms the "living curriculum". Wenger uses this to describe how an apprentice learns through a community of practice. For Wenger, the curriculum is the community of practice itself (1998, p. 4). On LEAD, the living curriculum is learnt with the help of the facilitators and the situated curriculum is co-constructed through the learning community (i.e. their cohort and the facilitators).

The following accounts demonstrate through how this cohort co-constructed the situated curriculum. The analysis explains how learning the situated curriculum of LEAD helps to understand how the delegates learn on LEAD. The first account is an observation of action learning set which involves six delegates and a facilitator. It shows, through three different episodes in the same set meeting, how the facilitator guides the delegates to act in a way appropriate to the learning intervention, thus bringing (part of) the situated curriculum to the surface.

This is the first set meeting after they had their introduction to action learning and a practice set a couple of weeks ago. [Facilitator] explained the purpose of ground rules within action learning and told them they are like a learning contract for which they have responsibility for. It is up to them what ground rules they have as they are unique to this set. The group make some suggestions for the ground rules and [facilitator] writes them on the flip chart paper in big, bold writing explaining that they can always revisit them and modify them as they go along.

[Facilitator] goes back over what they talked about during the introduction to action learning. [Facilitator] talks through the terminology of air time (where the presenter presents the issue) and the process review (where the set reflects on the process of action learning rather than the issue). [Facilitator] checks they are okay with the terminology and sits back down asking who would like to present their first issue. Gaynor says she definitely would not like to go first. Simon says he has something he would like to work on.

The facilitator makes the teaching curriculum of action learning explicit

....

At one point during Simon's air time, Gaynor keeps making suggestions [facilitator] says, "turn it into a question". She says, "How? I'm really struggling, I just want to tell him what I think" and Colin gives her a suggestion on how to do this. Colin says that Gaynor may have an observation to make. [Facilitator] chips in on another statement Gaynor makes later and says, "Is that your opinion or an observation you have for Simon?" It is okay to make an observation.

The situated curriculum begins to emerge

Excerpt from ethnographic diary

The action learning approach follows that advocated by Revans (1983) and matches the criteria set out by Pedler et al. (2005), whereby questioning is the main way to help participants proceed with their problems and learning is from reflection on actions taken. The facilitator helps the set members to learn how they should behave in an action learning set and learn the structured process of action learning. In the first part of the above account, the facilitator explains the purpose of the ground rules and the terminology of "air time" and "process review". These can be considered to be part of the teaching curriculum and Wenger's (1998) living curriculum. The situated curriculum, on the other hand, emphasises the local and symbolic social characteristics of the system of practices (Gherardi et al. 1998, p. 280).

The second part of the account shows that a situated curriculum is beginning to develop. This happens when the set member, Gaynor, struggles with the teaching/living curriculum, demonstrated through her wanting to tell another set member, Simon, what she thinks. The facilitator checks whether Gaynor is adhering to the guidelines within action learning and makes clear that an "observation" would be appropriate and in doing so infers that her opinion would not be appropriate. The use of the term "observation" became part of the set's discourse during all subsequent meetings and become an important tool in challenging the situated curriculum as is demonstrated further on. This is just one example of the delegates learning to function in the LEAD learning community and develop the practices of that community. However, here, the term "observation" is co-constructed by the community (including the facilitator) rather than assimilating a predetermined discourse.

This leads to the next finding which shows how the delegates conform to the situated curriculum but also challenge it. It is argued that challenging the situated curriculum makes it visible.

Challenging the Situated Curriculum

The pedagogical aims of LEAD are to help owner-managers develop their leadership capabilities. Identity is central to them to learn how to become delegates. To this end, to be a delegate means conforming to certain ways of behaving and therefore conforming to the situated curriculum. As the following post by Paul suggests, there is the "old me" or the "LEAD way":

I am starting to think about situations with a much more "step back" approach and finding the issues are far easily dealt with. The most difficult thing for me is making sure I do it all of the time, I find myself slipping into the "old me" and then realising that there is another way – The LEAD way!

LEAD forum post by Paul

It is argued that once the delegates learn the situated curriculum they also learn to challenge it. This is ever present in the action learning sets, where they persistently try to break the "rules" that they themselves have set for this space. In the first set meeting, all set members establish their own ground rules for their set; these included rules, such as committing to turning up to each session, respecting each other, treating each session as confidential and trying to ask open questions and not to give advice. The ground rules are revisited throughout the duration of the set meetings and are amended or added to as appropriate. The action learning set members all agreed to these ground rules and they were pinned up on the wall at every set meeting. The action learning sets are designed to help each other learn through reflection by asking open questions and, crucially, not offering one another advice (Smith 2009). The delegates often tried to break the ground rule of not giving advice by disguising advice by starting a sentence with "an observation I have is ..." or "observation ..." and then go on to explicitly give advice. The following account is taken from one of the set meetings, although similar accounts were observed in all of the set meetings. Three different parts of the observation are presented. The account shows some aspects of the situated curriculum of the action learning set that they have developed and learnt. For example, they have developed the practice of holding a pen up to indicate they want to say something (thus developing a situated curriculum). The facilitator tries to help them turn a statement into a question that might help the issue holder (thus making the situated curriculum explicit). The account then shows how they try to challenge the situated curriculum by asking for advice or offering advice which is disguised as an "observation" or a "story" as they put it.

Frances presents her issue and a couple of the set members ask some questions. This does not seem to be helping Frances. Gaynor puts her pen in front of her to indicate that she wants to chip in and makes an "observation", as she puts it, and suggests an action for Frances. [Facilitator] steps in and asks Gaynor if she can rephrase what she has just said and turn it into a question that could help Frances. Gaynor responds, "I just want to tell her what to do" to which Colin says, "Well, yeah we're all thinking that but you have to ask a question".

Adam says that he does not feel he is getting anywhere with his issue but he wants to know what to do, he wants a resolution. He shuffles back in his seat and sighs and asks the group to tell him what to do. Earlier on, he had been extolling the benefits of open questions when they did the process review on Frances' issue. And now, he is asking the group for explicit advice. He laughs a little and winks at the facilitator presumably acknowledging that this is not what the action learning set should do. Gaynor immediately says, "We're not allowed to do that" at the same time as Simon says, "We don't do that here".

(continued)

(continued)

> "A story, I think" says Gaynor and she tells Alan a story from her own company about her Managing Director. She begins to tell him that he could do the same. Alan asks if she can tell him a bit more about how she handled this situation. Gaynor giggles, "We're not allowed to tell you" to which Alan answers, "You can cheat".
>
> Ethnographic diary action learning set observation

This account shows how the situated curriculum is being developed, learnt and also challenged. The first part shows that Colin wants to challenge the situated curriculum by telling Gaynor, *"You have to ask a question"*. In the second part, Adam specifically asks the group to tell him what to do. By laughing and winking at the facilitator, he is showing that he knows he should not be asking for advice but working through the process of open questions instead. This is reinforced by Gaynor saying, *"We're not allowed to do that"* and Simon who says, *"We don't do that here"*. Gaynor and Simon are speaking on behalf of this group who have developed an understanding of what the correct behaviour should be. Despite the set members knowing what they should do, the third part shows how Gaynor tries to get around or renegotiate the situated curriculum. By using the term, *"a story"*, Gaynor disguises her advice for her fellow set member. Alan corroborates by telling Gaynor that she can cheat and tell him what to do. This account is light-hearted and the set members genuinely have each other's interests at heart. What it shows is that the situated curriculum is being surfaced and challenged.

Gherardi et al. (1998, p. 291) state that to the members of the community what they have called the situated curriculum amounts to nothing more than one of the many aspects of daily workplace activity that are taken for granted. They suggest that:

> once socialization to work has produced its effects, and newcomers have moved on from the role of peripheral participants to the status of fully legitimate members of the community, the learning they have acquired, together with its pattern and implicit complex logic, becomes part of their tacit knowledge. Such knowledge is not retained in the form of any sort of cognitive structure or plan or action, and is best understood as a custom ... sustained by the community.

As Gherardi et al. (1998) suggest, people become so used to the situated curriculum in their community that it renders itself invisible or at least hard to describe. Certainly, the researcher could never ask the delegates directly what the situated curriculum was or how they were learning it. By challenging the situated curriculum, it is argued that the delegates surface it and make it (or part of it) visible. Bringing the situated curriculum to the fore in this analysis highlights the importance of learning to be a delegate. Learning and developing the practices of the LEAD community develops the situated curriculum. This is also bound up with a shift in identity as participants become fuller participants through the process of legitimate peripheral participation (Lave and Wenger 1991).

Identity and Legitimate Peripheral Participation

The research builds upon the social learning theories proposed by Lave and Wenger (1991) and Wenger (1998) which view learning as situated or embedded within activity. Learning arises from participation in and gaining recognised membership within a community. This section uses Lave and Wenger's (1991) legitimate peripheral participation to explain how owner-managers *become* LEAD delegates. Following this, an alternative reading of legitimate peripheral participation relevant to this piece of research is presented.

Legitimate peripheral participation encompasses: "[the] process of being active participants in the *practices* of social communities and constructing *identities* in relation to these communities" (Wenger 1998, p. 4, emphasis in the original). Lave and Wenger's (1991) seminal work uses community of practice to refer to communities of practitioners, where newcomers enter and attempt to acquire the sociocultural practices of the community. Lave and Wenger use legitimate peripheral participation to characterize the process by which newcomers become included in a community of practice:

> It concerns the process by which newcomers become part of a CoP. A person's intentions to learn are engaged and the meaning of learning is configured through the process of becoming a full participant in a sociocultural practice (1991, p. 29).

The newcomers learn from old-timers, increasing their legitimacy within the group moving from peripheral participation to full participation as they identify more with the community of practice in question. This chapter uses the central concept within legitimate peripheral participation: How the learner's identity shifts as he or she becomes a fuller participant? Typically, a delegate's identity and behaviour change with increased participation. Joining the programme as owner-managers of small businesses, they often comment that at the beginning they do not feel like leaders, rather they feel they are impostors. Feelings of loneliness and isolation are common as demonstrated in the following quote: *"To many people it is very lonely, it's lonely being an owner-manager"* (Sarah, cohort 4). With no management team or hierarchical structure, and sitting at the head of the company in the "leader" role, the owner-managers have nobody around them to share thoughts with (Smith and Peters 2006). As they engage with the integrated learning model, the delegates learn from one another and develop a situated curriculum which becomes part of the practices of the learning community. Through their participation, they learn how to become a delegate which, in turn, develops their own leadership capabilities and results in an increased identification with being a leader. Remarks, such as *"I know that I am a leader"* or *"I have the confidence now to be a leader"*, are common. Participating in the development of the learning and learning/developing the situated curriculum brings the delegates closer to full participation as depicted in the Fig. 13.2 below.

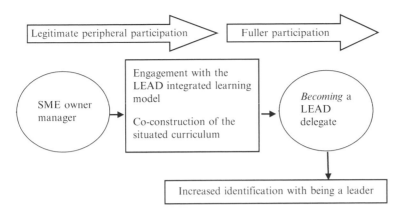

Fig. 13.2 Shift in identity through legitimate peripheral participation

Figure 13.2 shows that increased identification with leadership can be seen almost as a by-product of learning to be a delegate. Legitimate peripheral participation is linked with learning to become a delegate (rather than explicitly becoming a leader). Increased identification with leadership happens as a result of fuller participation as a delegate. The salience of the conversations the delegates have lies at the heart of the participative pedagogy of LEAD and the process of gaining fuller participation. The delegates' experiences resonate with one another which address the oft-quoted feelings of isolation as owner-managers and leads to an increase in confidence and an affirmation of their identity as they move towards a shift in identity from owner-manager towards that of leader.

Becoming LEAD delegates influences their practice of running small businesses and how and where they are accountable. Communities of practice have a regime of mutual accountability which becomes part of the practice (Wenger 1998, p. 81). As owner-managers of SMEs, the delegates are not only accountable to one another within LEAD, but are also accountable to their businesses. LEAD is a leadership pro-gramme, so if it achieves its pedagogic aims of developing leadership capabilities, accordingly an increased identification with leadership should be expected. In SLT, change in identity is inevitable with movement away from the periphery. Here, it is argued that it is through the process of learning to be a delegate and becoming a fuller participant that a shift in identity towards leadership happens. The following quote from Noel demonstrates this process:

"I feel that my attitude to running my company has most definitely changed in the short period that I have been on LEAD. I think that it is pretty much linked to confidence. I think that maybe my confidence has been increased in business, it has probably been increased socially but certainly in business it has, to be part of this cohort" (Interview: Noel).

For Noel, being part of his cohort affects his running of the business through an increase in confidence and a change in his attitude to risk. The joint enterprise within LEAD can be considered to be both learning how to be a delegate *and* a shift in identity and practice of being an owner-manager to becoming a leader. Gerber and Scott (2007, p. 463) argue that key factors in the process of identity development are the personal histories and perspectives of the learners. The following quote from Amy shows that the perspectives of the learners are indeed a key factor as to become a LEAD delegate they have to be ready to change their identity:

"You have to be open to changing your identity – Well LEAD was perfect for me, but you have to be ready for that change. You have to want it ... you have to desire that change or want to ... in order to do it ... I feel a bigger person for it, a better person, certainly business-wise, more informed and more able to deal with what I am going to have to deal with in the next 12 months" (Interview: Amy).

It has been argued that learning and developing the situated curriculum are part of the process of learning to be a LEAD delegate. Using Lave and Wenger's (1991) legitimate peripheral participation has shown that as delegates reach fuller participation their accountability lies not only to the learning community, but to their businesses also. Accordingly, fuller participation leads to a shift in identity and increased identification with leadership. This identity is socially constructed within the LEAD learning community through the circulation of knowledge through relational dialogue. In all of Lave's work, she urges us to use the environment as an analytic lens for the construction of particular identities (Chaiklin and Lave 1996; Rogoff and Lave 1984). Similarly, Eckert et al. (1997) argue that social relations form around the activities and that particular kinds of knowledge and expertise become part of individuals' identities and places in the community. The LEAD networked learning community is the environment for the construction of the LEAD delegate (and subsequently "leader" identity).

Enablers

This chapter argues that LEAD has a situated curriculum that is co-constructed between the facilitators and the delegates. It also shows that SME owner-managers learn how to become LEAD delegates and increase their identification with leadership through doing so. The practice or joint enterprise (Wenger 1998) is being, or learning to be, a delegate. An alternative reading of legitimate peripheral participation is used in the case of LEAD. It is proposed that learning to be a delegate is not learnt through seniors passing their knowledge on to novices as set out in SLT theory, but that this process is co-constructed between the delegates and facilitators dialogically and observationally. There are no old-timers as such to learn the act of learning to be a delegate. The facilitators who take the role of old-timers help the delegates become fuller participants. A different interpretation, using the term "enablers", may help to understand the process of legitimate peripheral participation within LEAD. The enablers are the facilitators. This is a departure from the SLT reading as the old-timers here are not owner-managers of small businesses but the facilitators within LEAD. Here, the enablers create the environment for learning. Gherardi et al. (1998, p. 283) state that newcomers are not "social dopes" but active actors who are as much product as producer of the social reality they live in. Although they are referring to newcomers in the workplace, this argument applies to newcomers into LEAD, i.e. the delegates are the products and producers of the social reality of LEAD. The following quote shows that through being "open" and sharing a common goal of wanting to develop their leadership, the delegates are both the products and producers of the LEAD social identity:

> "There is a link because everybody on LEAD wants to become a good leader, so there is a commonality there that sort of links you. ... I think because we are there because we want to do it better and you know that you can't do it better if you are closed. I think everyone recognises that in the openness is the growth and the learning" (Interview: Julie, cohort 5).

Guiding the delegates or role modelling is part of the social learning theory that underpins LEAD. The enablers are part of the process of imitation and modelling.

However, the role of the enablers is always different to that of the delegates because the delegates are learning to become delegates and therefore observe, imitate and model one another. The enablers create opportunities and spaces for this to take place. Enablers help the owner-managers learn how to become LEAD delegates and thus develop and learn the situated curriculum which, as has been shown, has an impact on their identity as they shift from owner-managers to leaders. It is not the intention to change the fundamental idea of legitimate peripheral participation, more so to propose a way of understanding how learning takes place on LEAD by using the concept of enablers. Cousin and Deepwell (2005, p. 61) note that participation enables learning and learning changes who we are. In relation to LEAD, it is argued that enablers create the opportunities for this shift in identity and therefore need to be critically reflexive in their practice, a point the chapter finishes with.

Reflexivity in Networked Learning

Many of the delegates refer to their time on LEAD as their "LEAD journey". This label has become part of the final learning and reflection day which involves them visually depicting their interpretations of their LEAD journey. As both director of the programme and researcher, the author is an integral part of their LEAD journey. She is part of the co-construction of the situated curriculum and an enabler of creating an environment, whereby the delegates' identity can shift in the process of legitimate peripheral participation. It is argued, therefore, that this role needs critical reflexivity. The responsibility facilitators take in LEAD and their role in the process of learning to be a delegate should be highlighted. Critical reflexivity is needed by course designers, teachers, facilitators and others who share a part of any student's learning. While the author was aware that she had a role in their learning journeys, undertaking this research and analysis has made this more explicit and given it labels through which to think and understand the learning processes within LEAD as a networked learning programme. This has enabled her to think more deeply about her own role in the co-construction of the situated curriculum and subsequently the delegates' learning.

As discussed, the relationship between facilitators and learners in networked learning is based on collaboration and co-construction of knowledge rather than on that of expert and acolyte (E-Quality Network 2002, p. 6). The principles of networked learning promote collaboration and connectivity across networks promoting learners to take an active role in the construction of their learning experiences. Facilitators within networked learning are part of this construction. Hodgson (2009) argues that critical reflection is needed for learning which is based on collaboration. Cousin and Deepwell (2005, p. 61) recognise that a difficulty for e-facilitators is that networked learning communities can form shared repertoires which can turn into congealed practices which are hard to change. This is true of any learning community. Cousin and Deepwell continue that there is "a risk for educationalists wanting to promote network learning – or any other pedagogy – in that they too may congeal their ideas and practices into new and even oppressive orthodoxies" (ibid). Finally, this chapter argues that as educators, course designers, facilitators and so on, we need to be critically reflexive about our own role within networked learning with a need to think about the role we play in the co-construction of social identities.

Summary

This chapter asked, "How do SME owner-managers learn to become leaders through networked learning?" Using Gherardi et al.'s (1998) concept of the situated curriculum, it was argued that the networked learning community, including the delegates and facilitators, develop and learn the situated curriculum. It was shown that delegates conform to it but also challenge it. Learning and developing the situated curriculum is essential in owner-managers' learning how to become LEAD delegates. Becoming a delegate was part of the process of becoming a fuller participant through legitimate peripheral participation. Identity is a key aspect of this process. Becoming a delegate in turn develops their leadership capabilities and a shift in identity towards that of a leader. It was argued that the practice within the learning community is that of being a LEAD delegate and as such there are no old-timers in the same way as outlined by Lave and Wenger (1991) in the process of legitimate peripheral participation. Therefore, it was suggested that the facilitators take the role of old-timers but that "enablers" is a more apt term as they create opportunities for learning within the CoP that lead to fuller participation. Finally, it was argued that as enablers, facilitators within networked learning need to adopt a critically reflexive stance in order to be aware of their own role in the circulation of knowledge and contribution to the shift in identity experienced by learners within networked learning.

Acknowledgements The author would like to thank all the delegates on LEAD for taking part in this research. Particular thanks goes to the members and facilitator of the observed action learning set who provided a valuable opportunity for the researcher to understand more fully the learning processes within LEAD.

References

Beaty, L., Cousin, G., and Hodgson, V. (2010). *Revisiting the E-Quality in Networked Learning Manifesto*, paper presented at the 7th International conference on Networked Learning, Aalborg, Denmark, 3rd and 4th May, 2010.

Blenkin, G. M., Edwards, G., & Kelly, A. V. (1992). *Change and the curriculum.* London: Paul Chapman.

Chaiklin, S., & Lave, J. (1996). *Understanding practice: perspectives on activity and context.* Cambridge: Cambridge University Press.

Cousin, G., & Deepwell, F. (2005). Designs for networked learning: a communities of practice perspective. *Studies in Higher Education, 30*(1), 57–66.

Curran, J., & Blackburn, R. A. (2001). *Researching the small enterprise.* London: Sage.

Eckert, P., Goldman, S., and Wenger, E. (1997). "The School as a Community of Engaged Learners" http://www.stanford.edu/~eckert/PDF/SasCEL.pdf. Accessed March 30, 2011.

E-Quality Network (2002). "E-quality in e-learning Manifesto" presented at the Networked Learning 2002 conference, Sheffield. http://csalt.lancs.ac.uk/esrc/. Accessed March 30, 2011.

Ferreday, D., Hodgson, V., & Jones, C. (2006). Dialogue, language and identity: critical issues for networked management learning. *Studies in Continuing Education, 28*(3), 223–239.

Fox, S. (2005). An actor-network critique of community in higher education: implications for networked learning. *Studies in Higher Education, 30*(1), 95–110.

Gerber, S., & Scott, L. (2007). Designing a learning curriculum and technology's role in it. *Education Technology Research Development, 55*, 461–478.

Gherardi, S., Nicolini, D., & Odella, F. (1998). Towards a social understanding of how people learn in organizations: the notion of situated curriculum. *Management Learning, 29*, 273–297.

Hine, C. (2000). *Virtual ethnography.* London: Sage.

Hodgson, V. (2009). Collaborative learning. In S. J. Armstrong & C. Fukami (Eds.), *The sage handbook of management learning, education and development* (pp. 126–140). London: Sage.

Hodgson, V., & Reynolds, M. (2005). Consensus, difference and "multiple communities" in networked learning. *Studies in Higher Education, 30*(1), 11–24.

Hodgson, V., & Watland, P. A. (2004). Researching networked management learning. *Management Learning, 35*(2), 99–116.

Jones, C., & Steeples, C. (2002). Perspectives and issues in networked learning. In C. Steeples & C. Jones (Eds.), *Networked learning: perspectives and issues* (pp. 1–14). London: Springer.

Lave, J., & Wenger, E. (1991). *Situated learning: legitimate peripheral participation.* Cambridge: Cambridge University Press.

Pedler, M., Burgoyne, J., & Brook, C. (2005). What has action learning learned to become? *Action Learning: Research and Practice, 2*(1), 49–68.

Revans, R. (1983). *The ABC of action learning.* Bromley: Chartwell-Bratt.

Rogoff, B., & Lave, J. (1984). *Everyday cognition: its development in social context.* Cambridge, MA: Harvard University Press.

Silverman, D. (2005). *Doing qualitative research.* London: Sage.

Smith, L. (2009). Experiences of action leaning in two SME business support programmes. *Action Learning Research and Practice, 6*(3), 335–341.

Smith, L., & Peters, S. (2006). *Leading by design: the case of LEAD full paper for symposium: entrepreneurial leadership learning.* Belfast: British Academy Management. September.

Tapscott, D., Ticoll, D., & Lowy, A. (2000). *Digital capital: harnessing the power of the business web.* Boston, MA: Harvard Business School Press.

Van Maanen, J. (1998). *Tales of the field: on writing ethnography.* Chicago: The University of Chicago Press.

Wenger, E. (1998). *Communities of practice: learning, meaning, and identity.* Cambridge: Cambridge University Press.

Wenger, E. (2004). Knowledge management as a donut: Shaping your knowledge strategy through communities of practice. *Ivey Business Journal* January/February.

Chapter 14
Innovating Design for Learning in the Networked Society

Karin Tweddell Levinsen and Janni Nielsen

Introduction

The transition from the industrial to the knowledge or networked society, together with the worldwide digitalization and e-permeation of our social, political and economic lives, has brought challenges to the educational system. The speed of change increases and actualizes questions, such as: What does it mean to be a well-functioning citizen? Which knowledge and competencies do people and societies need to adapt to cope with the emerging social formation of the networked society? How can the educational system meet the challenge of the changing conditions? During the last decade, some challenges to the educational system have become manifest. New key competencies have been described, and they have gradually become part of the overall learning objectives at all levels of education, along with the demand that information and communication technology (ICT) is integrated into education. In the same process, the educational system faces an increasing demand for productivity that tends to conflict with learning quality, as learning is a process that takes time.

Based on our experience with education at university level through two and three decades and the above-mentioned changes and challenges, this paper aims to present an innovation of learning in the networked society by contributing with a theoretical design for learning model.

K.T. Levinsen (✉)
Danish School of Education, Aarhus University, Aarhus, Denmark
e-mail: kale@dpu.dk

J. Nielsen
Centre for Applied ICT, Copenhagen Business School, Copenhagen, Denmark

L. Dirckinck-Holmfeld et al. (eds.), *Exploring the Theory, Pedagogy and Practice of Networked Learning*, DOI 10.1007/978-1-4614-0496-5_14,
© Springer Science+Business Media, LLC 2012

Background

The latest decades of transformation have produced new concepts and phenomena addressing globalization, the new economy and key competencies for the future, each of which, in turn, becomes dialectically constituting and constituted actors in the ongoing transformation. There are several designations for the outcome of the transformation: *information society, knowledge society* and *networked society*. The term information society came into use in the 1950s and relates to early digitalization and data management (Masuda 1980). Knowledge society (Stehr 1994) refers to a society, where knowledge has become a commodity – a dominant value and component of human activity. Networked society (Castells 2000) is a broad sociological term that refers to the principal organizational forms: ad hoc networks in a global economy that are made possible by worldwide e-permeation. We choose Castells's term, as it most adequately embraces the totality of the transition and the challenges that the educational system encounters.

Castells (ibid.) points to central characteristics that have already emerged from the transition from industrial to networked society, and describes the new societal structure in three dimensions. (1) *Informational*: The capacity to generate knowledge and process information determines productivity and competitiveness. (2) *Global*: Development of a worldwide IT infrastructure provides strategic activities with the capacity to work as a unit on a planetary scale. Globalization is highly selective and links to value anywhere while discarding anything (people, firms, territories, resources) that has no value or becomes devalued. (3) *Networked*: The connectivity of the global economy generates a new form of organization, the *network enterprise*, comprising either firms or segments of firms, where the unit of production is no longer the firm but the business project. In the New Economy, work and employment are defined through flexibility and mobility, and the people who work in this system are *fundamentally divided into two categories: self-programmable labour and generic labour.* Self-programmable labour is equipped with competencies for lifelong learning, in particular, the autonomous ability to retrain/adapt to new conditions and challenges. In contrast, generic labour is exchangeable and disposable. A third category is discarded, devalued people who are already becoming socially excluded not only in developing countries, but also in western countries.

> "... the fact that the world is e-permeated means that those who can understand and comfortably use e-facilities are significantly advantaged, in terms of educational success, employment prospects and other aspects of life" (Elearning Europa, 2006)

In the last decade, both national and international governments and business organizations (G8, OECD, UN) have focused on how to meet the challenge of the networked society. The general understanding is that a society meets the challenge when citizens and employees possess the competencies of the self-programmable labour. OECD's (2001) key competencies for a knowledge-based or networked society bear close resemblance to Castells's self-programmable labour. In 2006, the G8 World summit put focus on innovation and the subsequent demands on education in the twenty-first century and the European Parliament and the Council recommended that:

> "Key competences in the shape of knowledge, skills and attitudes appropriate to each context are fundamental for each individual in a knowledge-based society. They provide added value for the labour market, social cohesion and active citizenship by offering flexibility and adaptability, satisfaction and motivation. Because they should be acquired by everyone, this Recommendation proposes a reference tool for the Member States to ensure that these key competences are fully integrated into their strategies and infrastructures, particularly in the context of lifelong learning" (EU 2006).

In the following, we lean on Castells's concept of self-programmable labour, but as *self-programming* has technological connotations, we prefer to use designations, such as lifelong learning and self-initiated learning.

Educational Challenge

The above-mentioned challenges to the educational system represent forces that pull in contradicting directions and leave education and learning open for inter-pretation within at least two meta-discourses (Dyson 1999). The *political–ethical discourse* is ideological and philosophical. It focuses on the good life and what ought to be done; it also concentrates on the development of a new educational paradigm inspired by social constructivist and constructivist theory. The general consensus is that learning – including acquiring key competencies – needs time to mature. The *economic–pragmatic discourse* is currently based on liberalist eco-nomic theory and demands fast, efficient, predictable and controllable productivity from the educational institutions. Because they are based on entirely different grounds and objectives, the meta-discourses are mutually incompatible and generate a paradox. At the political level, the paradox appears as a tension between, on the one hand, New Public Management's quantitative demands for increasing productivity in terms of students per time unit and the institutions as economically profitable units, and, on the other hand, the qualitative focus of the learning paradigm on content and the demand for self-initiated lifelong learners. This paper addresses this paradox. The aim is to suggest strategies for innovation of learning in the networked society by contributing with a theoretical design for learning model.

Our point of departure is the didactic design approach based on Scandinavian constructivist and social constructivist traditions. The overall design for teaching and learning is based on Dewey's Experiential Learning (1974), Klafki's exemplary principle (1971) and the Critical Design for Learning, where the group is the organi-zational form of learning practice (Negt 1975; Schäfer and Schaller 1973). In Denmark, these strands have merged into problem-oriented project pedagogy (POPP) (Dirckinck-Holmfeld 2002; Illeris 1989). POPP is founded on exploration, dialogue, collaboration and the participants' own experience in relation to a given subject, and centres on problem formulation and enquiry of exemplary problems. In online and blended mode educations, POPP merged into computer-supported collaborative learning as an overall model of design for teaching and learning (Dirckinck-Holmfeld 2002).

The core principles in POPP are: the *experiential approach*, *abduction* (qualified guessing), *knowledge sharing* and *negotiation of meaning*. We also incorporate problem-based learning (PBL) (Barrows and Tamblyn 1980) and case-based learning (CBL) (Shulman 1992). POPP, PBL and CBL share the same constructivist and social constructivist learning principles. However, POPP is distinguished from PBL and CBL at the outset of the learning process. In POPP, it is the students who define their area of interest within the subject matter and choose the problem they want to investigate, whereas in PBL and CBL, it is the teacher who defines the problem.

Within designs for teaching and learning, such as POPP, the paradox appears as an increasing tension between the open design (political–ethical discourse) and the curriculum size, learning objectives, evaluation forms and demand for productivity (economic–pragmatic discourse). The Danish adjustment of the universities to the EU Bologna process (Europe Unit 2006) has turned the universities into business organizations, where future resources for teaching are dependent on previous productivity. The present consequence is that educational resources are reduced (economic–pragmatic discourse) while curricula are growing (political–ethical discourse). In practice, the contradicting forces confront students with a heavy workload and time pressure. The paradox appears as the students' personal cost-benefit analysis of the balance between in-depth studying (political–ethical discourse) and just passing a given course (economic–pragmatic discourse).

Students' personal negotiation of strategy under stressful circumstances tends to favour the economic–pragmatic side (Biggs 1999; Lawless and Allen 2004; Levinsen 2006). Phenomenologically, this manifests itself in students who have not read the theory before joining formally organized learning activities. They hope for or expect that teachers will FILL their knowledge gap by presenting a digested version of the literature. But educating students for the networked society means to educate them for an unpredictable future, to support their understanding of the emerging learning paradigm, and to scaffold their process of becoming self-initiated and critical lifelong learners. However, when performing POPP under the current conditions, we are confronted with the students' cost-benefit strategies as they navigate through the study programme under time pressure. The paradox exposes itself at this level as students who demand instructional teaching, where we stress constructivist and social constructivist approaches.

Our challenge is to maintain and develop the quality of learning under the present conditions. To do this, we find it necessary to circumvent the problems of time pressure and content. Incremental efforts in dealing with the paradox have turned time into a scarce resource and made stress the most prevalent disease in the western world. These efforts can be described using the concepts of *single-loop learning*=reflection *in* action, and *double-loop learning*=reflection *on* action (Argyris 1977):

- Efforts to do increasingly more of the same at a higher speed correspond to organizational single-loop learning.
- Efforts to FILL the knowledge gap represent a change of teacher strategy without a change of basic premises. This corresponds to organizational double-loop learning.

Single- and double-loop learning are reactive strategies (Ackoff 1976); however, instead of reacting to solve the paradox, we suggest that we exploit the paradox and its inherent power (Hastrup 1999). This implies a change from a reactive to a proactive and interactive strategy (Ackoff 1976) and a shift to organizational *triple-loop learning* – reflection on action (Hauen et al. 1998; Yuthas et al. 2004), which involves a larger context around the practice. Triple-loop learning also implies a radical change of the involved parties' mental models and basic assumptions. Hence, proactive and interactive strategies may move the paradox from a *Catch 22 – situation* into a *thinking out of the box – situation*. The paradox and its implications have to be met by a proactive strategy and radical innovation. This is the starting point for our explorative and experience-based work, which we present theoretically as the model of design for learning in the following.

The Vision: Design for Learning Model

In our teaching, we are confronted with the paradox at first hand:

- At the level of educational practice, the paradox appears as a tension between the quality of the educational outcome measured against the defined learning objectives.
- At the level of the individual, the paradox appears as a tension between students who perform cost-benefit strategies to deal with time pressure measured against learning as a time-consuming social activity, and immersion into the subject matter.

The challenges we encounter are twofold: first, at the level of society and organization, and second, at the level of education practice. At the level of society and organization, the questions are: How can we maintain the quality of education under the current conditions? How can we scaffold students' acquisition of key competencies for the networked society? And how can we scaffold students passing of exams? As mentioned, students hope that teachers will present a digested version of the literature at formalized sessions. They hope teachers will FILL their knowledge gap, establish the necessary set of concepts, and provide a reading guide for success during self-study periods.

However, *filling the gap* is a questionable approach for several reasons. *Filling the gap* equals the behaviourist theory of *transmission of information* between teacher and student. The theory is firmly rejected from the constructivist position and contradicts everything that the Scandinavian tradition stands for. It is also found that students – when exposed to stressful conditions – do not study the literature (Levinsen 2006). Instead, they begin to work on the assignment without exploring the topic, and perform only scattered ad hoc reading. Consequently, students reach deep understanding accompanied by productive frustration (Illeris 2006) only just before the assignment is to be handed in, all of which influences the quality of learning. Thus, *filling the gap* is an incremental and reactive solution that pushes the problems ahead.

The proactive strategy maintains that students *bridge* the knowledge gap themselves; accordingly, our design for learning must maintain a focus on transfer, knowledge construction and self-initiated learning (self-programming). At the level of educational practice, the question then becomes: How do we maintain the core principles: *experiential approach, abduction* (qualified guessing), *knowledge sharing* and *negotiation of meaning*?

For this purpose, we have developed the design for learning model that aims to scaffold students' internalization of important and framing concepts of the subject matter when they come unprepared for class. The challenge is extensive: (1) to construct a design for learning model that matches learning in a networked society and, at the same time, bypasses the consequences of the time pressure while still reaching the learning objectives; (2) to operationalize the model into various specific educational activities. The vision is to:

- Kick-start students' productive frustration and reflection.
- Bridge the knowledge gap and compensate for the lost time.
- Kick-start students' production of (new) knowledge.
- Provide students with a scaffold for approaching the theory, and support their reading reflection and operationalization of the theory during the self-study periods.

The empirical studies and experiments that ground the model were performed as part of the blended mode Danish Master's programme in ICT and Learning (MIL), which has been the subject of research from many perspectives during the 10 years since its establishment. The research and refinement of the model took place during a specific MIL course in *Interaction Design* over 3 years from 2007 to 2009. This paper is a theoretical presentation of the model, and we elaborate on our empirical work elsewhere (Levinsen 2009). The modifications based on MIL were supplemented by experiences gained from applying the model to a course in qualitative research methodology offered as part of the blended mode graduate programme *Psychological Pedagogy* at the Danish University School of Education.

The design for learning model is both an analytical tool for retrospective analysis and a design tool for the construction of new designs for teaching and learning. However, we delimit the scope of this paper to the theoretical presentation of the model as a design tool. In the following section, we present the theoretical framework of our design for the learning model that encompasses three stages of construction: (1) *conceptual modelling*, based on Darsø's (2001) dynamic knowledge map, (2) *orchestration,* staged as a complex framework based on Bohr's complementarity principle (1957), and (3) *operationalization*, containing the directions for students' performance in practice when the design model is applied in a specific context.

Conceptual Model: Based on Darsø

POPP and the Scandinavian constructivist tradition of *design for learning* are based on group work and projects. In the book *Innovation in the making* (2002), Darsø unfolds her theory of group dynamics and project management in relation to innovation and learning in organizations. Darsø's concepts *preject, pre-project* and *project* (ibid: pp 31) and their relation to time serves as a conceptual framework for the first step in our model: Development of a conceptual model for learning.

The *ideal* process of knowledge construction in POPP can be described along a timeline. To begin with, the students' body of knowledge consists of divergence along with ignorance. This is the period when students construct their bearings and identify landmarks of the new subject through exploration, meaning negotiation, knowledge construction and innovation. This early phase encompasses explorative, as well as non-linear and divergent activities, and aligns with Darsø's *preject*. Hereafter follows a period with goal-oriented research and refinement. This phase encompasses the problem statement and goal-oriented research, which are linear and product-driven activities that align with Darsø's *pre-project*. The goal-oriented period gradually transforms into a structured period with analysis when the assignment is produced. The activities in this phase are convergent and linear, aligning with Darsø's *project*.

However, as discussed above, the ideal process does not occur. The first phase which aligns with the preject (mandatory for POPP), as constructivist and social constructivist design for learning is missing because students do not prepare for the formally organized sessions. Any learning model must address this. The basic aim of our model is to create space for the preject activities to unfold, and the aim of the preject activities is to force students to *bridge* their knowledge gap.

Preject participants (and students too) bring whatever resources they possess into the preject (ibid, p. 321); thus, the prejects draw on divergent knowledge in terms of tacit knowledge, as well as conscious everyday and qualified knowledge. Prejects also draw on the participants' ignorance regarding the subject and on the emerging relations among participants. The conceptual model needs to build on students' resources prior to a formalized activity, and must therefore actualize students' knowledge from the everyday arena and bring it into the specialized arena of the subject matter.

In POPP, learning is linked to reflectivity and productive frustration. Darsø stresses that reflectivity depends on, and is initiated by, conscious awareness of what she calls *bifurcation points*, which appear when the participants are confronted with dilemmas and genuine problems. In other words, there are situations of productive frustration, where the participants have to negotiate choices in order to proceed. For every negotiation and choice, the time trajectory of the preject becomes a path of bifurcation points that Darsø describes as *"rather like 'forks in the road' leading to different futures"* (ibid, p 326). According to Darsø, reflectivity and learning are linked to the participants' awareness of their choices and deselections, as well as their awareness of how they negotiate decision-making. Thus, ongoing documentation of bifurcation points allows the participants to backtrack their process and explore alternative choices if necessary.

- Central specifications of the conceptual model are the support of the students' awareness of the trajectory of bifurcation points and the actualization of the students' prerequisites.

Based on her empirical studies, Darsø defines two dimensions of major importance for innovative and knowledge constructing group dynamics to succeed – the *Relational dimension* and the *Complexity dimension* (ibid, p. 332). The relational axis refers to the degree of collaboration and group dynamics, and the activities must pass beyond the *Sharing Barrier,* where it becomes "essential for the group to share." The complexity axis refers to the complexity of the challenge that the group faces. Here, the group's challenge must pass beyond the *Uncertainty barrier*, that is, the challenge must move from simple or complex puzzles for which an unambiguous solution can be found (first loop learning) onto genuine problems, where conditions and solutions are both ambiguous and uncertain (second and third loop learning). Darsø's model also operates with the concept of *The Edge of Chaos*. This is the area where the activity passes beyond barriers where the participants are challenged (1) to negotiate meaning and (2) to explore and construct (for them) new knowledge on the basis of their everyday and qualified knowledge, tacit knowledge and the realization of ignorance.

• The area at the Edge of Chaos is the area where the preject unfolds.

Activity Specifications

In the following, we focus on the preject and the activities that a preject may contemplate.

Our design aims to actualize the students' informal resources in terms of everyday and qualified knowledge through carefully designed activities at the *Edge of Chaos*. When everyday resources are externalized through practice, they may constitute a basis for constructing common grounds and clarifying concepts. Further, everyday resources may function as vehicles for reflectivity and knowledge construction, as teacher's direct awareness to their alignment with the theory of the subject matter. For example, the everyday activity of deciding what is practical to do when we want to know about something aligns with the specialized activity of methodological research design, and the everyday realization of ignorance aligns with the specialized activity of formulating research questions.

Applying these thoughts to Darsø's model (Fig. 14.1), the relational axis represents designed scenarios that aim to frame group work in order to push the participants' negotiation of meaning toward the establishment of common grounds, while their shared and collaborative activities are pushed above the sharing barrier. The complexity axis represents designed challenges that aim to confront participants with genuine dilemmas and problems, and to push their activities beyond the uncertainty barrier in order to reach the state of productive frustration that facilitates learning and reflectivity.

A successful design of the two axes may push the groups' shared activity into the area at the *Edge of Chaos*. This is where the roles that are designed for participants will scope the actions towards actualizing participants' qualified and everyday knowledge together with their tacit knowledge in a way that addresses theory in

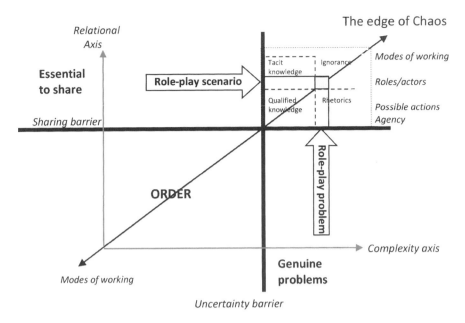

Fig. 14.1 Redesigning Darsø's model

everyday language. Pushing the activity into the Edge of Chaos creates a field of tension that may facilitate the actualization of the four core principles of POPP: experiential approach, abduction, knowledge sharing and negotiation of meaning.

However, the participants' practice must be supported in practice – not only framed and initiated. In order not to move out of the preject and into the succeeding pre-project, it is, according to Darsø, important that participants are aware not only of how they communicate, but also of their progress and bifurcation points. In order to achieve this, it is imperative that participants maintain an abductive approach and avoid making attempts at persuasion or jumping to conclusions. To support the participants' practice in this direction, our design for learning model faces the challenge of how to balance productive frustration with static deadlock or destructive chaos. Therefore, the last claims to our conceptual model relate the maintenance of the process and how to obtain that balance:

- The abductive approach is maintained through the description of the groups' task as open-ended and explorative.
- The awareness of bifurcation points and choices is heightened through a demand for documentation and the actual focus of the documentation: choices, deselections, decisions and arguments.
- The ongoing negotiation of structuring of the groups' collaboration is maintained through a script that defines the groups' task.

Thus far, Darsø's model has served as a vehicle to develop a general conceptual model and general specifications of our design for learning model. The next steps are how to orchestrate and then operationalize the conceptual model in specific cases.

Orchestration: Bohr's Principle of Complementarity

Orchestration can be understood in terms of a score of music or the script of a play. Here, orchestration means to transform the conceptual model claims into a script for concrete practice. The main challenge of our model is the general inherent contradiction in education between the complexity and scope of a curriculum as content and the time pressure on students. Students have no time to digest or touch upon the entire content and its implications. As it is currently defined, the conceptual model cannot deal with this challenge. This is where Bohr's complementarity principle becomes relevant.

Bohr's complementary principle relates to quantum physics, but already in 1934 Bohr saw its relevance in relation to the humanities and as a contribution to epistemology (Bohr 1957, 1964; Favrholdt 1992, 2009; Faye and Folse 1994; Levinsen 2005). According to Bohr, there exists a material world independent of our consciousness. However, any phenomenon is a construction that cannot be separated from the observer, the position or the context, and consequently all phenomena are situated and relative to the observer and observation as agency (Barad 2007). Bohr's epistemology bears strong resemblances, that is, to Heidegger's phenomenology, and this is not accidental, as Heidegger was inspired by Bohr and Quantum Physics when he developed his phenomenology (Glazebrook 2000). However, Heidegger did not elaborate on Bohr's complementary principle and Bohr's idea of the complementary image with regard to the humanities and social sciences and the relation between objectivity and construction regarding knowledge. Therefore, it is necessary to turn to Bohr's original writings (Bohr 1934, 1961) and present Bohr's complementary principle and the complementary image in order to explain the method of orchestrating the conceptual model.

Bohr's epistemology rejects the positivist correspondence principle, and recognizes that some objects and events cannot appear as phenomena. They can only appear indirectly as index signs, as they evade both observation and language – they are inexpressible. However, according to Bohr, it is possible to know something about objects that we can never observe as phenomena. The only way to obtain knowledge is through construction based on assumptions. In this sense, Bohr bears similarity to social constructivism. A classic example deals with the object of *light*. From one position, *light* appears as the phenomenon of waves, while from another position, it appears as particles. Bohr argues that in order to express the complex and inexpressible object of *light,* we have to accept that *light* (though we can never know what light *is*), can be both wave and particle, but it cannot be observed as both at the same time. In order to obtain knowledge, Bohr argues that we have to specify the conditions of observation and be precise in our use of language. This is what Bohr refers to as objectivity. The construction of knowledge is based on the use of metaphors that allow us to construct complementary images, which may serve as boundary objects or vehicles to communicate about and explore inexpressible objects and events (e.g. black holes).

In current humanities and social sciences, *complementarity* is generally understood holistically – as the construction of a whole out of complementary elements or perspectives, similar to the Yin-Yang Principle (see e.g. Wenger 1998, p. 232).

According to Bohr's complementary principle, there will always be blank areas in the image. Some of these gaps may be filled with new knowledge, as in the holistic interpretation of complementarity. Other areas are inexpressible and can only be bridged through interpretation and construction based on assumptions. According to Bohr, the complementary perspectives do not have to be logically consistent, compatible or even measurable. Thus, unlike other approaches, the different pieces or perspectives in a Bohrean complementary image cannot be expected to fit like the Yin-Yang principle or a jigsaw puzzle (Lemke 2000).

Bohr stresses that the only language we can use to share and explore our complementary images of the inexpressible and the knowledge gaps is everyday language. We have to be precise in our use of language in order to share the conditions of observation and the use of metaphors. In this sense, Bohr's complementary principle offers a dimension to Darsø's preject as a metaphor for the construction of meaning and the use of everyday language in the construction of knowledge at the Edge of Chaos.

In the humanities and social sciences, dynamic objects and events, such as life, learning, thoughts, practice and competencies, possess qualities similar to Bohr's inexpressible objects – they are complex and they possess dimensions that evade language and phenomenological appearance. Still, we can know something about them and negotiate their meaning. This is also the case with subject matters and curricula where our learning model may be applied. The assumption is that when students need to share the distributed knowledge later in the course, they may all contribute to their shared construction of a complementary image of the curriculum and the related practices. Therefore, the idea of applying the complementary principle to the conceptual model is to orchestrate the time-space relations in order to facilitate the distribution of knowledge and the construction of a shared complementary image of the curriculum.

- The model aims at exposing students to essential parts of the curriculum and to support the construction of a shared complementary image of the curriculum.

Operationalization

As previously described, our intentions are to pro-act and develop a *design for learning* aimed at learning in the networked society. Thus far, we have described the conceptual model and the orchestration. The last step in the process is *operationalization*, which can be understood as the score that a conductor follows during a concert or the directions that technical staff uses during the dramatic stage performance.

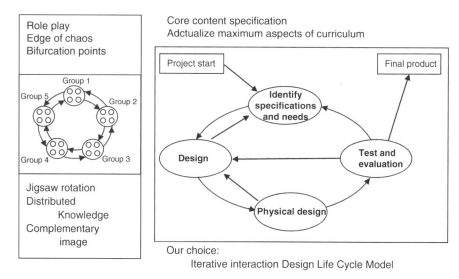

Fig. 14.2 Illustration of core content and choice of activity

In order to proceed from the conceptual level to application in practice, three steps are necessary. First, it is necessary to identify the core content of the curriculum that may serve as the backbone for the operationalization. Second, a suitable frame must be decided upon – pedagogic knowledge management – for the activity. Finally, the time–space relation must be formalized as a time–space relation script that both set the stage for the group activities and frame the maintenance of the preject.

Choice of Core Content

The design of the time–space–content relations in the actual practice must be centred on the core content. The core content of a curriculum is an individual and contextualized choice of a suitable backbone for designing the time–space relation. Therefore, the core content has to fulfil a set of requirements regarding the construction of a specific time–space operationalization (Fig. 14.2):

- The core content must facilitate the widest range of aspects of the full curriculum to be actualized and negotiated.
- The relation between activity and core content must exploit the participants' everyday experiences and language in a way that actualizes the theory.
- The core content may invite activities that align with the core principles of POPP: experiential approach, abduction, knowledge sharing and negotiation of meaning.

Usually, the core content is the content that formalized learning objectives are built on in terms of defined learning objectives and the description of course progression.

Accordingly, it is relatively easy to identify core content, but as the following case of applying the model demonstrates the nature and scope of core content may differ considerably, depending on the specific context.

In the blended mode MIL case of interaction design, the core is about designing and creating something new in the world (Cato 2001; Winograd 1996). Therefore, the curriculum covers the full process from initiating an idea to a final and released product. In this case, the core content was identified as a dynamic, iterative and progressive lifecycle model (Sharp et al. 2007). As everyone has tried to create something for a specific purpose and has experienced with projects in their everyday arena, students can be expected to actualize this knowledge during the performance of the activities. Similarly, as everyone in their everyday arena has tried to observe something for a specific purpose and has experienced gaining information and knowledge through inquiry and listening, we may expect students to actualize these everyday competencies during the performance of the designed activities.

Pedagogic Knowledge Management

The next step in the process addresses the challenge discussed above, namely, that students cannot be expected to know everything in a subject or a curriculum even though they must be aware of the totality and be able to address, reflect on and use it. *Pedagogic knowledge management* is coined by Holm Sørensen in relation to studies in the primary school (Sørensen et al. 2010), but according to Holm Sørensen the concept is applicable to all educational practices at all levels. Holm Sørensen defines *pedagogic knowledge management* as a strategy that aims to organize knowledge sharing and to facilitate an organizational culture, where allocation of time for dialogue and activities that externalize tacit knowledge and ignorance among learners becomes an obvious aspect of learning. It is central to pedagogic knowledge management that formal and informal learning strategies are given equal importance.

The adequate choice of pedagogic knowledge management design depends on the nature of the core content and the specific activities that the core content may contemplate. However, the specification demand for pedagogic knowledge management in this context is to facilitate the widest range of knowledge distribution among students in order to support the succeeding construction of shared complementary images of the curriculum. Hence, the demands for the strategic approach become:

- Mix participants as much as possible in various constellations according to the time available.
- Distribute core content as much as possible among participants.

No matter what the choice of organization is of the pedagogic knowledge management, the aim of the operationalized model is to support reflectivity and learning. Therefore, groups are requested to document their work process and the bifurcation points in terms of important arguments, choices and deselections. The tools for documentation are written notes, photos and video recordings.

Holm Sørensen suggests several models of organizing pedagogic knowledge management (ibid, p. 216) that may be useful in this context. However, some core contents and learning objectives require more complex designs of pedagogic knowledge management.

In MIL, the students were organized in semester study groups of four to five students. During the preject case work, the members of the study groups were mixed in core content-related activities according to a pedagogic knowledge management matrix that aims at a maximum distribution of students' experience with the core content. The matrix ensures that all semester groups will eventually have members that together have addressed all aspects of actualized theory. Therefore, the matrix also facilitates the semester groups in achieving a shared construction of a complementary image of the curriculum.

Jigsaw Rotation or the Café Model

Another way of initiating a wide distribution of knowledge is to organize students in groups and have each group work with a genuine problem for a specified amount of time, and then require some of the group members to change groups – and roles – before a new task is taken on. In our rotation, only two members stay in the original group. One acts as a host for the guests from other groups, the other acts as a participant observer.

The work up to this point is shared and challenged in the new group constellations. First, the host tells the guests about the original group's work, bifurcation points, decisions and doubts, what the group found important, etc. Afterwards, the guests are allowed to ask explorative questions, but they are not allowed to argue or air opinions. A specific time is allocated to this activity, after which all guests return to their original group and share their experiences: What did we learn from meeting the other groups? The teams are asked to present what they have learned in a video documented plenary session, which is also shared online after the session.

At the MIL course, the groups were given the task of designing and performing user-involving design interventions. Each group covered one step in the lifecycle; early conceptual exploration, proto-typing and final usability test. The rotation ensured that all semester groups had members who had experienced one of the core actor positions in interaction design. After the session, the groups shared their experiences and presented the most important things they had learned in the plenum. In this case, the whole session was recorded on video for students to use for further analysis.

Ideally, this set-up aims to ensure that all core actor positions and methodological considerations are actualized during the activity.

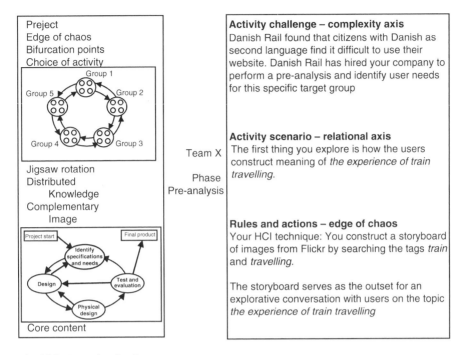

Preject
Edge of chaos
Bifurcation points
Choice of activity

Group 1
Group 5
Group 2
Group 4
Group 3

Jigsaw rotation
Distributed
Knowledge
Complementary
Image

Project start | Final product
Identify specifications and needs
Design
Test and evaluation
Physical design

Core content

Team X

Phase
Pre-analysis

Activity challenge – complexity axis
Danish Rail found that citizens with Danish as second language find it difficult to use their website. Danish Rail has hired your company to perform a pre-analysis and identify user needs for this specific target group

Activity scenario – relational axis
The first thing you explore is how the users construct meaning of *the experience of train travelling*.

Rules and actions – edge of chaos
Your HCI technique: You construct a storyboard of images from Flickr by searching the tags *train* and *travelling*.

The storyboard serves as the outset for an explorative conversation with users on the topic *the experience of train travelling*

Fig. 14.3 Operationalization

Operationalization – Script Specification: Team 1 Example

The stage for group work is set through a script that frames the time–space–content relations of the activity. The choices in our example cases lean on classic role-play theory (Johansen and Swiatek 1991) but could just as well lean on other frameworks. However, a role-play is a suitable choice, as it scopes specific challenges (complexity axis) and limits the participants to act within constraints (relational axis). The role-play scripts are built on a formula that forces the groups' task into the *Edge of Chaos*. The script is designed to drive the role-play through the POPP core principles: *experiential approach*, *abduction* (qualified guessing), *knowledge sharing* and *negotiation of meaning* in relation to an everyday approach to the theory of the subject matter (Fig. 14.3).

The reader may recall that we understand learning as linked to the participants' *conscious awareness of bifurcation points* and the *choices and deselections* related to these and the *negotiated decision-making* of how to proceed. In order to facilitate the awareness and to maintain the process in the preject phase, the script also instructs students in: *Who does what during the activity?*

In the MIL case, the script may look as follows:

Step 1: The team participates in the creative process of designing the storyboard and the set-up for the explorative conversation.
Step 2: Divide the following roles between you:

- One test leader
- One video recorder
- Two observers – to take notes
- The rest of the group members move to Team 2

Their role in Team 2 is: one acts as test subject and the other observes and
takes notes of the process
For those who stay in Team 1: You will have guests from Team 5. One acts
as your test subject and the others observe and take notes.
When the test is finished everybody returns to his or her original team.

Step 3: Analyze the process and data and prepare a short presentation based
on the following questions:

- How did the process evolve?
- What did you learn about designing test material?
- What did you learn about carrying out a test?
- To what one has to pay special attention?
- What turned out to be difficult or surprising?
- Are there any special challenges in your method?

Step 4: We meet in the plenary room where the teams and their findings –
followed by discussion.

Discussion of Initial Findings

The reader may recall that with our design for learning model the aim is to
scaffold students' framing of concepts of the subject matter. This model is developed
as an answer to the paradox of time pressure and growth of curriculum workload
to which students develop cost-benefit strategies, e.g. demanding instructional
teaching and coming unprepared for class. In the following, we touch upon some
initial findings. However, we must stress that our work is explorative. Our data
collection was motivated not only by the fact that our work was explorative and
iterative, and that we needed to be able to follow the learning process, but also by
the need to reflect upon the design for learning model. There are indications that
scaffolding was constructed during the 4-h teamwork session and was transferred
to the following period of online work, where students worked on a final eight-
page case assignment.

Scaffold to Enhance Quality of Learning

The 4-h set-up confronts students with the fact that they come to the shared activity from different positions with different preconceptions and horizons of understanding. The role-play forces students to externalize their different positions and make these positions tangible. Through this process, students may come to meta-reflect on the reality of their different positions, e.g. which strategies for negotiation and decision-making were chosen, and how they dealt with this complexity in practice. In this way, students may take on both the participant inside-out position and the contemplative outside-in position, and these positions allow for perception and externalization of emerging problems and support; plus, they enhance scaffolding.

At the 4-h seminar, the main themes for meta-reflections were:

- Pilot studies prior to actual tests.
- Role of test leader.
- Need for specifications of users' tasks in test design.
- Relationship between test leader and user.
- The applied HCI technique and the test purpose.

In the students' case reports 2 months after the online period – it must be remembered that the students were no longer in the seminar design teams, but had returned to their original semester groups, taking with them new knowledge and competencies – students reflected upon the same issues as in the F-2-F seminar. However, the students also unfolded new themes, e.g. how to manage unforeseen events during a test, such as a technological breakdown, users uninterested in the test task, or the meaning of core concepts. Students carried the issue of unforeseen events into a discussion of the test leader's role, leading to meta-reflection and the recognition that a test leader must be able to change roles. These reflections reveal complementary perspectives and include reflections on the language of the subject matter. One project group described surprise at the users' behaviour. The users were children and they did exactly as instructed, reading *the whole* text *very carefully* – which is atypical for Danish second graders. The group reflected critically on their choice of test leader – the children's teacher. They reasoned that children see and relate to the teacher as a teacher rather than as a test leader, and they behave accordingly. This led to the complementary perspective of the teacher, and the difficulties he may have had in assuming the role of test leader. The group reasoned that a relationship is an interaction, deeply embedded – in this case – in an established teacher–pupil relation. They concluded that a test leader must be a person the test subjects do not know.

In former MIL courses, before we introduced the design for learning model and the 4-h script, our experience as supervisors for the semester group assignments was that we had to force students to reflect critically on theories and methodologies (second and third loop learning). Students had difficulty understanding the assignment requirements and the intellectual learning goals of the course. Their theoretical work involved retelling the theory – or worse, applying theory mechanically – as if it could be used directly off the shelf.

In the new design, we found that students reflected critically upon the theoretical frame and concepts in the project reports. For example, one group carried out a theoretical analysis of an existing e-learning Web site. The first step was based on guidelines for the design of digital interfaces, enabling students to identify inconsistent use of graphics, problems with the layout and navigation, and lack of aesthetics. Their second analytical step was a clarification of the interactive functions (conversation and consultation) and the identification of the underlying grid structure of the Web site. They further enhanced their theoretical conceptual analysis with the qualitative dimensions: immersion and agency. In a final step, they uncovered the social constructivist learning perspective – the original basis for the Web site – and showed how the visual design, the navigation and other aspects did not support this. This last step may be perceived as an indication of triple-loop learning, implying that a radical change of students' mental models and basic assumptions has taken place.

Concluding Remarks

We suggest that the unfolding of new themes and the meta-reflections that embed complementary perspectives are indications that scaffolding has been constructed, i.e., it is transferable and does support students in their online project work. The scaffolding makes it possible for students to maintain progression of the learning process also in the online period as self-initiated learners. This suggests that our design for learning model does circumvent problems with time pressure and content, and enhances genuine learning. Moreover, the model shows potential in exploiting the power of the paradox.

A final reflection takes us back to international organizations, such as the G8 and the OECD. In their understanding, the future of the world will depend critically upon people's competencies in knowledge construction, skills, adaptability and ability to enter into lifelong learning. But as Castells (2000) points out in his theory on the networked society and in his notion of self-programmable labour, the essence is the ability of the human being to be self-initiated, retrain oneself and to adapt to new conditions and challenges. If we accept this claim, the learning needs and the educational system warrant innovation. We suggest that our model is a contribution to the innovation of the networked society's design for learning.

References

Ackoff, R. L. (1976). *En ny fremtid formes*. København: Nyt Nordisk Forlag.

Argyris, C. (1977). *Double-loop learning in organisations*. Harvard Business Review.

Barad, K. (2007). Meeting the Universe Halfway: Quantum Physics and the Entanglement of Matter and Meaning: Duke University Press

Barrows, H., & Tamblyn, R. (1980). *Problem-based learning: an approach to medical education* (Medical education, Vol. 1). New York: Springer.

Biggs, J. (1999). *Teaching for quality learning at university*. Buckingham: Open University Press.

Bohr, Niels (1934). Atomic theory and the description of nature. 1934: UP, Cambridge, England, 1961.

Bohr, N. (1957). *Atomfysik og menneskelig erkendelse*. København: Schultz.

Bohr, N. (1964). *Atomfysik og menneskelig erkendelse II*. København: J.H. Schultz Forlag.

Castells, M. (2000). Materials for an exploratory theory of the networked society. *British Journal of Sociology, 51*(1), 5–24.

Cato, J. (2001). *User-centred web design*. Pearson Education: Addison-Wesley.

Darsø, L. (2001). *Innovation in the making* (1st ed.). København: Samfundslitteratur.

Dewey, J. (1974 [1938]). *Erfaring og opdragelse*. København: Chr. Ejlers.

Dirckinck-Holmfeld, L. (2002). Designing virtual learning environments based on problem orientated pedagogy. In L. Dirckinck-Holmfeld & B. Fibiger (Eds.), *Learning in virtual environments* (pp. 31–54). København: Samfundslitteratur.

Dyson, A. (1999). Inclusion and inclusions: theories and discourses in inclusive education. In H. Daniels & P. Garner (Eds.), *World yearbook of education 1999: inclusive education* (pp. 36–53). London: Kogan Page.

EU (2006). Recommendation of the European Parliament and of the Council, of 18 December 2006, on key competences for lifelong learning. *Official Journal L 394 of 30.12.2006.*

Europe Unit (2006). *Bologna Process.* http://www.europeunit.ac.uk/bologna_process/index.cfm. Accessed 22 Jan 2011.

Favrholdt, D. (1992). *Niels Bohr's philosophical background*. København: DetKgl. Danske Videnskabernes Selskab, Historisk-Filosofiske Meddelelser.

Favrholdt, D. (2009). *Filosoffen Niels Bohr*. København: InformationsForlag.

Faye Jan & Henry J. Folse. (1994). Niels Bohr and contemporary philosophy: Springer.

Glazebrook, T. (2000) Heidegger´s philosophy of science: Fordham University Press.

G8 (2006). G8 Wold Summit in St. Petersburg – July 16, 2006. http://en.g8russia.ru/docs/12.html. Accessed 22 Jan 2011.

Hastrup, K. (1999). *Viljen til Viden. En humanistisk grundbog*. København: Gyldendal.

Hauen, F., van Strandgaard, V., & Kastberg, B. (1998). *Den lærende organisation* (2nd ed.). København: Peter Asschenfeldts Nye Forlag.

Illeris, K. (1989). *Pædagogikkens betydning*. København: Unge Pædagoger.

Illeris, K. (2006). *Læring*. Roskilde: Roskilde Universitets Forlag.

Johansen, C., & Swiatek, E. (1991). *Rollespil*. Frederiksberg: Bogfabrikken Fakta.

Klafki, W. (1971). *Bildungstheorie und didaktik*. Beltz: Weinheim.

Lawless, N., & Allen, J. (2004). Understanding and reducing stress in collaborative e-learning. *Electronic Journal of eLearning, 2*(1), 121–127.

Lemke, J. L. (2000). Material sign processes and emergent ecosocial organization. In P. B. Andersen, C. Emmeche, N. O. Finnemann, & P. V. Christiansen (Eds.), *Downward causation: minds, bodies and matter* (pp. 181–213). Århus, Sweden: Aarhus University Press.

Levinsen, K. (2005). *Virtuel Uddannelsespraksis. Master i IKT og Læring – et casestudie i hvordan proaktiv proceshåndtering kan forbedre praksis i virtuelle læringsmiljøer*. Ph.D. Thesis. København: Department of Informatics, Copenhagen Business School.

Levinsen, K. (2006). Collaborative on-line teaching: the inevitable path to deep learning and knowledge sharing? *Electronic Journal of eLearning, 4*(1), 41–48.

Levinsen, K. (2009). A didactic design experiment – towards a Network Society Learning Paradigm. *Designs for Learning, 2*(2), 34–55.

Masuda, Y. (1980). *The Information Society*. Tokyo: Institute for the Information Society.

Negt, O. (1975 [1968]). *Sociologisk fantasi og eksemplarisk læring*. Roskilde: RUC forlag.

OECD (2001). Meeting of the OECD education ministers – Paris, 3–4 April 2001. http://www.oecd.org/dataoecd/40/8/1924078.pdf. Accessed 22 Jan 2011.

Schäfer, K. H., & Schaller, K. (1973). *Kritische Erziehungswissenschaft und kummunikative didaktik*. Heidelberg: Quelle und Meyer.

Sharp, H., Rogers, Y., & Preece, J. (2007). *Interaction design* (2nd ed.). NY: Wiley.

Shulman, L. (1992). Toward a pedagogy of cases. In J. H. Shulman (Ed.), *Case method in teaching education* (pp. 1–30). New York: Teachers College Press.

Sørensen, B. H., Audon, L., & Levinsen, K. (2010). *Skole 2.0*. Aarhus: KLIM.

Stehr, N. (1994). *Knowledge societies*. London: Sage.

Wenger, Etienne (1998). Communities of practice:Learning, meaning and identity. Cambridge University Press.

Winograd, T. (1996). *Bringing design to software*. Stanford: Stanford University and Interval Research Corporation. Addison-Wesley.

Yuthas, K., Dillard, J. F., & Rogers, R. K. (2004). Beyond agency and structure: triple-loop learning. *Journal of Business Ethics, 51*, 229–243.

Chapter 15
Problem-Oriented Project Studies: The Role of the Teacher as Supervisor for the Study Group in Its Learning Processes

Jørgen Lerche Nielsen and Oluf Danielsen

Introduction

The paper contributes to the literature on problem-oriented project studies and problem-based learning (PBL), and it builds on and is a reflection of the experiences the authors have gained through decades of work with problem-oriented project pedagogy. Our primary focus will be on the Masters programme in ICT and Learning (MIL), where students from all over Denmark within a networked learning structure are studying in groups combining on-site seminars (four during a study year) with independent and challenging virtually organised project periods, which require a teacher who is flexible and aware of the different challenges in the new environment. We see the real challenge for a worthwhile education in the modern complex society with its ever changing conditions to open up for a personal, meaningful process, where new ways of thinking are made possible. Thus, students may learn to enter into new cultural patterns and to get involved in quite demanding but enriching practices. How can teachers through their supervision help students to meet these challenges?

Problem-Oriented Project Studies

The educational approach implemented by MIL goes back to the first half of the 1970s, when the new reform universities Roskilde and Aalborg University were founded in Denmark. The approach is called problem-oriented project pedagogy

J.L. Nielsen (✉) • O. Danielsen
Department of Communication, Business and Information Technologies,
Roskilde University, Roskilde, Denmark
e-mail: jln@ruc.dk; oluf@ruc.dk

L. Dirckinck-Holmfeld et al. (eds.), *Exploring the Theory, Pedagogy and Practice of Networked Learning*, DOI 10.1007/978-1-4614-0496-5_15,
© Springer Science+Business Media, LLC 2012

(Olesen and Jensen 1999). It not only shares certain characteristics with PBL, but it also differs from this approach (Kolmos et al. 2004). PBL goes back to the beginning of the 1970s, primarily not only in the USA and Canada, but also in Europe at Maastricht, The Netherlands, and Linköping Sweden (Barrett and Moore 2010). In PBL, the teacher finds and decides the questions and themes with which the students can work. It is the responsibility of the teacher as an expert to demonstrate how students in a constructive way can relate curriculum and theories to praxis. The professor assists the students in finding problems and challenging tasks in order to make it possible for them to work actively with theories and concepts. Within this framework designed by the teacher, the students are offered the opportunity to deal with some of the presented problems and shed light on the problem field using the recommended literature presented by the professor.

Problem-oriented project pedagogy, on the other hand, is characterised by collaborative project work in groups; it is an active kind of learning that is participatory-directed in a dialogue between students and the teacher as a supervisor. The teacher's role is to give the students critical constructive feedback as well as facilitating them in their learning processes. Furthermore, it is interdisciplinary in that it combines knowledge and ideas from different kinds of academic fields (Olsen and Pedersen 2005).

The starting point for the student groups is to investigate a topic or problem that the group is not familiar with and that represents a challenge for them. With a research question as a starting point, the group members embark on a dialogically organised process in which they collect relevant material, data and information; analyse it; and, guided by relevant theories and methods, work to transform this material with the goal of identifying and clarifying the research question.

The students draw conclusions that represent the range of differences in understanding among them, and they create a product that communicates their collective divergent insights to others.

It is the group members who jointly and in dialogue with the group supervisor discuss the formulation of an operative research question; the choice of theory and concepts; which methods to apply; and which practice field to analyse. The project work should be exemplary, which implies that analytical and methodological approaches are applied. The work with the theories and concepts goes beyond the specific project, thus helping to build and consolidate the students' broader study competence.

Through the acquisition and application of theory and method, the students ideally achieve an understanding of important aspects of the academic subject with which they are working. The goal of problem-oriented project pedagogy is that students relate their new insights to their previous experiences and hence through the study process construct new valuable skills and experiences.

Networked Learning in Relation to MIL's Project Work

According to Dirckinck-Holmfeld and Jones (2009, p. 261), two competing approaches can be found within networked learning: (1) *The broadcast model* – associated with the industrialised mode of e-learning – deliverance of content in large scale. This model has been part of the Open University e-learning. (2) *Discussion viewpoint* – closely associated with the social constructivist approach of networked learning. The MIL programme is an example of this model.

MIL, which has existed as a postgraduate Masters programme for 10 years, recruits professionals from all over Denmark and abroad. The programme implements new educational technology, which has made it possible to have flexible communicative patterns building upon the problem and the project-based pedagogical model within the structure of a networked learning environment. The virtual learning environment based on the First Class conference system is an integrative part of the teaching and learning environment. Students are organised in groups and have their personal folders within First Class. Here, they are able to write, store and organise their contributions. They constantly have dialogues and discussions both with their group partners and also with other students belonging to the cohort.

Furthermore, they have access to synchronous video (Adobe Acrobat, Connect Professional), peer-to-peer tools and Web 2.0 (Skype, Windows Messenger, Google Docs, blogs) and tools to support project and course work (Camtasia). They can also engage in discussions with their teachers during their group-based online project work, through the periods with online courses, and when they meet at the four yearly f2f-seminars. As teachers and researchers, we have been engaged in the MIL programme for 10 years. Thus, we have first-hand experience with the learning environment. The examples we will be referring to should be considered as generalised examples from our practice.

The Responsibility of the Students

In the problem-oriented project pedagogy, the students themselves are responsible for identifying which problem to work with, and the very act of formulating a problem is a large part of the learning process. To work in a group means that students must learn to work together in order to make decisions, and they must figure out how to share and coordinate work. Through these study processes, the students learn how to plan, manage and evaluate projects. We see this as part of the development of their study competences, which also must involve the ability to handle the large amounts of information that are within easy reach via the library, databases and the Internet. It is crucial that students learn to be information literate. This requires not only that students are able to locate data and information, but also that they are able to select critically within this huge body of information; that they are able to judge and evaluate the use of the information and that they are able to eventually succeed in letting this information contribute to the construction of knowledge within the group.

This understanding goes back to the definition of information literacy from the American Library Association (ALA):

> "To be information literate, a person must be able to recognize when information is needed and have the ability to locate, evaluate and use effectively the needed information [...] information literate people are those who have learned how to learn" (ALA, American Library Association 1989).

In this process, knowledge may be understood as the result of cooperative and collaborative actions in a context, where the students combine and connect relevant information with their previous knowledge and experiences. This knowledge creation takes place within an environment, where information and communication technology are

> "(…) used to promote connections: between one learner and other learners, between learners and tutors; between a learning community and its learning resources" (Goodyear et al. 2004, p. 1).

Thus, we see information literacy in the context of a modern, complex society, where it is a vital competence to be able to reflect on one's knowledge and learning in relation to ongoing changes and new challenges.

From this perspective, learning is not something that takes place exclusively in the individual's mind in a special, "clean" educational context detached from practical, work-related contexts. Learning is viewed as contextual, situational and dynamic, and it is taking place when we as active persons become involved in social interactions with others in specific social practices (Lave and Wenger 1991).

Negotiation Among the Participants

Our definition of problem-oriented project pedagogy is related to a social constructivist theory of learning, where concepts such as collaboration, communication, dialogue, negotiation and interpretation play important roles in constructing knowledge. The final step in this process is the evaluation, both as a self-reflexive process and as feedback from other students and the teacher.

The idea is that students should not just passively receive teaching but be actively involved as learners. Thus, students and teachers are working together in acquiring, constructing and negotiating the meaning of knowledge. What kinds of problem are the students working with, what is the goal, and how are they communicating, negotiating and working together? What kinds of knowledge are they constructing? Those are some of the dimensions that can provide motivation and give meaning for the individual person and for the group as a whole.

The real challenge is to open up for a personal, meaningful process, where new ways of thinking are made possible. Thus, students may learn to enter into new cultural patterns and to get involved in quite demanding but enriching practices. The goal of this problem-oriented project pedagogy is to help students become autonomous, yet collaborative and critically thinking individuals.

In relation to the challenges related to being involved in meaningful study activities, and being able to establish fruitful relations with others, we find it interesting to draw on some of the concepts developed by George Herbert Mead (1967 [1934]). According to Mead, it is in the intersubjective perspective that construction of meaning is created. Fundamentally, Mead uses the term "perspective" to describe the relationship between the experienced world and the experiencing subject. This means that the individual subject experiences his or her world in a situational, contextual and unique way. Perspective can furthermore be understood as a person's performance images or way of conceiving the world that will guide the social practice for this person in a contextual way (Mead 2005 [1934], p. 352).

John Dewey shares this point of view with Mead. They both have an understanding of learning as processes in intersubjective fields, participation in activities within various communities, of communication consisting of communities of learners, where meaning is negotiated and created. In this way of working, it is important that the students participating in group work with fellow students are able to relate to one another in an open way. The ability to take another person's perspective can be said to constitute the basis for learning. For the students, this ability is crucial. The Norwegian theorist Bråten discussing Mead writes: "It is through such a perspective construction, the ability to put yourself in someone else's place that students can enable their reflective capability" (Braåten 2000, p. 116).

Further on in his investigation Mead continues: "The individual becomes aware of his relations to that process as a whole, and to the other individuals participating in it with him; he becomes aware of that process as modified by the reactions and interactions of the individuals-including himself-who are carrying it on. The evolutionary appearance of mind or intelligence takes place when the whole social process of experience and behaviour is brought within the experience of any one of the separate individuals implicated therein, and when the individual's adjustment to the process is modified and refined by the awareness or consciousness which he thus has of it" (Mead 1967 [1934], p. 134).Other persons can also be seen as "generalised others", understood as an abstraction: "[...] representing the general societal position" (Vaage 2000, p. 103). A successful construction of perspective is thus a prerequisite for successful communication. In order to take the other persons' perspective in the group work, the participants should be open, reflexive and able to recognise new perspectives. In a group setting, it is important that the members are ready to acknowledge other people's wishes and life situations.

Stressing the importance of reflexivity Mead continues: "It is by means of reflexiveness-the turning-back of the experience of the individual upon himself-that the whole social process is thus brought into the experience of the individuals involved in it; it is by such means, which enable the individual to take the attitude of the other towards himself, that the individual is able consciously to adjust himself to that process, and to modify the resultant of that process in any given social act in terms of his adjustment to it. Reflexiveness, then, is the essential condition, within the social process, for the development of mind" (Mead 1967 [1934], p. 134).

> For teachers as well as for students, this concept of knowledge and learning "involves significant change in underlying values and knowledge structure – is always the subject of an organizational predicament", according to Donald Schön (1983, p. 328).

The Role of the Teacher as Supervisor for Students Doing Project Work

While students are working on their projects, they are receiving supervision from a teacher. In the next part of this chapter, we are going to analyse how supervision takes place in a networked learning environment. We further elaborate on the different roles that the supervisors take on as experts, facilitators and as social mediators, and how the different roles are supported and mediated by the learning infrastructure. The academic role as an expert can unfold with written communication through papers, giving feedback and advice within an asynchronously organised learning environment, such as a conference system. The other roles – especially that of a social mediator – require synchronous communication in personal meetings or, if that is not possible, through the use of Skype. This makes it easier for establishing a dialogical communication situation, where instant feedback and mutual response can take place. This is especially of importance since this supervisor role is in relation to social, cultural and psychological dimensions of the groups' work and learning processes.

The role of the supervisor is different from the role of the traditional teacher, who instructs, assigns works, finds texts, makes decisions regarding curriculum and evaluates the contributions of the students. In problem-oriented project studies, the supervisor is expected to provide extensive feedback to the work in progress that is submitted by the student group. Each paper from a student group for the "consultation meetings" can be up to 30 pages long. The supervisor offers his or her advice, discusses the various elements of the paper, and asks stimulating questions. The supervisor is responsible for providing the group with the required attention, drawing on his or her own experience, being able to relate to the students' experience, and thus helping the students to gain a deeper understanding of their own work. In this way, it is important that the teacher as supervisor is able to take the position of his or her students.

P. N. Dahl talks about student-tailored instruction (Dahl 2008). By this, he means that as a starting point the supervisor must go from the student's current "zone of development" and try to stimulate the "zone of proximal development". The zone of proximal development (ZPD) is the grey area between the things the learner can do alone and the things the learner can do with help from a more knowledgeable person or peer group (cf. Vygotsky 1978). By examining students' ZPD, we as teachers may have a window into the possibilities that the students can reach in the immediate future and thus we have a picture of the students' overall state of dynamic development. For a teacher as supervisor, it is not enough to be academically competent;

it is also crucial to be able to take the students' perspective, to try to interpret what kind of knowledge the students have, to be able to identify him- or herself with the specific kind of psychological and broader learning environment the students may need. A supervisor's ability to experience the ZPD of the students requires the capability to reflectively take the perspective of the other.

During the entire learning process, the supervisor as well as the students should make explicit their specific perspectives on supervision and guidance and inquire about the other's perceptions in order to be able to address possible differences in their mutual expectations. It is important to avoid defensive patterns by communicating openly and with respect for the other person's perspective. This is by no means easy, especially not for a teacher who is brought up in a traditional way. In such processes with challenges and no clear-cut answers, the supervisor must be able to cope with both his or her own and the students' uncertainty.

These understandings of imagination or horizons of understanding (Vaage 2003, p. 136) are constituted by the subject's experience, developed in an intersubjective and processual way. For example, a teacher has a specific perception of reality regarding the process of a learning sequence. This subjective perception may undergo changes during the learning process due to the self-reflection on the supervisor's side.

In a net-organised learning environment, the supervisor is expected to be even more flexible and sensitive in relation to the needs of the students. We take a look at some possible ways of filling out such a role

1. As the academically focused teacher, acting as an *expert* on a specific subject.
2. As the *process-oriented supervisor*, focusing on processes and methodological aspects.
3. As a *social mediator*, listening actively to what kind of psychological dimensions are taking place among the group members.

The Teacher as an Expert: Instructive Supervision

This kind of supervisor is providing guidance in relation to theories, methods and discussions within the philosophy of science. They see it as essential that the writings of the student group are thorough, coherent and adhering to the supervisor's norms. This supervision mode can be called *instructive* – the students are primed and instructed in how to provide answers to the research question. The students may ask questions such as: "can we" and "are we allowed". This type of supervisor can use terms, such as "shall", "please do", "don't do", "right" or "wrong".

Donald Schön, in discussing two different notions or contracts between the professional and the "client", outlines this traditional expert role in contrast to that of a democratically oriented, reflective practitioner. In our context, these two types of attitudes can shed light on the teacher–student relationship (Table 15.1).

As we have seen, Mead refers to the concept "to take another person's perspective" to describe the differentiation of experience in the common world of

Table 15.1 Two different dimensions of the expert role for the teacher – one the traditional expert approach – another as a reflective professional; borrowed from Schön 1983, p. 300

Expert	Reflective practitioner
I am presumed to know, and must claim to do so, regardless of my own uncertainty.	I am presumed to know, but I am not the only one in the situation to have relevant and important knowledge. My uncertainties may be a source of learning for me and for them.
Keep my distance from the client, and hold onto the expert's role. Give the client a sense of my expertise, but convey a feeling of warmth and sympathy as a "sweetener".	Seek out connections to the client's thoughts and feelings. Allow his respect for my knowledge to emerge from his discovery of it in the situation.
Look for deference and status in the client's response to my professional persona.	Look for the sense of freedom and of real connection to the client, as a consequence of no longer needing to maintain a professional facade.

experience, which we as persons are part of (Mead 2005, p. 353f). Mead's concept corresponds to the reflective practitioner, whereas the expert is more on the distance of the students.

Process Supervision – Focus on Methodological Questions, Epistemology: A Learning and Knowledge Process

This kind of supervisor is focused on aspects related to the research questions, the whole learning process and the continuing evaluation of the knowledge process. The supervisor aims to guide the group towards the final project through stimulating discussions, supporting the students' effort to reach a fruitful integration of the empirical data collected by the students and relevant theoretical positions. Important in this type of supervision is the students' heightened awareness of their study and work styles. The students should be able to constantly reflect on their way of acting and working with the material, what kind of choices they make, and what they are writing.

However, some students may find it difficult to involve themselves in an approach of reflexivity and to recognise the value of continual process evaluation. They seem only to focus their attention on constructing the product – their final project.

The supervisor can help by asking questions to clarify and further investigate the students' research question, theories and methods, and by indicating if working papers contain ambiguities and misunderstandings in relation to the study requirements.

Because the process supervisor has an open attitude, the students are using the supervisor as a qualified "opponent" – the supervisor poses "cheeky" questions, indicating there are no absolute answers – no solutions are entirely "wrong" or "right". It all depends.

The students will inform the supervisor about their work, using the supervisor as a sounding board for their ideas, so to speak. Thus, this kind of supervision is aiming at facilitating the entire learning and work process for the students.

Social Mediator: In Relation to the Interactions Among the Students

This kind of supervisor is focused on aspects related to the difficult and challenging elements of collaborative group work. When members of the group are talking at cross-purposes or even talking down to one another, the supervisor as a social mediator will intervene, for example, if students have difficulties making decisions and embarking on constructive dialogical processes, the supervisor will intervene. The method employed by this mediating supervisor is mainly inquiring and questioning in order to facilitate student engagement in explorative dialogues. The wellbeing of the group members is very important in this context.

The Relationship Between Student and Supervisor

In order to experience a successful supervising process, the group must make sure that the teacher as a supervisor is involved in the project study process.

The supervisor is a resource person whom the group must learn to make use of (depending on what type of supervisor they are and what the students' learning styles are). The students express their expectations to the supervision process explicitly, and they make the purpose of their project study and the level of their ambitions clear to the supervisor.

For example, a problem will arise if the students want to work with a practically oriented problem in communications, such as making a booklet or producing a video, and the supervisor wants to provide process-oriented supervision. These students may want concrete guidance on how to make productions and not a process orientated comment or intervention.

If such students feel insecure in relation to the requirements they must meet, they may be reluctant to expose their insecurity– consciously or unconsciously they may give their supervisor the impression that they are in possession of the competences and experiences that the supervisor wants.

The supervisor in this situation may take on a supervision style that actually *overestimates* the students.

In contrast, if a supervisor is downplaying the academically oriented product supervision, students may consciously or unconsciously give the impression that they are less competent than they really are in order to motivate the supervisor to be more academic and "professional".

Table 15.2 The teacher–student relationship seen as a traditional contract and a reflective contract, respectively; borrowed from Schön 1983, p. 302

Traditional contract	Reflective contract
I put myself into the professional's hands and, in doing this, I gain a sense of security based on faith.	I join the professional in making sense of my case, and in doing this I gain a sense of increased involvement and action.
I have the comfort of being in good hands. I need only comply with his advice and all will be well.	I can exercise some control over the situation. I am not wholly dependent on him; he is also dependent on information and action that only I can undertake.
I am pleased to be served by the best person available.	I am pleased to be able to test my judgments about his competence. I enjoy the excitement of discovery about his knowledge, about the phenomena of his practice, and about myself.

The supervisor may in this situation take on a supervision style that actually *underestimates* the students.

In relation to this teacher–student relationship, we refer again to the concepts proposed by Schön. This time the dichotomy is viewed from the perspective of "clients" – in our case students (Table 15.2).

When practitioners are unaware of their own frameworks for roles or problems, they do not experience the need to choose among them. They do not attend to the ways in which they construct the reality in which they function; for them, it is simply the given reality (Schön 1983, p. 310).

These three roles should not literally be understood as distinctively isolated differentiated roles. Rather they should be considered as an attempt to construct a methodological model through which to view the complex situation. In reality, a good supervisor should be able to take on all three kinds of roles depending on the phases of the project work and the situational mood among the students.

The Networked Learning Process: An Example

A project pedagogy process in MIL has a variety of different phases, ranging from face-to-face meetings with the student group to communication through digital media in virtual learning environments featuring written communication, audio and video. The roles of students and teachers change during a project working period.

The *students* identify the problem area they want to work with, based on the study declaration of the MIL. Then, they proceed to write a constructive problem formulation with a number of research questions by formulating one or two open-ended questions beginning with: Why, How and What …Next, the group members clarify which method they want to work with and the specific kind of philosophy of science the project must be based on.

The *supervisor* relates in a dialogical way to the situation described above of combining the roles of academically focused expert, process-oriented supervisor and social mediator. His or her approach is a kind of "joint inquiry" that allows the students in a qualified and informed way to make the preliminary crucial choices in their study process – knowing that further delimitation will be a necessary part of the learning process. The ideal and best way is that the outset of the project-driven study process takes place in a face-to-face setting.

Based on the group's independent work in literature searching, the completion of a number of interviews or other field work, and reading of relevant theory, the group will be able to present a comprehensive discussion paper covering 25–30 pages.

The supervisor acts as an *expert* relating to the students in an evaluating way as a starting point: Is the content presented in a coherent way? In the following phase, the teacher role will be more like a *facilitator*, helping to bring forward ideas for the continuing progress in the project work process. It may, for example, include assistance to the students in looking for supplemental references and additional literature.

The ability to write good papers is the focus of this phase of the work. It is beneficial if the students' contributions can be uploaded to a conference system, where all participants have access to read, write and print.

Disagreements may occasionally arise among the group members, leading to difficulties in collaboration, which can lead to disintegration in the project group. But disagreements or students' various viewpoints can also be seen as productive – even though they may be experienced as frustrating – and helping bringing different perspectives forward. At other times, they can be counter-productive and an obstacle to the continuing work in the group. In MIL, where students hold professional jobs while they are studying, they do not always have time and energy to deal with disagreements in a constructive way. There is consequently a tendency for more project groups to split up than we see in on-campus learning environments. A MIL group may split up into two smaller groups, or an individual student can continue as an associated member. This situation comes up once or twice nearly every year.

The supervisor functions as a social mediator for the students, asking questions to the two new groups separately. The questions concern (a) the participants' relation to the topic of the project work and (b) the relationship between the group members personally. Agreement is reached regarding how each new group can benefit from the previous empirical work to implement and analyse the content of the interviews. The result is "the division of property" as is the case in a "regular" divorce.

In this situation, the oral discussions unfold. Therefore, face-to-face meetings are best; however, if they are not possible, phone or Skype meetings can be used to replace them.

The work of the two groups progresses separately, and each group then later presents its new paper to the "joint teacher role" of: *academically focused expert and process-oriented supervisor.* It may turn out that the two projects have evolved in different directions, demonstrating that the disagreement largely had been of an academic character and therefore not just relating to personal conflicts.

Feedback to the students can either be given through Skype or by written comments uploaded to the conference system – or a combination of the two forms of communication.

The two groups, of course, take their exams separately. Both groups in this situation still experience their teacher in the role *of examiner* because the heart of the matter concerns the final evaluation. However, sometimes there is a possibility for more inquiry-oriented dialogues as part of the examination, which means that even at this occasion a genuine learning process among the participants may still take place.

Communication: A Basic Tool of Networked Learning

As part of the group's learning process, communication plays a central and important role. This applies to both the internal communication between group members and communication between the group and its supervisor. Communication within the group consists of two different types of messages, according to Alderfer (1986, p. 202):

- Messages associated with the specific issue of inquiry-based work as part of the learning process.
- Messages associated with the relationships between team members.

Messages linked to the explorative work with problem solutions to the investigations may, for example, be related to making proposals, expressing opinions and asking for other group members' opinions, and also requesting and providing information for the continued work on the group's research question. This is the professional, academic communication, where literature studies are combined with collection of empirical data through interviews and observations with external informants whose statements play an important role in the group's further work. This professional, academic communication should constantly be related to the research questions that were the group's starting point. However, development of the study explorations and the group's findings may make it necessary to revise the original problem formulation.

This ongoing development of the learning process contains a process of negotiation between group members and the supervisor. It is as part of the negotiation process that the relational communication between the members of the group will increase and eventually be quite time-consuming, in order for the learning process of the group to move on and evolve further. The messages associated with relationships between group members can be *positive*, where the participants act friendly towards each other, declare consensus, and dissolve any tension among them. However, the messages may also be *negative*, where opposing views are highlighted in statements of disagreements so that communication can be perceived as unfriendly and perhaps stressful for the group's continuing work.

Table 15.3 The negotiation processes among students viewed as a dichotomy between *dialogues* and *discussions;* borrowed from Alrø and Kristiansen 2004

Discussion	Dialogue
Convince – Winning	Joint investigation
We need not get smarter	We can all learn from each other
I have the right answers	Together we will find a solution
I show how you were wrong	We go for a new joint solution
I listen to find fault	I listen to understand
My opinions represent the truth	Let us examine our attitudes
I defend my views	We are improving each other's thinking
I keep cards close to my body	I am submitting my doubts
I do not take into account how you feel	We create together a safe space where stupid questions are OK

The communication in the group work is part of the ongoing negotiations within the learning process and typically will contain three different types of communicative processes; namely (Stewart and Logan 1993, p. 128):

- *Interpersonal communication* where the communicators address each other as unique individuals, as persons.
- *Social communication* that takes place between the social roles with no interest in the person behind the role.
- *Cultural communication*, where the communication depends on the person's views on for example gender, age, social class and ethnicity.

When the group members actively take part in a specific learning process, their interaction can be seen as *social communication*. This means that they communicate in their role as students, engaged in the literature and the methodological approaches of the project work. They have a shared interest in constructing a project that is as good as possible. However, during the ongoing negotiations various viewpoints and differences in opinion among the group members may arise. If no agreement or negotiated compromise can be reached, the interaction can change into *interpersonal communication*; i.e. each participant in the group declares his or her personal opinion as part of the negotiations. Maybe *cultural communication* will prevail if the interpersonal communication becomes prominent. In most cases, the group will achieve a compromise, perhaps with the assistance of the supervisor in their role as social mediator, and the students will be ready to continue with their learning process and work together. If not, the group may split into smaller groups, which will be experienced by them as a rupture that takes place in a potentially contentious and conflicted atmosphere.

From the outside, the negotiation processes might be viewed as a dichotomy between *dialogues* and *discussions* as part of the group members' either primarily negative or primarily positive relational communication. This may be set up as opposites (Alrø and Kristiansen 2004, p. 14) (Table 15.3)

Habermas's distinction between strategic and a communicative action represents another way of characterising the contrast between discussion and dialogue (Habermas 1986). Thus, discussion can be seen as a form of strategic communication;

i.e. instrumental communication, where the strategic actors' intentional behaviour are oriented towards cognition and success. A strategic actor communicates with the other group members with the purpose of influencing their perspectives according to his or her goals. Thus, strategic action aims at acquiring the definitional power. The outcome is experienced as an attempt to achieve one member's specific goal as part of a win–lose dynamic.

Conversely, dialogue can be seen as an effort of communicative action, where the communicative actors with their interactive competences and interests are oriented towards consensus and performative acts, including an orientation towards cognition. Such actors are striving to accomplish a more open communication without specific intentions to dominate the other participants. For Habermas, the goal is to reach a situation with "intersubjective mutuality of reciprocal understanding, shared knowledge, mutual trust and accord with one another" (Habermas 1979, p. 3). In other words, the underlying goal of reaching understanding is to foster enlightenment, deeper insight in the problem area, and consensus among the group members. In a specific project group, the communication at times alternate between discussion and dialogue in the sense that is described here.

Conclusion

In a networked learning environment, the participants only occasionally arrange face-to-face meetings; primarily, they are working together in groups via the Internet using an online conference system, Skype and video conferencing. It is therefore important that supervisors have a clear idea of how the physical and virtual means should be used. To meet face-to-face is important in the initial phase, where a project group is established. Meeting in person makes it easier for the supervisor and the students to achieve an alignment of expectations for their future relations and the group work. The communication in the group at this point focuses on constructing an initial problem formulation with some related research questions. In this phase of the project work, dialogues between supervisor and students contain Habermasian communicative action.

Any disagreements among the participants about the academic direction of the project work should preferably be resolved while the participants are physically together. A successful construction of interrelational perspective is thus a prerequisite for successful communication, as we have learned from our exploration into the world of Mead. As we saw, it can be difficult, but it is crucial that supervisors as well as students have the capability to take another person's perspective. It is important to avoid defensive and rigid patterns by communicating openly and with respect for the other person's perspective.

In subsequent phases, the collaboration is mediated through the Internet and the relevant digital tools, services and devices. In this phase, students have the opportunities to write collaborative texts and discuss them online. If disagreements or conflicts arise in the project work, the interpersonal communication among the participants cannot be confined to academic content alone. The participants' reciprocal, personal relationships come into focus; thus, each person must judge whether, for example, everyone's work performance has been adequate. If, for example, group members have different cultural backgrounds, it may also be necessary to clarify the more deep-seated perceptions of learning processes with the intent of bringing the project work back into a constructive direction. The supervisor must in these situations act as project manager and help negotiate differences, which is generally best done face-to-face. The supervisor as social mediator therefore from the viewpoint of Habermas has to understand and decode the strategic communication that is part of the discussions when students disagree.

To summarise, based on our experience and the ideas expressed in this chapter, we believe that successful network learning requires teachers or supervisors who are reflective and able to take the other's perspective. Further they should, in our view, be able to take on the three supervisory roles identified as important, of academic expert, process-orientated supervisor and social mediator.

References

ALA, American Library Association, Presidential Committee on Information Literacy. (1989). *Final report*, [online] Available at: http://www.ala.org/ala/mgrps/divs/acrl/publications/white-papers/presidential.cfm. Accessed 21 Apr 2011. Chicago: American Library Association.

Alderfer, C. (1986). An intergroup perspective on group dynamics. In J. W. Lorsch (Ed.), *Handbook of organizational behaviour*. Englewood Cliffs, NJ: Prentice Hall. Ch. 6.

Alrø, H., & Kristiansen, M. (2004). *Dialog og magt i organisationer*. Aalborg: Aalborg Universitetsforlag.

Barrett, T., & Moore, S. (Eds.). (2010). *New approaches to problem-based learning: revitalizing your practice in higher education*. New York/London: Routledge.

Bråaten, S. (2000). G.H. Meads filosofi som grundlag for dialogisk forståelse. In H. Thuen & S. Vaage (Eds.), *Opdragelse til det moderne – E. Durkheim, G.H. Mead, J. Dewey og P. Bourdieu* (pp. 107–132). Aarhus: Klim.

Dirckinck-Holmfeld, L., and Jones, C. (2009). Analysing networked learning practices – an introduction. L. Dirckinck-Holmfeld, C. Jones, & B. Lindström (Eds.), *Analysing networked learning practices in higher education and continuing professional development*. Rotterdam/Boston/Taipei: Sense Publishers, pp. 1–27.

Dahl, P. N. (2008). Studenter-afstemt vejledning og kommunikation. In L. Krogh, J. B. Olsen, & P. Rasmussen (Eds.), *Projektpædagogik – Perspektiver fra Aalborg Universitet* (pp. 89–106). Aalborg: Aalborg Universitetsforlag.

Goodyear, P., Banks, S., Hodgson, V., & McConnell, D. (Eds.). (2004). *Advances in research on networked learning*. London: Kluwer Academic Publishers.

Habermas, J. (1979). *Communication and the evolution of society*. Boston: Beacon.

Habermas, J. (1986). *Theory of communicative action* (Reason and the rationalization of society, Vol. 1). Cambridge: Polity.

Kolmos, A., Fink, F., & Krogh, L. (Eds.). (2004). *The Aalborg PBL Model – progress, diversity and challenges*. Aalborg: Aalborg University Press.

Lave, J., & Wenger, E. (1991). *Situated learning – legitimate peripheral participation*. Cambridge: Cambridge University Press.

Mead, G. H. (1967 [1934]). *Mind, self, and society: from the standpoint of a social behaviorist (Works of George Herbert Mead, Vol. 1)* (1st ed.). Chicago: University of Chicago Press.

Mead, G. H. (2005 [1934]). *Sindet, selvet og samfundet*. København: Akademisk Forlag.

Olesen, H. S., & Jensen, J. H. (Eds.). (1999). *Project studies – a late modern university reform?* Roskilde: Roskilde University Press.

Olsen, P. B., & Pedersen, K. (Eds.). (2005). *Problem-oriented project work – a workbook*. Roskilde: Roskilde University Press.

Schön, D. A. (1983). *The reflective practitioner – how professionals think in action*. New York: Basic.

Stewart, J., & Logan, C. (1993). *Together communicating interpersonally* (4th ed.). New York: McGraw-Hill.

Vaage, S. (2000). Handling og pædagogik – G.H. Mead om uddannelse og socialisering. In H. Thuen & S. Vaage (Eds.), *Opdragelse til det moderne – E. Durkheim, G.H. Mead, J. Dewey og P. Bourdieu* (pp. 83–105). Aarhus: Klim.

Vaage, S. (2003). Perspektivtagning, rekonstruktjon af erfaring og kreative læreprosesser: George Herbert Mead og John Dewey om læring. In O. Dysthe (Ed.), *Dialog, Samspil og Læring* (pp. 129–149). Aarhus: Klim.

Vygotsky, L. S. (1978). Mind in society. In M. Cole et al. (Eds.), *The development of higher psychological processes*. Cambridge, MA: Harvard University Press.

Chapter 16
Life Behind the Screen: Taking the Academic Online

Stuart Boon and Christine Sinclair

Introduction

The prospect of taking academic life online offers a range of challenges and opportunities for staff and students in higher education. This chapter focuses on some of the many transformative experiences encountered by academics in adjusting to, and participating in, networked learning environments. Moving on from our initial reluctance to "inhabit" social networking spaces, we adopt the well-used metaphor of the screen to find a framework for evaluating and developing questions raised in an earlier paper. We use personal experiences of becoming disconnected from traditional practices while at the same time drawing on the familiar to enable an effective transition to networked learning. We have conceptualized our route as involving a projection toward a screen, adjusting our focus to negotiate barriers and optimize enablers. But before we are fully immersed in a virtual world, we still have a stake in the real one. This has implications for our identity as academics when we find ourselves operating in both kinds of environment simultaneously. It affects language too as existing expressions become transformed or superseded to refer to new kinds of practice. It entails new relationships with time, where speed and lag both change the nature of the activities engaged in. And academic engagement itself must be looked at anew, amid competing demands for attention. Identity, language, time, and engagement are viewed as both barriers and enablers in the movement from behind the screen to full participation in networked learning environments. In exploring sites of transformation and highlighting the process of transition involved in taking the academic online, we identify potential challenges and opportunities experienced in stepping out from behind the screen and projecting ourselves into networked learning environments.

S. Boon (✉) • C. Sinclair
Centre for Academic Practice and Learning Enhancement,
University of Strathclyde, Glasgow, Scotland
e-mail: stuart.boon@strath.ac.uk

L. Dirckinck-Holmfeld et al. (eds.), *Exploring the Theory, Pedagogy and Practice*
of Networked Learning, DOI 10.1007/978-1-4614-0496-5_16,
© Springer Science+Business Media, LLC 2012

The Screen as Metaphor

In an earlier paper (Boon and Sinclair 2009), we described our disquiet and discomfort in using social networking and virtual environments, highlighting how this unease informed and impacted upon our relationships with networked learning. The first part of the title of that paper – "A World I Don't Inhabit" – was an expression picked up from a colleague in mathematics when we mentioned that we were exploring issues around Second Life and Facebook. More than 2 years on, we are still thinking about our engagement with networked learning environments and felt it would be useful to revisit the questions we raised in that previous paper. As a result, we have tracked our engagement with an emergent new understanding of networked learning, which we think can usefully be characterized as both a place and a set of practices. While we may still experience some disquiet in fully inhabiting these spaces, we are now participating more with and within them, and have found the metaphor of the screen has helped us to reframe our questions and move on.

The well-established metaphor of the screen neatly provides a portal as we cross the threshold to our new understanding. We use this metaphor to explore our experiences, emphasizing Stuart's role as a university teacher and Christine's time as a student undertaking an MSc in E-learning online at the University of Edinburgh. We are both educational developers, interested in learning as well as teaching and both work with students as well as staff. We have also drawn on our own dominant theoretical interests in phenomenography (Stuart) and activity theory (Christine) and our shared fascination with literacies required for higher education and beyond, although we are not using specific frameworks from these perspectives. Instead, our theoretical interests indicate the provenance of our treatment of our themes: variation in conceptions, capturing a transformative process in-flight before it becomes second nature, and the way that variations and actions are captured in language use. The themes themselves – identity, language, time, and engagement – emerged from our discussions with each other and a felt need to work out together whether what we were experiencing under these headings should be regarded positively or negatively in relation to participation in networked learning.

We have eclectically visited a range of theoretical perspectives in the process of unpacking our own understandings of networked learning. Our main emphasis, however, is empirical: using our own experiences to highlight barriers and enablers for staff and students in transitional states. We aim to capture snapshots of these transitional states to support our work as lecturers and educational developers, anticipating a future where we have to take on roles as projectors of new forms of practice. The process is raising questions about the extent to which academics can or should replicate old practices, and how we disaggregate and reaggregate academic habits and values. In exploring transformation in transition from traditional spaces to networked learning environments, we seek to highlight how academics are variously encouraged or discouraged, inspired or hindered, empowered or disconnected. Further research will consider the implications of our roles as projectors and complete our analysis of life of academics behind, on and through the screen.

As we inhabit transitional spaces variably differentiating and blending traditional and networked learning environments, our own conceptions of networked learning are still protean, fluid, and best described as works in progress. Although we have attended conferences on networked learning – and spoken, read, and written about it – the full implications of networked learning and its meaning for academic staff and students are still unfolding for us. Definitions that refer to connections and emphasize social understanding (Goodyear et al. 2004) are useful but may mask the complexity of that social nature. Networked learning has proved to be a threshold concept, with associated implications for how we engage as academics, students, and educational developers (Meyer and Land 2005). Those who write about threshold concepts seem particularly taken by Meyer and Land's defining expression "akin to a portal" (Meyer and Land 2006), as a Google search of this expression will reveal. Similarly, we feel we are passing through a portal of understanding to something previously inaccessible, and want to capture the experience before we have completely lost our old ways of viewing what is going on in academic practice. We shall suggest that networked learning is not only itself a threshold concept, but is also a site where threshold concepts abound. Networked learning can also be characterized as a set of practices that invoke threshold concepts, perhaps turning educational orthodoxies on their heads and requiring us to rethink what staff and students do and how they relate to each other (Wesch 2009):

> "And each digital innovation seems to shake us free from yet another assumption we once took for granted."

We are aware of some risks in trying to track where we are coming from as well as where we are going. Wesch (2009) warns that our cognitive habits make us try to hang on to our familiar ways of teaching and assessing. Yet, we know as educational developers working with both staff and students that we shall need an understanding of where our colleagues are coming from once we ourselves have passed through the threshold – or at least emerged from our current investigations of the screen as metaphor.

Some might even argue that the modern screen is not a metaphor; it refers to a physical item, a vital piece of hardware that we all use in day-to-day life. Indeed, recent findings showed that adults spend roughly 8.5 hours a day – a large proportion of their waking life – looking at screens of one sort of another (Council for Research Excellence 2009). Beyond the physical object, the screen is a word with many connotations and denotations, offering us multiple contextual overtones (Bakhtin 1981) to consider, some of which are metaphorical. As a metaphor, the screen is both potent and dynamic, having numerous and often-contradictory qualities: for example, it is capable of being simultaneously conceived of as both an enabling tool and a barrier to engagement.

The title of this chapter intentionally echoes Sherry Turkle's seminal work *Life on the Screen: Identity in the Age of the Internet* (1995), in which she prompts a range of associations (e.g., cinema, television, etc.) that might extend our analysis. These associations can have a powerful effect on academics' perceptions of networked learning and, particularly, in how academics see themselves in relation to networked learners. For example, the play on words "screen or monitor" in the title of a paper by Bayne and Land (2002) highlights issues of surveillance and power in the relationship between physical objects and their metaphorical associations. In this chapter, we concentrate on the positive side of the screen metaphor rather than its Orwellian descendents, though the connection has to be acknowledged as we try to find the boundaries of our framework.

Our title "Life Behind the Screen" deliberately adopts an alternative preposition to Turkle's: we are looking *behind* the screen, rather than *on* it. More specifically, our focus here is on the transformation from behind the screen to on the screen with its attendant issues, challenges, and opportunities. In future research, we will eventually extend this exploration to what happens *through* the screen: a construction that we see as particularly relevant for the relationship between staff and students. Herein, however, we will focus on our experiences in engaging with networked learning environments as both educators and students. In the 2 years following the publication of our previous paper, we have made progress in overcoming our initial feelings of discomfort and disquiet. However, the transition to online learners and educators has been neither simple nor seamless: rather we find ourselves surprised and intrigued by questions relating to our identities, the language that we use, our relationship with time and the ways in which we engage with online spaces. Reflecting on our own experiences, we look more closely below at these four sites of transition and transformation – identity, language, time, and engagement – examining how they can represent both barriers and enablers and how they have shaped our actions behind the screen.

The transformative journey we embark on when we enter into networked learning environments is not unlike Alice's journey in Lewis Carroll's *Through the Looking-Glass, and What Alice Found There* (1871): we encounter all manner of people, situations, and environments that may either attempt to replicate the familiar or provide totally alien experiences (e.g., Ball and Pearce 2009; Bayne 2008; Boon and Sinclair 2009; Castronova 2005; Wood and Smith 2005). These experiences may challenge or trouble us, intrigue or entertain us, aid or inform us, but each of them singly or as a whole will go some way to transform us and our relation to the world around us. Figure 16.1 below shows our conceptualization of our own journeys and the relationships involved.

Our main focus here is on our own experiences. We do have theoretical influences, both shared and individual, and their effects can be seen here. We are both interested in literacies, Stuart from the perspective of information literacy and Christine from literature on academic writing. We also draw on phenomenography and activity theory, though not adhering slavishly to either for our current purposes. From phenomenography, we emphasize the necessity of awareness of variation in experiences to allow for conceptualization of phenomena (Marton and Pang 1999) and Stuart explores the differences between the real and the virtual as he engages in different forms of academic participation. From activity theory, we recognize Leont'ev's (1981) distinction between action and operation and Christine's blog as an MSc student attempts to capture a "process in flight" (Vygotsky 1978, p. 64) before it has become fossilized. Once what we do as students and educators has become operationalized, it is hard to get back to an understanding of where it came from. It would therefore be difficult to support those who are still on the journey.

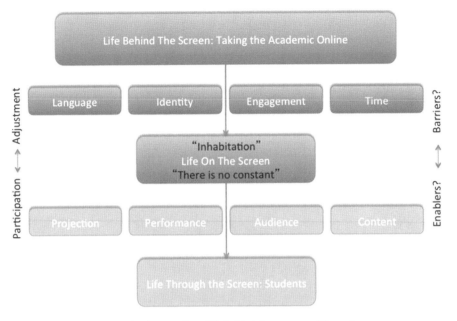

Fig. 16.1 The transformative journey from life behind the screen to life on the screen

As with our earlier paper, in this work, we use our own experiences as participants – as both students and educators – in online environments to illustrate and problematize these transformative experiences and encounters in networked learning. We use our immediate experience, recorded as reflections and as extracts from a student's blog (http://e-learningconfessions.blogspot.com). This chapter follows the journey of the first arrow in Fig. 16.1 (above) involving the transition from life behind the screen to inhabitation or life on the screen: we reserve the journey of the second arrow and its associated features for future work but are keen to anticipate it here.

Our use of the screen as both object and metaphor may be seen as an interaction with what Cousin (2005) describes as "transitional objects." Cousin points to the role of the virtual learning environment (VLE) in providing a link between familiar, traditional classroom practices and the new opportunities afforded by networked learning. In our own experience, we have noted that there are a number of adjustments that academics must make in order to participate effectively in online worlds – we cover four such adjustments or sites of transition below. As a transitional object, the screen – like Alice's looking glass – offers us passage through a liminal space in which our knowledge, our activities, and even ourselves are brought into conflict with the other. This transition and its concomitant transformation affect us directly, challenging the way we perceive and construct our world(s) and ourselves. In our own experience, for example, the seeming constants of language, identity, engagement, and time were shown to be inconstant and made unfamiliar through this transition or crossing. This inconstancy and unfamiliarity can be a very real barrier for academics and students alike. With one foot in the real and another in the virtual, users must come to terms with both difference and disquiet in order to participate effectively in networked learning environments.

One Foot in the Real and One in the Virtual: Implications for Identity

Identity in networked learning environments is an area of much interest, deliberation and debate (e.g., Mann 2003). For many academics, the transition to networked learning involves a move from the familiar and comfortable identities and activities of traditional practice to a new arena of engagement wherein identity and activity must be re/constructed and re/negotiated. As we argued in our previous paper, academics may well feel threatened by these processes and, in particular, by the need to edit or augment their identities (Boon and Sinclair 2009). Among our colleagues, we still see open resistance to participation in online environments and not only with the more senior members of the academy.

As academics in networked learning environments, we find ourselves often inhabiting or simultaneously straddling two worlds. For many of us, as the reflections below illustrate, our roles, our work, and our identities are in transition:

> My day is divided now: in the morning I stand in front of a class full of students, teaching in a traditional classroom to a traditional audience, but in the afternoon I'm online and then it's all different – I'm a different kind of teacher then with a different kind of audience in a space that's anything but traditional…. The strange thing is that we're all the same people from morning to afternoon and, yet, somehow we're not. In the online discussions and activities, I've got one foot in the real and one in the virtual: I'm still the traditional teacher, but now I'm something else, someone else, as well. I'm stretching between the two. It has to be real and yet it's also unreal or virtual. In the end, it sometimes feels like I'm the thing that's become divided – or maybe multiplied.
>
> (from Stuart's reflective diary)

This increased complexity and the concomitant challenge to identity and ways of thinking and practicing can be seen as a barrier to engagement with networked learning environments. On a symbolic level, immersion into a networked environment involves the dislocation of the individual – lecturer or student – from familiar structures and frameworks for teaching and learning (e.g., Anderson 2009; Wood and Smith 2005). For some, this can be a disorienting and disquieting process:

> I've found myself experiencing a kind of dislocation in my new role as an online educator. When I mentioned this to a colleague, she expressed a similar uncomfortable, almost nervous, feeling. In our discussion we came to realize that we felt as though the technology was essentially dislocating us from our established, disciplinary "communities of practice" (Lave and Wenger 1998). We both feel cut off in a sense, but then that makes sense. It is a new environment after all: the networked learning environment. I think I was assuming that the job of teaching online would be a seamless transition – taking what I know and applying it in a different context – but it isn't that easy. I can see that there's going to a lot more to it to become a part of a different community of practice.
>
> (from Stuart's reflective diary)

What is clear is that working effectively in online spaces necessitates a willingness and conscious decision to engage with and accept both the opportunities and challenges offered by networked learning. This virtual blurring and refocusing of identity, for example, simultaneously offers and threatens academics with potential changes in role, levels of engagement, and relationships between themselves and their students.

> My relationship to the students is different as well. It is often surprising how different they are online. But then I'm different online as well. It's a new environment for us all, I think. But for the students, I suspect the virtual is much more home to them than for me. For me, at this point in time, being there is still a challenge… but I see the opportunity too. It can still be strange from time to time. It's not uncomfortable usually – although I think it can be – but it requires a lot more work, a different kind of engagement, a different kind of knowledge, a different relationship and language. And, I guess, I'm still learning all that.
>
> (from Stuart's reflective diary)

Taking the academic online thus requires a re-examination and perhaps even redefining of academic identity. In transition, academics find themselves inhabiting liminal spaces in which identity, role, and activity are thrown into doubt, and ultimately require re-evaluation and reorientation. Encounters with and within networked learning environments thus raise a number of important questions regarding academic and professional identity: for example, how do we present or represent ourselves in networked learning environments? How are our identities negotiated or renegotiated in the process? How are our ways of thinking and practicing informed and/or challenged? These are questions that we have only begun to seek answers to. For now, we recognize the transitional journey from traditional to networked learning environments as a journey of change and transformation: the challenge for educators is to be open to develop new ways of being while taking advantage of opportunities for creating new relationships, roles, and practices that augment and enhance our traditional work.

Shifts in Perspective Transform Our Use of Language

The metaphors we use to describe what is happening online reveal how we conceptualize what is going on. In looking from behind the screen and becoming ready to step through it, we are invoking a complex metaphor of place. We need to think about what is going on in the places we encounter. Goodfellow and Lea (2007) argue that academic work online should be recognized as sites of literacy practice. This conception entails that the new medium is not, as some people would claim, just a "delivery truck" for content (Clark 1994), but rather is a place where identity and activity are constituted through textual exchanges. There are inevitable adjustments to be made, as illustrated by the following extract from a student's blog:

> I'm thinking about speech acts – though I've known about these for over 30 years, I now have a new take on them. …This issue [silence] is heightened online, through the whole idea of lurking and we're also very conscious of power structures and other effects such as the permanence of online text.
>
> (from Christine's blog as an MSc student)

Not only is silence different online, we have given it a new name (lurking) – though it is one that is shot through with negative connotations from its previous associations. Because the student here is clearly a (very) mature one, she has a wide repertoire of associations to draw on. The example shows how the new take can be an enabler, seen as expanding current understanding. For some students, though, the challenge to what is in the existing repertoire might act as a barrier, especially if the new use has negative connotations. For some of their teachers, too, such a new use of old language can have the effect of extending a repertoire or threatening to topple it.

A different student (and, equally, a different teacher) might regard the online meaning of lurking as the standard point of reference or definition. It might be the expression "speech acts" (Austin 1962) that is new to their repertoire. This student could also then have a new take on silence. Arguably, the concept of lurking for the older student and the concept of speech acts for the younger could scaffold a similar new scientific view of the everyday concept of silence (Vygotsky [1934] 1987). Looked at in this way, learning how to bring the familiar and unfamiliar together has implications that apply to new forms of participation through technology as well as those encountered in the disciplines.

New meanings, new expressions and alternative uses all have the potential to invoke change and prompt a new take on something in the existing repertoire. At the point of encounter, there may be a response to this that is quickly forgotten. Another extract from the blog illustrates a transformative, point-of-encounter response and its theme is also pertinent to our deliberations in this chapter. The initial stimulus for the reflections was a comment made by a respected colleague from another institution and an expert in e-learning. This was:

> "Students should all be encouraged to use aggregators. It's an essential part of digital literacy."

Aggregators are software or Web applications that collate Web content, such as RSS feeds. The comment about them prompted a set of responses recorded the following day in the blog:

> It is important to record something I recognized yesterday as frequently happening to me as a student, not just of e-learning but always. Someone makes a valuable comment that potentially leads to a change in what I do and/or how I think about things – but I have a sequence of internalized responses that attempt to filter it before that happens. I think I can identify each one. They were experienced very rapidly – and they are part of the process in flight; that is they will be forgotten when I have fully internalized it. I think I have captured all the stages below.
>
>   1. OMG, I do not do that.
>   2. Or do I? I perhaps do something a bit like it?
>   3. I did not know it was called that.
>   4. I do not think I want to do it.
>   5. I will find a rationale for not doing it.
>   6. Perhaps I should do it though.
>   7. I need to find out more about it – look it up, talk to other…
>   8. Well, X also suggested something on these lines but I had not picked up on it.
>   9. I am trying to imagine what it would be like doing this routinely and I am slightly uncomfortable with the picture.

10. I am not sure that I am the sort of person who does this.
11. Here is a simile/metaphor for it [tickertape].

(from Christine's blog as an MSc student; items 8–11 followed
after further reflection on the following day.)

This extract illustrates how coming to terms with new ideas in a new medium uses previous knowledge of self, ideas, and media in the attempt at assimilation. At the time of writing the present chapter, the process of adopting an aggregator is still incomplete, but the word and its new use are becoming firmly established. Thus in revisiting concepts from a book that referred (challengingly) to the effects of disaggregation (Brown and Duguid 2000) with respect to information technology, a new and transformative connection was made to the authors' arguments. What began as a barrier is eventually becoming an enabler. And this observation has made us both ask questions about disaggregation and disintermediation from older forms of pedagogy that are followed by reaggregation and reintermediation with the new. We were grateful to be alerted to potential shifts that are happening so quickly that they become second nature to some people before others even have the chance to encounter them.

A Time of Change: And a Change of Time

Time, like identity and language, is invariably shifted as we enter networked learning environments. One might argue that our relationship with time is one of the first things to undergo transformation when we participate in online spaces. Those working or participating in networked learning environments commonly experience a change in their relationship with time, often expressed alternatively as an acceleration or deceleration of time and/or speed of activity. As the following two reflections – first that of an academic and second that of a student – show, stepping over that threshold into the virtual requires a re-evaluation of time, speed, and activity:

> I am beginning to see a real issue with time here... certainly in the way I use it, the way I expect others to use it (and no doubt their expectations for me), and how networked learning impacts my relationship with time. I feel like I have to renegotiate the whole situation. In the real world, I feel like I have a good understanding of time and how much I can achieve in say 50 minutes. But online the idea of 50 minutes is utterly meaningless – the class is online 24 hours a day and people can be contributing and learning non-stop.

(from Stuart's reflective diary)

> I've been very conscious of the synchronous/asynchronous dichotomy for a while, but it's starting to dominate my thinking at the moment.... I have concerns about dichotomies but they are often useful in pointing to an issue for exploration.... My own preference in learning is for the asynchronous – blogs, discussion boards, reading – over the synchronous – instant messaging, Second Life, talk. But I wouldn't like my whole life to be asynchronous! I love to meet people face to face and talk things through with them. Part of that pleasure, though, is knowing that the ideas will keep developing.

(from Christine's blog as an MSc student)

Information technologies, the Internet and the blending of asynchronous and synchronous communication make it possible for us to be perpetually networked. The online presence of the academic or student need never sleep. Our Facebook profiles, blogs and various Web pages, for example, are ever-present and very nearly immortal. We are virtually omnipresent, but at a cost. Here again opportunity and challenge, barrier and enabler, are intertwined. While the common complaint among academics that working online takes up too much of their time and effort certainly factors into the perception of time as a barrier to participation (MacKeogh and Fox 2009), our interest focuses on how our perception of time is transformed in networked learning environment and what temporal adjustments academics must make to function effectively in online spaces.

Networked learning provides us with the potential for unparalleled connectivity and new levels of engagement but at the cost of compressed time and increased complexity and fragmentation. In *Tyranny of the Moment: Fast and Slow Time in the Information Age*, Eriksen (2001) argues that our use of information technologies has led us to adopt a logic of acceleration wherein time and events are compressed forcing us to alter our relationship with time and with one another. Periods of slow time, where we can think and communicate without interruption, he suggests are ever diminishing, as more and more aspects of our lives are taken online.

In networked learning, the Eriksen's tyranny of the moment might be expressed as the constant pressure to be online and available, to be fast in responding to students' needs, and to always be up to date. Time in online environments is inherently fast time. Lag – a reduction of speed and/or connectivity, which might also be seen as an expression of slow time – is not acceptable and a source of much frustration for users. This is closely connected to the cultural need to keep up, if not accelerate further, and can lead us to experience and perceive our own lives in the real world as lag. In that way, the virtual can begin to degrade the real, making it seem slow, uncoordinated, and out of touch. It is not uncommon, for example, to hear academics express the feeling that they should be online 24 hours a day and to even express guilt when operating in the real world. Statements like these can, in turn, lead others to dismiss the opportunities provided by networked learning environments, focusing only on the negative.

Ironically, the same processes enable students and academic staff to make more considered communications than they do in a classroom because of the need to write responses rather than say them (although even this is changing as voice plays an increasing role online). The challenge for academics is to find a balance between the demands of transformed time and the possibilities it provides us for facilitating and supporting student learning. In order to successfully navigate and participate in networked learning environments, academics must make the transition from tradition or real conceptions of time to new or virtual conceptions. This transition necessitates that academics reconsider their relationship with time both on a personal and professional level. We suggest that it may be important to acknowledge differing preferences in relation to time, especially in the synchronous/asynchronous spectrum to minimize barriers to participation, for example through under-engagement or over-engagement (Savin-Baden and Sinclair 2011).

Engagement in Networked Learning

Who we are online, the language available to us and our relationship to time all have an impact on the way we can engage – what we are able to do. The student blog contains examples of times where students feel under- and over-engaged, especially in relation to what other students are doing. As we learn about appropriate *academic* engagement online, the traces we leave can provide an opportunity to explore what we are actually doing. This particular example from the blog shows how such traces can be used for later analysis:

> A fellow student has written a draft that incorporates a Skype conversation in which I took part. It is fascinating – and sharing drafts is such a valuable (and brave) thing to do online, with all sorts of useful connections for all of us. If we all do this, it will be a rich source of support for writing. He's introduced an idea that really interests me and he makes an excellent case. I've still to add my comments, but have held back because the analysis and the transcript suggest that I go into the community in "tutor" mode – and this has got me thinking…
>
> The transcript does suggest that I have a tendency to try to frame the discussions in my course and this could disempower other students. This will now possibly make me want to contribute less – and that could lead to different types of silence (at least I can mention it in my essay!). I must be appearing to be more confident online than I actually am (and I think I may do this f2f too). The last thing I want to do is intimidate people, or appear to be a know-all (especially as I am not) but I do want to contribute to the thinking where I see opportunities.

(from Christine's blog as an MSc student)

The blog extract above contains evidence of how our four themes – identity, language, time, and engagement – interact. There are several layers of actions here. The blog author's actions referred to in the first paragraph as seen by herself were: participate in Skype (instant messaging) discussion, read draft, evaluate draft, reflect on own participation in discussion. The participation in Skype could be further broken down into actions – or speech acts (Austin 1962). From Christine's own memory, the actions included: express ideas, ask questions, summarize, suggest resources, and give reasons for a view. The negative action "held back" referred to in the blog extract is an interesting one, relating to the notions of silence and lurking that recur throughout the blog. There is much evidence in the blog of self-censorship online and the second paragraph elaborates on this in relation to the participation at this point of the course.

It was noted later that the fellow student had not expressed this view negatively or strongly and it was not his main point. Nevertheless, what was written – both synchronously in Skype and asynchronously in the draft – provided evidence of the action or speech act that might be defined as "framing a discussion" and of another student's response to this. The second paragraph captures reasoning for subsequent reduction in engagement at the time (though it has to be said that this was probably only a temporary effect).

However, there were also times of under-engagement for a variety of reasons. The example below comes from around the same time, during a module on language and culture, and the extract indicates the same obsessions with participation and silence and their relationship with the real world equivalents:

> The discussion board is fairly quiet at present with no tutor contributions and about four students doing some good stuff. I've realized that they're almost doing the reading for the

rest of us; by digesting and interpreting as a sort of advance party, they're putting up signposts that will help the rest of us. I've done a sort of comment to this effect, but am only just realizing how important this is. In fact, I remember some students telling me during an evaluation that they resented doing this kind of work for the rest of the class. But how different is it from students not speaking up in tutorials?

(from Christine's blog as an MSc student)

Here, it is other students' actions that can be seen in the extract – reading, digesting, interpreting, putting up signposts (in the forum).

There is a sense of guilt at lack of contribution and indeed that had been expressed more strongly in the previous paragraph. The previous example also suggests guilt at over-contribution. The fact that the entire blog is entitled *Confessions of an e-learning* student would highlight this effect for any external reader – and, indeed, the idea of engagement is rendered more complex by the fact that this blog was available for speech acts that felt wrong for other online spaces. Such public disclosures, however, may be inappropriate for younger students and there has been a subsequent concern by this writer that her student blog be regarded by other student readers as a model for online reflection. While it is useful for the current authors' purposes to capture a process in flight, it might not be helpful for some students to make public their own guilty feelings about their actions or lack of them. This observation highlights the complexity of issues facing academics and their students.

Both authors here have found that the move to networked environments of engagement has added an extra dimension to the way we interact both with students and staff. By engagement, here we are not simply referring to academics acquiring the skills to put things online; rather, we focus on social exchange – for example, the role of immediacy (e.g., Baker 2010) and presence (e.g., Picciano 2002) – which has implications for language and academic identity. Effective engagement offers a new track for learning, but requires some getting used to:

Engaging in a class or module online is significantly different, I would say. It feels different – it is a different kind of experience. I always feel like there's a lack of contact, or an imposed distance, but there's definitely less immediacy. It feels disembodied somehow. A little unreal. That throws things into confusion a bit for me.... I can engage fine, but it's not the same as face-to-face. I have to work harder to make sense of things. Maybe it is just a matter of getting used to it. I can see the point of it, thankfully, but I'm not sure I like the stress involved. I can see that it offers a different way of learning and it seems to work. I just need to find a way to make it less stressful and more meaningful for me.

(from Stuart's reflective diary)

Interestingly, the reflection above could be that of either a student or educator. As with other points of transition and transformation, engagement can be seen as an enabler, a barrier or both. Devoid of familiar signs, signals, and processes, networked learning requires foremost a willingness to adjust and to engage and participate differently. Like identity, language or time, effective engagement in networked learning environments relies on our openness to learn new ways of thinking, of being and of practicing.

Conclusions

These sites of transition and transformation – language, engagement, identity, and time – may, as noted throughout, appear to us as both barriers and enablers. It is the position and stance of the individual academic that informs whether these sites are encountered as opportunities or challenges or both. We ourselves find that our experiences are variable: our language, the way we engage with one another, our relationship to time and even our understandings of ourselves are in near constant flux in these networked environments.

In order to function successfully in networked learning environments then, the academic must come to terms with this new alien landscape and, perhaps more importantly, find a place in it for themselves. Our own experience has shown that many academics still prefer – knowingly or otherwise – to replicate the real in the virtual world, rather than unfetter themselves from tradition and the familiar and create new selves, constructs, relationships, and opportunities for engagement. It may yet take time before we as a profession overcome the alienation and otherness of online spaces and fully embrace the potential offered therein.

Academics who cannot make the necessary adjustments may find their progress halted by these barriers. Those who can make the adjustments may find that those self-same barriers are transformed and become enablers, offering academics new opportunities for interaction and involvement in networked learning environments.

Twenty-first century academic identity entails a number of roles. Both of us are simultaneously lecturers, researchers, students, and educational developers who support other lecturers, researchers, and students. We come from two generations, but there is a third generation now attending our university and we have to find appropriate ways of communicating with them. Like many of our colleagues, we are stepping out from behind the screen, but with a foot still in the old world.

Not only have we appropriated Turkle's metaphor of the screen, but we have also revisited some of her concerns about the tensions between the virtual and the real. At the time, she wrote that in 15 years the meaning of the computer had shifted from "a modernist culture of calculation toward a postmodernist culture of simulation" (Turkle 1995, p. 20). Another 15 years has passed since then and we feel that we are now going beyond simulation toward projection of a new, albeit reaggregated, reality. We are no longer simply replicating the real world in virtual spaces, but creating truly novel means of interacting and educating. Like Turkle, we believe that as we do this, we should not leave behind our values as human beings. But there is now a new context and this may also demand a new set of values.

In the (re)aggregation processes that may be required for current digital literacy, we may be buying in (both financially and politically) to particular ways of viewing the world – and projecting those ways to other people. This is a subject for future thought and research and a step beyond our attempt to "inhabit the virtual."

References

Anderson, T. (2009). Online instructor immediacy and instructor-student relationships in Second Life. In C. Wankel & J. Kingsley (Eds.), *Higher education in virtual worlds: teaching and learning in second life*. Bingley: Emerald.

Austin, J. (1962). *How to do things with words*. Oxford: Oxford University Press.

Baker, C. (2010). The impact of instructor immediacy and presence for online student affective learning, cognition, and motivation. *The Journal of Educators Online, 7*(1), 1–30.

Bakhtin, M. M. (1981). *The dialogic imagination: four essays by M.M. Bakhtin*. Austin, TX: University of Texas Press.

Ball, S., & Pearce, R. (2009). Inclusion benefits and barriers of 'once-removed' participation. In C. Wankel & J. Kingsley (Eds.), *Higher education in virtual worlds: teaching and learning in second life*. Bingley: Emerald.

Bayne, S. (2008). Uncanny spaces for higher education: teaching and learning in virtual worlds. *Research in Learning Technology, 16*(3), 197–205.

Boon, S., & Sinclair, C. (2009). A world I don't inhabit: disquiet and identity in Second Life and Facebook. *Educational Media International, 46*(2), 99–110. Based on a paper delivered at Sixth International Conference on Networked Learning, Halkidiki, Greece, 2008.

Brown, J. S., & Duguid, P. (2000). *The social life of information*. Boston, MA: Harvard Business School Press.

Carroll, L. (1871). *Through the looking-glass, and what Alice found there*. London: Macmillan.

Castronova, E. (2005). *Synthetic worlds: the business and culture of online games*. Chicago: University of Chicago Press.

Clark, R. E. (1994). Media will never influence learning. *Educational Technology Research and Development, 42*(2), 21–29.

Council for Research Excellence (2009). Video consumer mapping briefing paper. http://www.researchexcellence.com/committees/mediaconsumption_committee.php. Accessed 3 Feb 2010.

Cousin, G. (2005). Learning from cyberspace. In R. Land & S. Bayne (Eds.), *Education in cyberspace* (pp. 117–128). Abingdon: RoutledgeFalmer.

Eriksen, T. H. (2001). *Tyranny of the moment: fast and slow time in the information age*. London: Pluto Press.

Goodfellow, R., & Lea, M. (2007). *Challenging e-learning in the university*. Maidenhead: SRHE/Open University Press.

Goodyear, P., Banks, S., Hodgson, V., & McConnell, D. (2004). Research on networked learning: an overview. In P. Goodyear, S. Banks, V. Hodgson, & D. McConnell (Eds.), *Advances in research on networked learning* (pp. 1–11). Dordrecht: Kluwer.

Land, R., and Bayne, S. (2002). Screen or monitor? Surveillance and disciplinary power in online learning environments. In Rust, C. (Ed.) *Improving student learning using learning technology* (pp. 125–38). http://www.malts.ed.ac.uk/staff/sian/surveillancepaper.htm. Accessed 3 Nov 2009. Oxford: Oxford Center for Staff and Learning Development.

Lave, J., & Wenger, E. (1998). *Communities of practice: learning, meaning, and identity*. Cambridge: Cambridge University Press.

Leont'ev, A. N. (1981). The problem of activity in psychology. In J. V. Wertsch (Ed.), *The concept of activity in Soviet psychology*. Armonk, NY: M.E.Sharpe.

MacKeogh, K., & Fox, S. (2009). Strategies for embedding e-learning in traditional universities: drivers and barriers. *Electronic journal of E-learning, 7*(2), 147–154.

Mann, S. (2003). A personal inquiry into an experience of adult learning on-line. *Instructional Science, 31*, 111–125.

Marton, F., and Pang, M. (1999). Two faces of variation. Paper presented at the 8th European Conference for Learning and Instruction, University of Göteburg, Sweden.

Meyer, J., & Land, R. (2005). Threshold concepts and troublesome knowledge (2): epistemological considerations and a conceptual framework for teaching and learning. *Higher Education, 49*(3), 373–388.

Meyer, J., & Land, R. (Eds.). (2006). *Overcoming barriers to student understanding: threshold concepts and troublesome knowledge*. London: Routledge.

Picciano, A. (2002). Beyond student perceptions: issues of interaction, presence, and performance in an online course. *Journal of Asynchronous Learning Networks, 6*(1), 21–40.

Savin-Baden, M., & Sinclair, C. (2011). Lurking on the threshold: being learners in silent spaces. In R. Land & S. Bayne (Eds.), *Digital differences*. Rotterdam: Sense.

Turkle, S. (1995). *Life on the screen: identity in the age of the internet*. New York: Simon and Schuster.

Vygotsky, L. S. (1934/1987). Thinking and speech. In R. W. Rieber & A. S. Carton (Eds.), *The collected works of L. S. Vygotsky*. New York/London: Plenum.

Vygotsky, L. S. (1978). *Mind in society*. Cambridge, MA: Harvard University Press.

Wesch, M. (2009, January 7). From knowledgeable to knowledgeable: learning in new media environments. Retrieved 5 April 2009, from http://www.academiccommons.org/commons/essay/knowledgable-knowledge-able#comments

Wood, A., & Smith, M. (2005). *Online communication: linking technology, identity, and culture* (2nd ed.). London: Lawrence Erlbaum.

Part VII
Conclusions

Chapter 17
The Theory, Practice and Pedagogy of Networked Learning

Vivien Hodgson, David McConnell, and Lone Dirckinck-Holmfeld

Introduction

In Chapter One, we gave an account of the history and development of networked learning as it relates to research and practice in the UK and Denmark in particular and, more broadly, to the Networked Learning Conference itself.

We believe that the chapters from the Networked Learning Conference 2010 included in this book give us an opportunity to review where the theory, practice and pedagogy of networked learning is today, and where it is heading. In this final chapter, we would like to address the following four questions:

1. Is networked learning a theory, practice or a pedagogy?
2. What are the pedagogical values that underpin networked learning?
3. What is the relevance and challenges of networked learning to mainstream higher education?
4. What new possibilities and challenges is Web 2.0 bringing to networked learning?

We think that these are key questions moving forward and that the different chapters included in the book contribute to beginning to answer them and to thus progress our understanding of networked learning.

V. Hodgson (✉)
Lancaster University Management School, Lancaster University, Lancaster, UK
e-mail: v.hodgson@lancaster.ac.uk

D. McConnell
Independent Higher Education Consultant, Stirling, Scotland, UK

L. Dirckinck-Holmfeld
Aalborg University, Aalborg, Denmark

L. Dirckinck-Holmfeld et al. (eds.), *Exploring the Theory, Pedagogy and Practice of Networked Learning*, DOI 10.1007/978-1-4614-0496-5_17,
© Springer Science+Business Media, LLC 2012

The Ontology of Networked Learning

In asking ourselves is networked learning a theory, pedagogy or practice, we recognised it is all of these things. Indeed, the separation of theory from practice many would argue is an artificial one in the first place. There have been many debates on this issue in the wider social sciences to the extent that Willinsky (2000) observed that it might just be easier "to stop casting it as a division".

To consider the ontology of networked learning, we must identify what assumptions it makes about the nature of being and existence and how reality is seen. Our shared view of networked learning comes from an ontological position that assumes an understanding of the world and view of the world, including learning and teaching, is socio-culturally influenced and constructed. It is a view that aligns with the critical and humanistic traditions of the likes of Freire (1970), Dewey (1916) and Mead (1967), including the belief in the importance of focusing on making sense from one's own personal experiences and view of the world – or indeed one's own practice. As Nielsen and Danielsen explain in their chapter, learning in networked learning is achieved through participation in communities of learners where meaning is both negotiated and created through collaborative dialogue.

Equally important to us, however, is the nature of meaning and understanding of knowledge and of the world that is constructed and how it contributes to the wellbeing of society and the world in which we live. To this extent as explained by Levinsen and Nielsen in their chapter, networked learning, importantly, seeks to address the tensions between the two current primary but contradictory meta-discourses in education and in society itself; the *political–ethical discourse* on the one hand and the *economic–pragmatic discourse* on the other. In a political context of neo-liberalism, we feel both discourses need to be given attention. For us networked learning questions the nature of society and how we develop new knowledge of the world we live in, including societal form. It is equally, we believe, a way to conduct education that supports learners to contribute to a society that is literate and critically examines the way we work and live and take learning into the wider world. Several of the chapters point out (e.g. Alevizou, Galley and Conole, Boon and Sinclair, Nielsen and Danielsen and Ross) that to achieve this learners need to acquire new literacies, social literacy as well as a digital literacy. Networked learning, we believe, offers the theory and practice for a pedagogy that is appropriate or suited to live in a digitally connected and networked world where sharing and collaborative ways of working are the norm rather than the exception.

The Epistemology of Networked Learning

The learning theory that follows the ontology of networked learning is a social theory of learning. To this end it could be said, as Fox (2006) claims for other social theories of learning, such as activity theory and communities of practice, it attempts to transcend the dualism between abstract mind and concrete material social practice.

The epistemology of networked learning is in essence that knowledge emerges or is constructed in relational dialogue or collaborative interaction – knowledge is not a property but a social construction/way of knowing from our experience of the world.

If we take this a step further and perceive practice as a proxy for epistemology, we also move closer to overcoming the issue of separating theory from practice. Practice as epistemic, as a way of seeing or acting, particularly in the field of education and learning, becomes then an over-arching concept within which it can be argued resides theory *and* activity *and* learning in relationship to each other. By seeing practice as epistemic, networked learning can be claimed to exist inside practice and becomes itself an object of inquiry in terms of the theory and behaviours it creates as social action. What is more, the social action and associated behaviours that emerge from networked learning arguably emanate from the epistemology that underpins the pedagogy of networked learning.

As we explained in chapter one, technology is significant to any concept of networked learning. Technology meditates many of the connections within and between a learning community and its different actors. How technology is perceived impacts strongly on the epistemology of networked learning. Technology however only mediates, though as a number of chapters illustrate in its mediation capacity it has material affect, but it does not and cannot determine learning, learning design or the learning process.

The material affect of technology is explored by Thompson in her chapter. Thompson uses actor network theory (ANT) to analyse the relational and material connections within a networked learning situation in order to demonstrate the co-constituted and performative relations present between people and Web technologies. While Creanor and Walker in their chapter explain, from the perspective of socio-technical interaction network (STIN), the material and social are interlinked, and technology cannot be examined without reference to its use in social contexts.

The Pedagogy of Networked Learning

Based on several key sources on the topic Ryberg, Buus, and Georgsen identify e-quality, inclusion, critical reflexivity and relational dialogue as key theoretical perspectives and values associated with the pedagogical and socio-technical design of networked learning. They go on to explain that these differentiate networked learning from other ideas and concepts, such as personalised learning environments (PLE) and in particular connectivism.

As Ryberg, Buus, and Georgsen explain in connectivism, as purported by Siemens (2005, 2006), the most fundamental relationship is that between an individual and a resource or idea. Knowledge in this view becomes equated with content and learning remains ultimately an individual, cognitive, pursuit. Most telling, however, they point out in approaches like PLE and connectivism no attention is, apparently, given to issues of power, voice, access and inclusion.

Another field which many see as closely aligned with networked learning is computer supported collaborative learning (CSCL). There are it has to be said a lot of overlapping interests between CSCL and networked learning. Stahl et al. (2006, p. 15) explain in their essay on the history of CSCL that it is a field of study that "requires a focus on the meaning-making practices of collaborating groups and on the design of technological artefacts to mediate interaction, rather than a focus on individual learning".

The meaning making practices of collaborating groups in their description of CSCL is particularly pertinent to the research interests of networked learning. The design of technological artefacts to mediate interaction has been less of a focus of attention within networked learning. This said, much of the research done under the banner of CSCL could equally be seen as relevant to networked learning. However, unlike networked learning CSCL does not identify itself as part of the tradition of radical pedagogy based on a given ontology and epistemology. This radical tradition underpinning networked learning leads to an interest in researching and designing networked learning programmes and opportunities that are educationally rewarding but which do also give attention to issues of power, voice, access and inclusion – something many of the chapters in this book consider from different perspectives.

As we explained in Chapter One, problem and project-based learning (PBL) is another community with overlapping interest to networked learning. Historically, PBL in the Danish tradition shares pedagogical values with networked learning based on the critical and humanistic traditions of learning. Especially within a networked learning design the principles from PBL environments have proved to be productive with respect to students learning in the organisation between tight and loose ties (Dirckinck-Holmfeld et al. 2009). Nielsen and Danielsen; Ryberg, Buus, and Georgsen; Levinsen and Nielsen and Nyvang and Bygholm describe in their chapters a number of learning principles that problem and project-based learning integrates: participants" control, problem formulation, exemplary and interdisciplinary projects, team-work and forms of action learning, all of which work well with the principles of networked learning.

What Are the Pedagogical Values that Underpin Networked Learning

We have seen above that it is possible to describe networked learning in terms of its ontology and epistemology. These are underpinned by values and beliefs concerning the learning, teaching and assessment (LTA) processes of networked learning. These shared pedagogical values of networked learning do not, however, assume a given or taken-for-granted learning design. As demonstrated by the various chapters in this book, the shared pedagogical values of networked learning can lead to various and different designs, landscapes and spaces.

Implications for the Learning, Teaching and Assessment Process

Not all networked learning practitioners value the same things, nor when they do value shared learning and teaching beliefs are they valued in the same way or to the same degree. However, it is probably fair to say that most networked learning practitioners place a high value on the following:

- Cooperation and collaboration in the learning process.
- Working in groups and in communities.
- Discussion and dialogue.
- Self-determination in the learning process.
- Difference and its place as a central learning process.
- Trust and relationships: weak and strong ties.
- Reflexivity and investment of self in the networked learning processes.
- The role technology plays in connecting and mediating.

From this, we can say that the practice of networked learning is best seen from a holistic perspective. Each component of networked learning has to be integrated and has to contribute to the overall underpinning values and beliefs.

Learning, Teaching and Community

Networked learning is concerned with the development of a learning culture, in which the members' value supporting each other: no one individual is responsible for knowing everything. The community often works towards shared understandings. In networked learning, communities have to be "designed into" any learning event or course by the teacher, and not assumed to be in place or to exist without any intention. As Smith describes in her chapter, a networked learning community has the capacity to support a collective and shared process of learning that leads to acquiring a new identity and way of being in the world. Similarly, Raffaghelli and Richieri show that in intercultural settings, networked learning pedagogy has the capacity to provide appropriate support for teachers who are facilitating the learning process, and for learners who are working with people from other countries and other cultures.

It can be argued that when such social co-participation is valued, the focus is on each individual constructing their identity within the social space of the learning community. This occurs through collaborative and reflective learning processes: "The altered self has to be explored and constructed as part of a reflexive process of connecting personal and social change" (Giddens 1991, p. 33).

In their chapter, Boon and Sinclair consider the impact on what it takes to get the academic online. They explore the shift required from the way academics value conventional, face-to-face teaching and learning, towards a new set of values associated with networked learning. This requires the forging of new identities for academics themselves and acquiring sets of new values concerning learning and teaching, which is a complex and unsettling process. Networked learning is a new and alien landscape for many teachers, and they have to come to terms with it in their own way.

The new roles associated with the networked learning teacher are also explored by Nielsen and Danielsen in their chapter. They examine the emergence of new teacher pedagogies in problem-based networked learning, and indicate that teachers are coming to place an emphasis on new values and beliefs concerning their practice. Teachers are no longer valuing only the traditional roles of the "expert" teacher. They are realising that to engage in new forms of learning and teaching, such as we find in networked learning, they have to revalue their existing pedagogic practice in favour of values associated with the supervisor in various roles such as, academic instructor, a process-orientated supervisor and as social mediator. That is, where there is a greater value placed on processes, methodological dimensions and stressing the importance of a reflexive approach.

There is also a value point in relation to the nature of learning and *achievement*. Student learning is usually competitive and individualistic. In networked learning, where cooperation and collaboration has a high value, we ask the question: but what about cooperative and collaborative learning? How do these two forms of learning – competitive and individualistic learning, and cooperative and collaborative learning – differ in terms of the outcomes of student learning? As mentioned, the chapter by Levinsen and Nielsen discusses the presence of two contrasting meta-discourses. The *political–ethical discourse* which focuses on the good life and what ought to be done, and concentrates on the development of a new educational paradigm inspired by social constructivist and constructivist theory. As they explain complexities of learning in such a discourse require time to mature. In contrast to this is the *economic–pragmatic discourse* that demands fast, efficient, predictable and controllable productivity from the educational institutions. They point out that these opposing demands produce a paradox between the political demands of society and the qualitative demands of a learning paradigm, such as networked learning that asks for "self initiated lifelong learners".

This leads us to ask: what is the impact on *achievement* of competitive, individualistic and cooperative learning? There is evidence to suggest that in *cooperative/collaborative learning*, mastery and retention of material is higher; the quality of reasoning strategies is greater: focusing strategies are used more often in cooperative/collaborative learning; higher level reasoning is greater, and problems are solved faster. Process gains, such as the production of new ideas, are greater, and transference of learning from group to individual, is high (Johnson and Johnson 1990, 2003).

From this, two important questions arise in relation to networked learning:

What social engagements and processes provide the "proper" context for learning?
What forms of co-participation might be required when engaging learners in these forms of learning?

These value-laden questions have led to the design of networked learning as community. The value of "community" in networked learning contexts has been critically examined by many practitioners and researchers (for example, see Banks et al. 2008; Goodfellow 2008; Hodgson and Reynolds 2005; Koole 2010; McConnell 2006; Jones et al. 2006).

Conceptually, the "learning community", with a focus on learning together, sharing and developing relationships, is highly valued by many networked learning practitioners. (e.g. see Raffaghelli and Richieri in this book; Hodgson and Reynolds 2005; McConnell 2006). Other conceptual frameworks are however also valued, such as communities of practice (Wenger 1998), where the focus is on developing professional practice, as discussed by Smith in her chapter; communities of inquiry where members focus on inquiring about issues of common interest (e.g. see Suthers and Chu, in this book); and knowledge communities, which focus on developing knowledge (e.g. see Alevizou, Galley and Conole's chapter).

The diversity of conceptual frameworks suggests that when we design networked learning as community, we should be careful to define what we mean by "community", and then provide a pedagogic design that supports that definition and embodies the values therein (McConnell 2006).

The learning community attends to issues of climate, aspirations, resources, planning, action and evaluation. For some, the value of the democratic processes that this suggests is the driving force. There are certain expectations associated with this view of community. The central place of "difference" within the community is highly valued. The chapter in this book by Raffaghelli and Richieri indicates the complexity of working with difference in an intercultural setting. The authors show that networked learning pedagogy accepts differences, and that the *quality* of peoples' relations is an important characteristic in an online community. They place a high value on students learning how to belong to a learning community, and how to discover and practice how to take part in a learning community. The networked learner and teacher productively use and work with difference. They are, however, aware of the need not to uncritically believe that there is intrinsic good in the networked learning community, especially within communities made up of international members, where there are perhaps additional concerns over "difference" and the complexity that arises from that.

There is a tangible shift during the history of a learning community from seeing itself as a group of individual learners, to the members seeing themselves as people learning in a social environment where collaboration and cooperation is expected and rewarded. The learners come to own the value of seeing learning as "community", and we believe that this value can be transferred into the wider socio-political lives of the learners.

For many, the cornerstones of online communities lies in shared values associated with the development of privacy, authenticity and personal development (and, therefore implicitly, trust). These cornerstones of the networked learning community are highlighted in the chapter by Ross when she discusses new literacies for media practices. Ross argues that the new digital tools are "neither innocent nor culturally neutral" and require careful management by teachers and students alike so as to ensure the values of privacy, authenticity and trust are central to the learning process. A greater critical awareness of the processes of online reflective writing, and engagement with an understanding of the tensions produced in these processes is required. Networked learning teachers should have an ethical approach to the encouragement of students' engagement in these community environments.

In designing networked learning courses based on groups and communities, the incorporation of these characteristics into the teaching and learning processes is key. The paradox of the opposing demands of the political–ethical discourse and the economic–pragmatic discourse discussed by Levinsen and Nielsen, mentioned above, is highly relevant. They indicate that educating students for the network society means "to educate them for an unpredictable future, to support their understanding of the emerging learning paradigm and to scaffold their process of becoming self-initiated and critical lifelong learners ......The paradox exposes itself at this level as students who demand instructional teaching where we stress constructivist and social constructivist approaches". An important question to answer is: how do we design networked learning so that it supports those values and beliefs of learning in community that we hold to be so central to the practice of networked learning?

Reflexivity and Investment of Self in the Networked Learning Processes

In the context of networked learning, it has been suggested that collaborative assessment is central to changes required in making learning less instrumental and more participative: "....assessment is arguably the most important aspect of an educational programme in which to introduce collaborative principles. It is this intervention that develops the design from the instrumental to a more fundamentally participative approach" (Reynolds et al. 2002).

Many networked learning practitioners believe that if we ask students to value collaboration and cooperation, and produce collaborative and cooperative products and outcomes, we should design assessment processes so that they support and reward this. Many of the authors contributing chapters to this book practice a form of networked learning that requires learners to make judgments about their own learning, and that of others. Most often, learners are asked to participate in assessing in some way their own contribution to the collaborative and cooperative process, and also to assessing the contributions made by their group and community members. For example, this form of assessment is implicit in the learning designs described in the chapters by Nielsen and Danielsen, and Levinsen and Nielsen. The value of an inclusive and participatory assessment process is central to their practice.

In conventional higher education most assessment processes are closed and involve only the student and the tutor. In networked learning, it is considered important that the collaborative assessment process is underpinned by the value of openness, so as to mirror the openness in the learning process itself. The value of learning relationships is central, and they have to be developed and maintained, and trust developed, for it to be successful.

Networked collaborative assessment places a high value on the development of skill in judging one's own learning, and that of others. This is a skill that can be transferred to other lifelong learning situations and social contexts. We think that the value of equipping learners with such skills should be a key aspect of the so-called learning society.

The Role Technology Plays in Connecting and Mediating

With ICT support, networked learning has developed from being an isolated and uncoordinated endeavour of individual technology interested teachers and students to become an institutional commitment. If there is no institutional and managerial commitment, the network for learning is not likely to have many nodes or stretch across an institution. With few nodes, it is also not likely to foster the kind of connections and interactions needed for networked learning to take place. If the network stretches beyond the class of the individual teacher it is, however, also evident that the network of learners becomes quite complex. Actors (teachers, students, managers, others) have to develop their contributions and make sure that they fit into the network of other actors and resources. The chapters by Arnold et al. and Nyvang and Bygholm address the complexities involved in the development and adoption of networked learning infrastructure and tools. Nyvang and Bygholm are especially interested in the meso-level conditions under which institutional actors decide upon ICT strategies for networked learning purposes and to understand how to deal with the different rationales, priorities and values, which the different actors promote. In their case study based on an activity theory framework (Engeström 1987, 2009; Kuutti 1996), they focus on the following actors: the management, the support-organisation, and the teachers and students identifying different overall goals, values and attitudes towards the technology and its use. For networked learning practices to develop and become main stream, it is important to deepen the insights into these different goals and values as well as to develop strategies on how to cope with these differences within organisations.

What New Possibilities and Challenges Is Web 2.0 Bringing to Networked Learning

As Ryberg, Buus and Georgsen write in their chapter, the popularisation of Web 2.0 practices and technologies have revitalised the educational terms, such as collaboration, sharing, dialogue, participation, student-centred learning and the need to position students as producers, rather than consumers of knowledge. However, it is important to acknowledge that these are pedagogical ideals, which have been well established in the educational research and practitioners' community long before the Internet and prominent within research areas, such as networked learning, CSCL and CMC-research, well before the emergence of Web 2.0 (Jones and Dirckinck-Holmfeld 2009). In that sense this is not a new position; however, what may be new is that this participatory view through the wide adaptation of services, such as Facebook, Flickr and YouTube, are now becoming mainstream. These social networks have different organising principle when compared to the previous learning management systems (LMS) or virtual learning environments (VLE). While the previous LMS and VLE-systems were a kind of controlled learning environments by the institution, the Web 2.0 systems are organised around the user as a node in the network. These different organising principles offer new potentials, which also have to be considered within networked learning.

These technological developments have given rise to a number of different conceptual frameworks. On the one hand, we have networked learning, which sees new potential for mainstreaming of networked technologies, which can be made use of in order to strengthen collaborative, critical reflexive learning; and on the other hand, we see a revival of more individualistic positions, such as personal learning environments (PLE) and cognitive science positions, such as "connectivism".

Our point on Web 2.0 is a relational and transformative one, which is equally shaped by the underlying theoretical educational perspective and values with which we approach the pedagogical and socio-technical design of learning – and in particular how we view and design for the relational interdependencies and connections between learners in their mutual meaning constructions. We would call to re-pedagogize the networked learning environment taking into account the new practices, which is afforded by the socio-technical design of Web 2.0. The emergence of more dispersed networked technologies and "connective" patterns of interaction as well as active technologies that replicate aspects of human agency (cf. also Arnold et al., Jones, Ryberg et al.; Smith, and Thompson's chapters in this book) hold interesting opportunities for expanding existing designs for networked learning, for example networked problem- and project-oriented pedagogy and inquiry action learning based pedagogy to mention just two possibilities.

Following from this, networked learning environments can be designed and shaped in different ways depending on the underlying values and views of human cognition, learning, formation, the technology and pedagogy. At one extreme, they can be designed as constellations of technologies, where the individuals are free to form and control their learning processes by connecting to others for inspiration and resources and used across various levels of aggregation in the group, the network and the collective. While at the other extreme, networked learning environments can be designed as platforms for greater levels of mutual engagement and dedication, critical reflection, emancipatory formation and empowerments. The Network Learning community and the International Network Learning Conference are exploring the second line of development.

The Networked Generation and Digital Literacy

Several chapters in this book (Jones, Czerniewiez and Brown) critically examine the idea that has become common during the past 10 years, that young people have undergone a generational change in which their exposure to digital and networked technologies, the bits and bytes of the twenty-first Century, have caused a step change in the characteristics of a whole generation.

The argument, which among others has been brought forward by Prensky (2001, 2010) is based on a kind of technological determinism, that it is the technology in itself that has changed a whole generation of students' social character, and also the way they approach learning, having been exposed to and growing up with a range of digital and networked technologies. Alternative accounts understand young people as active agents in the process of engagement with technology, and also see them as brokers for new practices. Jones gives a strong and evidence-based account based on literature reviews and also his own empirical research against such determinism. Instead of championing a generational view he proposes to further develop the active agency perspective; while doing so, however, this needs to take account of and recognise that people necessarily enact roles within the relational constraints and affordances of the collective organisation.

Rather than showing a net generation of digital native students, who are naturally proficient with technology due to their exposure to the technology rich environment, the empirical evidence brought forward by Jones shows that students' experiences with technologies vary. Not all students are equally competent with technologies, and their patterns of use vary considerably when moved beyond basic and familiar technologies. There are variations among students within the Net generation age band, and students' selection of tools are related to other characteristics, including age, gender, socio-economic background, academic discipline and year of study. Both in the early work of Goodyear et al. (2005) and in the later work by Jones (Jones and Healing 2010), it seems to be the thoroughness with which new technologies are integrated into the design of a networked learning course that appears to be the significant factor in explaining differences in students' feelings and experiences about their learning and course. There is no evidence of a generational divide; rather it seems it is the well-integrated course of networked technologies, content and pedagogy that appears to be the key factor.

What is more there is much evidence to suggest the so-called net generation, as well as the academic who teach them, still require and are likely to require support in developing the new literacies required for working in a digital and information rich economy. As explained by a number of authors in this book this means online social literacy as well as digital and information literacy (Alevizou, Galley and Conole, Boon and Sinclair, Nielsen and Danielsen and Ross).

A Relational View on Agency

Agency, in contrast to structuralist approaches, is concerned with the shaping of processes by the intentions and actions of humans. Agency is emergent and cannot be reduced to structure nor vice versa. It is the individual who holds the power to be active and reflexive – in that sense agency is a fundamentally human characteristic. However, as also argued in the chapters by Jones and Czerniewicz and Brown, agency takes place in socio-cultural-mediated settings and on various levels of scale. Within networked learning the socio-technical learning infrastructure, the pedagogical principles and the organisational culture are some of the important factors mediating the agency of the learners as demonstrated in the chapters by Thompson, Creanor and Walker and Suthers and Chu.

Changing Cultural Capital

Even if we can not talk about generational characteristics of the networked learner, Czerniewicz and Brown show in their case study "investigating students access to and use of ICTs and mobile technologies in South Africa" that the capacity to use ICT as a kind of objectified cultural capital (Bordieu 1990) can provide students with new skills and competencies and strategies for learning, which becomes an integrated part of their agency and in that way reconfigures their identity to better cope with the learning culture. Their case study targets students from both a privileged and an under privileged socio-economic background. Both groups of students, however, benefit from the mastering of ICT. It would appear even for students coming from disadvantaged social backgrounds the opportunities afforded by ICT and mobile technology (here, the cell phone) fast track the appropriation of embodied cultural capital. The radical claim to Bordieus' theory on habitus and to the theory on agency is therefore, that the structures of habitus are not "set", but evolve. The appropriation of ICT and mobile technology for learning can change the structures of the cultural habitus of the learners.

These findings are relevant to understand how access to ICT may circumvent the constraints for some social groups of students imposed by social structures. Czerniewicz and Brown in their chapter focus on students from South Africa, however, an obvious conclusion would be that their findings can be generalised to other contexts and economies.

A Relational Model of Networked Learning

There is now a mounting empirical base on which we can begin to develop theories to adequately account for the changes that we can clearly see from research across the world on the so-called net generation. The availability of cheap computing, broadband and mobile networks and a range of web-based services is changing the way both students study and the way the universities they attend conduct their work. The chapters in this book have provided new insights building on a relational perspective between agency and structure. The book provides a theoretically and empirically informed body of research that takes us beyond simple dichotomies between structure and agency, technology and learners, the chapters exploring various aspects of how groups of learners – students and teachers – enact the use of ICT in the service of networked learning.

The relational model, which can be developed in relation to networked learning, based on the chapters in this book, integrates a number of dimensions:

- A pedagogical approach (values, principles, emancipatory perspectives).
- Organisation at different scales and levels (group, institution, the collective).
- The learner and the teacher (their individual choices).

The exposure to new technology, which is enacted and acted on differently by the different agents (learner, teacher, educational organisation) in becoming objectified and embodied cultural capital for the learner.

Concluding Comments

In this chapter, we have attempted to review where the theory, practice and pedagogy of networked learning are today, and where it is heading. We have explored four central questions concerning theory, practice and pedagogy, the values that underpin networked learning, the challenges facing networked learning in mainstream higher education, and the new possibilities and challenges to networked learning that Web 2.0 brings. We have shown how the papers presented at the Networked Learning Conference in 2010 critically address these questions, and how practitioners and researchers are vigorously engaged in actively bringing about change that is relevant to present-day higher education concerns, and presenting ways forward for a critical realisation of the theory, practice and pedagogy of networked learning.

Harasim et al. (1995) wrote over 15 years ago that "the paradigm for education in the twenty-first century that is emerging is networked learning". A view that we fully support and endorse. It remains unclear however whether the promise and potential of networked learning as described by ourselves in the first chapter and by Harasim et al. (1995) has yet been achieved. This is despite the changes and advances in technology software and infrastructure that could be assumed to make it more rather than less likely to have become the pedagogy of choice in a globalised and international world and economy. The chapters in this book go some way to help us to understand better some of the issues, constraints and difficulties that have until now prevented this being the case. They also help to reiterate the real possibilities and importance that networked learning can contribute.

We believe that in a global economy that is based on information and social networks a transformation of mainstream higher education is needed. Our view is the theory, practice and pedagogy of networked learning can contribute to this transformation.

References

Banks, S.B., McConnell, D., and Bowskill, N. (2008). A feeling or a practice? Achieving intercul-turality in an e-learning course (pp. 712–719). *Proceedings of the 6th International Conference on Networked Learning*. ISBN 978-1-86220-206-1.

Bordieu, P. (1990). *The logic of practice*. Cambridge: Polity.

Dewey, J. (1916). *Democracy and education: an introduction to the philosophy of education (1966 edn)*. New York: Free.

Dirckinck-Holmfeld, L., Nielsen, J., Fibiger, B., & Danielsen, O. (2009). Problem and project based learning. In L. Dirckinck-Holmfeld, C. Jones, & B. Lindström (Eds.), *Analysing networked learning practices in higher education and continuing professional development*. Rotterdam: Sense Publishers.

Engeström, Y. (1987). *Learning by expanding*. Helsinki: Orienta.

Engeström, Y. (2009). The future of activity theory: a rough draft. In A. Sannino, H. Daniels, & K. D. Gutiérrez (Eds.), *Learning and expanding with activity theory*. Cambridge: Cambridge University Press.

Fox, S. (2006). "Inquiries of every imaginable kind": ethnomethodology, practical action and the new socially situated learning theory. *Sociological Review, 54*(3), 426–445.

Freire, P. (1970). *Pedagogy of the oppressed*. New York, NY: Continum.

Giddens, A. (1991). *Modernity and self-identity: self and society in the late modern age*. Cambridge: Polity.

Goodfellow, R. (2008). New directions in research into learning cultures in online education (pp. 553–559). *Proceedings of the 6th International Conference on Networked Learning*. ISBN 978-1-86220-206-1.

Goodyear, P., Jones, C., Asensio, M., Hodgson, V., & Steeples, C. (2005). Networked learning in higher education: students' expectations and experiences. *Higher Education, 50*(3), 473–508.

Harasim, L., Hiltz, S. R., Teles, L., & Turoff, M. (1995). Network learning: a paradigm for the twenty-first century. In L. Harasim, S. R. Hiltz, L. Teles, & M. Turoff (Eds.), *Learning networks: a field guide to teaching and learning online* (pp. 272–278). Cambridge, MA: MIT.

Hodgson, V., & Reynolds, M. (2005). Consensus, difference and "multiple communities" in networked learning. *Studies in Higher Education, 30*(1), 11–24.

Johnson, D. W., & Johnson, R. T. (1990). Social skills for successful group work. *Educational Leadership, 47*(4), 29–33.

Johnson, D. W., & Johnson, R. T. (2003). *Learning together and alone: cooperative, competitive, and individualistic learning* (8th ed.). London: Allyn and Bacon.

Jones, C., & Dirckinck-Holmfeld, L. (2009). Analysing networked learning practices. In L. Dirckinck-Holmfeld, C. Jones, & B. Lindström (Eds.), *Analysing networked learning practices in higher education and continuing professional development*. Rotterdam: Sense Publishers.

Jones, C., Dirckinck-Holmfeld, L., & Lindström, B. (2006). A relational, indirect, meso-level approach to CSCL design in the next decade. *International Journal of Computer-Supported Collaborative Learning, 1*(1), 35–56.

Jones, C., & Healing, G. (2010). Networks and locations for student learning. *Learning Media and Technology., 35*(4), 369–385.

Koole, M. (2010). The web of identity: selfhood and belonging in online learning networks (pp. 241–248). *Proceedings of the 7th International Conference on Networked Learning 2010*, ISBN 978-1-86220-225-2.

Kuutti, K. (1996). Activity theory as a potential framework for human-computer interaction research. In B. Nardi (Ed.), *Context and consciousness: activity theory and human-computer interaction* (pp. 17–44). Cambridge MA: MIT.

Lave, J., & Wenger, E. (1991). *Situated learning: legitimate peripheral participation*. Cambridge: Cambridge University Press.

McConnell, D. (2006). *E-learning groups and communities*. Maidenhead: SRHE/OU Press.

Mead, G. H. (1967[1934]). *Mind, self, and society: from the standpoint of a social behaviorist (Works of George Herbert Mead, Vol. 1)* (1st ed.). Chicago: University of Chicago Press.

Prensky, M. (2001). Digital natives, digital immigrants. *On the Horizon, 9*(5), 1–6.

Prensky, M. (2010). *Teaching digital natives: partnering for real learning*. London: Sage.

Reynolds, M., Sclater, M., & Tickner, S. (2002). A critique of participative discourses adopted in networked learning. In S. Banks, P. Goodyear, V. Hodgson, & D. McConnell (Eds.), *Networked learning 2002: a research based conference on e-learning in higher education and lifelong learning* (p. 685). Sheffield, UK: University of Sheffield (ISBN 0902831 41 0).

Siemens, G. (2005). *Connectivism: a learning theory for the digital age.* http://itdl.org/journal/jan_05/article01.htm. Accessed April 1, 2011.

Siemens, G. (2006). *Connectivism: learning and knowledge today.* http://admin.edna.edu.au/dspace/bitstream/2150/34771/1/gs2006_siemens.pdf. Accessed April 1, 2011.

Stahl, G., Koschmann, T., & Suthers, D. (2006). Computer-supported collaborative learning: an historical perspective. In R. K. Sawyer (Ed.), *Cambridge handbook of the learning sciences* (pp. 409–426). Cambridge, UK: Cambridge University Press. Available at http://GerryStahl.net/cscl/CSCL_English.pdf. Accessed March 22, 2011.

Willinsky, J. (2000). The social sciences as information technology. A political economy of practice. In P. Trifonas (Ed.), *Revolutionary pedagogies*. New York: Routledge Falmer.

Index

L. Dirckinck-Holmfeld et al. (eds.), *Exploring the Theory, Pedagogy and Practice of Networked Learning*, DOI 10.1007/978-1-4614-0496-5,
© Springer Science+Business Media, LLC 2012

Printed by Printforce, the Netherlands